THE HUMAN COURSE

Collected Thoughts for Living

WILLIAM SENTMAN TAYLOR

AND

PHOEBE L. S. TAYLOR

EDITORS

A SCHENKMAN PUBLICATION

HALSTEAD PRESS DIVISION

JOHN WILEY & SONS

New York — London — Sydney — Toronto

Copyright © 1974 by Schenkman Publishing Company
3 Mount Auburn Place, Cambridge, Mass. 02138

136292

Distributed solely by Halsted Press, a Division
of John Wiley & Sons, Inc. New York.

Library of Congress Cataloging in Publication Data

Taylor, William Sentmen, 1894-   comp.
  The human course.

  "A Halsted Press book."
  1. Quotations, English.   I. Taylor Phoebe L. S.,
joint comp.   II. Title.
PN6081.T3   808.88'2   72-81517
ISBN 0-470-84832-4

Printed in the U.S.A.

ACKNOWLEDGMENTS

Copyright © materials are published in this book by permission of the copyright holders and representatives listed here. We thank them.

Any adaptation of form other than into modern English is marked by ellipsis points or square brackets in the text, or by "From" as the first word of the credit line. Any qualification or development of the original author's thought is indicated by "After" as the first word of the credit line.

COPYRIGHT HOLDERS

AAUP Bulletin, Washington

Harry N. Abrams, Inc., New York

Walter R. Agard, Madison, Wis.

George Allen & Unwin, Ltd., London

American Civil Liberties Union, Bristol, Conn.

American Psychological Association, Washington

The American-Scandinavian Foundation, New York

The American Scholar, Washington

American Scientist, New Haven

American Sunday-School Union, Philadelphia

Record, Amherst, Mass.

George Christian Anderson, New York

The Atlantic Monthly, Boston

A. S. Barnes & Company, Inc., New York

Barnes & Noble, Inc., New York

Basic Books, Inc., New York

Beacon Press, Boston

Behrman House Inc., New York

Ernest Benn Limited, London

Mrs. Dorothy Cheston Bennett, London

A & C Black Ltd., London

Brand Blanshard, New Haven

The Bobbs-Merrill Company, Inc., Indianapolis

Brandt & Brandt, New York

George Braziller, Inc., New York

J. Bronowski, San Diego

The Regents of the University of California, Berkeley

Cambridge University Press, New York

Jonathan Cape Limited, London

Capricorn Books, see Putnam

The Center for the Study of Democratic Institutions / Fund for the Republic, Inc., Santa Barbara

Chatto & Windus Ltd. London

The University of Chicago Press, Chicago: John Dewey, *Essays in Experimental Logic,* © 1916; Samuel Noah Kramer, *The Sumerians,* © 1963; Helen Harris Perlman, *Persona,* © 1968; Michael Polanyi, *Personal Knowledge,* © 1958; Giorgio de Santillana, *The Crime of Galileo,* © 1955; F. E. Sparshott, *Enquiry Into Goodness,* © 1958

Christianity and Crisis, New York

The Clarendon Press, Oxford

Clarke, Irwin & Company, Limited, Toronto

Hervey M. Cleckley, Atlanta

Columbia University Press, New York

Daniel Cory, care Braziller

Curtis Brown, Ltd., New York

The John Day Company, Inc., New York: Witter Bynner (tr.), *The Way of Life According to Laotzu,* © 1944 by Witter Bynner; Clifford Gessler, *Reasonable Life,* © 1959 by Clifford Gessler; Lin-Yutang, *The Importance of Living,* © 1937, © renewed 1965 by The John Day Company, Inc.

The Literary Trustees of Walter de la Mare, The Society of Authors, London

Dodd, Mead & Company, Inc., New York: *The Collected Poems of Rupert Brooke,* © 1915 by Dodd, Mead & Company, Inc. Copyright renewed 1945 by Edward Marsh

Doubleday & Company, Inc., New York: excerpts from William O. Douglas, *Almanac Of Liberty,* © 1954 by William O. Douglas; Jean Rostand, *Substance Of Man,* © 1962 by Doubleday & Company; W. Somerset Maugham, *Writer's Notebook,* © 1949 by W. Somerset Maugham

Theodora Dunkerley, Worthing, Sussex

E. P. Dutton & Co., Inc., New York

Lionel Elvin, London

Faber and Faber Ltd., London

Farrar, Straus & Giroux, Inc., New York

Fund for the Republic, see Center

Editions Gallimard, Paris

Marjorie Barstow Greenbie, Penobscot

Hamish Hamilton, London: From *The Plague* by Albert Camus, © 1947 Editions Gallimard, translation by Stuart Gilbert; © 1948

Harcourt Brace Jovanovich, Inc., New York

Trustees of the Hardy Estate, London

Harper & Row, New York

Harvard University Press, Cambridge

D. C. Heath & Co., Lexington, Mass.

William Heineman Ltd., London

Eric Hoffer, San Francisco

Holt, Rinehart and Winston, Inc., New York: Excerpts from "The Figure a Poem Makes" from *Selected Prose Of Robert Frost* edited by Hyde Cox and Edward Connery Lathem, © 1939, © 1967 by Holt, Rinehart and Winston,

Inc., and "The Constant Symbol" from *Selected Prose Of Robert Frost* edited by Hyde Cox and Edward Connery Lathem, © 1946 by Robert Frost; random lines from *The Poetry Of Robert Frost* edited by Edward Connery Lathem, © 1969 by Holt, Rinehart and Winston, Inc.

Horizon Press, New York

Houghton Mifflin Company, Boston

The Humanist, Buffalo

Hutchinson Publishing Group Ltd., London

Julian Huxley, London

University of Illinois Press, Urbana

Indiana University Press, Bloomington

Individual Psychology, Burlington, Vt.

Edgar Johnson, New York

Journal of Chemical Education, New York

The Julian Press, Inc., New York

Walter Kaufmann, Princeton

Walter Kerr, New York

Felix Klee, Bern

Alfred A. Knopf, Inc., see Random House

Robert Lantz — Candida Donadio Literary Agency, Inc.

Hazel Taft Lindeman and Robert Gessner, care Beacon

Lin-Yutang, Shihlin, Taiwan

J. B. Lippincott Company, New York

Little, Brown and Company, Boston

Longman Group Limited, Harlow, Essex

Louisiana State University Press, Baton Rouge

The Macmillan Company, New York

The Macmillan Company of Canada Limited, Toronto

Macmillan London and Basingstoke

Manas, Los Angeles

Massachusetts Review, Amherst

Literary Executor of W. Somerset Maugham, London

McClelland and Stewart Limited, Toronto

McGraw-Hill Book Company, New York

The Meeting House Press, Boston

J. B. Metzlersche Verlagsbuchhandlung, Stuttgart: Emblems listed at the end of Contents.

The University of Minnesota Press, Minneapolis

Minton, Balch & Co., see Putnam

The Modern Library, see Random House

Morehouse Barlow Co., Inc., New York

Arthur Ernest Morgan, Yellow Springs, Ohio

Willa Muir, care Faber

Thea Muller, Bloomington, Ind.

John Murray Ltd., London

National Council of the Churches of Christ, New York

New England Journal of Medicine, Boston

Newsweek, New York

The New York Times, New York

E. M. Nicholson, London

The University of North Carolina Press, Chapel Hill

Northwestern University Press, Evanston

W. W. Norton & Company, Inc., New York

Open Court Publishing Company, LaSalle, Ill.

Osmania University, see Sanskrit

Oxford University Press, New York

Pantheon Books, Inc., see Random House

University of Pennsylvania Law Review, Philadelphia

The University Press, University of Pennsylvania, Philadelphia

Peter Pauper Press, Mt. Vermont, N.Y.

A D Peters & Co., London

Phaidon Press, London

Philosophical Library, Inc., New York

Prentice-Hall, Inc., Englewood Cliffs, N.J.

Princeton University Press, Princeton: Arnold Brecht, *Political Theory*, © 1959; Joseph Fletcher, *Morals And Medicine*, © 1954; Jose Ortega y Gasset, *Mission Of The University*, © 1944; Philip Wheelwright, *Heraclitus*, © 1959; Richard Wilhelm (tr.), rendered into English by Cary F. Baynes, *The I Ching, Or Book Of Changes*, Bollingen Series XIX, © 1950, 1967

Psychiatry, Washington

G. P. Putnam's Sons, New York

Random House, Inc. Alfred A. Knopf, Inc., New York

Joseph Ratner, New York

Reader's Digest, Pleasantville, N.Y.

Revised Standard Version Bible, Nelson, see National Council

The Ronald Press Company, New York

Harry N. Rosenfield, Washington

Routledge & Kegan Paul Ltd, London

Rutgers University Press, New Brunswick

Lillian Steichman Sandburg, Asheville, N.C.

Sanskrit Academy, Osmania University, Hyderabad

Schocken Books Inc., New York

School & Society, New York

Science, Washington

Charles Scribner's Sons, New York

Cynthia Propper Seton, Northampton, Mass.

Sidgwick & Jackson Ltd., London

The Sierra Club, San Francisco

Simon & Schuster, Inc., New York: James R. Newman, *Science And Sensibility*, © 1961

The Society of Authors, London

Stanford University Press, Stanford

St. Martin's Press, Incorporated, New York

Lyle Stuart, Inc., New York

The Swallow Press, Inc., Chicago

Syracuse University Press, Syracuse

Frances Temple, Winchester, Hants

Thames and Hudson Ltd., London

Charles C Thomas, Springfield, Ill.

Helen Thurber, West Cornwall, Conn.

Time, Inc., New York

University of Toronto Press, Toronto

Mark van Doren, New York

Vanguard Press, Inc., New York

The Viking Press, Inc., New York

Ives Washburn, Inc., New York

The Washington Post, Washington

Washington Star, Washington

A. P. Watt & Son, London

Yale Alumni Magazine, New Haven

Yale University Press, New Haven

We thank also all who helped shape the book from sources to covers.

W. S. T. and P. L. S. T.

Northampton, Mass., 01060

Remembering
Sarah Wells Gallet Smith
ever wise and gentle

CONTENTS

In this table the references are to pages.

IX CHARACTER AND PERSONALITY (cont.)

EMBLEMS

The emblems that head the 17 chapters in this book are permitted by J. B. Metzlersche Verlagsbuchhandlung from their Henkel and Schöne, Emblemata: Handbuch der Sinnbildkunst des XVI. und XVII. Jahrhunderts, 1967. The emblems are these:

FOREWORD

This book is designed to be dipped into, to be consulted for suggestions, and for reading.

THE CONTENT

The book is a mosaic of aphorisms and other passages chosen as useful for human living.

The passages are selected from various authors and cultures, from the East and the West, from ancient times to the present. The passages are not, however, chosen to represent authors, cultures, times, doctrines, schools, or even contexts. They are chosen primarily for their content as likely worth while for thoughtful persons in every culture.

The passages are chosen further for form; especially for brevity and clearness, but also, when possible, for freshness and delight. Thus not only the occasional proverbs may have "the wisdom of many and the wit of one."

The passages so gathered are variously old, new, straight-forward, metaphorical, didactic, suggestive, sober, and playful. Each passage, however, is supposed to convey some useful truth.

All the passages are chosen according to a basic philosophic view which reflects substantial trends in art, literature, science, philosophy, and religion. This view is empirical, pragmatic, and humanistic. It is outlined in the last chapter of the book.

THE FORM

Most of the archaic passages have been changed into modern spelling and punctuation. Some passages are either new or synthesized translations.

Three dots show an omission from a quotation which is literal except for translation or modernized spelling and punctuation. Square brackets mark editorial additions.

Passages that come wholly or in parts from more than one independent author, or essentially from the editors' unpublished or out-of-print writings, are not referenced. Otherwise, so far as possible, each passage is followed by a reference to its source. For each passage that is adapted in form only, except by square brackets or by dots, the source is introduced by the word "From"; and for each that is significantly modified or developed in thought, by "After."

In the references, almost all initial articles (A, The, Der, etc.) are omitted. Many titles are shortened further, as shown by dots. Usually omitted from a poetry reference is a title that is the first-cited words or that seems unnecessary for reference. Likewise omitted are many publishers, dates, and easily found titles and pages of works published before 1915, especially works of which there are various editions.

The several forms of numerals mean as in this example:

2: volume; usually a periodical.
II "book," part, act, chapter, canto, or sonnet.
ii section, proposition, scene, or stanza.
2 page or, especially after a roman numeral, verse, rule, maxim, fragment, or line.

W. S. T. and P. L. S. T.

I

Introduction

1   Plants, animals, and men press toward perfect living.

A laurel bush is said to be "happy" when its native vigor and the right soil, filtered shade, and space let it shine green, blossom, and seed.

A dog has more life than the laurel. A dog sniffs, runs, barks, bays at the moon, learns his way around, and welcomes his master home.

A man is a unique organization of vegetative, animal, and higher levels. The higher levels differ enough from the lower to be different not only in degree but in kind: a Schubert song is not only a higher degree of anthropoid vocalization but is music. A man's living embodies a rich mental and social life with values, virtues, and graces. A man's knowledge and understanding increase, and his personality grows.

In living, we cannot but make judgments of bad and good, worse and better, in all areas from creature comforts to religion. Our judgments may be right or wrong; and, as William James said, no bell rings to tell us when they are right. The judgments develop out of our individual natures, experiences, and reflections. As we learn with Franklin that experience is of all teachers the most costly, we learn much from others' experiences as well. Communications, from grunts and gestures to language and electronics, and from folklore to the arts and sciences, bring to everyone some of the wisdom (and unwisdom) that his fellowmen have acquired.

What wisdom men have gained is largely piecemeal and scattered in divers literatures. We all have been surprised to learn how various human groups differ in languages, backgrounds, ways, and ideas. With fuller knowledge, however, we learn how much these same groups, or their most advanced representatives, agree as to how best to live.

2   Sensible men and conscientious men all over the world
are of one religion of well-doing and daring.

Emerson, Preacher

3   In faith and hope the world will disagree,
But all mankind's concern is charity.

Pope, Essay on Man III 303

4   Most likely, men will differ, throughout decades or
centuries, in theology, metaphysics, economics, and other areas
where human values so press, and facts, principles, and choices
are so hard to come by, that dogmas flourish. Possibly, however,
men will agree more and more in how to live as members of
humanity. Such agreement should increase with the spread of
enlightenment throughout the world, not merely from one culture but from the best of every culture.

5   East and West meet in every artist who is more than
an artist and whose love is not restricted to beauty; they meet
also in every great scientist who realizes that truth, however
precious, is not the whole of life, that it must be completed by
beauty and charity.   George Sarton,

History . . . 1937 108-109
Harvard University Press

6   We know that charity grows with understanding. Thus
we can understand that when men drive their workers and
hoard the gains, the workers are not the only slaves.

. . . To be just to these poor men of pelf,
Each does but hate his neighbor as himself:
Damned to the mines, an equal fate betides

The Slave that digs it, and the Slave that hides*.
Who suffers thus, mere Charity should own,
Must act on motives pow'rful, though unknown.

                Pope, Moral Essays III 108

  * hoards

7   Charity between men grows especially as men recognize their common interests.

8   The greatest aid to man is man . . . Men can satisfy their own needs best by mutual help; . . . only by uniting their forces can they escape from the dangers that on every side beset them.   Spinoza, Ethics IV xxxv

9   Common interests, also individual interests, are integral to living.

TOWARD FINDING THE GOOD LIFE

10   By necessity, by proclivity, and by delight, we all quote.
                                      Emerson,
                        Quotation and Originality

11   [Too often] we draw our water from standing pools, which never are filled but with sudden showers, and therefore we are dry so often.   Jeremy Taylor,
        Gest (ed.), House . . . 1954 103 Univ. Pa. Press

12   Be not concerned about the worth of the writer . . . Let your only motive to read be the love of truth.
                Thomas à Kempis, Imitation of Christ I v

13   **Light is good in** whatsoever lamp it is burning.

Abdul Baha

14   Just as a tree bears year after year the same fruit and yet fruit which is each year new, so must all permanently valuable ideas be continually born again in thought.

Schweitzer,
Out of My Life (Campion, tr.) 1933 259 G. Allen

15   All times share the same wide banquet, inexhaustively delightful to one who keeps his taste pure.   Atheneus

16   A great thought is a great boon.   Bovée

17   Often the shorter saying conveys the more wisdom.

Sophocles, Aletes 99

18   Sound precepts enlist the affections and are easily retained; and a few useful ones at hand do more towards a happy life than whole volumes of counsels that we know not where to find.   From Seneca

19   The truth is not always simple, and words often fail to convey it.

We must seek to distinguish between the unclear and the profound; the wordy and the substantial; the merely unconventional and the creative; the traditional that is not sound and the traditional that is sound; and the contemporary and the modern.

II

Over-all View

20 If we could first know where we are, and whither we are tending, we could better judge what to do, and how to do it.

Lincoln

21 The progress of knowledge is greatly retarded by attention to things which are not worth knowing or to such as are not knowable.   Goethe

22 Our trouble is not too much knowledge, but too little.

From Socrates

23 There is a time for small things, and a time for great things; a time for particulars, and a time for wholes.

From Cervantes

24 Solitude is as needful for thinking as society is wholesome for the character.

After J. R. Lowell, Among My Books

25   Though man a thinking being is defined,
Few use the grand prerogative of mind.
How few think justly of the thinking few!
How many never think, who think they do!

Jane Taylor, Essays in Rhyme

TO LIVE

26 Life comes as a gift, especially to one who makes the most of it.

27 Too largely, theologies have encouraged men to spurn the natural world, or to merely endure it, or to try to veneer it; to dream of living somehow above it.

True arts and sciences encourage men to see the world as the place for us to function, compete, and cooperate: to live.

28   Life is creation continuing.

Ansel Adams and Nancy Newhall,
This Is The American Earth 1960 52 Sierra Club

29   Man as invincibly tends to render himself happy as the flame to mount, the stone to descend, or water to find its level. Thus he strives to become wise and good.

Private happiness is allied to public good.

From Volney

30   We have found safety with all things undying,
The winds, and morning, tears of men and mirth,
The deep night, and birds singing, and clouds flying,
And sleep, and freedom, and the autumnal earth.

Rupert Brooke, Collected Poems,
Safety 1915 112 Dodd; Sidgwick; McClelland

31   Man is not against nature, but of nature; and for him to realize this relation is good for his material condition and his spirit.   From H. B. Hough,
Am. Scholar 1957 26:415

32   Man uses one part of nature to control another part.
John Dewey, Monist 1898 8:325

33   Our remedies in ourselves do lie,
Which we ascribe to Heaven.
Shakespeare, All's Well ...
I i 235-236

34   Man alone can see himself and his world in width and depth, and can choose his future course.

From Homer W. Smith,
Man and His Gods 1952 444 Little

35   We have no promise from the universe that we shall survive. We live for the growing of the human spirit, and we strive toward that growth up to the last moment of possibility.

From R. Redfield, Free Society 1958 10
Fund for the Rep.

36   An evil, foolish, intemperate, and irreligious life ought not to be called a bad life but, rather, dying long drawn out.

Democritus

37   The time to be happy is now. The place to be happy is here. The way to be happy is to make others so.

Ingersoll

38   It is not length of life, but depth of life.

Emerson, Immortality

39   If you have known how to compose your life, you have accomplished a great deal more than the man who knows how to compose a book.

From Montaigne, Right Enjoyment of Sensualities

40   He who has learned how to live well has learned also how to die well.   From Epicurus,
Strodach (tr.), Philosophy . . . 1962 181
Northwestern Univ. Press

41   For making a good voyage a pilot and wind are necessary: and for happiness reason and art.

Epictetus, Discourses . . . (Long, tr.) n.d. 443

42   Material things are superseded as spiritual things are not.   From Gilbert Murray

43   What you have inherited from your father you must earn again or it will not be yours.   Goethe

44   A free man meditates not about death; his wisdom is of and for life.   From Spinoza, Ethics IV lxvii

45   To assume that life is worth living helps make it so.

After William James, Will to Believe

46   Spiritual unhealth comes mainly from excessive love for undependable objects [material or immaterial].

From Spinoza, Ethics V xx Note

47   A sincere attachment to truth, moral and scientific, cures a thousand little infirmities of mind.

From Sydney Smith

48   It is good to live and learn.   Cervantes

QUEST FOR TRUTH

49   Every human being has a native need to open his mind to truth. Every human being has the right to freedom in searching for truth and in expressing and communicating his opinions.   From Angelo Giuseppe Roncalli,

Pope John XXIII, Pacem in Terris 1963

50   The mind no longer in the making is dead. Seek the truth, and the *quest* will make you free.   From Lessing

51   The scientific spirit is of more value than its products, and irrationally held truths may be more harmful than reasoned errors.

Thomas Huxley, Science and Culture 1881 312

52   [The open-minded approach to truth, beauty, and goodness has been called the modern spirit. This spirit is, primarily,] the disposition to accept nothing on authority, but to bring all reports to the test of experience. The modern spirit is . . . open on all sides to the influx of truth, *even from the past* . . . The modern spirit is marked, further, by an active curiosity, which grows by what it feeds upon . . . constantly sifting, . . . and holding fast that which is good, only till that which is better is within sight. This endless quest . . . requires labor, requires . . . courage; and so the modern spirit . . . is an heroic spirit. As a reward for difficulties gallantly undertaken, the gods bestow on the modern spirit a kind of eternal youth, with unfailing powers of recuperation and growth.

Stuart P. Sherman,
Genius of America 1925 74–75 Scribner

THE GOOD LIFE

53   There are two sentences inscribed upon the Delphic oracle, highly commended to the usages of man's life: "Know thyself" and "Nothing too much"; and upon these all other precepts depend.   Plutarch

54   Freely comply with every demand of your nature that does not hurt either your animal or your rational nature. The

rational requires what is good for mankind, of which you are
a part; and that good includes both refreshment and discipline.
After Marcus Aurelius, Meditations X 2

55   The sense of right grew up among healthy men and
was fixed by the practice of comradeship.
From William Kingdon Clifford,
Lectures . . . 1886 338

56   Can he be really virtuous who would give himself up
to vices if he did not fear future punishment?
After Kant

57   In the cold season we can tell which trees are ever-
greens.   From Confucius

VALUES AND VIRTUES

58   [Don Juan, speaking to The Devil]: Your friends are
all the dullest dogs I know. They are not beautiful: they are
only decorated. They are not clean: they are only shaved and
starched. They are not dignified: they are only fashionably
dressed. They are not educated: they are only college passmen.
They are not religious: they are only pewrenters. They are not
moral: they are only conventional. They are not virtuous: they
are only cowardly. They are not even vicious: they are only
"frail." They are not artistic: they are only lascivious. They
are not prosperous: they are only rich. They are not loyal,
they are only servile; not dutiful, only sheepish; not public-
spirited, only patriotic; not courageous, only quarrelsome; not
determined, only obstinate; not masterful, only domineering;
not self-controlled, only obtuse; not self-respecting, only vain;

not kind, only sentimental; not social, only gregarious; not considerate, only polite; not intelligent, only opinionated; not progressive, only factious; not imaginative, only superstitious; not just, only vindictive; not generous, only propitiatory; not disciplined, only cowed; and not truthful at all—liars every one of them, to the very backbone of their souls.

Bernard Shaw,
Man and Superman 1920 130–131 Brentano

59   Humility is a good thing, but over-humility is near to crookedness; silence is a virtue, but undue silence bespeaks a deceitful mind.

Confucius, in Lin-Yutang (ed.),
Wisdom of China and India 1942 1096 Open Court

60   Miserable indeed is a world in which we have knowledge without understanding, criticism without appreciation, beauty without love, truth without passion, righteousness without mercy, and courtesy without a warm heart!

Lin-Yutang,
Importance of Living 1937 142 Day; Heinemann

61   Beloved Pan, and all ye gods that haunt this place, make me beautiful within; and may the outward and inward man be at one. May I count the wise to be wealthy, and may I have only such worldly goods as a temperate man, and he alone, can use and support.   Socrates

62   To be honest, to be kind, to earn a little and to spend a little less, to make upon the whole a family happier for his presence, to renounce when that shall be necessary and not to be embittered, to keep a few friends, but these without capitu-

lation; above all, on the same condition, to keep friends with
himself; here is a task for all a man has of fortitude and
delicacy.   R. L. Stevenson, Christmas Sermon

63   To give birth without taking possession,
      To act without appropriation,
      To be chief among men without managing them—
      This is the Mystic Virtue.

                              Lao-tse, in Lin-Yutang (ed.),
              Wisdom of China and India 1942 588 Open Court

64   . . . Stoic, Christian, and Buddhist saints are practically
indistinguishable in their lives.

                  William James, Varieties . . . 1919 504 Longmans

65   Freedom and happiness are within, and virtue is its
own reward.   Stuart Hampshire,
                      Spinoza [1951] 155 Faber; Barnes & Noble

66   It seems to me that the supreme virtue is loyalty to the
adventure of life. This means doing the best we can for a good
way of life.   From Arthur E. Morgan,
                  Search for Purpose 1955 191 Antioch Press

67   If one strives to treat others as he would be treated by
them he will come near the perfect life.   Mencius

68   A human being at his best is a very precious thing.
                                          Ethel Sabin Smith,
                  Preface to a manuscript, God and Other Gods

THE HUMAN COURSE

69   One who has lost his traditional faith tends to find the shrine of some new god where he can kneel and be comforted and put on manacles to keep his hands from trembling.

From W. Lippmann,
Preface to Morals 1929 9 Macmillan

70   To be boosted by an illusion is not to live better than to live in harmony with the truth; it is not nearly so safe, not nearly so sweet, and not nearly so fruitful.

Santayana, Character . . . 1920 87 Scribner

71   To be genuinely civilized means to be able to walk straight and to live honorably without the props and crutches of any of the childish dreams which have supported many credulous men. That such a life can be lived will be difficult for men in general to learn; but many have learned it already.

From W. T. Stace, in Weeks and Flint (eds.),
Jubilee . . . 1957 385 Little

72   The right path (Tao) is near, yet men seek it afar off.

Mencius

73   Upon an everlasting tide
Into the silent seas we go;
But verdure laughs along the side,
And roses on the margin blow.

Nor life, nor death, nor aught they hold,
Rate thou above their natural height;
Yet learn that all our eyes behold,
Has value, if we mete it right.

Pluck then the flowers that line the stream,
Instead of fighting with its power;
But pluck as flowers, not gems, nor deem
That they will bloom beyond their hour.

Whate'er betides, from day to day,
An even pulse and spirit keep;
And like a child, worn out with play,
When wearied with existence, sleep.

Francis Hastings Doyle, Epicurean

74   The artist, the scientist, and the philosopher accept mystery but seek to replace mystification with light.

75   Religion lies deeper than the clergies, rituals, and theologies of all the sects; and in the same fashion, Art is not bound up with any doctrine, school or clique.

Albert Guérard

76   Every religion which proclaims love as the supreme value, and practices it, will be a form of the universal religion; every society which secures the freedom of the person to its members will be a part of the universal society.

From J. Middleton Murry,
Love . . . 1957 14 Cape, © Soc. of Authors

77   We who now live are parts of a humanity that extends into the remote past. The things in civilization we most prize exist by grace of the doings and sufferings of the continuous human community in which we are a link. We are privileged to conserve, transmit, rectify, and expand the heritage that those who come after us may receive it more solid and secure,

more widely accessible and more generously shared than we
have received it.

From John Dewey,
Common Faith 1934 87 Yale Univ. Press

78   Yesterday is but a dream
And tomorrow is only a vision;
But today well lived
Makes every yesterday a dream of happiness
And every tomorrow a vision of hope.
Look well, therefore, to this day.
Such is the salutation of the dawn.

Sanskrit teaching

79   Spirit of Beauty, that dost consecrate
With thine own hues all thou dost shine upon
Of human thought or form,—where art thou gone?

Ask why the sunlight not for ever
Weaves rainbows o'er yon mountain river,
Why aught should fail and fade that once is shown,
Why fear and dream and death and birth
Cast on the daylight of this earth
Such gloom,—why man has such a scope
For love and hate, despondency and hope?

No voice from some sublimer world hath ever
To sage or poet these responses given—
Therefore the names of Daemon, Ghost, and Heaven,
Remain the records of their vain endeavor,
Frail spells—whose uttered charm might not avail to
    sever,
From all we hear and all we see,
Doubt, chance, and mutability.

Thy light alone—like mist o'er mountains driven,
Or music by the night wind sent
Through strings of some still instrument,
Or moonlight on a midnight stream,
Gives grace and truth to life's unquiet dream.

Man were immortal, and omnipotent,
Didst thou, unknown, and awful as thou art,
Keep with thy glorious train firm state within his
   heart.

                    From Shelley, Hymn to Intellectual Beauty

FATO · PRVDENTIA · MAIOR ·

III

Fate and Fortune

80   ... How arrives it joy lies slain,
    And why unblooms the best hope ever sown?
    —Crass Casualty obstructs the sun and rain,
    And dicing Time for gladness casts a moan ...
    These purblind Doomsters had as readily strown
    Blisses about my pilgrimage as pain.
                        Thomas Hardy, Hap

81   We do not what we ought,
        What we ought not, we do,
        And lean upon the thought
        That chance will bring us through.
                   Matthew Arnold,
                   Empedocles on Etna

82   That power which erring men call Chance.
            From Milton, Mask (Comus) 586–587

83   Shallow men believe in luck; wise men in cause and effect ... Fate is unpenetrated causes.
        Emerson, latter, Conduct of Life 1904 32

84   We wrestle in our present state
    With bonds ourself we forged,—and call it Fate.
                  Paul Elmer More,
          Century ... 1898 76 LIV 11–12

85   ... They who await
    No gifts from chance have conquered Fate.
        From Matthew Arnold, Resignation

PAIN AND SUFFERING

86   The heart can ne'er a transport know
        That never knows a pain.
                        George Lyttelton, Song

87   Suffering is good only as it illumines what is not suffering, yields self-discipline, develops compassion, or prevents
greater suffering.

88   The patient who is victimized by serious ailments often
sublimates his suffering by sensitivity, wisdom, goodness, and
creativeness. He endorses the blessing of being alive even on its
most reduced and trying level.
                        From M. Gumpert,
                Anatomy of Happiness 1951 69 McGraw

89   Hope of gain lessens pain.   Proverb

90   Though there is much suffering in the world, there are
also many blessings. Among the blessings are ways to reduce
suffering.

IMPERFECTION

91   Sweet is the rose, but grows upon a brier;
        Sweet is the juniper, but sharp his bough;
        Sweet is the eglantine, but pricketh near;
        Sweet is the firbloom, but his branches rough;
        Sweet is the cypress, but his rind is tough.
                        Edmund Spenser, Amoretti XXVI

92   Everyone must know and admit that he is imperfect, that all other mortals are imperfect, and that it is childish to allow these imperfections to destroy all his hope and all his desire to love.   From O. Hammerstein II

93   In a ripe olive, the very imminence of decay lends a mysterious beauty to the fruit.
From Marcus Aurelius, Thoughts III 2

ADVERSITY

94   O, doth a bird deprived of wings
                     Go earth-bound willfully!
                     Thomas Hardy, Impercipient

95   Not all clouds bring rain.   Dutch proverb

96   There is always someone worse off than yourself.
Aesop

97   Childhood has no forebodings; but then, it is soothed by no memories of outlived sorrow.
George Eliot, Mill on the Floss

98   It would not be better if things happened to men just as they wish.   Heraclitus (Wheelwright, tr.),
1959 Frag. 52 Princeton Univ. Press

99   Before the evils of life come, one must foresee them, at least in general; and when they have come, one must foresee that one can console oneself.   Fontenelle, Du bonheur

100   Bear them we can, and if we can we must.

A. E. Housman

101   ... The darkest day,
Live till tomorrow, will have passed away.

William Cowper,
Needless Alarm, Moral

102   No life is so hard that you can't make it easier by the way you take it.   Ellen Glasgow

103   Every man has his chain and his clog: only it is looser and lighter to one man than to another.

Rule of Life 1800 57

104   It's no use crying over spilt milk: it only makes it salty for the cat.   Anon.

105   It is best to keep as tranquil as possible in misfortune. Nothing in human affairs deserves serious anxiety; impatience does not help us forwards; and grief hinders the self-succor that our duty requires.   From Plato, Republic X 604

106   ... Wise men ne'er sit and wail their loss,
But cheerly seek how to redress their harms.

Shakespeare, Henry VI III V iv 1–2

107   There is a budding morrow in mid-night.

Keats, To Homer

108   If any misfortune befall thee, behold it steadfastly, call it by name, and see what virtue it requires.

Marcus Aurelius

109   Calamity is the perfect glass wherein we truly see and know ourselves.   W. Davenant

110   Fire is the test of gold; adversity, of men.
                                                    From Seneca

111   There is no limit to trials; but the clever man learns by means of them.   Aristotle

112   Adversity elicits talents which in prosperity would have lain dormant.   Horace

113   Men of exceptional shrewdness and resource have usually been through hard times.
                        Mencius, Cranmer-Byng and Watts (eds.),
                        Book ... (Giles, tr.) 1942 110–111 Murray

114   How often the loss of one's fortune or power strengthens the body, perfects the moral qualities, and prolongs life!
                From Maimonides, On the Regulation of Health

115   Sweet are the uses of adversity.
                        Shakespeare, As You Like It II i 12

116   For one man who can stand prosperity there are a hundred that will stand adversity.
                        Carlyle, Hero as a Man of Letters

117   We have ideas yet that we haven't tried.
                        Poetry of Robert Frost (Lathem, ed.),
                        Riders 1969 268 Holt

GOOD FORTUNE

118   Good fortune favors the alert and industrious.

119   Good fortune brings out clearly our virtues and vices
. . . We need greater virtues to support good than bad fortune.
La Rochefoucauld, 1789 ed., Maxims 380 25

FAILURE AND SUCCESS

120   The men who try to do something and fail are infinitely better than those who try to do nothing and succeed.
Lloyd Jones

121   To be overcome by success or failure is to be the child
of circumstances.   From Tut-Tut

122   There is but one failure, and that is not to be true to
the best one knows.   F. W. Farrar

123   I would much rather lose in a good cause than win in
a bad one.   From Woodrow Wilson

124   The man who is successful is he who is useful to others'
spirits.   From Bourke Cockran

125   "To be a success you do not have to reach the top or
to outdistance others; you have only to make faithful use of
whatever ability you possess.

"Your success as a person has no relation to the success or
failure of anyone else."   Quoted by F. C. Brown,
Washington Star, Jan. 6, 1957

126　Even in self-development, nothing succeeds like success.

127　Talk not of your personal success to one who has failed; forget not your failures in your moment of success.

> Tut-Tut, in Lin-Yutang (ed.),
> Wisdom of China and India 1942 1094 Random House

128　A people is great that takes defeat as an opportunity and victory as an ordeal.

> Bernard Berenson Treasury (Kiel, ed.)
> 1962 152 Simon & Schuster

CYNICISM, PESSIMISM, AND OPTIMISM

129　A cynic distrusts mankind. A pessimist is without hope for the world. An optimist is more trusting and hopeful, perhaps too much so.

Such differences can come from native temperament. Often, however, one who is a cynic or a pessimist or both has tasted some grapes of life and found them sour, or has failed to reach the grapes and thinks they must be sour. The optimist has found sweet grapes, but also perhaps some sour ones that he thinks must be sweet.

Cynic, pessimist, optimist, any unrealistic person, may satisfy himself somewhat by thinking that he sees truth that most people fail to see.

130　It is easy to talk disparagingly of the best things.

> Peter Mere Latham

131　A dog starved at his master's gate
　　　Predicts the ruin of the state.

> William Blake, Auguries of Innocence

132   . . . Since the world has still
                Much good, but much less good than ill,
                And while the sun and moon endure
                Luck's a chance, but trouble's sure,
                I'd face it as a wise man would,
                And train for ill and not for good.
                               A. E. Housman,
                       Shropshire Lad Epilogue iii

133   The optimist proclaims that we live in the best of all possible worlds; and the pessimist fears this is true.
                                   J. B. Cabell,
                    Silver Stallion 1926 McBride

134   He that has so many and so great causes of joy is much in love with sorrow and peevishness who loses all these pleasures and chooses to sit down upon his little handful of thorns.
                              From Jeremy Taylor,
               in Gest (ed.), House . . . 1954 55 Univ. Pa. Press

135   One gets a bad habit of being unhappy.
                       George Eliot, Mill on the Floss

136   The optimist considers all the world good except the pessimist. The pessimist considers all the world bad except himself.   From Chesterton

137   Those who complain of the shortness of life let it slide by without making the most of its golden minutes.
               Hazlitt, Spirit of the Age 1825 336

138   Literary or dramatic tragedy, with its relief, enlightenment, and strengthening, is the decisive verdict against pessimism.   After Nietzsche

139   There is no doctrine of absolute negation. Every negation pronounced by men contains a hidden affirmation.
                                        H. Margolius, Gedanken—
                                        Thoughts 1964 Pandanus

140   This is a wretched world . . . a wretched world; and
the worst of it is, that nobody can live in it forever.
                                    Mrs. Darnley, in Santayana,
                                    Last Puritan 1936 535 Scribner

141   Animal optimism is a great renovator and disinfectant
in the world.
              Santayana, Reason in Religion 1905 125 Scribner

142   The lark . . .
              . . . Rises and begins to round,
              He drops the silver chain of sound,
              Of many links without a break,
              In chirrup, whistle, slur and shake,
              All intervolved and spreading wide,
              Like water-dimples down a tide
              Where ripple ripple overcurls
              And eddy into eddy whirls;
              . . .
              But wider over many heads
              The starry voice ascending spreads,
              Awakening, as it waxes thin,

The best in us to him akin;
And every face to watch him raised,
Puts on the light of children praised,
So rich our human pleasure ripes
When sweetness on sincereness pipes
Though naught be promised from the seas,
But only a soft ruffling breeze
Sweep glittering on a still content,
Serenity in ravishment.

For singing till his heaven fills,
'Tis love of earth that he instils,
And ever winging up and up,
Our valley is his golden cup;
And he the wine which overflows
To lift us with him as he goes,
But not from earth is he divorced,
He joyfully to fly enforced;
The woods and brooks, the sheep and kine,
He is, the hills, the human line,
The meadows green, the fallows brown,
The dreams of labor in the town;
He sings the sap, the quickened veins,
The wedding song of sun and rains
He is, the dance of children, thanks
Of sowers, shout of primrose-banks,
And eye of violets while they breathe;
All these the circling song will wreathe,
And you shall hear the herb and tree,
The better heart of men shall see,
Shall feel celestially, as long
As you crave nothing save the song.

    Meredith, The Lark Ascending 1–8 53–86

143   A foolishly sad man can know only foolish happiness.
W. Saroyan, Reporter June 4 1964 32

144   A fond illusion of life is not true, and a bitter dis-illusionment of life is also not true; so we must in good faith hold to our integrity.   From Hung,
Chinese Garden . . . (Chao, tr.) 1959 13
Peter Pauper

REALISM

145   Things and actions, including our own, are what they are, and the consequences of them will be what they will be; why, then, should we desire to be deceived?

From Joseph Butler

146   You throw the sand against the wind,
And the wind blows it back again.
William Blake, Poems 1800–3

147   Only when vitality is low do people find material things oppressive and ideal things unsubstantial.

Santayana

148   Like Antaeus the giant, who renewed his strength every time he touched Mother Earth, the human being grows in stature every time he comes in contact with reality in all its manifold and challenging variety.

Ethel Sabin Smith,
Dynamics of Aging 1956 80 Norton

149   Man's home is the natural world; his purposes and aims depend for execution upon natural conditions. When separate from such conditions they become empty dreams.

From John Dewey

150   The understanding of actuality requires a reference to ideality.   Whitehead

151   Nothing in the world is wholly prosaic, though in some things the poetry runs in thinner veins or lies a little deeper below the surface.   From R. W. Livingstone,
Education ... 1952 104–105 Oxford

152   A sense of right is a source of great strength and its absence one of weakness, but neither will decide a contest if the contestants are too unequal otherwise.

From H. G. Rickover,
Address Ind. Univ. Mar. 1960

153   To believe all men honest would be folly, to believe none so is something worse.

John Quincy Adams, Letter 1809

154   A living dog is better than a dead lion.

Ecclesiastes IX 4

155   The man who waits to make an entirely reasonable will dies intestate.   Bernard Shaw,
Androcles ... Preface 1916 cxxv Brentano

156   He is unreasonable who is overcome by the things which happen from the necessity of nature.

From Epictetus,
Discourses . . . (Long, tr.) n.d. 443

157   Philosopher! Let me not complain that "life is short and passing." For why so short, indeed, if not found sweet?

From Anthony Ashley Cooper,
Third Earl of Shaftsbury, Characteristicks . . . 1732 1:302

158   One must accept the security of the wingèd life, of ebb and flow, of intermittency.   Anne Morrow Lindbergh,

Gift From the Sea 1955 109 Pantheon

159   Knowledge of what is possible is the beginning of happiness.   Santayana,

Three Philosophical Poets 1930 204
Harvard Univ. Press

160   Happiness is nonetheless true happiness because it must come to an end, nor do thought and love lose their value because they are not everlasting.   Bertrand Russell,

Why I Am Not a Christian
1957 43 Simon & Schuster; G. Allen

161   So, again, our green world is going to ruin?

In the Nineteenth Century, Cold Misery portended a ruined State; but Charity grew.

At the turn of the century, Great Graft bore down; but Justice was stirred.

Now Power and Machines pound. Will they serve Humanity?

162   A healthy appraisal leads to joy that mankind, with all its handicaps, achieves much.

From Donald William Rogers, AAUP Bull. 1958 44:567

163   Life is seldom perfect, often good, and naturally interesting.

164   No man can produce great things who is not thoroughly sincere in dealing with himself, who would not exchange the finest pretense for the poorest reality.

J. R. Lowell

ACCEPTANCE

165   Let us imagine an extreme experiment:

There are six soldiers for six solitary posts. The men know nothing about one another. All of them are, by original nature, equally able to feel, perceive, think, and do well. Each one has been so fully trained that he is able and dependable in whatever he has to do as a soldier. Through earlier and perhaps incidental learning, however, each one has learned to react to difficult situations in his own way as a person.

All of the posts are equally isolated, uncongenial, and boring. Each soldier is assigned to one post, without liberty or means of communication, for a solid month.

After each man has been placed at his post, and has realized his situation, his individual response appears as follows.

The first man becomes apathetic. He does mechanically what the post requires, but, as a person, he is essentially vegetative. He merely surrenders to the situation.

The second man becomes melancholy. He surrenders to his situation, but with enough further reaction to be depressed.

The third man develops anxiety. Thus he surrenders with a stronger reaction.

The fourth is angry. He resents his situation; likely he blames it upon some person, a group, or fate; and he feels almost able to blast his way to freedom. Outwardly, he surrenders, but with a more effective emotion than anxiety and, in so far as he blames, with some thought.

The fifth daydreams. He imagines, and perhaps comes to believe, that he is an especially important victim, or that his present situation is perfect, or that he is happily somewhere else. Thus he surrenders physically, but with some thinking, possibly somewhat toward mastering his problem.

Every one of the men cited so far is only partly functioning, like a person more or less asleep; if he thinks about his problem at all, he thinks so narrowly that he is more or less deceived about himself, his immediate world, or both.

The sixth man is fully awake and realistic. He recognizes his situation as unavoidable, yet he neither surrenders to it, rebels against it, nor retreats into a distorted or irrelevant view. On the contrary, he makes the situation his own: he finds what is good in it—a chance to study the spiders, or to plan the house he intends to build; and he makes the most of that without being deceived about the rest. This is acceptance.

166　　We acknowledge, not that all is for the best in the best of all possible worlds (as Leibniz suggested), but that all must have come to be as it is in the only possible world.

From Stuart Hampshire,
Spinoza [1951] 125 Faber; Barnes & Noble

167　　Act for the best, hope for the best, and take what comes.
James Fitzjames Stephen

168   ... The worst is not
           So long as we can say, "This is the worst."
                        Shakespeare, King Lear IV i 27–28

169   To try to kick against natural necessity is to repeat the
folly of Ctesiphon, who undertook to outkick his mule.
                        From Montaigne, in Lowenthal (ed.),
                        Autobiography ... 1935 377 Houghton

170   A man must stoop sometimes to his ill star, but he
must never lie down to it.
                        From Savile, Complete Works ... 1912 238

171   What can't be cured must be endured.
                        Rabelais, Works V XV

172   When we have not what we like, we must like what
we have.   Bussy, Comte de Rabutin

173   [Often] our main business is not to see what lies dimly
at a distance but to do what lies clearly at hand.

                        Carlyle

174   Everything has two handles: one by which it can be
borne, another by which it cannot. If your brother acts un-
justly, lay hold of the affair not by the handle of his injustice,
for by that it cannot be borne, but by the handle that he is your
brother; thus it is to be borne.
                        From Epictetus, Enchiridion XLIII

175   There is some soul of goodness in things evil
           Would men observingly distill it out.
                        Shakespeare, Henry V IV i 4–5

176   To mourn a mischief that is past and gone
Is the next way to draw new mischiefs on.
What cannot be preserved when Fortune takes,
Patience her injury a mockery makes.
The robbed that smiles steals something from the
    thief;
He robs himself that spends a bootless grief.
              Shakespeare, Othello I iii 204–209

177   If you cannot catch fish, catch shrimps.
                Seven Hundred Chinese Proverbs
            (Hart, tr.), 1937 74 Stanford Univ. Press

178   Freedom is the recognition of necessity.   Hegel

ADVENTURE

179   Human nature craves novelty.   Pliny

180   He that leaves nothing to chance will do few things ill,
but he will do very few things.   From Savile,
              Complete Works . . . 1912 247

181   A life without adventure is likely to be unsatisfying,
but a life in which adventure is allowed to take whatever form
it will is sure to be short.   Bertrand Russell,
            Authority . . . 1949 25 G. Allen;
               Simon & Schuster

182   Without adventure civilization is in full decay.
                Whitehead

183 The search is worth the candle and must go on.
P. B. Sears, Am. Scholar 1957 26:450

184 A shipwrecked sailor buried on this coast
Bids you set sail.
Full many a bark, when we were lost,
Weathered the gale.

A Greek epitaph

185 If it is better to travel than to arrive, it is because traveling is a constant arriving. Arrival that precludes further traveling is most easily attained by going to sleep or dying.
From John Dewey,
Human Nature . . . 1922 282 Holt

186 The current of life flows on. Shall we enrich it in our time? Here is all possible scope for poetry, emotion, sentiment, endeavor, service, achievement, joy and pity.
H. B. Hough, Am. Scholar 1957 26:414

187 Adventure, struggle, and challenge require glorious effort, and are good for the soul.
From Marion Hilliard,
Woman Doctor . . . 1957 180 Doubleday

188 Difficulty of achievement stupifies the sluggard, terrifies the fearful, advises the prudent, and animates the courageous. From Rule of Life 1800 129

CHALLENGE

189 Progress is spurred when the difficulties almost equal the capacity to meet them. From R. Devereux

190   Great prophets and philosophers, poets and artists generally grow in unsettled societies, on the brink of some abyss.

> Walter Kaufmann,
> From Shakespeare to Existentialism 1960 23 Doubleday

191   High motivation is as precious as talent. Barriers which must be hurdled bring highly motivated people to the top.

> From John W. Gardner, Excellence 1961 100 Harper

HEROISM

192   Heroism is the glorious concentration of courage.

> From Amiel, Journal

193   We should rather die as men than live as animals.

> J. W. Krutch,
> Modern Temper 1929 249 Harcourt

194   He who is most fit to live welcomes the joy of life and the duty of life, and does not fear to die. Theodore Roosevelt considered "both life and death . . . parts of the same Great Adventure." Each person should serve the larger and continuing life of the whole.

> Quoting from Theodore Roosevelt,
> Great Adventure 1918 1 Scribner

195   'Tis better to have fought and lost,
Than never to have fought at all.

> Arthur Hugh Clough, Poems 1883 325

196   There is a heroism of omission no less profound, but much more difficult to exemplify, than the heroism that comes from the all-too-easy commitment to action.

> T. V. Smith, in Denise and Williams (eds.),
> Retrospect . . . 1956 138 Syracuse Univ. Press

197   The mighty dead, who humanized the sordid religious dogma of their time despite the terror of rack and thumb-screw and the other methods of torture invented to break not only the body but, infinitely worse, the spirit!

> From Oliver Watson May, Letter . . . Feb. 24 1958

198   Death in a good cause is no punishment, but an honor.

> From Spinoza, Theologico-political Treatise XX

199   Nor deem that acts heroic wait on chance:
The man's whole life preludes the single deed.

> J. R. Lowell,
> Under the Old Elm vii 3

200   Death, which threatens us daily and can never be far off, does not deter a wise man from making provision for his family and his country, and from regarding posterity as belonging to himself.   From Cicero

201   To the end of men's struggles a penalty will remain for those who sink from the ranks of the heroes into the crowd for whom the heroes fight and die.   George Eliot, Felix Holt

IV

Human Nature

202   The proper study of mankind is man:
        Sole judge of truth, in endless error hurled:
        The glory, jest, and riddle of the world!
                        From Pope, Essay on Man II 2 17–18

203   Man contains the animal, the animal the vegetable, the
vegetable the mineral, the mineral mathematics. Thoroughly
to understand man would be to find the universe an open book.
                From Amiel, V. Brooks and C. V. Brooks (trs.),
                        Private Journal ... 1935 xii Macmillan

BODY

204   I am fearfully and wonderfully made.
                                Psalms CXXXIX 14

205   In the parable of Jesus, the shepherd saves not merely
the soul of the lost sheep but the whole animal.
                Schweitzer, Out of My Life ... (Campion, tr.)
                        1933 270 Holt; G. Allen

206   The whole body is the vehicle for living.

207   That blessed internal peace and confidence that wells
up from every part of the muscularly well-trained human being
is, quite apart from its mechanical utility, an element of
spiritual hygiene.   From William James,
                        Talks to Teachers ... 1900 207

DISEASE

208   It is dainty to be sick, if you have leisure and convenience for it.   Emerson

209   Prevention is easier than cure.   Traditional

210   Some remedies are worse than the disease.
                              Publilius Syrus, Maxim 301

211   Sickness shows how much we are dependent on one another for comfort and even for necessities.
                              From Hosea Ballou

HEALTH

212   Health and a good constitution are better than all gold.
                              Ecclus. XXX 15

213   Health is so necessary to all the duties as well as pleasures of life that the crime of squandering it is equal to the folly.   From Samuel Johnson

214   Every diminution of the will-to-live is an ignorance of life or a definite symptom of ill-health.
                              After Schweitzer,
                    Civilization ... 1929 221 Macmillan; Black

215   With health a certain euphoria, a certain alacrity and sense of mastery are induced in the spirit.
                              From Santayana

216   Keep the body in good health to keep our mind strong
and clear.   Buddha, in Lin-Yutang (ed.),
        Wisdom of China and India 1942 360 Random House

217   Men of great abilities are generally of a vigorous animal nature.
                    From Henry Taylor, Statesman 1836 229

218   People who are always taking care of their health are
like misers hoarding up what they have not enough spirit to
enjoy.   From Sterne

219   The sick are often more sick in mind than in body.
                    From Manas, Apr. 10 1963 2

220   Good health and good sense are two of life's greatest
blessings.   Publilius Syrus, Maxim 827

221   My wealth is health and perfect ease;
            My conscience clear my chief defense.
                                    Edward Dyer,
                        My Mind to Me a Kingdom Is 43–44

FOOD AND DRINK

222   Keep him at least three paces distant who hates bread,
music, and the laugh of a child.
                    Lavater, Aphorism 318 (1787 ed.)

223   The best sauce for food is hunger.   Socrates

224   Appetite comes with eating.   Rabelais, Works I V

225   The stomach is a slave that must accept everything that is given to it, but which avenges wrongs as slyly as does a recalcitrant slave.   From Émile Souvestre

226   He who does not mind his belly will hardly mind anything else.   Samuel Johnson,
G. B. Hill (ed.), Boswell's Life . . . 1887

227   I never yet knew a man who was sad during his digestion of a good dinner. We like, at such moments, to remain in quietude, between the revery of a thinker and the comfort of the ruminating animals.   Balzac, Red Inn XXX

228   What neat repast shall feast us, light and choice, of Attic taste?   Milton, Lawrence

229   The vapors of wine may sometimes throw out sparks of wit; but they are like scattered pieces of ore, there is no vein to work upon.

Some men think they can drown their reason once a day, and that it will not be the worse for it; forgetting that, by too often diving, the understanding at last grows too weak to rise up again.

Nothing is a greater enemy to the brain than too much moisture; it can the least of anything bear being continually steeped. Thought may be likened to some creatures which can live only in a dry country.

From Savile, Some Cautions . . .

230   Better is a dinner of herbs, where love is, than a stalled ox and hatred with it.   Proverbs XV 17

231   When food is lacking in the larder, quarrel knocks at the door.
                                                    Baba Metzia

232   It is hard to tell the difference between right and wrong when the stomach is empty.
                                                    Chinese proverb

233   The thinker must have enough health and food and whatever else is necessary. Yet, though a man cannot be wholly happy without external goods, he needs only a modicum of them. A man can do noble acts without being ruler of land and sea.
                    From Aristotle, Nicomachean Ethics X viii

REST

234   Wayfarers on the dusty road
       By shaded wells their heavy load
       Undoing rest awhile, and then
       Pass on restored.—What cause of tears, O men?
                    Paul Elmer More, Century . . . LVIII

235   Rest is not quitting the busy career,
              Rest is the fitting of self to one's sphere.
                                        J. S. Dwight, Rest IV

SLEEP

236   Oh sleep! It is a gentle thing,
              Beloved from pole to pole.
                                                    Coleridge,
                            Rime of the Ancient Mariner, V 1–2

237   Tired Nature's sweet restorer, balmy Sleep!
> Edward Young, Night I 1

238   Sleep that knits up the ravelled sleave of care,
The death of each day's life, sore labor's bath,
Balm of hurt minds, great nature's second course,
Chief nourisher in life's feast.
> Shakespeare, Macbeth II ii 38–41

239   Heaven trims our lamps while we sleep.
> A. B. Alcott, Table-Talk 1877 70

240   Something attempted, something done,
Has earned a night's repose.
> Longfellow, Village Blacksmith

241   . . . Weariness
Can snore upon the flint, when resty sloth
Finds the down pillow hard.
> Shakespeare, Cymbeline III vi 33–35

242   . . . The cares that infest the day
Shall fold their tents like the Arabs,
And as silently steal away.
> Longfellow, Day is Done

243   He sleeps well who knows not that he sleeps ill.
> Publilius Syrus, Maxim 77

244   And all around
Mild apple boughs cool waters sound,

And from the rustling leaves o'erhead
Deep sleep is shed.

Sappho, Cool and Drowsy Orchard

245 There is sweet music here that softer falls
Than petals from blown roses on the grass,
Or night-dews on still waters between walls
Of shadowy granite, in a gleaming pass;
Music that gentlier on the spirit lies,
Than tired eyelids upon tired eyes;
Music that brings sweet sleep down from the
blissful skies.
Here are cool mosses deep,
And through the moss the ivies creep,
And in the stream the long-leaved flowers weep,
And from the craggy ledge the poppy hangs in
sleep.

Tennyson, Lotos-Eaters VI

246 Even sleepers collaborate in the processes of the universe.   From Heraclitus, Frag. 41

247   Each night we die,
Each morn are born anew; each day a life!
Edward Young, Night II 286–287

SENSES AND ELEMENTARY FEELINGS

248   The eye of man hath not heard, the ear of man hath
not seen, man's hand is not able to taste, his tongue to conceive, nor his heart to report, what my dream was.
Shakespeare, Midsummer Night's Dream IV i 218–221

249 The devotee who contemns all sensations has no point of reference by which to judge even the ones he claims are false. From Epicurus (Strodach, tr.), Philosophy . . . 1962 200 Northwestern Univ. Press

250 Lights, sounds, odors, skin pressures, muscle pulls, and the like, as we get them apart from their meanings, reduce to elementary sensations, primal experiences through the senses. Sensations are more or less localized in the body and discriminating between stimuli. Sensations seem to have developed later in evolution than the elementary feelings.

The elementary feelings, also called hedonic reactions, are two, pleasantness and unpleasantness (not to be confused with pleasure and displeasure, which are more complex affective states). Pleasantness and unpleasantness are neither localized nor in themselves discriminating; though pleasantness is likely to accompany good tastes, odors, and so on, and unpleasantness is likely to accompany pains, bad tastes, and such. Apparently the two feelings are general, basic reactions, which are mutually exclusive, and either of which, whether weak or strong, pervades the whole person. Thus, unless there are times with no elementary feeling, at any given moment either pleasantness or unpleasantness is one's hedonic tone. This tone occurs with every mental state, from relatively simple ones, of which "sheer pleasantness" would be an example, to the most complex states, affective, cognitive, or conative (striving or doing), and their combinations.

The complex affective states include emotions.

FEAR AND ANGER: EMERGENCY EMOTIONS

251 Fear ranges from anxiety to terror; anger, from irritation to fury.

Fear or anger occurs when the individual feels severely hurt, thwarted, or threatened; fear when he feels relatively unable, and anger, relatively able, to meet what for him at the moment is an emergency. These emotions have therefore been called emergency emotions.

252   We boil at different degrees.
                    Emerson, Society and Solitude, Eloquence

253   Anger is a wind which blows out the lamp of the mind.
                                            Anon.

254   The first part of anger is madness and the second is regret.   Wortabet (tr.), Arabian Wisdom 1910 46

255   Many a violent antipathy betrays a secret affinity.
                                            After Hazlitt

256   Anxiety is not permissible.
                            Shayast-La-Shayast XX 12

257   Where ill nature is not predominant, anger cannot hold out a long course; for our emotions, like our limbs, are tired with being long in one posture.
    There is in good sense a dignity that is offended and defaced by anger.
                    From Savile, Moral Thoughts . . . Of Anger

258   A tranquil mind is health for the body; passion is a rot in the bones.   Proverbs XIV 30

259   The greatest remedy for anger is delay.   Seneca

260   Only the ignorant man becomes angry. The wise man understands.   East Indian teaching

261   As many children quail in the dark, so we in the light of day are often terrified by things which are no more to be feared than what those children think is going to happen. This terror must be routed by the rational inspection of nature.

From Lucretius (Strodach, tr.),
Philosophy ... 1962 70–71 Northwestern Univ. Press

262   Explosions of temper and needless fear are simply bad habits. By ventilation and illumination of the mind it is possible to cultivate tolerance, poise, and real courage.

From Metchnikoff

SORROWFUL EMOTIONS

263   A feeling of sadness and longing
               That is not akin to pain,
               And resembles sorrow only
               As the mist resembles the rain.

Longfellow, Day is Done

264   Light griefs are loquacious, but the great are dumb.

Seneca, Hippolytus II iii 607

265   Oftentimes we call a man cold when he is only sad.

Longfellow

266   The secret of being miserable is to have leisure to bother about whether you are happy or not.

Bernard Shaw, Misalliance, Preface 1914

PLEASANT EMOTIONS

267   Some people think that whatever is done solemnly
must make sense.   G. C. Lichtenberg

268   Joy is the sweet voice, Joy the luminous cloud.
        We in ourselves rejoice!
        And thence flows all that charms or ear or sight,
        All melodies the echoes of that voice,
        All colors a suffusion from that light.
                    Coleridge, Dejection v

269   Our affections are our life. They supply our warmth.
                    From W. E. Channing

270   Sex is such a strong, recurrent motive, even before
physical and mental maturity, and is so freighted with actual
and potential values and disvalues, that commonly it enlists
more thinking for or against than about it.

Until well into the Twentieth Century, in our culture there
was little enlightenment about sex. (Sexual adventures and enlightenment are not synonymous.) There was some sex instruction, both official and unofficial. The official kind was intended
to keep the young chaste. Much of this instruction was presented "in a modest way," that is, in the half-light of taboos,
hence was prejudiced, partial, and often erroneous. The
unofficial kind was produced clandestinely to tell the young
what they wanted to know. Most of this kind was presented in
a ribald way, in a spirit of truancy from the taboos, and was
correspondingly prejudiced, partial, and often erroneous. Thus
the young were given two general impressions about sexual
motivation, one that it is bad under any conditions, and another that it is good despite traditional condemnation. Nat-

urally these impressions conflicted with each other and with normal impulse, judgment, and idealism.

Under modern social conditions, most people find some enlightenment about sex, but little about ethics. Many resent the previous lack of enlightenment about sex but overlook the lack of enlightenment about ethics. If they think about ethics at all, they tend to confuse ethics with behests of theology or of propriety, especially when the behests are more commended than practiced. Consequently, many people either overvalue sex, perhaps taking it to be the only real source of personal and marital happiness, or cheapen sex, so losing its reinforcement for familial interests. Either error leads to conflicts with other motives.

What we know of sexual motivation is no argument for licentiousness. Many "emancipated" persons merely flounder out of traditional taboos and into worse thwartings, and even develop psychoneuroses in consequence. Psychologically and ethically, good living means maximal integration; not indulgence of some interests, such as the sexual, through denial of other interests, such as the altruistic and idealistic. As Spinoza said, "A thing can be bad for us not through the quality which it has in common with our nature, but in so far as it is contrary to our nature."

Sexual motivation ought not to be confused with other pleasant states such as esthetic emotion, tender emotion (love for one's pet, child, parent, friend), sympathy, or altruism. Nor can we say that these pleasant states are but diverted or refined forms of sexual motivation. True, they often accompany sexual motivation; they blend in sexual love and with one another; and naturally they and sexual emotion reinforce one another. Often, however, they occur quite apart from sexual motivation. They all seem to be pleasant emotions, or at least pleasant states of mind, in their own right.

271   Loving is part of one's warm appreciation of life, and enhances that appreciation.

272   Love . . . moves between two poles: on one side, pure delight in contemplation; on the other, pure benevolence . . . well-wishing.
                                                Bertrand Russell,
                        Why I Am Not a Christian 1957 45 46
                                G. Allen; Simon & Schuster

273   What is love? Love is a feeling which takes various forms. Love can wax ardent or blow lightly in delight; love can be blinding or illumining.

Perhaps the form of love that we think of first is *sexual* love. This is a fusion of lust with personal appreciations and tender feelings. The pattern of fusion varies from culture to culture, from person to person, and from youth to maturity. *Marital* love includes mutual respect and congeniality which together can create a life of the spirit. Often this life needs to be cultivated. *Parental* love is a bond of hope and care for a child's good. *Love for relatives and friends,* grown from common experiences, interests, and pleasures, at its best expands the spirit. *Compassion,* or *charity* in the King James usage, is a desire, a fervent hope, for comfort and peace of someone through sympathy, understanding, and benevolence.

There is a degree of love in the *attachment* to a domestic pet, a delicate vase, a familiar greenwood, not as an echo of another love. We say that love is *a part of creative activity,* as in the devotion to express a deep personal experience or insight.

These several loves, together with turns of fortune, the cruelties and beauties of nature, her mysterious processes, the order in the universe, and infinity evoke feelings of wonder, awe, submission, and perhaps participation. The source of all may seem otherworldly, supernatural, or inherent. A person may take the source, or the whole, or evolution, or a goal such as happiness for mankind to be the highest good. His accordant communion or devotion is *religious* love.

The several loves are not wholly different one from another. They all have degrees of warm or heightened feeling that is uniquely pleasant. Each, too, is a blend of different elements.

Common to most of the loves is tender emotion, as in love for a pet, for a person, and in many an instance of charity. Most if not all loves include also esthetic appreciation. Many loves contain admiration, pride, congeniality, and altruism.

Yet the several loves are not wholly alike. Each love has its realm, its living-path. There the love has its special object, such as a mate or a child, and the special feelings, thoughts, and actions that relate to that object.

Different blends vary the loves. And within each type of love there are individual blends. Within sexual love, one person's blend may contain much sense of beauty; another's, little.

Difference in the blend may produe one-season love or sustained love. Through idealizing a person, one can float upon imaginative thought into romantic love. This ranges from puppy love, and attachment through being "in love with love," to medieval courtly love of verse and song, and such zestful married life as that of Robert and Elizabeth Browning. Though some American tradition and the cinema place all romantic love higher than the rainbow, romantic love without realistic thought can hardly create a fruitful marriage. Unrealistic romantic love may fail to gain the good earth of mutual respect, sufficiently common style of life, and thoughts and deeds for posterity.

Parental loves differ also. In one parent, the love may be

almost wholly tender and protective; in another, it may be tinged with egoistic pride, parental extension of the self in the offspring.

Any kind of love can be corrupted by untoward circumstances or poor judgment. Love can be ego-laden, or lapse into satiety; in either case it is directed away from the poised art of loving and living. Overimpulsive love can lead to infatuations which prevent clear thought and perspective.

Every kind of love can be harmed by failure to realize that, within the limits of human attention, the several kinds of love are naturally compatible and tend to reinforce each other. Esthetic appreciation for a person is likely to arouse tender feeling; and tender feeling, esthetic appreciation. Enhancement of any love makes the world more beautiful; and finding the world more beautiful enhances one's loves.

Various well-meaning mentors have tried to teach that lust and tender emotion are incompatible. "Lust," they say, "is egoistic, and tender emotion is altruistic." It is true that lust can occur without tender emotion, and that tender emotion occurs frequently without lust. It is also true that, of the two emotions, lust is commonly the more impulsive. It is the more primitive.

In evolution, mating occurred earlier than parental care, family affection, and nonsexual friendliness. Tender emotion is more highly evolved than lust. It is also the more encouraged by society because the consequences of tender emotion are usually benign.

Naturally, however, each of the two emotions *in itself* is merely impulsive, wholly without altruism. Simple lust merely seeks expression. Every mother wants to fondle her child. An unthinking mother may fondle her child so much that she cramps its development. Therein she is not altruistic. Altruism takes learning and thought. Tender emotion, being a relatively calm state, is more conducive to thought than is lust, hence is more conducive to altruism.

Given freedom from prejudice, lust and tender emotion naturally reinforce each other, and so tend to converge upon the same loved person. Altruism can check lust and tender emotion somewhat alike. It can also enhance either or both.

Of course, neither sexual love, nor any love, can solve all problems, cure all unhappiness, or substitute for all other values.

Personal styles vary from extreme exuberance to quiet tastes with little overt expression. Restraint can be mistaken to be coldness, lacking love; exuberance can be found intrusive, undisciplined, unintellectual, romantic, even sentimental. Persons with opposite qualities are not easily compatible.

Some say that everyone is lonely unless "completed" by sexual love. Loneliness can come from a lack of resourcefulness. A solitary person in an absorbing project is not lonely. A self-sufficient person may relish his own thought and spirit of adventure. Even a socially-minded person may be moved not so much by compassion as by intellectual curiosity and the urge to find answers. Also, creative outgoing love can find an incoming benevolence intrusive.

Anyone who tries to live by and for "nothing but love" must fail in self-guidance and contribution. At best, he can become like a too-serene wanderer in a lovely fog.

Since there are limits of human attention, no one can enjoy all the human values of fun, learning, and the loves either at once or successively. Life is so abundant that often one must choose. Socrates taught that one needs to choose knowingly.

274   When the enterprising burglar's not a-burgling,
       When cut-throat isn't occupied in crime,
       He loves to hear the little brook a-gurgling,
       And listen to the merry village chime.
                          W. S. Gilbert, Policeman's Lot

275   A cheerful heart has a continual feast.
                                   Proverbs XV 15

276   The spirit of delight comes often on small wings.
                          R. L. Stevenson, Ordered South

277   Men's muscles move better when their souls are making merry music.   George Eliot, Adam Bede

278   A merry heart goes all the day,
              Your sad tires in a mile-a.
                  Shakespeare, Winter's Tale IV ii 135–136

279   A merry heart is a good medicine; but a broken spirit
drieth the bones.   Proverbs XVII 22

280   It is as healthy to enjoy sentiment as to enjoy jam.
                                              Chesterton

281   Ability to turn to elementary beauties is a test that
judgment remains sound.
                    Santayana, Reason in Art 1905 197 Scribner

282   In the man whose childhood has known caresses there
is always a fiber of memory that can be touched to gentle
issues.   George Eliot, Janet's Repentance

283   Pleasantness, pleasure, and happiness are not the same. Pleasantness is an elementary feeling. Pleasure includes pleasantness, also sensations from without and from within the body, and further reactions, including some thought. Happiness includes some pleasure, also especially thought, understanding, and likely some philosophy and religion. Yet it seems possible that all pleasant experience, from pleasantness to happiness, may occur with passage toward the most-perfect functioning of the organism in itself, and unpleasant experience, toward the least-perfect functioning of the organism in itself.

This view does not make goals and practical effects unimportant. On the contrary, goals and effects naturally influence the functioning: worthy goals and good consequences make for perfect functioning and pleasant experience, and unworthy goals and bad consequences make for imperfect functioning and unpleasant experience.

This does not mean that one should live intent on one's own pleasure or even happiness. Any *direct* attempt to get pleasure or happiness makes it vanish. Good living is for good goals, and in good activities, for themselves; and therein occurs pleasant experience, from pleasantness to happiness.

After Spinoza, Ethics III,
Definition of the Emotions 2, IV xlv Note, and passim;
Ethel D. Puffer, Psychology of Beauty 1907;
Everett, Moral Values 1918 Holt

284   No pleasure endures unseasoned by variety.
Publilius Syrus, Maxim 406

285   Pleasure is far sweeter as a recreation than a business.
Roswell Hitchcock

286   Headlong joy is ever on the wing.

Milton, Passion 5

287   A wise man refreshes and invigorates himself with moderate and pleasant eating and drinking, sweet scents, green plants, ornaments, music, sports, the theatre, and all things that one can enjoy without hurting another. For the human body is composed of a great number of parts which constantly need new and varied nourishment in order that the whole body and the mind may be equally fit.

From Spinoza, Ethics IV xv Note

288   The ceasing of a pain, the change from cold to warm, sunshine, young animals, flowers, the taste of food, the discovery of a book or a painting, melody, some new knowledge, the looking at happiness, the absence of hostility, being listened to, being well groomed, being liked, giving to others, some usefulness, silence, being tired after work, sleeping, being well rested, leisure, and humor—for those who are able and willing, there is no end to the enjoyment of being alive.

After M. Gumpert,
Anatomy of Happiness 1951 211 McGraw

289   He who bends to himself a joy
               Doth the wingèd life destroy:
               But he who kisses the joy as it flies
               Lives in eternity's sunrise.

William Blake, Eternity

290   The joy of life is to put out one's power in some natural and useful or harmless way.

Lin-Yutang,
On the Wisdom of America 1950 450 Day

291   In Joy one does not only feel secure, but something goes out from oneself to the universe, a warm, possessive effluence of love.   John Buchan,
Pilgrim's Way 1940 117 Houghton

292   Blessed are the joymakers.   N. P. Willis

MOODS

293   Wrapt in a pleasing fit of melancholy.
Milton, Mask (Comus) 546

294   One basic emotion drives out another. Thus fear displaces anger, or anger, love, at least momentarily.
Moods based on such emotions likewise displace one another; though more subtly based emotions may blend.
Often a person says he is "not in the mood" to practice a musical instrument, or to do creative work, when he means only that he is not well mobilized to do just that.
An occasional person says "I can't do it until I am in the mood." He means that he can do it only when he is in a particular affective state, such as anger, anxiety, or love, in which habitually he does his practicing or creative work.
Any such mood—an affective state—tends to recur with its specially associated memories, thoughts, and actions. It embodies a rather limited and stereotyped pattern of reactions. This pattern is relatively compartmented from other moods and from the rest of the mental life.
Though love may be relatively little compartmenting, any real mood as habitual for the practicing makes it not well organized with the total person, hence not most fruitful. Likewise, to confine creativity within a habitual mood may isolate the creative effort from so many data and perspectives as to

make the product more ingrown and peculiar than sound and beautiful.

"A moody person" is not so well put together, integrated, as one who is not "given to moods."

295   The taste for emotion may become a dangerous taste; we should be careful not to squeeze out of life more ecstasy and paroxysm than it can afford.

From Sydney Smith

MIND

296   Man is the highest type produced by over two-and-a-half billion years of the blind opportunistic workings of natural selection; if he does not destroy himself, he has at least an equal stretch of evolutionary time before him.

During the later part of biological evolution there emerged mind—our word for the mental activities and properties of organisms. Eventually it became the main source of further evolution, which is less biological than cultural.

Thus the cosmos reveals, in man especially, an evolutionary trend toward mind, with its richness of being.

After Julian Huxley (ed.),
Humanist Frame 1961 17–19 G. Allen

297   The mind is within the world as a part of the world's own ongoing process.

From John Dewey, Quest . . . 1929 291 Minton

298   Mental organization correlates with anatomical and physiological organization of the brain.

After Russell Brain, in Julian Huxley (ed.),
Humanist Frame 1961 57 G. Allen

299   The elementary sensations directly making up our ordinary sensations are themselves compounded of sensations of less intensity and duration, and so on. As to the elements, consciousness does not attain to them, reasoning concludes that they exist; they are to sensations what molecules and atoms are to bodies; we have but an abstract conception of them, and what represents them to us is not an image, but a notation. We only perceive the highest points, the lighted-up peaks of a continent whose lower levels remain in the shade. By the side of ordinary images and ideas are their collaterals, the latent images and ideas, which must take their turn of preponderance and ascendancy in order to reach consciousness.

We recognize intelligent mental activity by its results, which often suddenly appear from some unexpected source. This darkened sphere is much greater and more characteristic for the individuality than the relatively small number of impressions which pass into the state of consciousness.

From Taine and from W. Griesinger,
in Lancelot Law Whyte, Unconscious Before Freud
1960 174 160–161 Basic Books; G. Allen

300   Many theorists and practitioners have assumed that the subconscious holds repressed emotion, and that this is unhealthy, though perhaps safer than to express the emotion in a proper society. From this assumption it follows that, for his best health, so far as his society will permit, the person who has repressed emotion should "get it out of his system" as soon as he can; whenever he is emotionally aroused he should express the emotion at once if possible; and, if his honest expression of the emotion hurts his reputation, or hurts someone else (as when a young man was told, "You must express to your

stepfather your hatred of him"), that is a comparatively small price to pay for keeping a sound mind.

So far as we can judge, those assumptions reflect some truths. One's anger, fear, love, any emotion, can become so strongly linked with a particular person, topic, or other object that that object continually evokes or threatens to evoke it, as though the emotion were a fluid stuff somehow stored up and pressing to be let out. To merely hold in any strong emotion is wearing, and, if long continued without at least alternative satisfaction, can be pathogenic. Self-deception that one does not have the emotion is more pathogenic, or is actual pathology.

Nevertheless, the assumptions that emotion is stored and that repression and expression are the only ways to handle it are contrary to what seems our best understanding of emotion. Though any emotion derives partly from and contributes to divers hormones and other fluids of the body, it is not itself a stuff that can be stored anywhere, even in the subconscious. The negative or unpleasant emotions, namely, fear, anger, and their congeners, which are integral to many if not all neuroses, accompany patterns of response that arise from psychological stress. Pleasant emotions accompany patterns of response that arise from happy events. Whatever the emotion, it recurs whenever its source, or a conditioned excitant that means that source, occurs; and this goes on until some different pattern of response is developed for the given source or in lieu of reaction to it. Fortunately, to many a natural or conditioned source of negative emotion especially, repression and expression are not the only possible responses. Clear understanding, reassessment, effective planning and action, and reasonable turning to other interests, including some with pleasant emotions, are all to the good. Confer Spinoza!

W. S. Taylor, Am. J. Clin. Hypn. 1966 8:156–157;
referring to Spinoza, Ethics III IV

301   As consciousness is the latest development in human evolution, it is the most vulnerable, though the most significant, of our general powers.

From John Hughlings-Jackson

302   To see how our motives are various and often conflicting, let us consider a case. This case is not historical; it is partly from Benavente's play, The Passion Flower. It is, however, typical of the rather extreme cases which are most illuminating.

Phila is a girl, 15 years old, and an only child. Her father dies. She and her widowed mother live together.

The mother remarries and is happy. Phila is glad on her mother's account, yet feels displaced. As she does not want to be selfish, she helps make the home pleasant for the man, and finds him to be a pleasant person. Soon, however, she begins to notice things about him that she does not like. Before long they irritate her so much that she "can't stand the man"; indeed, she hates him, and even screams that she hates him.

All three persons become so disturbed that the girl pours out her troubles to a woman friend who lives nearby. The friend listens, and asks questions. Finally she suggests that perhaps Phila does, as she says, hate the man partly because he has seemed to preempt some of her mother's love for her, and partly because of his idiosyncrasies; but especially because, naturally in her situation, she had unwittingly fallen in love with him, her mother's husband. That she had so fallen in love seemed clear from many little acts, such as always waiting up for him when he came home late "so she could scold him for coming home so late."

"I'm *not* in love with him!" Phila shouts. "You don't *know* how I hate him!" But even as she protests, she begins to recall sundry feelings, fancies, and acts that she had not assessed;

and before she leaves she realizes that her friend's analysis is true.

At first furious, then crestfallen, and finally hopeful and grateful, she goes home.

The next day she returns and talks further with the friend. Now Phila realizes clearly that she had been unaware of a special root of her intense reactions to her stepfather; that that root was subconscious fantasy; and that she has other, more fruitful, interests.

Through some more talks with her friend, and reading George Eliot, and developing additional interests, she gains further perspective; and within a few weeks the family life is normal.—

Everyone has various needs and interests, such as food, love, ambition, altruism; various motives.

Some motives are essentially physical; others are higher, mental or spiritual.

Within each person, at times, some motives conflict: physical with physical, physical with higher, or higher with higher. Most such conflicts get resolved or dissolved quickly: if A is jealous of B, yet wants to be a nice person, he humiliates B with too much kindness; or he becomes interested in something else, and has no time to be jealous. Some conflicts persist until, after days, months, or years, the individual develops a new attitude or a somewhat revised way of living: A comes to understand and appreciate B, and is no longer jealous of him; or A moves into work where B is not a rival. Some conflicts in some persons are never settled.

Some motives, whether physical or higher, are less acceptable to the individual than others, according to his lights. Unacceptable to many a puritanical person are sex, greed, fear, jealousy, any motive the individual considers sinful or unworthy.

Even when the individual has not realized that he has such a motive, he may fear or hate it, and, without knowing why, may fear or hate himself as an inadequate person.

When an unwelcome motive continues to press against other motives and the conflict becomes wearing, the person may try not to think about the unwelcome motive, and may even make himself think that it does not exist.

Often a physical or a higher motive must be bypassed or checked for the sake of other motives; even, in an emergency, that the individual or something dear to him may survive. Anyone, however, who insists that an actual physical or a higher motive within him does not exist gets a warped, too-limited view of himself and of human nature; a view that contravenes the freshest and fullest living. He needs to apply Socrates' maxim, "Know thyself"; to weigh values ethically; and to have realistic ideals.

Aristotle taught that human nature is essentially vegetative, animal, and rational. Of these, the vegetative level is the lowest (in a functional, not pejorative, sense), and the rational is the highest. The three levels are, however, interdependent; and each person is a unique organization of the three levels.

We know that the three levels shade into one another, and that they have evolved from the simplest forms of life. Normally, the lower levels support the higher, and the higher conserve and guide the lower, unto the best life for the whole organism.

Any usurpation by a lower level, or any presumption by the highest that a lower level does not exist, is self-defeating. Only as each level is, in effect, recognized and allowed to function so far as best for the whole organism, with its long-range and idealistic interests, can there be the best life for the individual and the group.

303   The healthy mind loves life.

From Emerson, Immortality

304   The mind of man is keener than it is rational and embraces more than man is able to clearly explain.

Vauvenargues, Reflection 2

305   To be affected psychologically by objects, such as stones, plants, persons, or ideas, as particulars and in groups, means more than to be exposed to the objects or even bombarded with them.

Other things equal, the greater the number of ways in which a person can be affected by objects, and the number of ways in which he can affect objects, the greater is his ability to think.

After Spinoza,
Ethics IV App. 27 and passim

306   All too often we think of the mind as a storehouse to be filled when we should be thinking of it as an instrument to be used.

From John W. Gardner,
Self-Renewal . . . 1964 21 Harper

307   The mind, like the body, is able to maintain itself only by constant nourishment.

From Vauvenargues, Reflection 194

308   The mind is its own place, and in itself
Can make a heaven of hell, a hell of heaven.

Milton, Paradise Lost I 254–255

309   The more there is of mind in your employments, the more dignity there is in your character.

From Lavater, Aphorism 272 (1787 ed.)

HUMAN LIFE

310   Our deepest human need is to make sense of our lives.

A. MacLeish,

Poetry and Experience 1961 149 Houghton

311   Even in their activities, all living things are obeying things: they conform to natural law.

After Nietzsche, Thus Spake Zarathustra

312   The life of plants is essentially nutrition and reproduction; of animals, those same vegetative functions together with sensation and movement; and of men, the vegetative and animal functions and reason.

The essential goal of vegetative living is integrated functioning of the vegetative capacities as a whole plant; of animal living, of the vegetative and animal capacities as a whole animal; and of human living, of the vegetative, animal, and human capacities as a whole man.   From Aristotle

313   Man is born with rainbows in his heart and you'll never read him unless you consider rainbows.

Carl Sandburg,

The People, Yes 1936 208 Harcourt

314   As when the sun approaches towards the gates of the morning, he first opens a little eye of heaven, and sends away the spirits of darkness, and gives light to a cock, and calls up the lark to matins, and by and by gilds the fringes of a cloud, and peeps over the eastern hills, thrusting out his golden horns . . . and still while a man tells the story, the sun gets up higher, till he shows a fair face and a full light, and then he shines one whole day, under a cloud often, and sometimes weeping

great and little showers, and sets quickly: so is a man's reason
and his life. From Jeremy Taylor,
in Gest (ed.), House . . . 1954 92 Univ. Pa. Press

315   Stop and consider! Life is but a day;
A fragile dewdrop on its perilous way
From a tree's summit; a poor Indian's sleep
While his boat hastens to the monstrous steep
Of Montmorenci. Why so sad a moan?
Life is the rose's hope while yet unblown;
The reading of an ever-changing tale;
The light uplifting of a maiden's veil;
A pigeon tumbling in clear summer air;
A laughing school boy, without grief or care,
Riding the springy branches of an elm.
Keats, Sleep and Poetry

316   Today the world is fair.
Tomorrow, if dark clouds rebellious run
In flaming rack athwart the seas of heaven,
I shall not less have lived.
Santayana, Lucifer 1899 177

317   . . . Whoe'er can know,
As the long days go,
That To Live is happy, hath found his Heaven!
Euripides, Bacchae (Murray, tr.), Chorus

318   Self-preservation is the first law of nature.
Samuel Butler, Remains c. 1675

319   Out of a higher form of self-preservation we strive for
the ideal. From Giordano Bruno

320   We are never happier than when strong feeling determines us to live in *this* world.

From G. C. Lichtenberg, Stern (ed.),
Lichtenberg 1959 224 Ind. Univ. Press

321   Otherworldliness slights the power of man.

Walter Kaufmann,
From Shakespeare to Existentialism
1960 260 Doubleday

322   The best of men have their moments of enthusiasm, absence of mind, faint-heartedness, stupidity. If you allow not for these, your criticisms on man will be a mass of accusations or caricatures.

From Lavater, Aphorism 620 (1787 ed.)

323   The fickle mob ever changes along with the prince.

Claudian, Panegyricus de Quarto
Consulatu Honorii Augusti 302

324   The imagination can be purged and the judgment ripened only by an awareness of the slow, hesitant, wayward course of human life, its failures, its successes, its indomitable will to endure.   Learned Hand, Address 1952

325   Life is too serious to be taken too seriously.

G. L. Walton, Peg Along 1915 81

326   There is no possible ground for maintaining life at the cost of demoralization and depersonalization. Life is to be maintained at spiritual standards.

From J. Fletcher,
Morals and Medicine 1954 215 Princeton Univ. Press

327   Sometimes, without being irrational, the totality of existence may be sacrificed for one of its moments, as a single verse may be preferred to the whole poem.

J. M. Guyau, Sketch of Morality . . . 1898 130

328   Better a glorious death than a shameful life.

Georgian proverb,
Champion (ed.), Racial . . . 1938 liv Macmillan,
ⓒ Routledge; Barnes & Noble

329   As the pleasure the ear finds in rhyme is said to arise from its recurrence at measured intervals, so it is in life: the recurrence of things same or similar, the content in the fulfillment of expectations so familiar and so gentle that we are scarcely conscious that they were formed, have a harmony and a charm, and, where life is enriched by no loftier genius, often make the only difference between its poetry and its prose.

From E. G. Bulwer-Lytton

330   Too busy with the crowded hour to fear to live or die.

Emerson, Quatrains, Nature

331   Not the fruit of experience, but experience itself, is an end in itself.   Walter Pater

332   The desirable life involves wealth of experience.

Certain experiences exclude each other: one cannot both take bribes and feel honorable.

The deliberate choice not to have a given experience is itself an experience which, for the total meaning of life, may be one of the best and richest.

From Everett, Moral Values 1918 329 Holt

333   Man's need to love and be creative is quite as verifiable as his need for calcium or security.

Walter Kaufman,
Critique of Religion and Philosophy 1958 302 Harper

334   There is more to life than increasing its speed.

Gandhi

335   Reason's whole pleasure, all the joys of sense,
Lie in three words—health, peace, and competence.

Pope, Essay on Man IV 79

336   What we get out of life is in direct proportion to what we put into it.   H. H. Lehman

337   There is nothing so handsome as to play the man properly and well. Of all our diseases, the worst is to despise our own being.   From Montaigne, Lowenthal (ed.),
Autobiography . . . 1935 379 Houghton

338   . . . The privilege of being a person.

W. A. Neilson

339   There are many wonders, but none is more wondrous than man.   Sophocles

340   Man is evolution become conscious of itself.

From Julian Huxley

341   The supreme end of life, so far as we can see it, is to produce such values as beauty, truth, and justice.

From G. Sarton,
History . . . 1937 xiv 9 Harvard Univ. Press

342 . . . Life is Color and Warmth and Light,
And a striving evermore for these.

Julian Grenfell, Into Battle 5–6

343 The great difference between cultures is between those which say Yes and those which say No to human life.

From H. J. Blackham,
Six Existentialist Thinkers 1959 33 Harper, © Macmillan

V

Individual Background
and Growth

ANCESTRY

344   A hen is only an egg's way of making another egg.
            Samuel Butler, Life and Habit 1923 109 Dutton; Cape

345   Ye shall know them by their fruits. Do men gather
grapes of thorns, or figs of thistles?   Matthew VII 16

346   Straw eaten by cows turns into milk, while milk drunk
by serpents turns into poison.
                        Sharma and Raghavacharya (trs.),
                        Gems from Sanskrit . . . 1959 33 Osmania

347   No man is his own sire.   Melville

348   Sagacious people who look forward to posterity look
backward to their ancestors.
            From Edmund Burke, Reflections on Revolution . . .

349   It is indeed desirable to be well descended, but the
glory belongs to our ancestors.
                        Plutarch, On the Training of Children

350   Brainless sons boast of their ancestors.
                                        Chinese proverb

351   It shames many a man if he be worse than his ancestors.
                        Boethius, Consolations . . . XXX

352   The nobler the blood the less the pride.
                                        Danish proverb

NATIVE ENDOWMENT

353   A duck's legs, though short, cannot be lengthened without pain to the duck, and a crane's legs, though long, cannot be shortened without misery to the crane.

> Chuang Tzu, in Champion (ed.),
> Eleven Religions 1945 279 Dutton; Routledge

354   What is bred in the bone will never come out of the flesh.   Pilpay, Two Fishermen

355   Of every one to whom much is given, much will be required.   From Luke XII 48

356   What is more foolish than being self-satisfied about something which one has not accomplished by one's own efforts?   Seneca

357   The people cannot get on without men of talent; yet often they have not treated them well.   After Goethe

358   From fairest creatures we desire increase,
        That thereby beauty's rose might never die.

> Shakespeare, Sonnet I

360   According to systematic data, gifted individuals are apt to be more stable than the less gifted.

> From John W. Gardner,
> Excellence 1961 61 Harper

361   Remember that you are not more indebted to your parents for your nature than for their love and care for you.

> William Penn

362   We cannot raise fine human beings without attending to both nature and nurture.

> From S. J. Holmes,
> Life and Morals 1948 207 Macmillan

363   The Pedigree of Honey
Does not concern the Bee—
A Clover, any time, to him,
Is Aristocracy—

> Emily Dickinson, Thomas H. Johnson (ed.),
> Complete Poems . . . 1960 669 Little

ABILITY AND GENIUS

364   To each is given a certain inward talent, a certain outward environment; to each, by wisest combination of these two, a certain maximum of capability.   Carlyle

365   The pitcher at the well is filled, nor more
Draws at the ocean-shore.

> Paul Elmer More, Century . . . 1898 XLVI 68

366   Every normal man has it in his own power, by natural reason, to avoid falling into presumption or dejection.

> From L'Estrange

367   Let each man learn to row with the oars he has.

> Dutch proverb

368   The majority of men dwell within a little circle of ideas which have not been derived from their own resources. Perhaps there are fewer loose minds than sterile ones.

> Vauvenargues, Reflection 238

369   Much of the good work of the world has been that of dull people who have done their best.   G. F. Hoar

370   Each honest calling, each walk of life, has its own elite, its own aristocracy based upon excellence of performance.

J. B. Conant
in John W. Gardner, Excellence 1961 132 Harper

371   Who in the same given time can produce more than many others, has vigor; who can produce more and better, has talents; who can produce what none else can, has genius.

Lavater, Aphorism 23

372   Talent can, genius must.

373   . . . O, it is excellent
To have a giant's strength, but it is tyrannous
To use it like a giant.

Shakespeare,
Measure for Measure II 2 107–108

374   Talent unguided is a child at large.

375   The virtues come neither by nature or against nature; but nature gives the capacity for acquiring them, and they are developed by training.

From Aristotle, Nicomachean Ethics II i

376   The good society does not ignore individual differences but deals with them wisely and humanely.

From John W. Gardner,
Excellence 1961 75 Harper

EARLY YEARS

377   In a child, we have pleasure not only from what we see but even more from what we hope for.   From Goethe

378   Youth's a stuff will not endure.
                              Shakespeare, Twelfth Night II iii 55

379   Rejoice, O young man, in thy youth.
                                        Ecclesiastes XI 9

380   Young men think old men are fools; old men know young men are fools.
                              George Chapman, All Fools V i

381   Youth thinks intelligence a good substitute for experience. His elders think experience a substitute for intelligence.
                                        From L. Bryson,
                              Drive Toward Reason 1954 75 Harper

382   Youthful ignorance the days correct.   Proverbial

383   My youth may wear and fade, but it shall never rust.
                  From William Congreve, Way of the World II i

PERSONAL GROWTH

384   One can stand still in a flowing stream, but not in a world of men.   Japanese proverb

385   The way I happen to be is no necessary measure of what I may be.   Arthur E. Morgan,
                              Observations 1968 14 Antioch Press

386   The business of life is to go forward.
                          From Samuel Johnson, Idler No. 72

387   Socrates used to express surprise that sculptors should take pains to make a block of marble into a man, and should take no pains lest they themselves turn out mere blocks, not men.   From Diogenes Laertius,
                          Lives ... Hicks (tr.), 1925 1:163 Putnam

388   It is never too late to start becoming a better person.
                          George Lawton,
          How to Be Happy Though Young 1949 238 Vanguard

389   In order to become better, we need to learn our failings through either the admonitions of friends or the invectives of enemies.   Diogenes

390   Our goal rises ever higher as we progress.
                          Giordano Bruno

390a   In the same naturalistic, scientific sense that an acorn may be said to "press toward" being an oak tree, the human being presses toward fuller and fuller being. This means pressing toward knowledge, courage, love, kindness, unselfishness, honesty, and serenity.

                          From A. H. Maslow,
          New Knowledge ... 1959 130 126 Harper

391   The playwright Naughton knows that a man is not a man because he is tough, or queer because he is tender; and

that gentleness, far from blurring any line between man and woman, only sharpens the line between man and beast.

From J. Morgenstern,
Newsweek July 24 1967 75

392   Character is destiny.
            Heraclitus

393   It is a dangerous illusion to believe that one can . . . write without reading, talk without listening, produce without feeding oneself, to give of oneself without recovering one's strength.

Péguy, Basic Verities (Green, tr.) 1943 99 Pantheon

INTEREST

394   In the ideal sense nothing is uninteresting; there are only uninterested people.   B. Atkinson 1955

395   One can be bored because one is empty, or lazy, or inhibited.   From M. Gumpert,
Anatomy of Happiness 1951 36 McGraw

396   Man is not a grazing animal, and he would never stay long in a paradise where everybody has four meals a day and nothing else ever happens.

From Santayana, Mercury 1961 37:377

397   Empty leisure is wont to make men hate their lives.
                    From Seneca,
Ad Lucilium . . . (Gummere, tr.) 1918 2:199 Putnam

397a   What makes life dreary is the want of motive.
George Eliot, Daniel Deronda

398   There is surprising variation in everything if we watch
for it. Things change, our environment changes, our outlook
on life changes.   From M. Gumpert,
Anatomy of Happiness 1951 37 McGraw

399   Not by years but by disposition is wisdom acquired.
Plautus, Trinummus II ii 86

400   In general, time that is filled with varied and interesting experiences seems short in passing but long in retrospect;
and time that is empty of experiences seems long in passing
but short in retrospect.

From William James,
Psychology: Briefer Course 1892 283

401   He who desires to keep body and soul in perfect health
must concern himself with the general affairs of mankind.
From E. von Feuchtersleben,
Lewisohn (tr.), Health and Suggestion 1910 164

402   Every enlarging interest in non-self breaks down the
outer boundaries of selfhood so that a person feels that he is
what he includes.
From Ethel Sabin Smith, Dynamics of Aging 1956 80 Norton

EXPERIENCE

403   The years teach much which the days never know . . .
A chief event of life is the day in which we have encountered
a mind that startled us.   Emerson

404   Students claim the right to choose their own goals, which includes the right to choose unwisely and to repent later.

K. H. Mueller,
Educating Women 1954 7 Univ. Minn. Press

405   Respect for the things of experience alone brings with it respect for others, who are the other centers of experience; and such respect precludes patronage, domination, and the will to impose. Intellectual piety toward experience is a precondition of the wise direction of life and of tolerant and generous cooperation among men.

After John Dewey,
Experience and Nature 1925 39 Open Court

406   Experience, unless enlightened by imagination and philosophy, may teach little.

Arthur E. Morgan,
Observations 1968 184 Antioch Press

407   When we truly comprehend and enter into the rhythm of life, we shall be able to bring together the daring of youth with the discipline of age in a way that does justice to both.

J. S. Bixler,
Two Blessings of Joseph 1964 15-16 Carleton College

ACTIVITY AND EFFORT

408   An object is achieved by effort, not merely by wishes. The prey will not of itself enter the mouth of a sleeping lion.

From Sharma and Raghavacharya (trs.),
Gems from Sanskrit . . . 1959 15

409   If all ends were already reached, and no art were requisite, life could not exist at all, much less a life of reason.

Santayana, in Logan Pearsall Smith (ed.),
Little Essays 1920 5 Scribner

410   Whoever remains unwilling to help himself can be helped by no one.

From Pestalozzi,
Education . . . 1953 54 Philos. Lib.

411   Inaction saps the vigors of the mind.

From Leonardo da Vinci

412   The real fault is to have faults and not try to amend them.

Confucius

413   The glory is not in never falling, but in rising every time you fall.

Chinese proverb

414   A man should never be ashamed to say he has been in the wrong, which is but saying in other words that he is wiser today than he was yesterday.

Pope

415   Perfection is obtained by slow degrees; it requires the hand of time.

Voltaire

416   A wise man will make more opportunities than he finds.

Francis Bacon

417   Live each day free from agitation, from torpor, and from insincerity.

Marcus Aurelius, Meditations VII 69

VI

Training and Education

418   ... As the twig is bent the tree's inclined.
                                    Pope, Moral Essays I 150

419   Whoso neglects learning loses the past and is dead for
the future.   From Euripides, Frag. 927

420   Education includes learning what you didn't even
know you didn't know.
                        From D. J. Boorstin, Newsweek July 6 1970 29

421   It is better to learn late than never.
                                    Publilius Syrus, Maxim 864

422   To be fond of learning is near to wisdom.
                                                    Confucius

423   The child is to become able to take away from others
as little as possible and to bring them as much as possible.
                                        From Paul Valéry,
                        History ... 1962 148 c Bollingen Found.

424   Manhood, not scholarship, is the first aim of education.
                                                    E. T. Seton

425   A pupil should be taught what it means to know something, and what it means not to know it; what should be the
design and end of study; what valor, temperance, and justice
are; the difference between ambition and greed, loyalty and
servitude, liberty and license; the marks of true and solid con-

tentment; the true springs of our actions and the reasons for
our varied thoughts and desires.

> From Montaigne, in Lowenthal (ed.),
> Autobiography . . . 1935 32-34 Houghton

426   The object of education is to supply the equipment
and the stimulus for making a life.

In education, appreciation of relative values is the beginning
of wisdom.

A well-planned educational system could go far toward making universal men and women, each to the limit of innate
capacity. This education will give more power of action to
intellectual men, and more intelligence to men of action.

> From Arthur E. Morgan,
> Observations 1968 165 185 175 Antioch Press

427   The common core of all religions, theistic and non-
theistic, and of all enlightened ethical codes, should be taught
in all schools.

428   Education is an ornament in prosperity and a refuge in
adversity.   Aristotle

429   To learn and know, and thence to do; to perform
justly, skillfully, and magnanimously.

> From Milton, Areopagitica, and Of Education

430   The proper study of the liberal arts can help produce
the surest guarantee of personal integrity: an enlightened conscience, based on a moral code which the student has achieved
through reasoned judgment and knowledge.

> From T. C. Mendenhall, Smith Alum. Q. Nov. 1962

431   A liberal education should be as good for a foreman as for an executive.

B. C. Keeney,
Brown Alumni Mo. Dec. 1957

432   Liberty without learning is always in peril, and learning without liberty is always in vain.

J. F. Kennedy,
address at Vanderbilt University 1963

433   In my view, the gaining of knowledge and understanding is the most moral motivation of man.

A. W. Melton,
Am. Psychologist 1970 25:xi [sic]

434   The usual young person wants to be somehow liked, recognized, and contributory. Many a one develops well physically, mentally, morally, and socially.

To be completely undeveloped in any one of those ways would be monstrous or even fatal. An occasional earnest spirit, however, seems never to have thought of developing well socially, to be good company.

Ordinarily, to develop in any of the ways, say the mental way, helps one to develop somewhat in the other ways. One develops well mentally partly through relevant give-and-take with associates in individual interests and ideas.

Social life involves such give-and-take, especially in mutual interests. The interests, however, are chosen as pleasant, even recreational.

Any social give-and-take requires considerateness, fair play, and good manners.

Considerateness, fair play, and good manners are the essentials of vital humanism.

Each essential, likewise their common humanism, is good in itself.

IGNORANCE AND FOLLY

435   Ignorance is the greatest enemy of freedom and happiness.
From Jefferson

436   Ignorance is the greatest poverty.
Wortabet (tr.), Arabian Wisdom 1910 30

437   Ignorant persons raise questions which have been answered by the wise thousands of years ago . . .
Nothing is more frightful than ignorance in action.
Goethe

438   "Good will" can do as much damage as "ill will," if it is not enlightened.   Camus, La Peste 1947
150 Gallimard; Knopf; Hamish Hamilton

439   Of all hatreds, there is none greater than that of ignorance against knowledge.
Galileo, in Giorgio de Santillana,
Crime . . . 1955 137 Univ. Chicago Press

440   To be ignorant of one's ignorance is the malady of the ignorant.   Unknown

441   Ignorance is everywhere a stranger; unwelcome, ill at ease and out of place.   M. F. Tupper,
Proverbial Philosophy 1849 138

442   The world is full of fools,
         And he who would not see an ass
         Must bide at home and bolt the door
         And break his looking glass.
                 Unknown, in G. L. Walton, Peg Along 1915 107

443   A fool must now and then be right by chance.
                         William Cowper, Conversation 96

444   The fool who knows his foolishness is wise at least so
far; but a fool who thinks himself wise is a fool indeed.
                                     The Dhammapada V

445   The greatest fool is he who thinks he is not one and
all others are. He does not see who does not see that others see.
         From Balthasar Gracian (Jacobs, tr.) Maxim 201

446   Folly is as often owing to a want of proper sentiments
as to a want of understanding.
                                                 Hazlitt,
             Characters of Shakespear's [sic] Plays 1906 7

447   He must be a thorough fool who can learn nothing
from his own folly.   Anon.

448   A rebuke goes deeper into a man of understanding
than a hundred lashes into a fool.   Proverbs XVII 10

449   . . . Heaven is hell with folly's bell,
         And hell is heaven, with wisdom's leaven.
                 Hindu, Gems of the Orient (Alger, tr.)

450   A wise man's day is worth a fool's life.

Arabic saying

451   What in me is dark,
        Illumine; what is low, raise and support.

Milton, Paradise Lost I

LEARNING AS A PROCESS

452   When the infant becomes able to seize a small stone, it
inspires him to put it in his mouth. Essentially, the stone
affects him in only one way, and he affects it in only one way.

In later years, the stone stimulates him by its size, shape,
colors, weight, texture, and associations to react to it in different ways, as a treasure, a paperweight, a geological clue. The
stone affects him in more ways, and he affects it in more ways,
as he becomes more capable and learns more perceptions and
responses. Therein his life is richer.

After Spinoza, Ethics IV xxxviii

453   In a man's life, domestic lore is what the trunk is to a
tree, for on it all the twigs and branches of our human wisdom
and destiny must grow.   From Pestalozzi,

Education . . . 1953 25 Philos. Lib.

454   Learning is ever in the freshness of its youth, even for
the old.   Aeschylus, Agamemnon 584

455   Sit down before fact as a little child, be prepared to
give up every preconceived notion, follow humbly wherever
and to whatever abysses nature leads, or you shall learn noth-

ing. I have only begun to learn content and peace of mind since I have resolved at all risks to do this.

Thomas H. Huxley,
letter to Kingsley

456   An error once learned is difficult to unlearn.

Baba Batra

457   He who knows only his own side of the case knows little of that.   From John Stuart Mill

458   Whenever walking in a company I can always find my teacher among them. I select a good person and follow his example, or I see a bad person and correct myself.

From Confucius

459   Repeat to children the names and deeds of those who have loved their country and people and have striven to help them. Instil into their hearts the strength to resist injustice and oppression. Let them learn how lovely is the path of Virtue; how noble it is to become apostles of the Truth; how holy to sacrifice themselves, if need be, for their fellows.

From Mazzini, Duties of Man 1864

460   Learning is but an adjunct to ourself.

Shakespeare,
Love's Labour's Lost IV iii 314

461   Men have entered into learning and knowledge, sometimes upon a natural curiosity and inquisitive appetite; sometimes to entertain their mind with variety and delight; sometimes for ornament and reputation; sometimes to enable them to victory of wit and contradiction; and most times for lucre

and profession; but too seldom for the benefit and use of mankind. This would indeed dignify and exalt knowledge, if contemplation and action be conjoined.

From Francis Bacon,
Advancement of Learning I V xi

462   Learning has no particular relation to any of the five
senses, but without it they cannot be regulated.

Confucius

463   As long as you live, keep learning how to live.
Ancient proverb, cited by Seneca,
Ad Lucilium . . . (Gummere, tr.) 1918 149 Putnam

464   He who understands the why and wherefore of what
he learns does not forget it quickly.
Talmud Jerushalmi, Berakot

DISCIPLINE, CORRECTION

465   Soap and education are not as sudden as a massacre,
but they are more deadly in the long run.
Mark Twain,
Sketches Old and New, Facts . . . 1917 322 Harper

466   Correction given in anger, however reasonable, is never
so effective as that which is given without anger.
From Francis de Sales,
Devout Life 1890 III VIII

467   Punishment and retribution seldom if ever make men
better unless they are accompanied by kindness and love.
Pestalozzi, Education . . . 1953 61 Philos. Library

468   In order to succeed with children, we should not appear astonished or irritated at their bad dispositions; we should be compassionate to their weakness. Generally confidence and sincerity are more useful to them than rigorous authority.

It is necessary always to make children understand what we require of them; for joy and confidence must be their ordinary disposition, otherwise we shall damp their spirit and abate their courage. The mind led by fear always becomes weaker.

It is most important that the mentor know his faults as well as the child will know them, and that the mentor desire his best friends to point them out to him. Generally, those who govern children pardon nothing in them, though they pardon everything in themselves. Consequently, when the children discover any fault in their governors they are delighted, and feel only contempt for them.

From Fénelon,
Education of a Daughter 1847 41–42 45 49–50

469   A most effective criticism is indifference.

From E. W. Howe

470   Let your children be more in awe of your kindness than of your power.

From Savile, . . Advice to a Daughter, House . . .

TRAINING

471   Anyone can hold the helm in a calm sea.

Publilius Syrus

472   The unpolished diamond is but a stone.

R. L. Stevenson,
Letter to Henry James Dec. 8, 1884

473   Every kind of excellence needs some polish.
> Balthasar Gracian (Jacobs, tr.) Maxim 12

474   The opposite of slovenliness is to be in form. To be in form the individual must go into training, and give up many things, in the determination to surpass himself.
> From Ortega y Gasset,
> Mission . . . 1944 43 Princeton Univ. Press

475   All genuine education *terminates* in discipline, but it *proceeds* by engaging the mind in activities worth while for their own sake.
> John Dewey, How We Think 1933 87 Heath

476   The novice in any field is hobbled by his lack of skill. If he is creative, the discipline of apprenticeship frees him to work creatively.

477   A great carpenter teaches his apprentice to use squares and compasses. The man who wants to cultivate himself must also have squares and compasses for his conduct.
> Lin-Yutang (ed.),
> Wisdom of Confucius 1938 290 Modern Lib.

478   Every form of education should give the pupil a technique, a science, an assortment of general ideas, and aesthetic appreciation. Each of these sides of his training should illuminate the others.
> From Whitehead,
> Aims . . . 1929 75 Macmillan, © Cambridge; Benn

TEACHING

479   Good teaching wins the people's heart.

Mencius

480   He who has insights that can broaden his neighbor's life and does not offer them is robbing his neighbor of his due. The gifts of the spirit, like the gifts of substance, are a trust to be shared with others.

From The Talmud, in Bokser,
Wisdom . . . 1951 107–108 Philos. Lib.

481   Teaching should make men fall in love with the lesson, and not with the teacher. What is given is for the auditor, not for the author.   From Francis Bacon,
Advancement of Learning II XX ii

482   Whenever any person is helped to think a clearer thought, or face a more difficult fact, or feel a quicker beauty, that is so much gained.   L. Bryson
Drive Toward Reason 1954 144 Harper

483   A teacher affects eternity; he can never tell where his influence stops.

Henry Brooks Adams, Education . . . 1906

484   Is the lamp injured in aught that thou hast lit the others from it?

Abbot John, in Helen Waddell (tr.),
Desert Fathers 1936 148 Holt; Curtis

485   And gladly would he learn and gladly teach.

Chaucer, Canterbury Tales, Prologue

486   Being willing to teach means being willing to give.
                                          From H. Margolius,
                    Aphorisms . . . n.d. 9, 15 Black Mt. News

487   . . . No legacy is so rich as honesty.
                                               Shakespeare,
                            All's Well that Ends Well III v 13

488   The teacher must be free to be critical and objective
in his own way, and above all he must work in the clear daylight without hidden allegiances or obligations which require
him to distort his research or teaching in accord with dictates
from without.   J. R. Killian, Jr.,
                    statement for Mass. Inst. Tech., May 3, 1949

489   The schoolteacher must not be the representative of
the government. . . . He is the only and priceless representative
of poets and artists, of philosophers and scholars, of the men
who have made and maintained humanity.
              Péguy, Basic Verities (Green, tr.) 1943 97 Pantheon

490   The authority of those who teach is often an obstacle
to those who want to learn.   Cicero

491   Once you get people believing that there is an authoritative well of wisdom to which they can turn for absolutes, you
have dried up the springs on which they must in the end draw.
                              Learned Hand, I. Dilliard (ed.),
                       Spirit of Liberty 1952 153 Knopf

492   As Plato says, man needs to be so trained from his
youth up as to find pleasure and pain in the right objects.
                    Aristotle, Nicomachean Ethics II iii 2

493   The great end of instruction is not to stamp our minds on the young but to stir up their own; not to make them see with our eyes but with their own; to inspire a love of truth; to quicken thought, and awaken conscience, so that they may discern and approve for themselves what is right and good.

From W. E. Channing, Sunday School

494   In teaching you will come to grief as soon as you forget that your pupils have bodies.   Whitehead, Aims . . . 1929 78

Macmillan, © Cambridge; Benn

495   It is not a mind we are educating, nor a body: it is a man.   From Montaigne, in Lowenthal (ed.),

Autobiography . . . 1935 36 Houghton

496   It is man whom the educator must understand . . . His profession calls for a deep understanding of human nature and skill in guiding it.

From Pestalozzi, Education . . . 1953 33 Philos. Lib.

497   We need a method by which teachers teach less and learners learn more.   From Comenius

498   To many things their prohibition is their only temp-tation.   After Hazlitt,

Characteristics CXL, CXLII

499   Precept must be upon precept, line upon line; here a little, and there a little.   From Isaiah XXVIII 10

500   The sight of a drunkard is a better sermon against that vice than the best that was ever preached.

From Savile . . . Advice to a Daughter, Vanity . . .

501   A good way to make children tell the truth is to tell it yourself.   Ingersoll

502   There are many ways of teaching. By the very things I do not think worth teaching, I teach a man something.
Mencius (Dobson, tr.),
1963 56 Univ. Toronto Press; Oxford

503   What comes from the heart will reach the heart.
Pestalozzi, Education . . . 1953 43 Philos. Lib.

504   One repays a teacher badly if one always remains nothing but a pupil.
Nietzsche, in Walter Kaufmann (tr.),
The Portable Nietzsche 1954 190 Viking

COUNSELING

505   Here thou, great Anna! whom three realms obey,
Dost sometimes counsel take — and sometimes tea.
Pope, Rape of the Lock III 7

506   We are prone to censure others where we will not endure advice ourselves.   William Penn

507   To give advice to a friend, either asked or unasked, is a duty; but if a man love to give advice, he himself needs it.
From Savile, Complete . . . 1912 244

508   No man can be sorry for seeking advice critically, or happy if he blindly follows out his own thoughts.
After Wortabet (tr.), Arabian Wisdom 1910 32

509   A knife of the keenest steel requires the whetstone, and the wisest man needs advice.   Shayast-La-Shayast X 28

510   Apt words have power to suage
                The tumours of a troubl'd mind.
                                Milton, Samson Agonistes

511   Words are the physician of a mind diseased.
                                Aeschylus, Prometheus 378

512   There is no such remedy against flattery of a man's self as the liberty of a friend.   Francis Bacon, Of Friendship

513   In multitude of counselors there is safety.
                                Proverbs XXIV 6

514   Advice is like snow; the softer it falls, the longer it dwells upon and the deeper it sinks into the mind.
                                Coleridge

515   How to profit from good advice often requires as much good sense as how to give it.   La Rochefoucauld

516   Men are so pleased with the prudent shape of an adviser that, when one is an adviser, it may, rightly or wrongly, raise the value he has of himself.
  A man whilst he is advising puts his understanding up, on tiptoes, and is unwilling to bring it down again.
                                From Savile,
                Miscellaneous Thought . . ., Of Advice . . .

517   He must be wise who can distinguish a wise counselor.
                                Diogenes

SKILL AND METHOD

518   Do you see a man skilful in his work? He will stand before kings.

Proverbs XXII 29
Rev. Stand. Ver. Bible 1952 © Nat. Coun. Churches

519   We must learn to honor excellence in every socially acceptable activity ... An excellent plumber is infinitely more admirable than an incompetent philosopher. The society which scorns excellence in plumbing because plumbing is a humble activity and tolerates shoddiness in philosophy because it is an exalted activity will have neither good plumbing nor good philosophy. Neither its pipes nor its theories will hold water.

John W. Gardner, Excellence ... 1961 86 Harper

520   The minimum of effort with the maximum of success: such is the way of the sage.

From Chuang Tze, Infinite Tao (Ballou, ed.),
Bible of the World 1939 526 Viking

521   He who grasps a sword unskilfully does but inflict a wound upon his hand.   Buddha

522   The man who works wholly by exact rule and discipline is weak; the least deflection ruins him.   Montaigne

523   True ease in writing comes from art, not chance,
As those move easiest who have learn'd to dance.

Pope, Essay on Criticism II

524   **No man** can with all the wealth in the world buy so much skill as to be a good lutenist; he must go the same way that poor people do, he must learn and take pains.

Jeremy Taylor, in Gest (ed.),
House . . . 1954 46 Univ. Pa. Press

525   More haste, less speed.   Proverbial

526   A mistake of a hair's breadth at the beginning will lead to an error of a thousand *li*.   Yi

527   All strong interests easily become impersonal, the love of a good job well done.   Whitehead,
Adventures . . . 1933 371
Macmillan; Cambridge

STUDY

528   When shall I cease to wonder?

Sagredo, in de Santillana,
Crime of Galileo 1955 175 Univ. Chicago Press

529   There is an unspeakable pleasure attending the life of a voluntary student.   Oliver Goldsmith

530   The pupils have got to be made to feel that they are studying something, and are not merely executing intellectual minuets.   Whitehead, Aims . . . 1929 15
Macmillan, © Cambridge; Benn

531   If a man does not love study, his moral aspirations will suffer. For example, if he loves kindness, his kindness will fall short through ignorance; if he loves wisdom, his wisdom will

fall short through having fanciful or unsound ideas; honesty, through spoiling or upsetting things; simplicity, through sheer following of routine; courage, through unruliness or violence; and decision of character, through self-will or headstrong belief in himself.   From Confucius

532   The wise man becomes full of good even if he gather it little by little.

From Buddha, The Dhammapada IX

533   Some books are to be tasted, others to be swallowed, and some few are to be chewed and digested.

Francis Bacon, Of Studies

534   The neglect of technical education as an ingredient in the complete development of ideal human beings has arisen partly from the mistaken antitheses between mind and body and between thought and action.

After Whitehead, Aims . . . 1929
77–78 Macmillan, © Cambridge; Benn

535   In a life of study, every now and then be completely idle—do nothing at all.

From Sydney Smith,
Sketches of Moral Philosophy, Habits of Study

HABIT

536   No man ever became extremely wicked all at once.

Juvenal, Satire II 83

537   . . . Habits gather by unseen degrees,—
           As brooks make rivers, rivers run to seas.
                     Ovid, Metamorphoses (Dryden, tr.) XV 155

538   What one does, one becomes.   Japanese proverb

539   As men become builders by building, harp players by
playing on the harp, by doing just actions we become just;
temperate actions, temperate; and brave actions, brave.
                                   Aristotle, Ethics II i

540   Practice yourself in little things, and thence proceed to
greater.   From Epictetus, Discourses I XVIII

541   Avoid even a minor transgression lest it lead you to a
major one.   The Talmud, in Bokser, Wisdom . . .
                                   1951 153 Philos. Lib.

542   Habit is a cable; we weave a thread of it every day, and
at last we can not break it.   Horace Mann

543   Habit with him was all the test of truth;
        "It must be right: I've done it from my youth."
                     George Crabbe, Borough, Letter III 138

544   To make anything a habit, do it; to not make it a habit,
do not do it; to unmake a habit, do something else in place of
it.   After Epictetus, Discourses II XVIII

545   One habit overcomes another.
                     Thomas à Kempis, Imitation of Christ I XXI 2

546   . . . Use almost can change the stamp of nature.
                                    Shakespeare, Hamlet III iv 168

547   Civilization advances by extending the number of
important operations which we can perform without thinking
about them.   Whitehead, Introduction . . . 1911 61

548   . . . Habit is but long practice, friend,
            And this becomes men's nature in the end.
            Evenus, in Aristotle, Nicomachean Ethics VII x

MANNERS AND DRESS

549   The rules of propriety serve as dikes for mankind.
   The young people should be good sons and daughters at
home, polite and respectful in society; they should be careful
in their conduct and faithful, love the people, and associate
themselves with the kind people. If, after learning all this, they
still have energy left, let them read books.

                                        From Lin-Yutang (ed.),
                        Wisdom of Confucius 1938 204 Modern Lib.

550   Dishonor not a man in his old age; for even some of us
wax old.   Ecclus. VIII 6

551   Manners are more important than laws. Upon them, in
large measure, the laws depend. The law touches us but here
and there, and now and then. Manners are what vex or soothe,
corrupt or purify, barbarize or refine us, by a constant, insensible operation like that of the air we breathe.
            From Edmund Burke, Letters on a Regicide Peace

552   . . . A man by nothing is so revealed
          As by his manners.
                              Edmund Spenser, Faerie Queene VI III i

553   Manners impress as they indicate real power.
                                                  Emerson, Behavior

554   Rudeness is the weak man's imitation of strength.
                                                  Eric Hoffer,
                              Passionate State of Mind 1955 138 Harper

555   A beautiful behavior is better than a beautiful form; it
gives a higher pleasure than statues or pictures; it is the finest
of the fine arts.
   Manners must be inspired by the good heart, marked by fine
perception, the acquaintance with real beauty. There is no
beautifier of complexion, or form, or behavior, like the wish to
scatter joy and not pain around us.
                                      Emerson, Manners; Behavior

556   Real manners have their basis in respect for self and
others. As Kant insisted, a man exists as an end in himself, and
not merely to be used.   After N. M. Butler

557   We must be as courteous to a man as to a picture to
which we give a good light.   From Emerson, Behavior

558   Politeness is to do and say
          The kindest thing in the kindest way.
                                                  Proverbial

559   Manners are the happy ways of doing things.
                                                  Emerson, Culture

560   Right good manners require much sense.

We cannot recommend an affected clown who renounces clean linen or good manners. On the other hand, there are superfine gentlemen, carpet-knights, whose understanding is strictly appropriated to their dress; a too earnest application to have their clothes right strikes too deep into their small stock of thoughts.   From Savile,

Miscellaneous Thoughts . . ., Good Manners;

Some Cautions . . .

561   The world is good-natured to people who are good-natured.   Thackeray

562   A cheerful countenance is a presage of good.

Wortabet (tr.), Arabian Wisdom 1910

563   Of manners gentle, of affections mild,
            In wit a man, simplicity a child.

Pope, Epitaph on Gay

564   A gentleman is a person continually considerate.

Will Durant, Address, June 6, 1958

565   Be familiar but by no means vulgar.

From Shakespeare, Hamlet I iii 61

566   Return a salutation by something better, or at least by something as good.

The Koran, Wortabet (tr.), Arabian Wisdom 1910 58

567   . . . Mend your speech a little,
            Lest you may mar your fortunes.

Shakespeare, King Lear I i 96–97

568   . . . Her voice was ever soft,
     Gentle and low, an excellent thing in woman.
                         Shakespeare, King Lear V iii 274–275

569   A gentle tongue is a tree of life.   Proverbs XV iv

570   It is an ornament of the heart to hear kindly.
               Ptahhotep, in Breasted, Dawn . . . 1933 136 Scribner

571   A gentle answer turns away wrath; a harsh word stirs
up anger.   Proverbs XV i

572   Be swift to hear, slow to speak, slow to wrath.
                                          James I 19

573   The art of making those people easy with whom we
converse is good manners.   From Swift

574   The spirit of politeness is to make others pleased with
us and with themselves.   From Montesquieu

575   He that is truly polite knows how to contradict with
respect and to please without adulation.
                              Rule of Life 1800 68

576   A time to test a gentleman is to observe him when he
is in contact with individuals of a group that is less fortunate
than his own.
               From Booker T. Washington, Up from Slavery

577   There is always time enough for courtesy.
                              Emerson, Social Aims

578   Living agreeably is inseparable from the virtues.

Epicurus

579   Virtue and learning, like gold, have their intrinsic value: but if they are not polished, they lose much of their luster.   From Chesterfield

580   Grace, when gained, is effortless.

581   The warmth of genial courtesy,
             The calm of self-reliance.

Whittier

582   Grace has been defined as the outward expression of the inward harmony of the soul.   From Hazlitt

583   Many men have failed to recognize the tremendous increase of insight, power, and well-being which can result from refinement of conduct.

Arthur E. Morgan,
Observations 1968 305 Antioch Press

KNOWLEDGE

584   A little knowledge is a dangerous thing, but a little lack of knowledge is also a dangerous thing.

From Samuel Butler

585   To think clearly on a basis of ignorance is merely to rearrange one's prejudices.   F. E. Sparshott,
Enquiry into Goodness 1958 22
Univ. Chicago Press

586   In the realm of nature, ignorance is punished just as severely as willful wrong.

Thomas H. Huxley, Evolution and Ethics 1902 58

587   Only an unenlightened mind thinks the walls of its own dungeon the limits of the universe, and the reach of its own chain the outer verge of intelligence.

From Longfellow

588   Where there are no dark corners there is very little foulness or infection.

From H. G. Wells, Salvaging . . . 1921 114 Macmillan

589   Knowledge is a lamp from which men light their candles.

Wortabet (tr.), Arabian Wisdom 1910 27

590   Unless one knows, one does not truly live.

Balthasar Gracian (Jacobs, tr.), Maxim 247

591   Learning is a treasure which follows its owner everywhere.

Seven Hundred Chinese Proverbs (Hart, tr.), 1937 18
Stanford Univ. Press

592   Knowledge in youth is wisdom in age.   Proverb

593   Any subject matter which liberates human intelligence and human sympathy is humane, and any subject matter which does not is not even educational.

From John Dewey, Democracy . . . 1916 269 Macmillan

595   Without knowledge love is in vain.
                    Stanton Coit, Message of Man 1894 288

596   Zeal without knowledge is like expedition to a man in
the dark.   John Newton

597   Knowledge without courage is sterile.
                    Balthasar Gracian (Jacobs, tr.) Maxim 4

598   The world must be known before it can be reformed.
                    Santayana, Reason in Science, 1905 91 Scribner

599   Good and evil we know in this world grow up together,
and the knowledge of good is involved with the knowledge of
evil. What wisdom can there be to choose, what continence to
forbear, without the knowledge of evil?
                    From Milton, Aeropagitica 17–18

600   The ambition of a man of parts should be, not to know
books, but *things;* not to show other men that he has read
Locke . . . and Beccaria, and Dumont, but to show them that
he knows the subjects on which Locke and Beccaria and Dumont have written.   Sydney Smith

601   The tritest lessons are still the most imperiously
needed.   Albert Guérard,
                    Bottle in the Sea 1954 23 Harvard Univ. Press

602   There are so many connections between things that
no one science or art can be known thoroughly without knowledge of other sciences and arts.
                    After Anthony Collins, Discourse . . . 1713 8–9

603   To attain the full altitude of the knowable, whatever that may be, should be our earnest aim, and more than this is not for humanity.   [Walter Richard Cassels]
Supernatural Religion 1879 3:585

604   The conclusions of prior knowledge are the *instruments* of new inquiries, not the norm which determines their validity.

Continued progress in knowledge is the only sure way of protecting old knowledge from degeneration into dogmatic doctrines received on authority, or from imperceptible decay into superstition and old wives' tales.

From John Dewey, Quest . . . 1929 186
Minton, Reconstruction . . . 1948 34 Beacon

605   What we think we know prevents us from learning.
From Claude Bernard

606   The confession of ignorance is the beginning of all wisdom.   A. B. Alcott,
after Socrates, Table-Talk 1877 89

607   Knowledge and practice are a unit.
Wang Yang-Ming (Henke, tr.),
Philosophy . . . 1916 55 Open Court

608   The traces of forgotten knowledge may yet guide one's way.

609   Deep versed in books and shallow in himself.
Milton, Paradise Regained IV 327

610   To be proud of learning is the greatest ignorance.

> Jeremy Taylor

611   An honest heart being the first blessing, a knowing head is the second.   Jefferson, Letter . . . 1785

612   He that knows not, and knows not that he knows not, is a fool. Shun him.

He that knows not, and knows that he knows not, is simple. Teach him.

He that knows, and knows not that he knows, is asleep. Wake him.

He that knows, and knows that he knows, is wise. Follow him.

> Persian proverb

SELF-KNOWLEDGE

613   Know thyself.

> Thales, in Diogenes Laertius XIII,
> Lives . . . (Hicks, tr.) 1925 41 Putnam

614   A man can lose his god but he cannot lose himself.

> Homer W. Smith, Man and His Gods 1952 444 Little

615   At first one suffers from things which seem to come from other persons, or from circumstances outside oneself. Gradually one finds that many or most of one's troubles are in oneself.   From (Dom) John Chapman,

> in D. B. Phillips et al. (eds.),
> Choice . . . 1948 149 R. R. Smith

616   Men and women make sad mistakes taking their vague, uneasy longing sometimes for genius, sometimes for religion, and oftener still for a mighty love.

From George Eliot, Middlemarch

617   The most frequent impediment to men's turning their minds inward upon themselves is that they are afraid of what they will find there.

From Coleridge, Aids to Reflection

618   Those who remain in the dark about their own motives are as it were strangers to themselves. No one is truly literate who cannot read his own heart.

Over-seriousness is one means of camouflage.

Often the reckless wasting of one's vigor is a blind striving to "liquidate" an unwanted self.

Often the thing we pursue most passionately is but a substitute for the one thing we really want and cannot have.

It seems that we are most busy when we do not do the one thing we ought to do; most greedy when we cannot have the one thing we really want; most hurried when we can never arrive; most self-righteous when irrevocably in the wrong.

The craving to change the world may be a reflection of the craving to change ourselves.

From Eric Hoffer,
Passionate State of Mind 1955 95 97 60 5 2 66 Harper

619   Many a prude is trying to cover his own unwelcome desires.

620   In some cases, in running away from ourselves we either fall on our neighbor's shoulder or fly at his throat.

From Eric Hoffer, True Believer 1951 14 Harper

621   Weak natures take to daydreaming as a refuge as strong ones do to fanaticism.

> From John Dewey,
> Common Faith 1934 22 Yale Univ. Press

622   A neurosis is a stupidly stereotyped reaction in a non-stupid person.

> After Albert Ellis, J. Gen. Psychol., 1958 59:38

623   Self-deception can be more or less unconscious.

624   Self-understanding rather than self-condemnation is the way to inner peace and mature conscience.

> J. L. Liebman,
> Peace of Mind 1946 33 Simon & Schuster

625   If you have assumed a character above your strength, you have acted in an unbecoming way and have neglected that which you might have fulfilled.

> From Epictetus,
> Discourses . . . (Long, tr.) n.d. 406

626   Even superior talents will be obscured, defeated, and destroyed if a man does not recognize the limits of his powers.

> Goethe

627   We are all apt to believe what the world believes about us.   George Eliot, Mill on the Floss

628   Envy is ignorance. Every man must take himself for better, for worse, as his portion.

> From Emerson, Self-Reliance

629   I shall never be a Milo, yet I do not neglect my body; nor a Croesus, and yet I do not neglect my property; nor, in a word, do we abandon our effort in any field because we despair of the first place.
Epictetus,
Discourses and Manual (Matheson, tr.) I ii

630   O wad some Power the giftie gie us
          To see oursels as ithers see us!
          It wad frae monie a blunder free us.
Burns, To a Louse . . .

631   It is generally easier to discover egoism in others than in oneself, for its discovery in others raises one's own ego.
From F. Künkel,
Let's Be Normal (Jensen, tr.) 1929 33 Washburn

632   The greatest of faults is to be conscious of none.
From Carlyle, Hero as Prophet

633   Few admit their faults as readily as their virtues.
S. J. Hurwitt, Treasury . . . 1961 4 Philos. Lib.

634   It is silly to be inconsolable at seeing one's own imperfections.
After Fénelon

635   To belittle yourself is not modesty so much as stupidity; but to overpraise yourself is not only presumption but folly.
From Montaigne, in Lowenthal (ed.),
Autobiography . . . 1935 163–164 Houghton

636   . . . Oft-times nothing profits more
Than self-esteem, grounded on just and right
Well managed.

Milton, Paradise Lost VIII 571

637   Only he who knows whence he comes, where he is, and whither he tends is wise.   Lavater, Aphorism 88

638   Let each man proportion his efforts to his powers.
Cicero (Shuckburgh, tr.), Essay on Old Age

639   They are great men who follow that part of them which is great.   Mencius

640   This above all: to thine own self be true,
And it must follow, as the night the day,
Thou canst not then be false to any man.
Shakespeare, Hamlet I iii 78–80

641   We understand others as we understand ourselves.

642   Self-knowledge is the forerunner of compassion, rational conduct, creativity—all of these basic to the extension of life.   Unknown

EDUCATION

643   Whatever is preached, and whatever we learn, we must remember that it is man who gives and man who receives, a mortal hand that offers and a mortal hand that takes.
From Montaigne, in Lowenthal (ed.),
Autobiography . . . 1935 239 Houghton

644   Orthodox regimes try to give their pupils "censored enlightenment." This is not education but dogmatic indoctrination. Most likely it conveys some truth, but also error; it obscures further truth; and it cramps the teachers and stunts the pupils.

645   The world needs open hearts and open minds, and it is not through rigid systems, whether old or new, that these can be derived.   Bertrand Russell, Why I Am Not a Christian
1957 xiii G. Allen; Simon & Schuster

646   Education is a kind of continuing dialogue, and a dialogue assumes . . . different points of view.
R. M. Hutchins, before a House Com. 1952

647   The essence of liberal education is the freedom of mind that grows out of an indomitable quest for truth.
From Bentley Glass,
Science . . . 1960 54 La. State Univ. Press

648   Education is not a process of packing articles in a trunk . . . Its nearest analogue is the assimilation of food by a living organism.   Whitehead, Aims . . . 1929 51
Macmillan, © Cambridge; Benn

649   A child educated only at school is an uneducated child.
Santayana, Modern Mo. 1935 9:77

650   Be not proud because of thy learning. Take counsel with the unlearned as with the learned . . . Worthy speech is found even among slave-women at the millstone.
Ptahhotep,
in Breasted, Dawn . . . 1933 129–130 Scribner

651   A function of education is to train people to say what they mean.

Max Salvadori, Smith Alum. Q., Feb. 1970 5

652   Reading makes a full man; conference a ready man; and writing an exact man.   Francis Bacon, Of Studies

653   The more a man is able to comprehend a regular chain of causes and effects the more fully is the human quality developed in him.   From ibn Khaldun (Issawi, tr.), Arab Philosophy . . . 1950 166 Murray

654   In the preparation of the citizen for his political duties, the humanities are as important as acquaintance with the persons and the current events upon which he is to pass. There is no substitute for an open mind enriched by reading and the arts.   From Learned Hand

655   To omit the teaching of science and the scientific spirit from education would condemn students to a medieval outlook.
    We need to achieve the value of specialization without giving up the completeness of the individual.

From Arthur E. Morgan,
Observations 1968 177 66 Antioch Press

656   Education is learning the laws of Nature, not merely things and their forces, but men and their ways; and the fashioning of the affections and of the will to move in harmony with those laws.   From Thomas Huxley

657   Education is the best provision for old age.

Aristotle

658   The man who has not been tested knows not how much he knows.

From Ecclus. XXXIV 10

659   An educated person knows when a thing is proved.

John Morley

660   The vindication of the obvious is sometimes more important than the elucidation of the obscure.

(Justice) O. W. Holmes

661   Of practical wisdom there are the three fruits: to deliberate well, to speak to the point, to do what is right.

Democritus

662   When the solid qualities exceed the accomplishments, there is rusticity. When the accomplishments exceed the solid qualities, there are the manners of the upstart. When the accomplishments and the solid qualities blend, there is the man of complete virtue.

From Confucius

HIGHER EDUCATION

663   A university is the temple of the open-minded.

From C. E. Wyzanski, Jr.,
Harvard Alum. Bull. Jan. 23 1954 316

664   The classroom is where problems are pursued to the horizon—problems not only of the material world but of man, rights, and wrongs.

From W. O. Douglas, speech,
Center for the Study of Dem. Inst. 1961

665   The university is the chief custodian of the life of reason. The life of reason seeks to fuse the ideal and the real, to make what is done correspond to what is professed.

From B. N. Schilling, AAUP Bull. 1959 45:269

666   The university must assert itself as a major "spiritual power," higher than the press, standing for serenity in the midst of frenzy, for seriousness and the grasp of intellect in the face of frivolity and unashamed stupidity.

Ortega y Gasset,
Mission . . . 1944 99 Princeton Univ. Press

667   To impose any straitjacket upon the intellectual leaders in our colleges and universities would imperil the future of our civilization. Teachers and students must always remain free to inquire, to study and to evaluate, to gain new maturity and understanding.   From the Supreme Court opinion on the New York Feinberg Law

668   The universities must be the intellectual powerhouses for human living, not just the feeder stations for technological empires.   After C. B. MacPherson,
AAUP Bull. 1969 55:437–438

669   The universities must not acquiesce in the desire of the impatient to escape the moral responsibility for rational choice.   From Kingman Brewster, Jr.,
Am. Scientist 1970 58:175

670   The essence of liberalism in every field is to find out what evidence there is as to possible alternatives, each to receive the same logical treatment before we can determine which is best grounded.   Morris R. Cohen

671   If there is to be toleration in the world, one of the things taught in schools must be the habit of weighing evidence.
Bertrand Russell,
Free Thought . . . 1922 49 Huebsch

672   Men of science reckon him who explodes old error as next in rank to him who discovers new truth.
From Thomas Huxley, Life and Letters

673   Nobody can detect the error of his teacher until he knows varying opinions.
ibn Gabirol

674   Not only the grounds of the opinion are forgotten in the absence of discussion, but too often the meaning of the opinion itself.
John Stuart Mill, On Liberty 1892 23

675   Nothing should be left undone to impress upon the young that freedom of thought is an axiom of human progress.
J. B. Bury, History . . . 1913 251

676   Ever since the founding of the University of Bologna in the twelfth century, college students and faculties have been suspected as subversives. In reality, the students' world is the world of the future. As long as there is progress, especially technological progress, the humanities and social sciences will strive to conserve both it and human values.
After A. H. Kittell, AAUP Bull. 1965 51:363

677   A true humanist must know the life, the essential stream, of science as he knows the life of art and the life of religion.
After George Sarton,
History . . . 1937 xvi Harvard Univ. Press

678   The problem of education is to make the pupil see the wood by means of the trees.   Whitehead, Aims ... 1929
Macmillan, © Cambridge; Benn

679   The schools have the responsibility to see that those who go out have ideas that are worth thinking and expressing, as well as the courage to express them.
From John Dewey,
Intelligence ... 1939 723 Random House, © Ratner

680   The colleges should at least try to give us the feeling for a good human job anywhere, the admiration of the really admirable, the disesteem of what is cheap. This is what we call the critical sense, the sense for ideal values. It is the better part of what men know as wisdom.
From William James,
Memories and Studies 1911 34

681   A Bachelor of Arts degree is a license to acquire an education.
From Gerald W. Johnson, Am. Scholar 1957 26:424

682   The university is not engaged in making ideas safe for students. It is engaged in making students safe for ideas.
Clark Kerr, statement at Univ. Calif. 1958

683   To improve the education of women is to improve the education of men also.   From Sydney Smith

684   Education should implant important facts, principles, and techniques; enlarge perspective; facilitate learning; strengthen judgment, and foster contribution.

685   Through reading, looking, and listening, one can observe with Aristotle, behold with Euripides, stand erect with Bruno, reflect with Spinoza, inquire with Hume, enjoy with Mozart, feel with Beethoven, understand with George Eliot, glimpse human life with Hardy, see with Mary Cassatt. Thus one is increased.

Broad and deep education, academic or other, develops mental fiber and sap. It makes a person more even-tempered and resilient, objective and engaged, idealistic and realistic, aware and effective, industrious and playful, wise and considerate. At the same time he lives more and is more livable.

TRAVEL

686   The fool wanders, the wise man travels.

English proverb

687   The world is a great book, of which they who never stir from home read only a page.   Augustine

688   In traveling, a man must carry knowledge with him if he would bring home knowledge.

From Samuel Johnson

689   We can never learn what sort of persons people are, when they come to us; we must go to them, if we would know what stuff they are made of and how they manage or mismanage their surroundings.

Goethe

690   Travel gives a character of experience to our knowledge, and brings the figures on the tablet of memory into strong relief.

H. T. Tuckerman

691　　When a man is acquainted only with the habits of his own country, they seem so much a matter of course that he ascribes them to nature, but when he travels abroad and finds totally different habits and standards of conduct prevailing, he begins to understand the power of custom.

J. B. Bury, History ... 1913 26–27

692　　Travel regulates imagination by reality.

From Samuel Johnson

PERSONAL CULTURE

693　　Man is born a barbarian, and only raises himself above the beast by culture . . . Nothing contributes so much to culture as knowledge. But even knowledge is coarse if without elegance.

Balthasar Gracian (Jacobs, tr.) Maxim 87

694　　Culture is precisely the opposite of external ornament.

From Ortega y Gasset,
Mission ... 1944 43 Princeton Univ. Press

695　　Culture is the art of aristocrats, the art of enriching life.

From Mary M. Colum

696　　What we should aim at producing is men who possess both culture and expert knowledge in some special direction. Their expert knowledge will give them the ground to start from, and their culture will lead them as deep as philosophy and as high as art.

Whitehead, Aims ...
1929 1 Macmillan © Cambridge; Benn

697   Let us be manysided! Turnips are pleasing to the taste, especially when mixed with chestnuts; and these two noble products grow far apart.   Goethe

698   He who gives preferential treatment to the lesser parts of the body becomes a lesser man . . . to the greater parts . . . a greater man . . . Men despise one who lives only to eat and drink.   Mencius (Dobson, tr.),
1963 145 Univ. Toronto Press; Oxford

699   The result of the educative process is capacity for further education.
John Dewey, Democracy . . . 1916 79 Macmillan

700   The growth of higher feeling within us brings with it a sense of added strength.   George Eliot, Adam Bede

701   As the hidden spring comes to light in the river, so must a man's knowledge come to the surface in his actions.
From Pestalozzi,
Education . . . 1953 36–37 Philos. Lib.

702   The cistern contains; the fountain overflows.
William Blake, Marriage of Heaven and Hell

703   Learn the art of entertaining yourself alone, without being weary or melancholy.   Rule of Life 1800 139

704   When the Way prevails everywhere, use it to pursue your personal cultivation. When the Way does not prevail, use your personal cultivation to pursue the Way.
Mencius (Dobson, tr.),
1963 189 Univ. Toronto Press; Oxford

705   To continue to observe, to think, to learn—that alone can arouse our sympathy for the life of man; that alone can keep our own life in its course.

From E. von Feuchtersleben, Lewisohn (tr.),
Health and Suggestion 1910 164–165

706   Man is born to live, not to prepare for life.

Boris Pasternak

VII

Recreation and Leisure

707   High from the earth I heard a bird;
             He trod upon the trees
             As he esteemed them trifles,
             And then he spied a breeze,
             And situated softly
             Upon a pile of wind
             Which in a perturbation
             Nature had left behind.
             A joyous-going fellow
             I gathered from his talk,
             Which both of benediction
             And badinage partook,
             Without apparent burden,
             I learned, in leafy wood
             He was the faithful father
             Of a dependent brood;
             And this untoward transport
             His remedy for care,—
             A contrast to our respites.
             How different we are!

                                   Emily Dickinson,
                          Thomas H. Johnson (ed.),
                     Complete Poems 1960 699 Little

708   He ate and drank the precious Words—
             His spirit grew robust—
             He knew no more that he was poor,
             Nor that his frame was Dust—

             He danced along the dingy Days
             And this Bequest of Wings

Was but a Book—What Liberty
A loosened spirit brings—

Emily Dickinson,
Thomas H. Johnson (ed.),
Complete Poems . . . 1960 658 Little

709   To unbend our thoughts, when they are too much
stretched by our cares, is not more natural than it is necessary;
but to turn our whole life into a holiday is not only ridiculous,
but destroys pleasure instead of promoting it.

The mind, like the body, is tired by being always in one
posture; too serious breaks it, and too diverting loosens it.

From Savile, Advice to a Daughter, Diversions

710   Good blocks of oak it was I split . . .
The blows that a life of self-control
Spares to strike for the common good,
That day, giving a loose to my soul,
I spent on the unimportant wood.

Poetry of Robert Frost (Lathem, ed.),
Two Tramps in Mud Time 1960 275 Holt

711   Recreation is to the mind as whetting is to the scythe,
to sharpen the edge which otherwise would grow dull. He that
spends his whole time in recreation is ever whetting, never
mowing. Contrariwise, he that always toils is ever mowing,
never whetting; laboring much to little purpose; as good no
scythe as no edge.   From Joseph Hall

712   Caricature Prints ought not to abound so much as they do. Fun I love, but too much Fun is loathsome. Mirth is better than Fun, and Happiness is better than Mirth.

From William Blake,
Letter to the Revd. Dr. Trusler August 23, 1799

713   Even Eden grew tiresome after a time; else why would Eve have looked for diversion?

From H. H. Perlman,
Persona 1968 96 Univ. Chicago Press

PLAY

714   The bow too tensely strung is easily broken.

Publilius Syrus, Maxim 388

715   To the art of working well a civilized race would add the art of playing well. To play with nature and make it decorative, to play with the overtones of life—the colors, sounds, feelings, emotions, questions, mysteries—in creative dreams, including myths, is delightful. If, however, we do not know our environment as an order of natural law, we shall mistake our dreams for a part of that environment, and so spoil our science by making it fantastic, and our dreams by making them obligatory, not to be doubted. The art and the religion of the past have fallen into this error. To correct it requires moral courage.

From Santayana,
Three Philosophical Poets 1910 214 and passim

FUN

716   A little nonsense now and then
Is relished by the wisest men.
Old nursery rhyme

717   Behold the child, by nature's kindly law
Pleased with a rattle, tickled with a straw:
Some livelier plaything gives his youth delight,
A little louder, but as empty quite:
Scarfs, garters, gold, amuse his riper stage,
And beads and prayer-books are the toys of age.
Pope, Essay on Man II 275

718   A grain of gaiety seasons all.
Balthasar Gracian (Jacobs, tr.), Maxim 79

719   When I play with my cat, who knows whether I do not make her more sport than she makes me?
Montaigne, Apology for Raimond Sebond

MIRTH

720   A man without mirth is like a wagon without springs.
H. W. Beecher

721   Every smile or laugh from the heart adds something to life.
After Sterne

722   . . . It sort o' rests your face—
Just smiling.
Unknown, Try Smiling

723   We should never be too deadly serious; always laugh in time, especially at our own sublimities.   Augustine

724   We know the degree of refinement in men by the matter they will laugh at, and the ring of the laugh; but we know likewise that the larger natures are distinguished by the great breadth of their power of laughter.   Meredith

725   One inch of joy surmounts of grief a span,
           Because to laugh is proper to the man.
                 Rabelais, To the Reader

726   It isn't *things* that make us laugh, it's our own lightness or gaiety of heart.

                       Edgar Johnson,
       Treasury of Satire 1945 32 Simon & Schuster

727   Laughter is healthy, and joy a balm; but peace of mind is the source of laughter and of joy.

                            Pestalozzi,
          Education . . . 1953 80 Philos. Lib.

RECREATION

728   In times of loneliness or perplexity, how comforting and clarifying is the companionship of inanimate objects, the touching or handling of wood or stone; and how steadying is the performance of familiar manual tasks!

       From Jan Struthers, Reader's Digest Sept. 1945

729   I have found that all people in the world who are dull in their conversation and hateful to look at in their faces are those who have no hobbies.

Yuan Chung Lang, in George Lawton,
Aging . . . 1946 104 Columbia Univ. Press

730   Genial or spritely talk renews the spirit.

After Aristotle

731   The simple pleasures are always pleasures, and they cost nothing.   Fontenelle, Du bonheur

732   It is sweet to dance to violins
            When Love and Life are fair:
            To dance to flutes, to dance to lutes,
            Is delicate and rare.

Oscar Wilde,
Ballad of Reading Gaol

733   There is nothing more notable in Socrates than that he found time, when he was an old man, to learn music and dancing, and thought it time well spent.   Montaigne

734   A life without a holiday is like a long journey without an inn.   Democritus, Frag. 230

LEISURE

735   Leisure to those who know how to use it is the most beautiful of possessions.

From A. B. Alcott, Table-Talk, 1877 52

736   For a noble mind leisure is good when it alternates with hard work.
                                                        Giordano Bruno

737   Life would be poor without the power to look quietly around, without the restful glance at other lives.
                                            From Hans Margolius,
                                    Aphorisms ... n.d. Black Mt. News

738   There is a quality of quietness
               Which quickens people by no stress.
                                            Witter Bynner,
                                Way of Life according to Laotzu
                                            1944 69 Day

739   In some easy, idle days we absorb impressions and are enriched; in some full days we strain our eyes and mind and miss much that enriches.   After C. M. Skinner

740   It is better to have loafed and lost than never to have loafed at all.   James Thurber,
                            Fables for Our Time 1940 55 Harper,
                                    © 1968 Helen Thurber

741   In the emerging social order, leisure is coming to mean recreation rather than mere recuperation. Leisure activities are becoming discovery and development of new personal resources and style, the realization of self in everyday life.
                                            From G. G. Stern,
                                    AAUP Bull. 1966 52:412–413

SILENCE

742 On the tongue of the temple bell
A butterfly sleeps.
Buson

743 Muddy water, if allowed to remain still, will become
clear of itself. From Mencius

744 . . . Silence like a poultice comes
To heal the blows of sound.
(Doctor) O. W. Holmes

745 There is in stillness oft a magic power
To calm the breast when struggling passions lower.
John Henry Newman, Solitude

746 Silence is the element in which great things fashion
themselves. Carlyle, Sartor Resartus

SOLITUDE

747 . . . Solitude sometimes is best society,
And short retirement urges sweet return.
Milton, Paradise Lost IX 249–250

748 Where is the wise, or the learned, or the good that
sought not solitude for thinking?
Seek thou solitude, but neither in excess nor morosely.
From M. F. Tupper,
Proverbial Philosophy 1849 358

749   With some people solitariness is an escape not from others but from themselves; for they see in the eyes of others only an unhappy reflection of themselves.

After Eric Hoffer,
Passionate State of Mind 1955 128 Harper

750   Many a gregarious animal seems unable to live comfortably when not with the herd. If the animal is kept solitary for a while, then released, he rushes back into the herd and presses against the other members.

Many a person seems to want constant company. Aristotle observed that man is gregarious, but not only so. Most of us find companionship and even crowds good, within limits. Perpetual socializing may cure overindividualism, but it can stifle the individuality that everyone needs both in himself and in others.

751   Men that cannot entertain themselves want somebody, even though they care for nobody.

From Savile, Moral Thoughts . . ., Of Company

752   Be able to be alone.

Thomas Browne, Christian Morals III ix

753   There is a pleasure in being in one's own company, when a man has made himself worth enjoying.

From Seneca (Gummere, tr.),
Ad Lucilium . . . 1918 1:407 Putnam

VIII

Perception, Thought, and Action

754   The roots of our conscious being are in a dark soil, but this does not diminish the worth of the light.

From Morris R. Cohen,
Reason and Nature 1931 8 Harcourt, © Rosenfield

755   All the instincts, impulses, and emotions which push man into action outside the treadmill of use and habit are irrational. The business of reason is not to extinguish the fires which keep the cauldron of vitality seething, nor yet to supply the ingredients which are in vital stir. Its task is to see that they boil to some purpose.   From John Dewey,

Characters . . . 1929 587 Holt

756   A fool has no dialog within himself; the first thought carries him without the reply of a second.   Savile

757   To deny, believe, and doubt well are to a man what to race is to a horse.   Pascal

758   No one is subject to more mistakes than the one who functions only through reflection.

Vauvenargues, Reflection 131

759   Some are realists out of idealism. Some are fighters for the sake of peace. Some are sarcastic out of love for man.

H. Margolius,
Gedanken—Thoughts 1964 10 Pandanus

760   In extremely complex matters the unseen processes of the mind, emerging as ready judgment or intuition, may be better guides than reasoning. But intuition should always be subject to examination. Intuition and intelligence should constantly discipline each other.

The habit of objective thinking, of being open with one's self, of becoming aware of one's unconscious conditioning, and of bringing such conditioning under critical appraisal, may result in more significant and dependable intuitions.

From Arthur E. Morgan,
Observations 1968 219 277 Antioch Press

761   Act as men of thought; think as men of action.

Henri Bergson

IMPULSES AND PASSIONS

762   The inchoate and scattered impulses of an infant co-ordinate into serviceable powers through social dependencies and companionships.

Impulse brings with it the possibility of reorganization of habits to meet new elements in new situations.

From John Dewey,
Human Nature ... 1922 94 104 Holt

763   Every one of our elementary motivations, even those which are necessary to our preservation, without training would fill the world with misery.

From John Stuart Mill, Three Essays ... 1885 57

764   As an empty building echoes sounds, a vacant mind responds to suggestions.   Oriental proverb

765   A man without passion is only a latent force.

Amiel, Journal

766   For one heat, all know, doth drive out another,
       One passion doth expel another still.
                          George Chapman, Monsieur D'Olive V i

767   The ruling passion, be it what it will,
           The ruling passion conquers reason still.
                          Pope, Moral Essays III 153–154

768   Every spendthrift to passion is a debtor to thought.
                          Unknown

769   All passions that suffer themselves to be relished and
digested are but moderate.   Montaigne, Of Sorrow

770   Passion holds up the bottom of the world, while genius
paints its roof.   From Chang Ch'ao

WISH AND DESIRE

771   If wishes were horses, beggars would ride.
                          Proverbial

772   Wishes at least are the easy pleasures of the poor.
                          D. Jerrold

773   Inclination snatches arguments
       To make indulgence seem judicious choice.
                          George Eliot, Spanish Gypsy I

774   Too many men wish to have a castle but do not wish
to build it.   After Goethe

775   Those who are slaves of desire are slaves of the world; but those who make desire their slave have the world at their service.   From Sharma and Raghavacharya (trs.), Gems from Sanskrit ... 1959 13 Osmania

776   [For self-direction, one asks]: What will happen to me if the object of my desire is achieved? And what will happen if it is not?   From Epicurus, Strodach (tr.), Philosophy ... 1962 207 Northwestern Univ. Press

777   It is difficult to satisfy one's appetite by painting pictures of cakes.   Seven Hundred Chinese Proverbs (Hart, tr.) 1937 52 Stanford Univ. Press

778   The best way to make your dreams come true is to wake up.   J. M. Power

779   Leave something to wish for, so as not to be miserable from very happiness.   Balthasar Gracian

OBSERVATION

780   Nature, to be led, must be followed.
                    After Francis Bacon, Novum Organum

781   Expect the unexpected, or you will never find truth.
                    Heraclitus, Frag. 19

782   Slight not what's near through aiming at what's far.
                    Euripides, Rhesus 482

783   He who can take no interest in what is small will take false interest in what is great.

From Ruskin

784   Close observation of little things is essential to success in business, in art, in science and in every pursuit in life.

From S. Smiles

785   What amazing differences appear in the objects around us, according to the point of view from which we regard them!

From Peter Mere Latham

PERCEPTION

786   Why fly into eternities?
        What man perceives, that he can seize.

Goethe, in Walter Kaufman,
From Shakespeare to Existentialism
1960 70 Doubleday

787   In the night all cats are gray.

Proverbial

788   Colors seen by candle-light
        Will not look the same by day.

Elizabeth Barrett Browning, Lady's Yes

789   Mountains at a distance appear airy and smooth.

Diogenes Laertius, Pyrrho IX

790   . . . Swans seem whiter if swart crows be by.

Guillaume Salluste du Bartas,
Divine Weekes . . . Ii

791   Mud sometimes gives the illusion of depth. Extra items do likewise. These effects appear in landscaping, painting, music, diction, and other arts.

> After Stanislaw J. Lec,
> Unkempt Thoughts 1962 45 St. Martin's Press

792   He that I am reading seems always to have the most force.

> Montaigne,
> Apology for Raimond Sebond

793   All seems infected that th' infected spy,
As all looks yellow to the jaundiced eye.

> Pope, Essay on Criticism II 558

794   Bad-tempered persons are like men who stand on their heads: they see all things the wrong way.   From Plato

795   To observations which ourselves we make,
We grow more partial for th' observer's sake.

> Pope, Moral Essays I 11–12

796   A fool sees not the same tree that a wise man sees.

> William Blake, Marriage of Heaven and Hell

797   Two men look out through the same bars:
One sees the mud, and one the stars.

> F. Langbridge,
> Cluster of Quiet Thoughts 1896 31

798   None so deaf as those that will not hear.

> Matthew Henry, Commentaries: Psalms lviii

799   When one shuts one eye, one does not hear everything.
                            Swiss-German proverb, Champion (ed.),
                                 Racial . . . 1938 319 Macmillan,
                                  © Routledge; Barnes & Noble

800   We are prone to see what lies behind our eyes rather
than what appears before them.
                            Anon., Contemporary Psychol. 1959 4:139

801   It's as you throw a picture on a screen:
           The meaning of it all is out of you;
           The voices give you what you wish to hear.
                              Poetry of Robert Frost (Lathem, ed.),
                              The Generations of Men 1969 78 Holt

802   To the eyes of a miser a guinea is far more beautiful
than the sun, and a bag worn with the use of money has more
beautiful proportions than a vine filled with grapes. The tree
which moves some to tears of joy is in the eyes of others only
a green thing which stands in the way. As a man is, so he sees.
                                      From William Blake,
                      Letter to the Revd. Dr. Trusler August 23 1799

803   Only in calm waters things mirror themselves undis-
torted. Only in a calm mind is adequate perception of the
world.   From H. Margolius,
                      Thoughts . . . 1962 24 Lib. of Humane Lit.

804   The proof of the pudding is in the eating.
                                          Proverbial

805   The value of systematic training in perception as a
preparation for enlightenment in the everyday world was

stressed many centuries ago by certain of the Tantric philos-
opher-psychologists of India. Shiva says: "When eating or
drinking, become the taste of the food or drink and be filled."
"While being caressed, enter the caressing as everlasting life."
"Intone a sound audibly, then less and less audibly, as feeling
deepens into this silent harmony." "See as if for the first time
a beauteous person or ordinary object." "Wherever your attention alights, at that point *experience.*"

It is useless to preach the life of reason to people who find
that life is flat, stale, and unprofitable. But if the life of reason
could be combined with the life of cleansed perceptions and a
capacity for mystico-sensuous enjoyment, rationality could
make a wider, stronger appeal, and the idiocies and delin-
quencies to which, in our boredom, we now resort would be
less alluring.   From Julian Huxley,
          Humanist Frame 1961 424–426 G. Allen

806   To see a world in a grain of sand,
         And a heaven in a wild flower,
         To hold infinity in the palm of your hand,
         And eternity in an hour.
                    William Blake, Auguries of Innocence

MEMORY

807   Like Some Old Fashioned Miracle
            When Summertime is done—
            Seems Summer's Recollection
            And the Affairs of June
                              Emily Dickinson,
                         Thomas H. Johnson (ed.),
                    Complete Poems . . . 1960 142 Little

808　　. . . Shapes return,
　　　　Some frequently, some seldom, some by night
　　　　And some by day, some night and day: we learn,
　　　　The while all change and many vanish quite,
　　　　In their recurrence with recurrent changes
　　　　A certain seeming order; where this ranges
　　　　We count things real; such is memory's might.
　　　　　　　　　James Thomson, City of Dreadful Night

809　　Memory, the daughter of Attention, is the teeming
nurse of Wisdom.　　　　　　　　　　After M. F. Tupper,
　　　　　　　　　　　　Proverbial Philosophy 1849 105

810　　Could we know what men are most apt to remember,
we might know what they are most apt to do.
　　　　　　　　　Savile, Complete Works . . . 1912 252

811　　A learning creature uses its past stupidities and successes to inform its present. Thus the values of experience
become means to new desires and aims.

　　　　　　　　　　　　　　From John Dewey,
　　　　　　　　　　Art as Experience 1934 Minton
　　　　　　　　　　and Liberalism . . . 1934 Minton

BELIEF

812　　When one dog barks at a shadow, ten thousand dogs
turn it into a reality.　　　　　　　　　　Chinese proverb

813　　Men are born to believe and to love, and, without true
objects of belief and love, they turn to false ones.　　Pascal

814   Every idea is an incitement. It offers itself for belief and if believed it is acted on unless some other belief outweighs it or some failure of energy stifles the movement at its birth.   (Justice) O. W. Holmes

815   Some men persuade the world that they believe what at heart they disbelieve. Many men persuade themselves that they believe—not knowing what it means really to believe.
From Montaigne, in Lowenthal (ed.),
Autobiography . . . 1935 269 Houghton

816   Do not confuse opinions with certainties.
Arabian proverb

817   With most people disbelief of one thing is founded upon blind belief of another.
G. C. Lichtenberg, Stern (ed.),
Lichtenberg 1959 314 Ind. Univ. Press

818   Certitude is not the test of certainty. We have been cocksure of many things that were not so.
(Justice) O. W. Holmes,
Collected Legal Papers 1920 311 Harcourt

819   A man must not swallow more beliefs than he can digest.
Havelock Ellis, Dance of Life 1923 Houghton

820   We are not free to believe what we like; we are only free to test by reason, to weigh according to evidence, to follow truth.   From Arthur Foote,
Letter to an Orthodox Colleague
1955 Am. Unitarian Assn.

821   No one has ever proved the non-existence of Apollo or Aphrodite; belief in them merely declined when it corresponded no longer with general intellectual conditions.

Maugham, Writer's Notebook
1949 80 Doubleday; Heinemann

822   Ah! What a dusty answer gets the soul
        When hot for certainties in this our life!

Meredith, Modern Love L

823   Any human belief, however defensible it may seem, is only a probable belief. Our widest and safest generalizations are simply statements of the highest probability.

From Thomas Huxley,
American Addresses 1877 3

824   He is no mean philosopher who can give a reason for half of what he thinks.

Hazlitt, Characteristics CCCXXXIX

825   The problem of integration and cooperation between man's beliefs about the world, and his beliefs about the values and purposes that should direct his conduct, is the deepest problem of modern life.

From John Dewey, Quest . . . 1929 255 Minton

826   Some beliefs restrict men's interests, sympathies, and self-direction, cramp their personalities, and let them either over- or underestimate themselves.

Other beliefs broaden men's interests, develop sympathies, and encourage self-direction and personal growth.

DOUBT

827   [Often,]
             If your Soul Seesaw—
             Lift the Flesh door—
             The Poltroon wants Oxygen—
             Nothing more—
                      Emily Dickinson, Thomas H. Johnson (ed.),
                      Complete Poems . . . 1960 136 Little

828   The complete sceptic is a dogmatist. He enjoys the
delusion of complete futility.
                                        After Whitehead,
                      Essays in Science . . . 1947 102 Philos. Lib.

829   A well-founded confusion is often better than an ill-
founded certainty.   J. B. Furst

830   Truth often loses by blind obedience, but gains by
inquiry.   From William Penn

831   The courage of one's doubts can be a strength.
                                        After A. MacLeish,
                      tribute to Adlai Stevenson 1965

832   A weakening of belief can be due as much to a gain in
power, skill, and experience as to a loss of vigor and drive.
A fading of belief does not necessarily spell decline.
                                        From Eric Hoffer,
                      Temper of Our Time 1967 102 Harper

833   The capacity to cultivate doubt should be cherished
and nurtured by those who know its price and its value. The

substitution of one intense conviction for another does not count here. Consistent scientific skepticism is dispassionate, impartial, broadly interested.

After S. S. Stevens,
Contemporary Psychol. 1967 12:2

834   No scientist will doubt everything equally strongly. While he might admit in principle all scientific knowledge is open to revision, that does not mean that he is questioning everything all of the time.

H. Feigl,
The Humanist, Sept.-Oct. 1968 21

835   The closed orthodox mind can be intense, but the open scientific mind, secure.

836   Anyone who takes life seriously enough to consider religion in its substance and express any honest doubts is more truly religious, devoted to highest good, than those who accept doctrine without question, even though his inquiry may bring him to extremely unorthodox conclusions.

After P. B. Sears,
Sci. Mo. 1956 82:317

IMAGINATION

837   Were there only dreaming, there would be no dreaming.
Ralph Barton Perry

838   To make a prairie it takes a clover and one bee,—
And revery.

The revery alone will do
If bees are few.

> Emily Dickinson, Thomas H. Johnson (ed.),
> Complete Poems . . . 1960 710 Little

839   Such tricks hath strong imagination
        That, if it would but apprehend some joy,
        It comprehends some bringer of that joy;
        Or in the night, imagining some fear,
        How easy is a bush supposed a bear!

> Shakespeare,
> Midsummer-Night's Dream V i 18–22

840   There is no fantasy without a kernel of wheat in the
mass of chaff.   Zohar, Tosefta

841   If you have built castles in the air your work need not
be lost; that is where they should be built; now put foundations under them.   Thoreau

842   Life's gift outruns my fancies far,
           And flows the dream
           Into larger stream,
           As morning engulfs the morning star!

> After D. A. Wasson, All's Well

843   Fools act on imagination without knowledge; pedants
act on knowledge without imagination.

> Whitehead, Aims . . .
> 1929 140 Macmillan, © Cambridge; Benn

844   It does not pay to tether one's thoughts to the post of use with too short a rope. Power in action requires largeness of vision which can be had only through imagination.

From John Dewey,
How We Think 1933 224 Heath

HOPE

845   . . . Hope is swift, and flies with swallow's wings;
Kings it makes gods, and meaner creatures kings.
Shakespeare, King Richard III V ii 23–24

846   None without hope e'er loved the brightest fair,
But love can hope where reason would despair.
George Lyttleton, Epigram

847   Man toils for some far heaven, wherefrom
The enthronèd gods were fain released.
Paul Elmer More, Century . . . 1898 XLII 64

848   He that lives on hope will die fasting.
Franklin, Speech of Father Abraham

849   Hope deferred is not proved false.
Albert Guérard,
Bottle in the Sea 1954 51 Harvard Univ. Press

850   The most ridiculous and the boldest hopes have sometimes been the cause of the most extraordinary successes.
Vauvenargues, Reflection 231

851   Hope would not exist but for uncertainty if not fear. The more we are guided by reason, the less we depend on

hope; we reduce uncertainty and fear as we acknowledge the unknown and the unavoidable, and make the most of the useful and the worth while.

From Spinoza,
Ethics IV xlvii Proof Note and passim

852   Hope is generally a wrong guide, though it is very good company by the way. It brushes through hedge and ditch till it comes to a great leap, and there it is apt to fall and break its bones.

The hopes of a fool are blind guides; those of a man of sense doubt often of their way.

Men should do with their hopes as they do with tame fowl, clip their wings that they may not fly over the wall.

From Savile, Moral Thoughts . . . Of Hope

THOUGHT

853   . . . Thought has a pair of dauntless wings.

Poetry of Robert Frost
(Lathem, ed.), Bond and Free 1969 120 Holt

854   Freedom is inherent in thought.

Albert Guérard,
Bottle in the Sea 1954 16 Harvard Univ. Press

855   Thought is the algebra of the world.

Guyau, Education . . . 1891 294

856   The great conquerors, from Alexander to . . . Napoleon, influenced profoundly the lives of subsequent genera-

tions. But the total effect of this influence shrinks to insignifi-cance, if compared to the entire transformation of human habits and human mentality produced by the long line of men of thought from Thales to the present day, men individu-ally powerless, but ultimately the rulers of the world.

Whitehead,
Science . . . 1925 299–300 Macmillan; Cambridge

857   The manner in which one single ray of light, one single precious hint, will clarify and energize the whole mental life of him who receives it, is most wonderful.

From Arnold Bennett

858   Glory to the man who first seized fire from the heavens, and greater glory to him who first laid hold of the concept of fire.

Edmond Cahn,
Moral Decision 1955 241 Ind. Univ. Press

859   Nothing is more powerful than an idea whose time has come.

Victor Hugo

860   What he greatly thought, he nobly dared.

Homer, Odyssey II 312

861   All wrong conduct means some limitation or disturb-ance in thinking.

From Everett,
Moral Values 1918 212 Holt

862   There are people with a voracious and indiscriminate appetite for knowledge who could not be called thoughtful

persons, and there are profoundly thoughtful persons whose knowledge is very limited.   From Brand Blanshard,
Reason and Goodness 1961 437 Macmillan

863   Learning without thought is vain; thought without learning is perilous.   Chinese proverb

864   Only when reflecting on our experiences do we remove them from the evanescence of the moment.

At times our ideas about the world and about man are clearer than experience and come nearer to the truth.

From H. Margolius,
Thoughts . . . 1962 9 29 Lib. of Humane Lit.

865   Consideration often would prevent what the best skill in the world cannot recover.   William Penn

866   As a man thinks, so he becomes.

Ramakrishna, in Brian Brown (ed.),
Wisdom of the Hindus 1921 271 Brentano

867   [Too often, it seems that] there is no expedient to which a man will not resort to avoid the arduous task of thinking.   Joshua Reynolds

868   It is better to think and sometimes think wrong than not to think at all.   W. J. Mayo,
Collected Papers . . . 27:1212–1216 1935

869   The person who really thinks learns quite as much from his failures as from his successes.

John Dewey, How We Think 1933 114 Heath

870   The True Gentleman spends a lifetime of careful thought, but not a day in worrying.

Mencius (Dobson, tr.),
1963 134 Univ. Toronto Press; Oxford

871   Sensitiveness to ideas means curiosity, adventure, change.

Whitehead,
Adventures . . . 1933 105 Macmillan, Cambridge

872   . . . We must not think of thought as passive, as arising out of perceptions, as steam rises from heated water, but as an activity, a doing, a going out towards, as grasping and manipulating the data of sense.

From W. Macneile Dixon,
Human Situation, n.d. 58–59 St. Martin's

873   The objective of the world of ideas as a whole is not the portrayal of reality—this would be an utterly impossible task—but rather to provide us with an *instrument for finding our way about more easily in this world.*

From H. Vaihinger,
Philosophy of "As If" (Ogden, tr.), 1925 15–16
Harcourt, © Barnes & Noble; Routledge

874   We must not put off thought till we are up to the chin in mire . . . It is better to sleep on things beforehand than lie awake about them afterwards . . . Rumination and foresight enable one to determine the line of life.

Balthasar Gracian (Jacobs, tr.) Maxim 151

875   In human life second thoughts often prove to be wiser.

Euripides, Hippolytus
(Vellacott, tr.) 1953 40 Penguin, © G. Allen

876   To seek after ideas for conducting practical operations is to help create a world in which the springs of realistic thinking will be clear and ever-flowing.

From John Dewey, Quest . . . 1929 138 Minton

877   A richer plexus of emotions is concerned in producing or contemplating something humanly necessary than something idly conceived.

Santayana, Reason in Art 1905 210 Scribner

REASON

878   If man is not an entirely rational animal, neither is he entirely an irrational one.

R. L. Jenkins,
Breaking Patterns . . . 1954 231 Lippincott

878a   Impulse pushes. Reason beckons, and beckons.

879   Reason cannot recognize arbitrary prohibitions or barriers without being untrue to herself. The universe of experience is her province, and, as its parts are all linked together and interdependent, it is impossible for her to recognize any territory on which she may not tread, or to surrender any of her rights to an authority whose credentials she had not examined and approved.   J. B. Bury, History . . . 1913 18

880   He who cannot reason is a fool; he who will not is a bigot; and he who dares not is a slave.

From W. Drummond, Academical Questions

881   Logical consequences are the scarecrows of fools and the beacons of wise men.

Thomas Huxley, Animal Automatism 1874 15

882   Our logical thoughts dominate experience only as the parallels and meridians make a checkerboard of the sea.

Santayana, Interpretations . . . 1900 261 Scribner

883   Only rational processes can reveal the areas of irrationality. Thus the knowledge of our own irrationality is a triumph for rationality.

From E. R. Hilgard,
Unconscious Processes . . . [1958] 18 Univ. Ill. Press

884   There are whole worlds of fact waiting to be discovered by inference.   Woodrow Wilson

885   To say that our aim should be consistent thought in all areas except that of the supreme experiences of the spirit is unwillingness to face the facts of human rationality.

From J. S. Bixler,
Harv. Found. Adv. Study . . . Dec. 30, 1961 4

886   There are many faiths, and we may not share that of others, as others may not share ours, or we may not even share any faith whatsoever. But all men without exception may share in reason and its conquests, and it should be our common concern to extend its domain as far as we can, and not to accept any attempt to reduce it. Our life and our person are not made of reason alone, and the more we are aware of this fact, the better it is. But reason is the only tool we have for bringing a ray of light and order into the great, dark chaos from which

we were born, into which we shall return, and by which we are surrounded on all sides.

P. O. Kristeller,
Eight Philosophers . . . 1964 90 Stanford Univ. Press

887   When reason and authority conflict, there is no recourse but the appeal to reason. We must use it even in deciding which authority we shall follow. Furthermore, if we think, we shall see that nothing in the end is true because an authority says it; the authority, if he *is* an authority, would merely give you the evidence, assuming that man's common reason is the last and highest authority.

Intellectual openness can give tone to a whole character. As John Locke said, "The love of truth is the major part of human perfection in this world, and the seedplot of all other virtues."

From Brand Blanshard,
The Humanist May/June 1968 28: No. 3 14

888   We ought to call in reason like a good physician as a help in misfortune.

Epictetus, Discourses . . . (Long, tr.) n.d. 443

889   Men, in so far as they live rationally, are useful to their fellow man.   Spinoza, Ethics IV xxxvii Proof

890   Many human problems call for limited answers. It is foolish to first require the power to solve all the riddles of the universe.   From J. A. C. F. Auer,
Auer and Hartt,
Humanism . . . 1951 64 Antioch Press

891 What can we reason but from what we know?
Pope, Essay on Man I 17

892 It is always a windfall for truth when well-established facts collide with a well-constructed theory.
Jean Rostand,
Substance of Man 1962 94 Doubleday

893 A question rightly asked is half answered.
C. G. J. Jacobi

894 "For example" is not proof. Yiddish proverb

895 Who reasons wisely is not therefore wise;
His pride in reasoning, not in acting, lies.
Pope, Moral Essays I 117–118

896 Reason is the path, not the goal. Albert Guérard

897 Reasoning is not the principal thing in us. It is only like a staircase by which we can climb up to the desired place, or like a good genius which brings us tidings of the highest good, thereby to stimulate us to lose ourselves in that good.
From Spinoza,
L. Roth, Spinoza 1929 161–162 Little

898 When reason is not unduly curbed, it leads on ahead of belief.
Walter Kaufmann,
Critique of Religion and Philosophy
1958 307 Harper

THEORY AND HYPOTHESIS

899   Those who "refuse to go beyond fact" into theory and hypothesis, as distinguished from belief, rarely get to important further facts.   After Huxley,
                    in Bibby, T. H. Huxley 1959 38 Horizon

900   Without theory, practice is but the routine of habit. Theory alone can bring forth and develop the spirit of invention.   Pasteur

901   Too often, what is put forward as a theory is the over-hasty effort of an impatient mind which, eager to avoid many facts, sets up in their place images, notions, or mere words.
                                              From Goethe

902   The need to create sound syntheses and systematization of knowledge calls for a special kind of scientific genius, the genius of integration.   From Ortega y Gasset

903   Nothing is so practical as a good theory.
                                          From Kurt Lewin

904   Hypotheses are fruitful when they are suggested by actual need, are bulwarked by knowledge already attained, and are tested by the consequences of the operations they evoke.   John Dewey,
                        Quest . . . 1929 310–311 Minton

905   The principles of scientific method form a feedback loop of hypothesis formation, hypothesis testing, hypothesis

revision, re-testing, and successive revision until deviations of reality from the hypothesized reality fall within tolerable limits.
R. F. Simmons,
Synthex ... 1961 380 System Development Corp.

906 The most abstract statements or propositions in science are *hypothetical.*
From William Kingdon Clifford, Lectures ... 1886 289

907 The guiding motto in the life of every natural philosopher should be, seek simplicity and distrust it.
Whitehead, Concept of Nature 1926 163 Cambridge

908 Carry theory lightly that you may follow where fact may lead.
K. M. Dallenbach,
Psychol. Rev. 1953 60:35

909 Though the dogmatist may seem to think and act decisively, his response is essentially mechanical. The open-minded person can weigh, choose, and act more wisely.

910 There is realistic conjecture as well as realistic certainty; and each saves many lives.
After Peter Mere Latham

UNDERSTANDING

911 In vain sedate reflections we would make
When half our knowledge we must snatch, not take.
Pope, Moral Essays I 39–40

912   No true appreciation of anything is possible without a
sense of its *naturalness,* of the innocent necessity by which it
has assumed its special and perhaps extraordinary form.

Santayana,
Genteel Tradition ... 1931 73 Scribner

913   In all instances the unknown is to be explained by the
known and never the known by the unknown.

From J. A. C. F. Auer,
Auer and Hartt, Humanism ... 1951 6 Antioch Press

914   Understanding, and action proceeding from it, is the
one instrument by which liberty, health, and joy may be shaped
or shaped towards.   From J. Agee,
Let Us Now Praise Famous Men
1960 289 Houghton

915   [In any philosophical or other system of thought,] to
acquiesce in discrepancy is destructive of candor and of moral
excellence.   Whitehead

916   No man can do well what he does not understand well.
From Richard Baxter, Christian Politics

917   In so far as the mind conceives a thing according to
reason, it is affected equally, whether the idea be of a thing
future, past, or present.

In proportion as the mind understands more things, it is less
subject to those emotions which are evil.

The mind has greater power over the emotions and is less
subject thereto, in so far as it understands all things as caused.

From Spinoza, Ethics IV lxii, V xxxviii vi

918   Our affections, when they are enlightened by understanding, are organs by which we enter into the meaning of the natural world as genuinely as by ["intellectual"] knowing, and with greater fullness and intimacy.

John Dewey, Quest . . . 1929 297 Minton

919   The world is enlarged for us not so much by new objects as by finding more affinities and potencies in those we have.   Emerson

920   So far as we discern causes and effects we understand, and can act wisely.

921   Understanding shapes the will.

From Francis Bacon,
Advancement of Learning I VIII iii

INTELLECT

922   The intellect remains unsatisfied with its own work, and is always turning up afresh the soil of past opinion.

From J. Tulloch, Movements . . . 1885 335

923   Without moral force to whip it into action, the achievements of the intellect would be poor indeed.

John Tyndall, Address . . . 1874 61

ANTICIPATION

925   Shed no tear—O shed no tear!
The flower will bloom another year.

Weep no more—O weep no more!
Young buds sleep in the root's white core.
Keats, Faery Song I

926   It is worth a thousand pounds a year to have the habit
of looking on the bright side of things.   Samuel Johnson

927   [Often] it is worse to apprehend than to suffer.
Jean de la Bruyère

928   That which has been long expected comes more gently.
Seneca,
Ad Lucilium . . . (Gummere, tr.) 1918 2:199 Putnam

929   Anticipation quickens energy in action.
After E. G. Bulwer-Lytton

IDEALISM

930   'Tis but a base ignoble mind,
That mounts no higher than a bird can soar.
Shakespeare, Henry VI II i 13

931   . . . Spirits are not finely touched
But to fine issues.
Shakespeare, Measure for Measure I i 35–36

932   Life enlightened is spirit; the voice of life, and therefore aspiring to all the perfections to which life aspires.
Santayana,
in Cardiff (ed.), Atoms . . . 1950 192 Philos. Lib.

933   The quest of man at his best is for excellence—at least to know what it is, and, so far as possible, to practice it.

After R. W. Livingstone,
Standards and Values, a lecture 1956

934   The ideals which have always shone before me and filled me with the joy of living are goodness, beauty, and truth.

Einstein,
Living Philosophies 1931 Simon & Schuster

935   The idealism which becomes visible is small compared with what men and women bear locked in their hearts.

From Schweitzer,
Out of My Life . . . (Campion, tr.) 1933 114 Holt

936   The indwelling ideal lends all the gods their divinity.

Santayana,
Reason in Religion 1905 190 Scribner

937   God represents a challenge to man to change his life and become loving and just.   Walter Kaufmann,
Critique of Religion and Philosophy
1958 305 Harper

938   [For man] the supernatural . . . points to the satisfaction of his earthly interests . . .

Only in reference to what is not itself life—to ideals that cannot be experienced but may only be conceived—can life become rational and truly progressive . . .

The distinction between the ideal and the real is one which human idealism itself insists should be preserved.

Santayana,
Reason in Science 1905 298 Scribner,
Three Philosophical Poets 1910 178,
Reason in Art 1905 29 Scribner

940   Idealism and realism are the two great forces molding human progress.   Lin-Yutang,
Importance of Living
1937 4 Day; Heinemann

941   We grant that human life is imperfect; but how did we find out that it was imperfect?   After Emerson

942   Presentment of better things on earth
Sweeps in with every force that stirs our souls.
From George Eliot, Minor Prophet

943   The ideal itself has its roots in natural conditions; it emerges when the imagination idealizes existence by laying hold of the possibilities offered to thought and action.

John Dewey,
Common Faith 1934 48 Yale Univ. Press

944   An ideal is often a calculation by an intellect as logical as that of Euclid.   From D. Swing

945   Everything ideal has a natural basis and everything natural an ideal development.   Santayana,
Reason in Common Sense
1905 21 Scribner

946   It is important that man dreams, but it is perhaps equally important that he can laugh at his own dreams.

Lin-Yutang,
Importance of Living 1937 4–5 Day; Heinemann

947   [There is a] rare advance in wisdom which consists in abandoning our illusions the better to attain our ideals.

Santayana,
Interpretations . . . 1900 250 Scribner

948   Ideals must be built on the real.   Stanton Coit

949   For idealism to be effective, creative imagination must know the materials it works with. The idealist must be a realist in appraising the nature of things.

From Arthur E. Morgan,
Observations 1968 35 Antioch Press

950   [Saving money can be a means to wealth for economic security and social prestige. The saving can become, however, hoarding as an end in itself.

In some circumstances, wealth is gained through corrupt means such as theft and bribery.]

When we take means for ends we fall into moral materialism. But when we take ends without regard to means we degenerate into fanaticism.

Our idealism will never prosper until it involves the greater forces of modern life: industry, commerce, finance, scientific inquiry and discussion, and human companionship.

After John Dewey, Reconstruction . . .
1948 73 Beacon, Characters . . . 1929 635 Holt

951   No man can set up an ideal for another nor . . . realize it for him.

Santayana, Soliloquies . . . 1922 259 Scribner

952   Somehow, evolution has made us happiest over those things which in the long run yield the greatest good to the greatest number.   Stefansson

953   In a noble ideal there is something like the sun which coaxes a June out of a winter.   From D. Swing

954   When the ideal shifts, one must change one's perspective. The sunflower remains faithful to the sun.

Jean Rostand,
Substance of Man 1962 192 Doubleday

955   To relish life, to be aware of what the good life is, and to contribute, ever in a light spirit, leads us toward the perfect life.

956   Our angels only go out that archangels may come in.
Emerson, Compensation

VISION

957   Where there is no vision, the people perish.
Proverbs XXIX 18

958   The future lies
With those whose eyes
Are wide to the necessities,

And wider still
With fervent will,
To all the possibilities.

John Oxenham, in Wallis (ed.),
Selected Poems 1948 56 Harper, © Dunkerley

959   The freer our faith is from delusions, the more effective it will prove.

Albert Guérard,
Bottle in the Sea
1954 122 Harvard Univ. Press

960   Analysis is only a step to real knowledge.

Art, music, poetry, philosophy, religion, can develop capacities of vision, and enable us to become aware of realities, without which we shall have a very inadequate idea of the world.

After R. W. Livingstone,
Education . . . 1952 87 104 Oxford

TASTE

961   Creative intelligence and taste are brothers of the same womb, sons of capacity, and of equal excellence. A refined taste finds satisfaction in good things.

There are as many tastes as vocations and inclinations.

From Balthasar Gracian, El Heroe

962   Next to achieving excellence is the appreciation of it.

From Thackeray

963   Good taste, besides being inwardly clear, has to be outwardly fit.

Santayana, Reason in Art 1905 199 Scribner

964   Good taste is the flower of good sense.

Achille Poincelot

965   Good taste requires a finely gifted mind, purified into harmony with itself, into keenness and justness of vision.

From Carlyle

966   When our integrity declines, our taste does also.

La Rochefoucauld

CRITICAL JUDGMENT

967   Criticism is a disinterested endeavor to learn and propagate the best.

Matthew Arnold, Essays in Criticism I

968   Wit is brushwood, judgment is timber. The first makes the brightest flame, but the other gives the most lasting heat.

Hebrew proverb

969   Art, science, and conduct depend on rational discrimination.

From Morris R. Cohen,
Reason and Nature
1931 457 Harcourt, © Rosenfield

970   Every person complains of the badness of his Memory, but none of his defective Judgment.

La Rochefoucauld, Maxim 89

971   A great many people are perfectly willing to sit on a porcupine if you first exhibit it at the Museum of Modern Art and say that it is a chair.

R. Jarrell,
Lecture, Lib. Cong. 1956

972   One who is educated knows that there is a difference between sound and sense, between what is emphatic and what is distinctive, between what is conspicuous and what is important.
From John Dewey,
Characters . . . 1929 776 Holt

973   It is much easier to be critical than to be correct.
Disraeli

974   Man is the measure of all things.   Protagoras

975   A man whose greatest achievement is to detect flaws sentences himself to live in a world of flaws.
Albert Guérard,
Bottle in the Sea 1954 59 Harvard Univ. Press

976   A small spring pleases the thirsty as the great ocean does not.
From Sharma and Raghavacharya (trs.),
Gems from Sanskrit 1959 31 Osmania

977   The critic himself should have a determinate character and a sane capacity for happiness.
Santayana,
Reason in Common Sense 1905 xi Scribner

978   The fact that millions of people share the same vices does not make these vices virtues, and that millions share many errors does not make the errors truths.
From Erich Fromm,
Sane Society 1955 15 Rinehart; Routledge

979   To err is human; but, in the long run, human judgment of worth is more likely to be right than wrong, otherwise
the race could not have continued.

> From J. A. C. F. Auer,
> Auer and Hartt,
> Humanism . . . 1951 74 Antioch Press

980   One does not have to be a master baker to know that
a loaf has a bad taste.   After Fritz Reuter

981   Common Sense is genius in homespun.

> A. N. Whitehead

982   The youth reaches for too many books. The older
person is more selective.

> From Max Roden,
> Spiegelungen 1951 18 Johannes-Presse

983   Be not deceived with the first appearances of things,
but give yourself time to be in the right.   William Penn

984   It is wonderful what a different view we take of the
same event four-and-twenty hours after it has happened . . .
   A thing is not good just because it is new or because it is old.

> From Sydney Smith

985   What is the worth of anything
            But for the happiness 'twill bring?

> R. O. Cambridge, Learning

986   The area of immediate experience open to any individual is a mere slit in the world's expanse; most of what we

believe about the world rests on some sort of authority. We must use reason to determine which authority to follow, which men and institutions present the most reason for being trusted.

From D. E. Trueblood,
Logic of Belief 1942 66 67 72 Harper

CONFLICT AND CHOICE

987   As a person is a union of divers elements, he is pulled in different directions.   From Pythagoras

988   The good that I would I do not; but the evil which I would not, that I do.   Romans VII 19

989   In the inanimate world, conflict occurs between various physical forces. Sociological conflict involves competition or combat between groups, between individuals, or between a group and an individual. Psychological conflict occurs within the individual, between his own interests or components; more exactly, between their responses.

Here we are concerned with psychological conflicts.

Such conflicts may occur between two or more conscious processes; between conscious and subconscious processes; between subconscious processes; or in any combination of these.

Though conflict often moves men to improved ways and insights, continued conflict is uncomfortable, inefficient, and wearing, and can lead to pathological effects. As Seneca observed, woeful is he that is at enmity with himself.

"Choice," Dewey showed, "is the emergence of a unified preference out of competing preferences." Unintegrated choice is unreasonable, in that it lets some habit or impulse sweep the field regardless of other habits and impulses. Integrated choice is reasonable; it represents a free interplay of all the person's interests, immediate and long-range.

Quoting Dewey, Human Nature . . . 1922 193 Holt

990   There are hurricanes in human affairs, tempests of passion, when it is wise to retire to a harbour and ride at anchor. You cannot act for yourself if you are not yourself, and passion always drives out reason. As soon as you notice that you are losing your temper beat a wise retreat. It takes a wise doctor to know when not to intervene.

From Balthasar Gracian (Jacobs, tr.) Maxims 138 287 138

991   No man ever *knowingly* chooses the worse of two alternatives.   From Socrates

992   That we learn to decide by making decisions is somewhat true, but it seems more true that we learn how to make decisions by learning what to make decisions for. We make good decisions when we learn what goodness is; and part of this knowledge we get from others.

From J. S. Bixler,
Two Blessings of Joseph 1964 13 Carleton College

993   It is difficult to weigh alternatives unless one has cultivated some tolerance of uncertainty.

From J. C. Whitehorn,
Perspectives in Biol. & Med. 1963 7:121

994   Every radical adjustment is a crisis in self-esteem: we undergo a test, we have to prove ourselves.

Eric Hoffer,
Ordeal of Change 1963 1 Harper

995   There's will as motor and there's will as brakes.
       Reason is, I suppose, the steering gear.
                            Poetry of Robert Frost (Lathem, ed.),
                            Masque of Reason 1969 481 Holt

ACTION

996   Be lord and master of your own actions.
                            Thomas à Kempis,
                            Imitation of Christ III XLIII

997   As our thoughts and our acts are, so will our lives be.
                            Seneca,
                            Ad Lucilium . . . (Gummere, tr.) 1918 3:87 Putnam

998   Action without study is folly, and study without action
is futile.   Confucius

999   It is well to know when we have done enough.
                            From Rule of Life 1800 123

999a   He who does not act as he thinks he should thinks
badly.   Guyau

1000   Man's noblest activity is that in which he is not aware
of himself. Once he makes himself an object, the *whole* man no
longer acts, for he has stopped a part of his activity in order to
reflect about himself. [Sometimes he may need to examine himself to improve his noblest activity.]   From Schelling

1001   The more we do, the more we can do.   Hazlitt

MORAL RESPONSIBILITY

1002   When the sot in the gutter watched the successful man drive by in a fine car, he said, "There, but for me, go I."

From T. V. Smith,
in Denise and Williams (eds.),
Retrospect . . . 1956 131 Syracuse Univ. Press

1003   All persons are *accountable* for what they do, as a tree that falls on a wagon is accountable for what it does to the wagon. Not all persons, however, are *responsible*. Society must hold responsible all those persons, and only those, who are *accountable and educable* as to what they do. Thus the very immature, unintelligent, or insane are not responsible.

From Everett,
Moral Values 1918 369–374 Holt

1004   Most of us want to feel not responsible for acts prompted by our own questionable impulses. The weak person may act dishonorably because he "has to obey orders." The stronger one may proclaim himself "the chosen instrument of a higher power"—God, history, fate, nation, or humanity.

After Eric Hoffer,
Passionate State of Mind 1955 54 Harper

1005   Faith in science, or reason, or duty, or self-direction, or Christ, if it stands between the individual and his total responsibility, hides him from himself.

From H. J. Blackham,
Six Existentialist Thinkers
1959 163 Harper, © Macmillan

1006   Evil is wrought by want of Thought
            As well as want of Heart.

Thomas Hood, Lady's Dream

1007   Mere reward and punishment cannot give children the kind of moral training they need today. A civilized society rests on a morality rooted in understanding.

After J. R. Moskin,
Morality in America 1966 257 Random House

VIRTVTIS RA DICES ALTÆ

IX

Character and Personality

MOTIVATION

1008   Hunger relishes the homeliest food, fatigue turns the hardest bed to down; and the difficulty and uncertainty of pursuit enhance the value of possession.

From Hazlitt, Characteristics CCLXXXVII

1009   Have a care where there is more sail than ballast.

William Penn

1010   Bitterness is the sister of half-heartedness.

The Shepherd (second century)

1011   The justice that one receives as the result of other people's efforts in the name of humanity most certainly comes later than that one achieves for oneself.   Alf Ross,

Why Democracy?

1952 115 Harvard Univ. Press

GREED, AVARICE, COVETOUSNESS

1012   The sun and the moon and the stars would have disappeared long ago . . . had they happened to be within the reach of predatory human hands.   Havelock Ellis

1013   An avaricious man is like barren sandy ground which sucks in all the rain and dews but yields no fruitful plants.

From Zeno

1014   Covetousness numbs the apprehension of anything above the sensory.

From Thomas Browne, Christian Morals I viii

1015   Only that which is honestly got is gain.
                                    Rule of Life 1800 124

1016   Sometimes it is better to lose than to gain.
                            After Plautus, Captivi II ii 77 (327)

1017   The poor man lacks much; the greedy man lacks all.
                        Syri Sententiae, Ribbeck (ed.), Frag. 236

1018   Lessen your wants, husband your powers.
                                    Chuang Tzu

1019   The greedy search for money or success will almost
always lead men into unhappiness. Why? Because that kind of
life makes them depend on things outside themselves.
                                    André Maurois

1020   A greedy man may be materially rich, but spiritually
poor; a contented man may be materially poor, but spiritually
rich. One who holds a high position may feel physically at ease,
but mentally fatigued; one who has a low position may feel
physically fatigued, but mentally at ease. Which of these is a
gain, and which a loss, a man of insight can distinguish for
himself.   From Hung,
                                    Chinese Garden . . .
                            (Chao, tr.) 1959 49 Peter Pauper

GENEROSITY

1021   A mean person knows how to harm others' interests,
but not how to help further them.
                            From Sharma and Raghavacharya (trs.),
                            Gems from Sanskrit . . . 1959 25 Osmania

1022   The poor who envies not the rich, who pities his companions of poverty, and who can spare something for him that
is still poorer, is, in the realms of humanity, a king of kings.

Lavater, Aphorism 632 (1787 ed.)

1023   The gift without the giver is bare.

J. R. Lowell,
Vision of Sir Launfal, II 8

1024   We make a living by what we get, but we make a life
by what we give.   H. van Dyke

1025   His heart and hand both open and both free;
For what he has he gives, what thinks he shows;
Yet gives he not till judgment guide his bounty.

Shakespeare, Troilus and Cressida IV v 100–103

1026   Nothing is generous if it is not also just.   Cicero

EGOTISM, CONCEIT

1027   Pride may be reasonable or unreasonable. Reasonable
pride reflects objectivity and insight. Unreasonable pride is
subjective, likely egotistic or defensory, so is relatively unenlightened. Often the bare term, pride, is used for unreasonable
pride.

1028   A child is inclined to exaggerate its own importance.

Sukkah

1029   Self-love is the greatest of all flatterers.

La Rochefoucauld, Maxim 2

1030   He was like the cock who thought the sun had risen to hear him crow.   George Eliot, Adam Bede XXXIII

1031   A habit of sneering marks the egotist, or the fool, or the knave—or all three.   Lavater, Aphorism 115

1032   Conceit is to nature what paint is to beauty; it is not only needless, but impairs what it would improve.   Pope

1033   Vanity is the mother, and affectation is the darling daughter; vanity is the sin, and affectation is the punishment; the first may be called the root of self-love, the other the fruit. Vanity is never at its full growth till it spreads into affectation, and then it is complete.   From Savile,
. . . Advice to a Daughter, Vanity . . .

1034   [Unreasonable] pride defends not only itself but every other fault.   From Richard Baxter,
Works 1830 III 48

1035   A proud man watches for your downfall; he tries to entrap you, turning good into evil, and in things worth praise will lay blame upon you.   From Ecclus. XI 30–31

1036   Contempt is a kind of gangrene, which if it seizes one part of a character corrupts all the rest.   Samuel Johnson,
Works . . . 1787 3:186

1037   He that falls in love with himself will have no rivals.
Franklin,
Poor Richard's Almanac 1739 May

1038   Pride goes before a fall.   From Proverbs XVI 18

1039   In its swelling pride, the bubble doubts the truth of the sea, and laughs, and bursts forth into emptiness.

Tagore

1040   The vain person wishes to be honored and sought after not on account of his good qualities or achievements but of his mere existence.   From Goethe

1041   Fools take to themselves the respect that is shown to their office.   Aesop, Fables, Donkey in Office

1042   The less promise and potency in the self, the more imperative is the "need" for pride.

From Eric Hoffer,
Passionate State of Mind 1955 23 Harper

1043   It is the persons with scanty learning who are exceedingly vain.   Sharma and Raghavacharya (trs.),
Gems from Sanskrit . . . 1959 69 Osmania

1044   Snobbery is the pride of those who are not sure of their position.   B. Braley

1045   [Often] our fancied superiority to others is in some one thing, which we think most of, because we excel in it, or have paid most attention to it; whilst we overlook their superiority to us in something else, which they set equal and exclusive store by.   Hazlitt, Characteristics LII

1046   Men exalt themselves on their principles, which they think separate them as sheep from the goats, who prove, after all, to be only the other sheep.

From Walter Raleigh,
Complete Works of George Savile . . . 1912 x

1047   When one man talks down to another, there is seldom any reason for supposing that the best-qualified chromosomes are on the side of the insolence.

Jean Rostand,
Substance of Man 1962 12 Doubleday

1048   Heroes, according to Rousseau, are not known by the loftiness of their carriage; as great braggarts are mere cowards.

From Hazlitt, Characteristics X

1049   We never despise others except when we do not reflect upon ourselves.   From T. Wilson, Maxims . . . 1898 57

1050   Think not that your word alone must be right.

From Sophocles, Antigone 706

1051   A little society is needful to show a man his failings.

R. L. Stevenson,
Works 1924 82 Ryerson Press

1052   There is no better corrective of undue pride, there is no more potent inciter of modesty, than the frequent attempt to pattern ourselves on the masters.

Brander Matthews,
Study of Versification 1911 vii Houghton

1053   Our virtues would be proud if our faults whipped
them not.
                                           Shakespeare,
                        All's Well That Ends Well IV iii 84–85

1054   Vanity is an absurd human weakness.
                                        From Henri Bergson

1055   Keep clear of the pride of humility.   Unknown

HUMILITY, MODESTY

1056   Humility, that low, sweet root
            From which all heavenly virtues shoot.

                                        Thomas Moore,
                    Loves of the Angels, Third Angel's Story

1057   Wisdom is ofttimes nearer when we stoop
            Than when we soar.

                                        Wordsworth

1058   Humility is often feigned to master others; it is pride
humbling itself to exalt itself.
                        From La Rochefoucauld, Maxim 254

1059   Many people confound humility with weakness. Genuine humility is planting our foot upon the rock of fact.
                                        After H. P. Liddon

1060   It is a great mistake to overestimate or to underestimate one's worth.   From Goethe

1061   The boaster pretends to more than he has; the mock-
modest one, to less than he has; and between these two, the

sincere man, in word and deed, confesses the simple truth
about himself.   From Aristotle,
                                        Nicomachean Ethics IV vii

1062   If thou hast become great after thou wert little, and
hast gained possessions after thou wert formerly in want . . .
be not unmindful of how it was with thee before . . . Thou
art not greater than another like thee to whom the same has
happened.   Ptahhotep,
                             in Breasted, Dawn . . . 1933 132 Scribner

1063   Modesty implies esteem of others.
                                                 After H. Margolius,
                             Aphorisms . . . n.d. 11 Black Mt. News

1064   The wise man discerns all in his mind but speaks
simply; and he is capable but does not boast of his deeds.
                                                 Motse (Y.-P. Mei, tr.),
                                    Ethical . . . 1929 7 Probsthain

1065   People who are unsure of themselves brag and assert
themselves. Commonly, self-respect and modesty are found together.   From Arthur E. Morgan,
                                    Observations 1968 57 Antioch Press

1066   When your work speaks for itself, don't interrupt.
                                                       H. J. Kaiser

1067   [It is a] critical moment in the life of a man and a
nation . . . [when] they are first conscience-stricken and con-
victed of vanity.   Santayana,
                                 Reason in Religion 1905 204 Scribner

1068   Humble because of knowledge, mighty by sacrifice.
                                             Kipling, Islanders

1069   The show-off does not shine.   Lao-tse

1070   Knowledge is proud that she knows so much. Wisdom
is humble that she knows no more.
                                    G. Stanley Hall, in A. E. Hamilton,
                                    Psychology and "The Great God Fun"
                                                  1955 179 Julian

1071   Modesty prepares the mind for knowledge and the
heart for truth.   Guizot

1072   When we do not crave to seem important we are not
awed by the importance of others.
                                                Eric Hoffer,
                                Passionate State of Mind 1955 83 Harper

1073   Those who have exerted themselves to the utmost feel
the limitation of their powers and show neither admiration of
themselves nor triumph over others.
                                From Hazlitt, Characteristics LXX

1074   Thy modesty's a candle to thy merit.   H. Fielding

1075   The humility that does not demand the impossible of
ourselves makes for psychic peace.
                                            After J. L. Liebman,
                                Peace of Mind 1946 54 Simon & Schuster

HYPOCRISY

1076   Hypocrisy is the homage vice pays to virtue.
                          La Rochefoucauld, Maxim 218

1077   A truth that's told with bad intent
            Beats all the lies you can invent.
                          William Blake, Auguries of Innocence

1078   O, that there might in England be
            A duty on Hypocrisy,
            A tax on humbug, an excise
            On solemn plausibilities.
                          Henry Luttrell, Aspiration

1079   To provincial prudes, the most beautiful thing is hypocrisy adorned with a blush.   From Ingersoll

1080   It is easier to make a saint out of a libertine than out
of a prig.   Santayana,
                      Reason in Religion 1905 201 Scribner

1081   There is no vice so simple but assumes
            Some mark of virtue on his outward parts.
                          Shakespeare, Merchant of Venice III ii 81–82

1082   Suspicion always haunts the guilty mind;
            The thief doth fear each bush an officer.
                          Shakespeare, King Henry VI III V vi 11–12

1083   When, in the name of morality, a society heaps injuries on human nature, that nature even in "good" persons
may take revenge through bad behavior.

From John Dewey,
Human Nature ... 1922 4 Holt

1084   We assume that by virtue of being bad we are at least
safe from being hypocrites. But are we any such thing? . . .
The bad . . . must often have to pass for large-hearted when
it is nothing but a strain on the heart that makes the heart
secretly sick. That is one curse that is laid on them; and another is that in every out-and-out clash with the righteous they
must try to make themselves out more right than the righteous.
You can see what that would lead to. No, I am afraid hypocrisy
is as increasing to evil as it is diminishing to good.

Selected Prose of Robert Frost
(Cox and Latham, eds.), 1956 82 Holt

1085   Some hypocrites are great dupes. This is either because
they think only of deceiving others and are off their guard, or
because they know little about the feelings or characters of
others. Perhaps they resort to artifice in the first place from
not only callousness of feeling but obtuseness of intellect which
cannot get on by fair means.

A hypocrite despises those whom he deceives, but cannot
respect himself. He would make a dupe of himself too, if he
could.

When a society becomes more permissive as to morals, vice
becomes less secret, but virtue, more genuine than before.

Simple integrity can result partly from profound thought.

From Hazlitt,
Characteristics CIII CCCXCVIII CXXX CXXV

HONESTY, INTEGRITY

1086   A self-contained man thinks it more graceful to go on foot than to drive in a carriage under false pretenses.

> From I Ching (Wilhelm, tr., Baynes, tr.)
> 1967 92 Princeton Univ. Press; Routledge

1087   Sincerity is to speak as we are; to do as we profess; to perform what we promise; and to be what we would seem.

> From J. Tillotson

1088   An honest man speaks truth though it may give offence; a malicious man, in order that it may.

> After Hazlitt, Characteristics CCCLXXXVII

1089   It is not the oath that makes us believe the man, but the man the oath.   Aeschylus, Frag. 385 Nauck

1091   Openness is the sweet fresh air of our moral life.

> George Eliot, Daniel Deronda XXXIII

1092   The truth is always the strongest argument.

> Sophocles

1098   There is no substitute for integrity.

> Brandeis, in H. W. Schneider,
> Three Dimensions . . . 1956 116 Ind. Univ. Press

1099   Keep to the truth though it may harm you, and keep away from falsehood though it may profit you.

> Wortabet (tr.), Arabian Wisdom 1910 35

1100   He who lies for you will lie against you.

Bosnian proverb

1101   Every violation of truth is a sort of suicide in the liar and a stab at human society.

From Emerson, Prudence

1102   O, what a tangled web we weave,
              When first we practice to deceive!

Walter Scott, Marmion VI

1103   No man has a good enough memory to be a successful liar.   Lincoln

1104   This is the punishment of a liar: he is not believed even when he speaks the truth.

The Babylonian Talmud, Sanhedrin

1105   The cruelest lies are often told in silence.

R. L. Stevenson, Virginibus Puerisque

1107   The thief steals from himself.

Emerson, Compensation

1109   Affectation is a greater enemy to the face than the small-pox.   Saint-Évremond

1110   He who has a brazen face has a craven heart.

Wortabet (tr.), Arabian Wisdom 1910 21

1114   Lies and perfidy are the refuge of fools and cowards.
                    Chesterfield, Miscellaneous Works 1777–9

1115   With fortune gone, little is lost; health gone, much is
lost; honor gone, all is lost.   Estonian proverb

1116   The superior man is never in a position in which he is
not himself.   Confucius

1117   The great man . . . does not think beforehand that his
words shall be sincere, or that his acts shall be resolute; he
simply abides in the right . . .
    One cannot procure a true gentleman with a bribe . . .
    The wailing at the lament for the dead must not be for the
benefit of the living.
    The pursuit . . . of virtue . . . must not be for . . . the
emoluments.
    A man must tell the truth, but not merely as a matter of
conventional rectitude.
                            Mencius, mostly from Dobson (tr.)
                        1963 50 159 Univ. Toronto; Oxford Press

1118   Better keep yourself clean and bright: you are the win-
dow through which you must see the world.
                                                Bernard Shaw,
                    Man and Superman, Maxims . . . 1903 233

1119   Really frank natures have tremendous strength.
                            From Balzac, La Cousine Bette

1120   Who can keep you from being good and simple?
                    Marcus Aurelius, Meditations X 32

1121   Naturalness is the easiest thing in the world to acquire, if you will but forget yourself—forget about the impression you are trying to make.

> From Dale Carnegie, . . . Scrapbook
> (Dorothy Carnegie, ed.) 1959 16 Simon & Schuster

1124   Give freely and receive, but take from none
   By greed, or force, or fraud, what is his own.

> Buddha, Light of Asia (Arnold, tr.) VIII

1126   The man who makes it his business to please the multitude is never done. Let us follow reason, and the public follow us if it will. Said the sailor of olden days: "O Neptune, you may save or destroy me as you will; but meanwhile I will hold my rudder true."

> From Montaigne, in Lowenthal (ed.),
> Autobiography . . . 1935 378 Houghton

1128   Deal so plainly with man and woman as to compel the utmost sincerity, and destroy all hope of trifling with you. It is the highest compliment you can pay.

> From Emerson, Over-Soul

1129   Insincerity in a man's own heart must make all his enjoyments, all that concerns him, unreal; so that his whole life must seem like a merely dramatic representation.

> Hawthorne

1131   He's armed without that's innocent within.

> Pope, Epistles of Horace I i 94

1132   Pure gold does not fear the furnace.
                        Seven Hundred Chinese Proverbs (Hart, tr.)
                            1937 37 Stanford Univ. Press

1133   A sense of one's own integrity will make one pass by
injuries more easily.
                        Thomas Wilson, Sacra Privata, On Anger

1134   ... Truth hath a quiet breast.
                        Shakespeare, King Richard II I iii 96

1136   Simplicity of character is no hindrance to subtlety of
intellect.   John Morley, Life of Gladstone

1138   How happy is he born and taught
                That serveth not another's will;
                Whose armor is his honest thought,
                And simple truth his utmost skill!

                Whose passions not his masters are;
                Whose soul is still prepared for death;
                Not tied unto the world with care
                Of public fame or private breath;

                This man is freed from servile bands
                Of hope to rise, or fear to fall;
                Lord of himself, though not of lands;
                And having nothing, yet hath all.
                                From Henry Wotton

1139   It takes great resources of mind and heart to appreciate
sincerity when it hurts, or to practise it without offending.
                        From Vauvenargues, Reflection 235

TACT

1140   Always speak truth, but do not always tell it.

Nikita Ivanovitch Panin

1141   Only he has a right to be perfectly frank who first of all is perfectly kind.

From A. W. Hummel,
in Anshen (ed.), Moral . . . 1952 605 Harper

1142   Fair and softly goes far.

Cervantes, Don Quixote I III II

AMBITION AND ASPIRATION

1143   This secret spake Life herself unto me: "Behold, I am that which must ever surpass itself."   From Nietzsche

1144   One something sees beyond his reach
            From childhood to his journey's end.

Gustave Nadaud, Carcassonne v

1145   Trifles make perfection, and perfection is no trifle.

Michelangelo

1146   The archer ought not to hit the mark only sometimes; he ought to miss it only sometimes.

Seneca, Ad Lucilium . . .
(Gummere, tr.) 1918 1:205 Putnam

1147   All ambitions are lawful except those which climb upward on the miseries or credulities of mankind.

Joseph Conrad, Personal Record

1148   If our secret ideals were always pure and high, we should rarely be envious of what others possess or do.

I. W. Hart

1149   Great men undertake great things because they believe those things are great; and the fools because they believe they are easy.   Vauvenargues, Reflection 90

1150   The aspiring man needs to recognize the merits of his older contemporaries without letting himself be hindered by their shortcomings.   From Goethe

1151   There are two kinds of discontent: the discontent that works, and the discontent that wrings its hands. The first may get what it wants, while the second loses what it has.

From Gordon Graham

1152   Existence is infinite, not to be defined;
      And, although it seem but a bit of wood in
         your hand, to carve as you please,
      It is not to be lightly played with and laid down.

Witter Bynner,
Way of Life according to Laotzu 1944 45 Day

1153   Be good for something while it is in your power.

Rule of Life 1800 146

1154   Hitch your wagon to a star.   Emerson, Civilization

1155   He that strives to touch a star often stumbles at a straw.

From Edmund Spenser,
Shepheardes Calendar July 97

1156   Stretching his hand out to catch the stars, too often man forgets the flowers at his feet.

From Jeremy Bentham, Deontology 2 I 52

1157   I know what I can, what I cannot, and consequently what I ought to do.   Chesterfield, Letters ... 1892

1158   Honour and shame from no condition rise:
        Act well your part, there all the honour lies.

Pope, Essay on Man IV 4

1159   ... He who seeks all things, wherever he goes
        Only reaps from the hopes which around he sows
        A harvest of barren regrets.

E. R. Lytton, Lucile II ii

1160   The youth gets together his materials to build a bridge to the moon, or, perchance, a palace or temple on the earth, and at length the middle-aged man concludes to build a woodshed with them.   Thoreau

1161   Be careful that too broad and high an aim does not paralyze your effort.   Learned Hand,
Irving Dilliard (ed.),
Spirit ... 1952 9 Knopf

1162   He who stands on tiptoe does not stand firm;
        He who strains his strides does not walk well.

Lao-tse, in Lin-Yutang (ed.),
Wisdom of China and India
1942 596 Random House

1163   At no time in the world will a man who is
          wholly sane
       Over-reach himself,
       Over-spend himself,
       Over-rate himself.

From Witter Bynner,
Way of Life according to Laotzu 1944 43 Day

1164   Let not one set oneself too great nor too small tasks.
From Francis Bacon, Of Nature in Men

1165   How slow to him who haunts preferment's door
       The long days drag! how lightly hurry o'er,
       When the awakened soul hath thrown aside
       Its load of worldly pride!

Indian epigram,
Paul Elmer More, Century . . . 1898 121

1166   If any man seeks for greatness, let him forget greatness
and ask for truth, and he may find both.

After Horace Mann

1167   What I aspired to be,
                     And was not, comforts me.
                          R. Browning, Rabbi Ben Ezra

1168   Who cannot what he will, let him will what he can.
Leonardo da Vinci

1169   Though our garden be small, let us cultivate it. The
adjoining parks make it no smaller.

From C. Richet,
Impotence of Man n.d. 149 Stratford

1170   He who demands much from himself and little from others will be spared resentment.

> Confucius,
> Analects XV XIV, Soothill (ed.), 1910

1171   Great is their peace who know a limit to their ambitious minds.   William Penn

1172   Let not Ambition mock their useful toil,
Their homely joys and destiny obscure;
Nor Grandeur hear with disdainful smile
The short and simple annals of the poor.

> Thomas Gray, Elegy

1173   Aim at soundness in every word and every act.

> Marcus Aurelius, Thoughts IV 51

1174   I am to see that the world is the better for me, and to find my reward in the act.   Emerson, Man the Reformer

DEDICATION AND PURPOSE

1175   No life grows great until it is focused, dedicated, disciplined.   From H. E. Fosdick

1176   Human life, by its very nature, has to be dedicated to something.

> Ortega y Gasset,
> Revolt of the Masses 1932 154 Norton

1177   We work for what we love, but we may love something far greater than the individual life.   Giordano Bruno

1178   . . . He is dead who will not fight,
              And he who dies fighting has increase.
                                   Julian Grenfell, Into Battle 7–8

1179   To a man who is determined to achieve his goal, the
earth is like a platform in his own yard, the ocean like a canal,
the abyss like a piece of land, and the Sumeru mountain like
an ant hill.

                              From Sharma and Raghavacharya (trs.),
                              Gems from Sanskrit . . . 1959 3 Osmania

1180   Great minds have purposes, others have wishes.
                                        Washington Irving

1181   I judge a man by his commitments—and by his de-
tachments.   Robert Frost

1182   He is already dead who lives only to keep himself
alive.   Goethe

1183   It is a mistake to speak of dedication as a sacrifice.
Every man can know that there is exhilaration in intense effort
applied toward a meaningful end.

                                   From John W. Gardner,
                              Life June 13 1960 100 © Time

1184   Wise men always have held that real happiness comes
from devotion, not to our own pleasure, comfort, or influence
but to something outside of ourselves, as we see in the life of a
saint or religious mystic, a social reformer, a research scientist,
a philosopher, an artist.   George Lawton,
                              How to be Happy though Young
                                   1949 274 Vanguard

1185   The dedicated person may often be tense, worried, fatigued; he has little of the leisure one associates with the storybook conception of happiness; but he has found a more meaningful happiness.   From John W. Gardner,
Excellence 1961 149 Harper

1186   A life fixed on a rational purpose is its own reward.

1187   Faith in a holy cause is too often a substitute for the lost confidence in ourselves.

From Eric Hoffer,
True Believer 1951 14 Harper

1188   "Means" and "ends" are not separate: the "means" become part of the "ends."

From Adelbert Ames, Jr., in Cantril (ed.),
Morning Notes . . . 1960 27 Rutgers Univ. Press

1189   Purpose must issue in acts and habits, or it is only a kind of intoxication.   Arthur E. Morgan,
Observations 1968 17 Antioch Press

1190   I do the best I know how, and I mean to keep on doing it to the end. If the end brings me out all right, what is said against me will not amount to anything. If the end brings me out all wrong, ten angels swearing I was right would make no difference.   From Lincoln

1191   Be ashamed to die until you have won something for humanity.   Horace Mann

CONSTANCY

1192   Wide is the gate, and broad is the way, that leads to destruction.
Matthew VII 13

1193   I know not what death is; it may be good, and I am not afraid of it. But I know that it is bad to desert one's post; and I prefer what may be good to what I know to be bad.
Socrates

1194   Constancy is the foundation of all the virtues.
Latin maxim

1195   Ceaseless change of activity yields monotony.

1196   Light abandonment of ties because they had ceased to be pleasant would uproot social and personal virtue.
From George Eliot, Romola LVI

1197   If one has many irons in the fire, some will cool.
From Hazlitt, English Proverbs

1198   It is often a higher constancy to change the mind.
After J. Hoole

1199   We can set a watch over our affections and our constancy as over other treasures.
From George Eliot, Middlemarch LVII

DUTY, OBLIGATION

1200   Duty is the call that the ideal makes upon the self.
The duty that is not happily performed is not rightly performed.   From J. A. Hadfield,
                        Psychology and Morals 1923 92–93 Methuen

1201   [Usually] it isn't the load that breaks us down; it's the
way we carry it.   Morris M. Brill

1202   Anything can be endured when taken because of interest or duty.   From Marcus Aurelius, Meditations X 3

1203   Who escapes a duty avoids a gain.   Theodore Parker

1204   Life is not made up of great sacrifices and duties;
        But mostly of little things; in which smiles
        And kindness and small obligations,
        Given habitually, are what win and
        Preserve the heart and secure comfort.

                                    From Humphrey Davy

1205   It is surprising how practical duty enriches the fancy
and the heart, and action clears and deepens the affections.

                                              J. Martineau

1206   Let us have faith that right makes might, and in that
faith, let us, to the end, dare to do our duty as we understand
it.   Lincoln, Speech, Feb. 27, 1860

1207   When Duty whispers low, Thou must,
            The youth replies, I can!

                                    Emerson, Voluntaries

1208   This that I see is not all, and this that I do is
           but little;
       Nevertheless it is good, though there is better
           than it.
                        Arthur Hugh Clough, Poems 1883 139

1209   The reward of one duty is the power to fulfill another.
                                    George Eliot, Daniel Deronda

1210   It is they who do their duties
           In everyday and trivial matters
           Who fulfill them on great occasions.
                                              Charles Kingsley

CONSCIENCE

1211   A man may as well cease to be a man as to be wholly
without conscience.   Jeremy Taylor, in Gest (ed.),
                               House . . . 1954 60 Univ. Pa. Press

1212   I desire so to conduct the affairs of this administration
that if, at the end, I have lost every other friend on earth, I
shall at least have one friend left, and that friend shall be
down inside of me.   From Lincoln

1213   Conscience came with recognition of consequences.
                                          From Bentley Glass,
                                       Science and Ethical Values
                                    1965 33–34 Univ. N. C. Press

1214   Conscience, psychologically considered, is the individual's moral attitudes, his characteristic reactions to what he
takes to be right and wrong.

The consciences of different individuals range from poorly integrated to well integrated.

A poorly integrated conscience is made up of moral attitudes that are relatively undeveloped or unorganized or both. Such a conscience may reduce to little more than conventional or even neurotic habits, rites, taboos, and superstitions which likely are inconsistent among themselves and are largely inconsistent with whatever rational views the individual may have developed. Consequently the individual is poorly integrated and ethically unenlightened.

A well-integrated conscience is composed of moral attitudes that are well developed and organized. They embody ethical insights, are highly consistent, and are integral to a whole, well-organized person. This person is ethically enlightened and welcomes ethical progress.

An integrated conscience is developed through education, not dogmatic indoctrination.

1215   Fanaticism is "conscience without science." The path chosen by enlightened conscience will be that of reasonableness.
                                    From Albert Guérard,
                                    Battle in the Sea
                        1954 39 40 Harvard Univ. Press

1216   One does not show a man as a finger points to a stone or a piece of wood; but when one shows the man's principles, he shows him as a man.   From Epictetus,
                        Discourses . . . (Long, tr.) n.d. 207

1217   He that has light within his own clear breast
        May sit i'th' center, and enjoy bright day;

But he that hides a dark soul and foul thoughts,
Himself is his own dungeon.

From Milton, A Mask, Comus 380–384

1219   We know for certain that there is a heaven, when a
good deed has been done; and a hell, in the dark heart no
longer able to live openly.   From E. Dowden,

Studies in Literature 1889 117

1220   A peace above all earthly dignities,
          A still and quiet conscience.

Shakespeare, King Henry VIII III ii 380–381

1221   If, as our daily experience teaches us, the moral sense
gains by the constant endeavor to find out what is right and
what is wrong, it must be moral suicide to delegate our conscience to another man. It is true that when we are in difficulties we seek counsel; but such counsel is to help private judgment.

From William Kingdon Clifford, Lectures . . . 1886 374

1222   When true principles have taken hold, even the simplest precept keeps one from brooding and fear.

In applying principles be like the boxer, not the swordsman;
for the swordsman drops his sword and is killed, but the boxer's hand is always ready.

Marcus Aurelius, Meditations X 34 XII 9

1223   Bread won by fraud tastes sweet to a man, but after-
ward his mouth will be filled with gravel.

Proverbs XX 17

1224   Nought's had, all's spent,
Where our desire is got without content:
'Tis safer to be that which we destroy
Than by destruction dwell in doubtful joy.
Shakespeare, Macbeth III ii 4–7

1225   Suspicion always haunts the guilty mind;
The thief doth fear each bush an officer.
Shakespeare, King Henry VI III V vi 11–12

1226   Guilty consciences make men cowards.
Pilpay, Two Fishermen VII Fable iii

1227   Though the night is dark, the conscience has insomnia.
R. L. Jenkins,
Breaking Patterns . . . 1954 214 Lippincott

1228   . . . Infected minds
To their deaf pillows will discharge their secrets.
Shakespeare, Macbeth V i 75–76

1229   Spend the day well, and you will rejoice at night.
Rule of Life 1800 140

1230   Self-respect . . . comes to us when we are alone, in quiet moments, in quiet places, when we suddenly realize that, knowing the good, we have done it; knowing the beautiful, we have served it; knowing the truth, we have spoken it.
A. Whitney Griswold, Address, New Haven 1957

1231   A good conscience is both the testimony and the reward of a good life.
From Seneca

DILIGENCE AND PERSEVERANCE

1232   The difference between perseverance and obstinacy is that one often comes from a strong will, and the other from a strong won't.   H. W. Beecher

1233   One must not depend on miracles.   The Talmud

1234   Short as life is, we make it shorter by the careless waste of time.   Victor Hugo

1235   There is no substitute for hard work.
                                                    T. A. Edison

1236   Drudgery is as necessary to call out the treasures of the mind as plowing and planting are for those of the earth.
                                            From Margaret Fuller

1237   He who has genius without patience and energy (if indeed such genius be possible) might as well have no genius.
                                        From E. G. Bulwer-Lytton

1238   The greatest poets, orators, statesmen, and historians, men of the most brilliant and imposing talents, have taken more pains than other men.   From Sydney Smith

1239   Diligence increases the fruit of toil.
                                    Hesiod, Works and Days 412

1240   Keep thy shop, and thy shop will keep thee.
                                    George Chapman, Eastward Hoe

1241   A man with a heart full of determination and perseverance can enjoy the myriad miracles of his mind.

> Hung, Chinese Garden . . .
> (Chao, tr.) 1959 58 Peter Pauper

1242   Many things which cannot be overcome when together
yield when taken little by little.   Plutarch,
> Life of Sertorius

1243   . . . Many strokes, though with a little axe,
Hew down and fell the hardest-timbered oak.
> Shakespeare, King Henry VI III II i 54–55

1244   We need not hope to succeed in order to persevere.
> From William of Orange

1245   Seven falls, eight rises.
> Japanese proverb, Champion (ed.),
> Racial . . . 1938 440 Macmillan, © Routledge;
> Barnes & Noble

1246   In retrospect, our achievements speak for themselves.
We tend to forget the many false starts and painful gropings.
We see our present vain attempts as signs of decay and decline.
> From Eric Hoffer, Harper's Nov. 1966 91

1247   It is much more to conclude than to begin well.
> Rule of Life 1800 130

1248   Wise to resolve, and patient to perform.
> Homer, Odyssey (Pope, tr.) IV 372

1249   Often hard work disguises opportunity.

ALERTNESS

1250   There is a tide in the affairs of men,
Which, taken at the flood, leads on to fortune.
... We must take the current when it serves,
Or lose our ventures.

Shakespeare,
Julius Caesar IV iii 217–218 222–223

1251   Late beginners seldom attain their end without difficulty.   Gandhi,
Indian Business Calendar

1252   A little fire is quickly trodden out,
Which, being suffered, rivers cannot quench.
Shakespeare, King Henry VI III IV viii 7–8

1253   A pebble turns the streamlet, whose proud sway
Unbridled sweeps the granite rocks away.

Unknown

1254   The unexpected always happens.   Proverb

1255   Opportunities come to all, but many do not know they
have met them.   A. E. Dunning

PRUDENCE

1256   The hasty leaps over his opportunities.
Albanian proverb, Champion (ed.),
Racial ... 1938 14 Macmillan, © Routledge;
Barnes & Noble

1257   Haste is the sister of repentance.

> Moroccan proverb, Westermarck (ed.),
> Wit and Wisdom . . . 1931 1323 H. Liveright,
> © Routledge

1258   Do not sell the bearskin before you kill the bear.

> French proverb

1259   For the want of a nail a shoe was lost,
For the want of a shoe the horse was lost,
For the want of a horse the rider was lost,
For the want of a rider the battle was lost,
For the want of a battle the kingdom was lost
And all for the want of a horseshoe-nail.

> Franklin,
> Poor Richard's Almanac 1758

1260   Those whose care extends not far ahead will find their troubles near at hand.   Confucius

1261   It is far easier to prevent than to rectify.

> Balthasar Gracian (Jacobs, tr.) Maxim 86

1262   One should think beforehand of a remedy against possible misfortune. It is not wise to try to sink a well when the house is on fire.

> From Sharma and Raghavacharya (trs.),
> Gems from Sanskrit . . . 1959 25 Osmania

1263   The mouse does not entrust its life to one hole.

> After Plautus, Truculentus IV iv 15

1264   Moor your bark with two anchors.

Publilius Syrus, Maxim 119

1265   Prudence is not synonymous with cowardice. At times, the better part of discretion is valor.

From Hazlitt, Characteristics CCCLXXXIII

1266   It is the part of prudent men to provide against difficulties, and of courageous men to deal with them.

From Pittacus

BOLDNESS, COURAGE AND FORTITUDE

1267   There is a nobility which . . . has its roots among the most primitive instincts of the human being . . .

I think there is in the heroic courage with which man confronts the . . . world a beauty greater than the beauty of art. I find it in the defiant gesture of Paddy Finucane when, plunging to his death, he transmitted the message to the airmen in his squadron: "This is it, chaps." I find it in the cool determination of Captain Oates when he went out to his death in the arctic night rather than be a burden to his comrades. I find it in the loyalty of Helen Vagliano, a woman not very young, not very pretty, not very intelligent, who suffered hellish torture and accepted death . . . rather than betray her friends.

. . . Man for all his weakness and sin is capable on occasion of such splendor of spirit . . .

Maugham, Writer's Notebook
1949 366 Doubleday; Heinemann

1268   Perfect courage is to do without a witness all that we could do before the whole world.

La Rochefoucauld, Maxim 216

1269   True courage is cool and calm.
                    Anthony Ashley Cooper, Third Earl of Shaftsbury

1270   The coward calls the brave man rash; and because the brave man is judiciously cautious, the rash man calls him a coward.   After Aristotle,
                              Nicomachean Ethics II viii

1271   Courage is, properly, contempt of hazards according to reason. Contempt of hazards without or against reason is rather a brutal fierceness.   From Roger L'Estrange,
                              Seneca's Morals . . . 1756 416

1272   Sometimes it is an act of bravery even to live.
                              Seneca, Ad Lucilium . . .
                      (Gummere, tr.) 1918 2:183 Putnam

1273   A misfortune becomes two to the impatient.
                    Wortabet (tr.), Arabian Wisdom 1910 43

1274   Though we be sick and tired and faint and
              worn,—
         Lo, all things can be borne!
                        Elizabeth Akers Allen, Endurance

1275   Fortune is not on the side of the faint-hearted.
                              Sophocles, Frag. 842

1276   He who is afraid of a thing gives it power over him.
                    Moroccan proverb, Westermarck (ed.),
                      Wit and Wisdom . . . 1930 1427 Routledge

1277   Cowards die many times before their deaths;
        The valiant never taste of death but once.
                            Shakespeare, Julius Caesar II ii 32–33

1278   A great deal of talent is lost in the world for want of
a little courage.   Sydney Smith

1279   He is condemned to depend on no man's modesty and
honor who dares not depend on his own.
                            Lavater, Aphorism 455 (1787 ed.)

1280   A Moment—We uncertain step
                    For newness of the night—
                    Then—fit our Vision to the Dark—
                    And meet the Road—erect—

                    Either the Darkness alters—
                    Or something in the sight
                    Adjusts itself to Midnight—
                    And Life steps almost straight.
                    Emily Dickinson, in Thomas H. Johnson (ed.),
                        Complete Poems . . . 1960 200 Little

1281   Courage in danger is half the battle.   Plautus

1282   When a resolute young fellow steps up to the great
bully, the world, and takes him boldly by the beard, he is often
surprised to find it come off in his hand, and that it was only
tied on to scare away timid adventurers.
                    (Doctor) O. W. Holmes, Elsie Venner 1861 10

1283   He alone is happy who requires neither to command
nor to obey.   Goethe

1284   Courage and truth are the pillars of one's being.
From Ruskin,
Sesame and Lilies, Of Queens' Gardens LXXX

1285   That man is happy who leans upon none but himself;
for one who sustains himself by any prop may fall.
From Seneca, Ad Lucilium . . .
(Gummere, tr.) 1918 2:447–449 Putnam

1286   The most important consequence of self-sufficiency is
freedom.   Epicurus, (Strodach tr.),
Philosophy of Epicurus 1962 207
Northwestern Univ. Press

1287   A decent boldness ever meets with friends.
Homer, Odyssey (Pope, tr.) VII 66

1288   Virtue is bold, and goodness never fearful.
Shakespeare, Measure for Measure III i 214–215

1289   Wise venturing is the upper story of prudence.
From Savile,
Miscellaneous Thoughts . . . , Boldness

1290   The spirit of the brave and earnest grows with the
difficulty of his task.   From Seneca, Ad Lucilium . . .
(Gummere, tr.) 1918 1:153 Putnam

1291   He that flies when he should can fight again.
Traditional

1292   Learn from your earliest days to inure your principles
against the perils of ridicule: you can no more exercise your

reason, if you live in the constant dread of laughter, than you can enjoy your life, if you are in the constant terror of death. If you think it right to differ from the times, do it, not for insolence. Resistance soon converts unprincipled wit into sincere respect; and no aftertime can tear from you those feelings which every man carries within him who has made a noble and successful exertion in a virtuous cause.

From Sydney Smith

1293   Better be the hammer than the anvil.

French proverb

1294   I dare do all that may become a man;
            Who dares do more is none.

Shakespeare, Macbeth I vii 46–47

1295   Whoever are least disturbed in mind by calamities, and in act struggle against them, these are the best men in state and in private life.

Epictetus, Discourses . . . (Long, tr.) n.d. 442

MORALE

1296   There is nothing so easy but that it becomes difficult when you do it with reluctance.

Terence, Heaut. IV vi 1 (805)

1297   Any coward can fight a battle when he's sure of winning; but give me the man who has pluck to fight when he's sure of losing.   George Eliot, Janet's Repentance

1298   To fight aloud is very brave,
                But *gallanter*, I know,

Who charge within the bosom
The cavalry of woe.
Emily Dickinson, Thomas H. Johnson (ed.),
Complete Poems 1960 59 Little

1299   He who loses wealth, loses much; he who loses a friend, loses more; but he that loses his spirits, loses all.

Spanish maxim

1300   No morale, no excellence!
John W. Gardner, Excellence 1961 85 Harper

1301   Many are naturally pugnacious, or irascible, or enthusiastic, and these passions when strongly excited may render them insensible to fear. But take away the conflicting emotion, and fear reasserts its dominion: consistent courage is always the effect of cultivation.   John Stuart Mill,
Three Essays on Religion 1885 47

1302   A righteous man falls seven times, and rises again; but the wicked are overthrown by calamity.
Proverbs XXIV 16 Rev. Stan. Ver. Bible 1952

1303   A heart unspotted is not easily daunted.
Shakespeare, Henry VI II III i 100

1304   The enthusiasm which comes from thought has the same relation to that which is produced by mere random feeling as the wind which sweeps the heights has to that which eddies about between the hills.
Schweitzer, Decay . . . 1932 88 Black

1305   A good cause makes a courageous heart.

> Rule of Life 1800 129

1306   To contribute something, however little, towards the victory of the good is a thought more vitalising and strengthening than any other by which men can be inspired.

> After John Stuart Mill

1307   The best morale is enlightened courage.

1308   Say not, the struggle nought availeth,
             The labor and the wounds are vain,
             The enemy faints not, nor faileth,
             And as things have been they remain.

             If hopes were dupes, fears may be liars;
             It may be, in yon smoke concealed,
             Your comrades chase e'en now the fliers,
             And, but for you, possess the field.

> Arthur Hugh Clough, Poems 1883 326

1309   Our greatest glory is not in never falling but in rising every time we fall.

> Confucius

1310   Never give up while there is hope; but hope not beyond reason, for that shows more desire than judgment.

> From William Penn

1311   Be like the promontory against which the waves continually break.

> Marcus Aurelius,
> Thoughts (Long, tr.) n.d. IV xlix

BALANCE AND PERSPECTIVE

1312   Man always travels along precipices, and, whether he will or no, his truest obligation is to keep his balance.

Ortega y Gasset,
Man and People 1957 32 Norton

1313   . . . How sour sweet music is
When time is broke and no proportion kept!
So is it in the music of men's lives.

Shakespeare, Richard II V v 42–44

1314   It is a law of life that any one value [e.g., beauty, parental love], when isolated from other values and converted into an absolute, must destroy itself.

R. E. Fitch,
Decline and Fall of Sex 1951 99 Harcourt

1315   Who is narrow of vision cannot be big-hearted; who is narrow of spirit cannot take long, easy strides.

Tut-Tut, in Lin-Yutang (ed.),
Wisdom of China and India 1942 1095
Random House

1316   All superfluity is annoying, especially in things that annoy. To keep hovering around the object of your annoyance is a kind of mania.

Balthasar Gracian (Jacobs, tr.) Maxim 88

1317   Excessive longings for any object blind the soul to other things.   Democritus

1318   Lose not the substance by grasping at the shadow.
                                Aesop, Dog and the Shadow

1319   . . . Small to greater matters must give way.
                        Shakespeare, Antony and Cleopatra II ii 11

1320   To put oneself in another's place is to lose jealousy and
hatred; and to put another in one's own place is to lose pride
and conceit.   From Goethe

1321   He who sets before him, as in a picture, this vast image
of our mother Nature in her entire majesty; . . . who discerns
himself therein, and not himself only but a whole kingdom, to
be but a most delicate dot—he alone esteems things according
to the just measure of their greatness.   Montaigne

1322   To know what to relinquish and what to keep is one
of the final tests of art and of living.
                                After Ethel Sabin Smith

1323   The more we understand life as a whole, the better our
sense of truth and human values.

FLEXIBILITY AND OPEN-MINDEDNESS

1324   It is good to be firm in temperament but flexible in
thought.   Vauvenargues, Reflection 191

1325   Have many strings to your bow.
                                John Heywood, Proverbes I XI

1326   The uncompromising attitude may be more indicative of an inner uncertainty than of deep conviction.

From Eric Hoffer,
Passionate State of Mind 1955 41 Harper

1327   Conceit inclines one to indoctrinate; the love of truth, to educate.

1328   Beware of a man of one book.   Proverbial

1329   A mind is less than fully sane if any of its ideas have become closed to free circulation from the rest of the mental organism.   From Brand Blanshard,
Reason and Goodness 1961 435 Macmillan

1330   The greatest natural genius cannot subsist on its own stock: he who resolves never to ransack any mind but his own, will be soon reduced to imitate himself, and to repeat what he has before repeated.   From Joshua Reynolds

1331   Open-mindedness includes an active desire to listen to more sides than one; to give heed to facts from whatever source they come; to give full attention to alternative possibilities; to recognize the possibility of error even in the beliefs that are dearest to us.

John Dewey, How We Think 1933 30 Heath

1332   Neither despise nor oppose what you do not understand.   William Penn

1333   To change one's way upon good advice does not decrease one's freedom.

Marcus Aurelius, Meditations VIII 16

1334   If through the years one has developed a love of adventure, a willingness to accept change in ideas, in customs, and in values, the spirit of youth has been preserved.

From Ethel Sabin Smith,
Dynamics of Aging 1956 128–129 Norton

MODERATION, TEMPERANCE

1335   Nothing in excess.   Solon

1336   He who lives according to reason is master of himself. The reasonable man desires what, as, and when he ought.

Aristotle, Nicomachean Ethics III xii

1337   Too far east is west.   Dutch proverb

1338   Extreme straightness is as bad as crookedness. Extreme cleverness is as bad as folly. Extreme fluency is as bad as stammering.   Mencius

1339   Press all the juice from an orange and it becomes bitter.

Balthasar Gracian (Jacobs, tr.) Maxim 81

1340   [Too often,] first the man takes a drink, then the drink takes a drink, then the drink takes the man.

Japanese proverb, Champion (ed.),
Racial . . . 1938 440 Macmillan, © Routledge;
Barnes & Noble

1341   . . . That men should put an enemy in their mouths to steal away their brains!   Shakespeare, Othello II iii 92

1342   . . . The taste of sweetness, whereof a little
More than a little is by much too much.
Shakespeare, King Henry IV I III ii 72–73

1343   Enough is as good as a feast.   Proverbial

1344   The short-range hedonistic philosophy of "Eat, drink,
and be merry, for tomorrow you may die" is unrealistic: since
most of the time you do not die tomorrow but live and rue the
consequences of too much eating, drinking, and merrymaking
today.   From Albert Ellis,
Reason and Emotion in Psychotherapy
1962 363 Lyle Stuart

1345   Better than fortune's best is mastery in the using.
Unknown, Temperance

SELF-CONTROL

1346   I can resist everything except temptation.
Oscar Wilde 1946

1347   Men imagine that they are free when subject to their
passions. They do not realize the weariness, mishaps, disappointments, humiliations, that must follow.
From Fénelon, Spiritual Letters to Men CXX iii

1348   Temper, if ungoverned, governs the whole man.
Anthony Ashley Cooper, Third Earl of Shaftsbury

1349   Anger begins in folly, and ends in repentance.
Pythagoras

1350   A Slip of the Foot you may soon recover,
       But a Slip of the Tongue you may never get over.
                                        Franklin

1351   Call not yourself a man so long as you are angry.
                        Wortabet (tr.), Arabian Wisdom 1910 47

1352   A man without self-control is like a city broken into
and left without walls.
                     Proverbs XXV 28 Rev. Stan. Ver. Bible 1952

1353   No one is free who is not master of himself.
                                        Pythagoras

1354   Let us possess one world: each hath one and is one.
                                        John Donne

1355   Self-control is self-completion.
                                        E. G. Bulwer-Lytton

1356   Give me that man
       That is not passion's slave, and I will wear him
       In my heart's core, ay, in my heart of heart.
                        Shakespeare, Hamlet III ii 76–78

1357   He that is slow to anger is better than the mighty; and
he that ruleth his spirit than he that taketh a city.
                                        Proverbs XVI 32

1358   Be gentle, and you can be bold; be frugal, and you can
be liberal; avoid putting yourself ahead of others, and you can
become a leader among men.   Mencius

1359   As rain breaks through an ill-thatched house, harmful passion will break through an unreflecting mind.

From The Dhammapada I

1360   Check your passions, that you may not be punished by them.

Epictetus, Discourses . . . (Long, tr.) n.d. 414

1361   When angry count ten before you speak; if very angry, a hundred.   Jefferson, Letter 1825

1362   Whenever Socrates felt any disposition to anger, he checked it by speaking low.   From Rule of Life 1800 18

1363   True freedom consists not in following our impulses but in subjecting them to the thought of the best.

W. M. Salter, Ethical Religion 1891

1364   When right, you can afford to keep your temper; when wrong, you cannot afford to lose it.   From Frank E. Park

1365   Two things a man should never be angry at: what he can help and what he cannot.

English proverb, Champion (ed.),
Racial . . . 1938 21 Macmillan, © Routledge;
Barnes & Noble

1366   Whenever vexed, remember that life is short.

Marcus Aurelius, Meditations XI 18

1367   Everyone can clearly understand himself and his emotions, at least in part, and so can become less subject to them.

From Spinoza, Ethics V iv Note

1368 A wrathful man stirs up strife; but he that is slow to anger appeases strife.   Proverbs XV 18

1369 By a little self-control, a normal individual can culti- vate the habit of finding satisfaction in the present.

After James T. Fisher and Hawley Lowell,
Diary . . . 1952 248 Hutchinson

SELF-DENIAL AND SELF-DISCIPLINE

1370 The cat would eat fish, and would not wet her feet.
John Heywood, Proverbes I XI

1371 Keep the faculty of effort alive in you by a little gratu- itous exercise every day; that is, every day or two be sys- tematically ascetic, or do something for no other reason than that you would rather not do it, so that, when the hour of need draws nigh, it may find you not untrained to stand the test.

From William James, Psychology 1892 149

1372 If you wish to conquer your weakness, you must not give in to it.   From William Penn

REPOSE, CALM, SERENITY

1373 . . . A state, like the region above the moon, always clear and serene.   From Montaigne, Essays I XXV

1374 . . . Bless'd are those
Whose blood and judgment are so well com-
mingled

That they are not a pipe for fortune's finger
To sound what stop she please.

Shakespeare, Hamlet III ii 73–76

1375   No one ever saw Socrates too elated or too depressed.

Seneca, Ad Lucilium . . .
(Gummere, tr.), 1918 3:207 Putnam

1376   It was said that Socrates, whether teaching the principles of morality, or answering his corrupt judges, or receiving sentence of death, or swallowing the poison, was ever the same man, calm and courageous; in a word, wise to the last.

From Rule of Life 1800 171–172

1377   . . . To bear all naked truths,
             And to envisage circumstance, all calm,
             That is the top of Sovereignty . . .

Keats, Hyperion II

1378   Serving Heaven consists in nourishing one's real being, not anxious about life or death.   Mencius

1379   A man is as big as the things that annoy him.

George E. Allen,
Presidents . . . 1950 194 Simon & Schuster

1380   Flurried men lack wisdom.   Proverb

1381   Good temper is an estate for life.

Hazlitt, Plain Speaker 1826 2:106

1382   Only serenity gives tenderness strength and firmness.

H. Margolius, Aphorisms . . . n.d. 6

1383   It is the greatest manifestation of power to be calm.
Vivekanandi

1384   A mind is never right until it is at peace with itself.
Seneca

1385   An easygoing person is probably more able to realize
eternity—the endless flow of life and death—than the one who
is overserious. The overserious are the truly shallow.
After Eric Hoffer,
Passionate State of Mind 1955 63 Harper

1386   The unwise get highly agitated while undertaking
something trivial. The wise, though undertaking great tasks,
remain calm.
From Sharma and Raghavacharya (trs.),
Gems from Sanskrit . . . 1959 13 Osmania

1387   Heroic deeds and magnificent plans are often initiated
by leisurely and serene people.
Hung, Chinese Garden . . .
(Chao, tr.) 1959 57 Peter Pauper

1388   Passionate intensity often indicates a lack of proficiency
and power.   From Eric Hoffer,
Passionate State of Mind 1955 6 Harper

1389   By a tranquil mind I mean nothing else but a mind
well ordered.   Marcus Aurelius, Meditations IV 3

1390   Pose is not poise, no matter how habit-forming.
Emerson Shuck, AAUP Bull. 1960 46:270

1391   He who neither presses life nor withdraws from it finds that many a right solution comes at the right time. The roses of patience bloom in countless gardens.

After Max Roden,
Spiegelungen 1951 33 Johannes-Presse

1392   Waste not your heart with futile cares.

From Plutarch

1393   Nothing in human affairs deserves serious anxiety, and grief hinders the self-succor that our duty requires.

Plato, Republic 604 B

1394   When laziness lets things alone, it is a disease; but when skill does it, it is a virtue.

From Savile, Moral Thoughts . . ., Of Apologies

1395   If you are disquieted at any thing, ask yourself, "Is that thing of such worth that I should so lose my tranquility?"

From Marcus Aurelius

1396   You cannot choose the lower against the higher and have peace of mind.

A. Powell Davies,
Temptation to be Good 1952 137 Farrar

1397   He who wants to enjoy tranquility of mind must not engage in too many activities.   Democritus

1398   The more intelligent the acts, the more they yield repose.   From Montessori

1399   . . . This is peace— . . .
         To lay up lasting treasure
         Of perfect service rendered, duties done
         In charity, soft speech, and stainless days:
         These riches shall not fade away in life,
         Nor any death dispraise.
                         Buddha, Light of Asia (Arnold, tr.) VIII

1400   Empty vessels make much noise.
                         Sharma and Raghavacharya (trs.),
                         Gems from Sanskrit . . . 1959 69 Osmania

1401   Smooth runs the water where the brook is deep.
                         Shakespeare, Henry VI II III i 53

1402   The human spirit can be stirred as profoundly in calm
         as in the emotional state, and by silence as by tempest.
                         From Balzac, Jesus Christ in Flanders

1403   Back of tranquility often lies conquered unhappiness.
                         Unknown

CONTENTMENT

1404   If a man is moderate and contented, then even age is
         no burden; if he is not, then even youth is full of cares.
                         Plato

1405   Calmness should be tested in a place of turmoil; con-
         tentment, in a world of vanity.
                         From Hung, Chinese Garden . . .
                         (Chao, tr.) 1959 45 Peter Pauper

1406   It happens as with cages: the birds without despair to get in, and those within despair to get out.

Montaigne, Upon some Verses of Virgil

1407   Tomorrow I will live, the fool does say.

Martial, (Cowley, tr.) Epigrams V 58

1408   It is related that the monk Basle, being excommunicated by the Pope, at death was sent in charge of an angel to find a fit place of suffering in hell. Such was the contented spirit of the monk that he found something to praise in every place and company, and made a kind of heaven of it. At last the escorting angel returned with his prisoner saying that, in whatever condition, Basle remained incorrigibly Basle. His sentence was remitted, and he was allowed to go into heaven and was canonized as a saint.   From Emerson, Behavior

1409   Stone walls do not a prison make,
            Nor iron bars a cage.

Richard Lovelace, To Althea from Prison

1410   Contentment is true riches.

Latin proverb, Champion (ed.), Racial ... 1938 216
Macmillan, © Routledge; Barnes & Noble

1411   Without contentment, it becomes almost as difficult to please others as ourselves.   From Fulke Greville

1412   Lightly an ignorant boor is made content,
        And lightlier yet a sage;

But minds by half-way knowledge warped and
    bent,
Not Brahma's self their fury may assuage.
        Paul Elmer More, Century . . . 1898 XXX 52

1413   A man's hatred of his own condition no more helps to
improve it than hatred of other people tends to improve them.
        Santayana,
        Reason in Common Sense 1905 225 Scribner

1414   If a man cannot find ease within himself, it is to little
purpose to seek it anywhere else.   Rule of Life 1800 135

1415   Be a man adapted to the daily round, which if not the
highest is the most necessary thing in life.
        Balthasar Gracian (Jacobs, tr.) Maxim 232

1416   Patience is the key of contentment.   Mohammed

1417   . . . 'Tis better to be lowly born,
    And range with humble livers in content,
    Than to be perked up in a glist'ring grief
    And wear a golden sorrow.
        Shakespeare, King Henry VIII II iii 19–22

CHEERFULNESS

1419   Be cheerful as long as you live.

1421   All things do help th'unhappy man to fall.
        John Webster, Duchess of Malfi III iv

1422   It costs us more to be miserable than would make us
perfectly happy.   Rule of Life 1800 173

1423   Health and cheerfulness mutually beget each other.
                                                        Addison

1424   A merry heart doeth good like a medicine.
        He that is of a merry heart hath a continual
            feast.
                                          Proverbs XVII 22 XV 15

1425   Good temper is the sweetener of toil and the soother
of disquietude.   Washington Irving

1426   O, blest with temper whose unclouded ray
            Can make tomorrow cheerful as today.
                                    Pope, Moral Essays II 257–258

1428   Eternal smiles his emptiness betray,
        As shallow streams run dimpling all the way.
                                Pope, Prologue to the Satires 315–316

1429   Always miserable are the envious, the censorious, the
· discontented, the wrathful, the ever-suspicious, and the parasitic.   From Sharma and Raghavacharya (trs.),
                                Gems from Sanskrit . . . 1959 13 Osmania

1430   . . . Smiles from Reason flow,
            To brute denied, and are of Love the food.
                                    Milton, Paradise Lost IX 239

1431   Keep your face to the sun and the shadows will fall
behind.   Unknown

1432   To be vexed is to forget that everything happens according to nature.   Marcus Aurelius, Meditations XII 26

1433   The cheerful live longest in years, and afterwards in our regards.   Bovée

1434   Every heart that has beat strongly and cheerfully has left a hopeful impulse in the world.
                    From R. L. Stevenson, Virginibus Puerisque

HUMOR

1435   The man who has no sense of humor rides through life on a wagon with no springs.   From B. Baruch

1436   Only man has intellect and laughter; the latter to compensate for the awesome responsibilities of the former.
                                From Alfred Hitchcock, address, 1963

1437   Socrates' gay seriousness and wisdom full of pranks constitutes the best state of the soul of man.
                            Nietzsche, in Walter Kaufman,
                Nietzsche 1968 400 Princeton Univ. Press

1438   The best humor is that which contains most humanity, that which is flavored throughout with tenderness and kindness.   Thackeray

1439   Good humor is the seasoning of Truth.   Pestalozzi

1440   Many a true word is spoken in jest.   English proverb

1441   Do not mind a jest; salt thrown at you is harmless unless your skin is sore.   Junius

1442   Humor keeps piety from becoming sticky, and piety prevents humor from becoming cruel.

T. V. Smith,
Non-Existent Man 1962 23 Univ. of Tex.

1443   Joking decides great things
         Stronger and better oft than earnest can.

Horace

1444   Better a witty fool than a foolish wit.

Shakespeare, Twelfth Night I v

1445   No mind is thoroughly well organized that is deficient in a sense of humor.

Coleridge, Table Talk

1447   Humor goes with good nature, and good nature is the climate of reason.   Ingersoll

1448   True wit is the distillation of a generous, richly-gifted nature, founded on seriousness.   From Evert A. Duyckinck

1449   Brevity is the soul of wit.

Shakespeare, Hamlet II ii 90

1450   What a man finds ridiculous reveals his character.

From Goethe

DIGNITY

1451   The nobler sort of man is dignified but not self-important; the inferior man is self-important but not dignified.

Confucius, Analects XIII XXVI

1452   True dignity is never gained by place, and never lost when honors are withdrawn.   P. Massinger

1453   The ideal man bears the accidents of life with dignity and grace, making the best of the circumstances.

Aristotle

1455   The consciousness of having reflected seriously and conclusively on important questions, whether social or spiritual, augments dignity while it does not lessen humility.

John Morley, On Compromise 1913 121

MORAL CHARACTER

1456   Often our courtesy is only a selfish worldly discretion; our modesty a superficial and hypocritical means of keeping within the bounds of good manners and winning praise; our zeal merely a matter of temperament or pride; our frankness only bluntness; and so on.

Fénelon, Elizabeth C. Fenn (tr.),
Meditations . . . 1952 16 Morehouse

1457   Take heed therefore that the light which is within thee be not darkness.   Luke XI 35

1458   Often, man is less moral than moralizing.

From M. Edel and A. Edel,
Anthropology and Ethics 1959 29 Thomas

1459   The early Romans built temples and offered sacrifices to Valor, to Truth, to Good Faith, to Modesty, to Charity, to Concord.   From J. A. Froude, Caesar II

1460   A virtue is no less virtue because many possess it.

H. Margolius,
Thoughts ... 1962 6 Lib. Humane Lit.

1461   I cannot praise a fugitive and cloistered virtue, unexercised and unbreathed, that never sallies out and sees her adversary, but slinks out of the race, where the immortal garland is to be run for not without dust and heat.

Milton, Areopagitica

1462   It is with certain good qualities as with the senses: those who wholly lack them can neither appreciate nor comprehend them.   La Rochefoucauld, Maxim 337

1463   Tell me what you like and I will tell you what you are.

Ruskin, Crown of Wild Olives 64

1464   You can tell the man who rings true from the man who rings false not by his deeds alone but also by his desires.

Democritus

1465   Character is what you are in the dark.

D. L. Moody, Sermons

1466   He who needs witnesses in order to be good has neither
virtue nor religion.   Lavater, Aphorism 535 (1787 ed.)

1467   . . . Not that you won or lost—but how you played the
game.   G. Rice,
                            Final Answer 1955 69 A. S. Barnes

1468   Men love and hate their vices at the same time.
                                        Seneca, Ad Lucilium . . .
                                (Gummere, tr.) 1918 3:281 Putnam

1469   . . . Sweetest things turn sourest by their deeds;
        Lilies that fester smell far worse than weeds.
                                        Shakespeare, Sonnet XCIV

1470   Of the mind, good thoughts; of the tongue, good words;
of the hand, good works; these make the virtuous life.
                    Tahmura's Fragments of the Nasks XXVIII 57

1471   Virtue lies in a free choice of what is good, not in blind
obedience.   Edgar Johnson,
                    Treasury of Satire 1945 126 Simon & Schuster

1472   Often unjust men are rich and just men are poor; yet
we will not exchange our virtue for their money, since excellence lasts, but wealth comes and goes.   Solon

1473   The superior man refrains from resting on his virtue.
                        From I Ching (Wilhelm, tr., Baynes, tr.)
                            1967 167 Princeton Univ. Press; Routledge

1474   Virtue is sociable and gentle: free, **steady, and fearless;** content within itself; full of inexhaustible delights; and valued for itself.   From Seneca,

R. L'Estrange, . . . Morals 1756 98–99

1475   Character is a diamond that resists every stone.

From A. Bartol

1476   A man who lives right has more power in his silence than another by his words. Character is like bells which ring out sweet notes and which, when touched accidentally even, resound with music.   Phillips Brooks

1477   Character calls forth character.   Goethe

1478   He who practices virtue is not left forever to stand alone; he will gain companions.   From Confucius

1479   To be prudent, honest, and good are infinitely higher accomplishments than being learned.   From Charron

1480   Virtue is never the less venerable for being out of fashion.   Roger L'Estrange

1481   Like light, when virtue moves among the impure, it is not polluted.

From Augustine, In Johannis Evangelum 5 xv

1482   Silver and gold are not the only coin; virtue, too, passes current all over the world.   Euripides, Oedipus 546

1483   The bad are never completely happy and at ease, though possessed of everything that this world can bestow; and the good are never completely miserable, though deprived of everything that this world can take away. The worst men cannot thoroughly esteem a bad man, though he be their dearest friend, nor thoroughly despise a good man, though he be their bitterest enemy.   From C. C. Colton, Lacon 1832 93

1484   Wealth does not bring virtue; rather, virtue brings wealth and other human goods, private and public.

From Socrates, in Plato, Apology

1485   A man's character is his guardian divinity.

Heraclitus, Wheelwright (tr.)
1959 Frag. 69 Princeton Univ. Press

1486   Strength of body is nobility in beasts of burden; strength of character is nobility in men.

Democritus, Frag. 57

1487   Character is nature in the highest form.

Emerson, Character

1488   Character is nurtured midst the tempests of the world.
From Goethe, Torquato Tasso I 2

1489   It is by its promise of a sense of power that evil often attracts the weak . . .

There is probably as much effort involved in being exquisitely wicked as in being exquisitely good.

Eric Hoffer,
Passionate State of Mind 1955 58 41 Harper

1490   The spirit of Evil, even if one gives it no more than a single hair, will eventually carry away the head.

> Baudelaire, Prose and Poetry
> (Symons, tr.) 1926 239 A. & C. Boni

1491   Most sin consists in preferring a lesser good to a greater.
> From Richard Baxter, Works 6 8–9 Christian Politics

1492   Sin should mean what is self- or society-defeating.
> From Albert Ellis, Reason and
> Emotion in Psychotherapy 1962 144 Lyle Stuart

1493   Let the enlightened man lay well to heart that false and fruitless things become him not.   Buddha

1494   He who finds pleasure in vice and pain in virtue is a novice in both.   Chinese proverb

1495   The good are wise.
> Euripides, Alcestis antistrophe 2

1496   A real attachment to virtue does not need to bolster itself with an outrageous or affected antipathy to vice.
> From Hazlitt,
> Characters of Shakespear's Plays, Cymbeline

1497   Be not overcome by evil, but overcome evil with good.
> Romans XII 21

1498   Whatsoever things are true, whatsoever things are honest, whatsoever things are just, whatsoever things are pure, whatsoever things are lovely, whatsoever things are of good report: if there be any virtue, and if there be any praise, think on these things.   Philippians IV 8

1499   All virtues grow with practice.   Socrates

1500   If you do right, your character will take care of itself.
                          J. G. Holland, Gold-Foil ... 1881 205

1501   A man of virtue is a benefactor to the world.
                          From Rule of Life 1800 17–18

DEEDS AND CONDUCT

1502   To be good means not merely not doing wrong, but not wanting to do wrong; and it means good deeds.
                                              From Democritus

1503   ... If our virtues
            Did not go forth of us, 't were all alike
            As if we had them not.
                   Shakespeare, Measure for Measure I i 33–35

1504   It is easier to fight for one's principles than to live up to them.   Alfred Adler

1505   Saying is one thing, doing another.
                                       Montaigne, Of Anger

1506   Deed and word should be in accord.
                                       Seneca, Ad Lucilium ...
                          (Gummere, tr.) 1918 1:135 Putnam

1507   A gentleman is ashamed that his words are better than his deeds.

> Confucius, in Lin-Yutang (ed.),
> Wisdom of China and India 1942 193 Random House

1508   You do not pay a man for his intentions; you pay him for his work.   Mencius, Cranmer-Byng and Watts (eds.)
> (Giles, tr.) Book ... 1942 66

1509   A good deed strengthens the doer; an evil deed weakens him.   After Emerson and Spinoza

1510   Ahead of every act lies a habit; habit is nine-tenths of conduct; conduct is character in the making; and character ends in destiny.

> From G. H. Betts, Fathers and Mothers 1915 56-57

1511   Virtuous actions are pleasant in themselves.
> Aristotle, Nicomachean Ethics I viii

1512   Life is given to him who does what is loved.
> From the Memphite Drama (ca. 3400 B.C.),
> Homer W. Smith,
> Man and His Gods 1952 46 108 Little

1513   Actions speak louder than words.   Proverb

1514   By their fruits ye shall know them.   Matthew VII 20

1515   Good words gain honor in the marketplace, but good deeds gain friends among men.

> Lao-tse, Sayings ... (Giles, tr.) 1905 50

1516   How far that little candle throws his beams!
        So shines a good deed in a naughty world.
                        Shakespeare, Merchant of Venice V i 89–90

1517   Only achievement endures.
                        Balthasar Gracian (Jacobs, tr.) Maxim 57

1518   Greater is he who acts from love than he who acts from
fear.   Simeon ben Eleazar, Sotah 31

1519   Good deeds come from good thoughts only.
                        The Brahmans, in Brian Brown (ed.),
                        Wisdom of the Hindus 1921 13–14 Brentano

1520   If you want to hit a bird on the wing, you must have
all your will in a focus, you must not be thinking about yourself, and equally, you must not be thinking about your neighbor; you must be living in your eye on that bird. Every achievement is a bird on the wing.   (Justice) O. W. Holmes

1521   The deed is all, the honor nothing.   Goethe

1522   A man that has done a good deed does not proclaim it
but goes on to do another, as a vine that bears grapes again in
season . . .
        Be not discouraged if you do not always act according to
principle; try again, and be glad if most of your acts are worthy
of human nature.   Marcus Aurelius, Meditations V 6 9

1524   The way to do is to be.
                        Witter Bynner,
                        Way of Life according to Laotzu 1944 55 Day

1525   Like threads of silver seen through crystal beads
         Let love through good deeds show.
                              Buddha, Light of Asia (Arnold, tr.) VIII

1526   I expect to pass through life but once. If, therefore,
there be any kindness I can do any fellow-being, let me do
it now.   From William Penn

BUSYNESS

1527   One coin in a bottle rattles, but a bottle full of coins
makes no sound.   Baba Metzia

1528   ... He seemed busier than he was.
                                      Chaucer, Prologue 323

1529   Work expands so as to fill the time available for its
completion.
         C. Northcote, Parkinson's Law 1957 Houghton

1530   The feeling of being hurried can result from a vague
fear that we are wasting our lives.
                    From Eric Hoffer, Harper's No. 1966 91

VOCATION

1531   A wholesome person will find more satisfaction in his
actual work than in his dreams.
                              From Arthur E. Morgan,
                    Observations 1968 285 Antioch Press

1532   So much does the soul require an object to work upon that, when it does not have one, it will turn upon itself and create problems.   From Montaigne, Essays I iv

1533   Many a person takes to the useless side of life because he fears that he will be defeated if he remains on the useful side.   From Alfred Adler,
What Life Should Mean to You 1931 115 Little

1534   Know what you can work at, and do it. In many senses, true work is worship.
From Carlyle, Past and Present III XI

1535   That man is truly free who desires what he is able to perform, and does what he desires, reasonably considered.
After Rousseau

1536   Aristotle meant, I suppose, . . . that the Good Life begins only when one's satisfactions are not derivative, but immediate; that what one gives one's time to should be an end in itself, not a means.

Learned Hand,
Irving Dilliard (ed.), Spirit . . . 1952 85 Knopf

1537   A man's business may be like a shoe: if too big it will trip him, and if too small will chafe him.
From Horace, Epistles

1538   It is important to choose a vocation in which you will grow rather than stagnate.   H. W. Dodds

1539   Sloth, like rust, consumes faster than labor wears. The used key is always bright.   B. Franklin

1540   Labor is wholesome for thy body and good for thy mind.
From William Penn

1541   The busier we are the more acutely we feel we live.
Kant

1542   What a man can do is his greatest ornament.
Bonaparte, in Emerson, Literary Ethics

1543   No group can prosper till it learns that there is as much dignity in tilling a field as in writing a poem.
After Booker T. Washington, Up from Slavery

1544   A ploughman on his legs is higher than a gentleman on his knees.
B. Franklin

1545   Each honest calling, each walk of life, has its own elite, its own aristocracy based on excellence of performance.
J. B. Conant

1546   Always take your job seriously, never yourself.
D. D. Eisenhower

1547   Art thou little, do that little well, and for thy comfort know
The biggest man can do his biggest work no better than just so.

Goethe

1548   If you are doing the best you can, the results, immediate or eventual, you should leave to the universe.
After Bolton Hall

1549   The reward of a thing well done is to have done it.
                                Emerson, New England Reformers

1550   My share of the work of the world may be limited, but
the fact that it is work makes it precious.   Helen Keller

1551   Heaven doth with us as we with torches do,
        Not light them for themselves.
                        Shakespeare, Measure for Measure I i 32–33

1552   The day is short and the work is great. You are not
called upon to complete the work, yet you are not free to
evade it.   From Ethics of the Fathers IV 20–21

1553   Let us cultivate our garden.   Voltaire, Candide

CREATIVE WORK

1554   The nobility, greatness, and magnificence which make
our actions and enterprises marvelous and excellent do not
consist only in what is necessary but also in the unnecessary.
                                Galileo, in de Santillana,
                        Crime . . . 1955 174 Univ. Chicago Press

1555   When love and skill work together expect a master-
piece.   Ruskin

1556   In the long run, we trust generous ideas will survive
ungenerous ones; justice, injustice; beautiful things, ugly ones;
and truth, error. We can share in this ideal so far as we do our
best within our own little field.
                                From G. Sarton,
                in Anshen (ed.), Moral . . . 1952 442 Harper

1557   The creator's vision, imagination, dreams, through trial and error yield the inventions, creations, that the merely able use and live by.

From B. Berenson,
Sunset and Twilight 1963 422 432 Harcourt

WISDOM

1558   Hardly anybody, except possibly the Greeks at their best, has realised the sweetness and glory of being a rational animal.   Santayana,
Character and Opinions . . . 1920 18 Scribner

1559   Many know many things, yet lack wisdom.

Democritus, Frag. 64

1560   Wisdom is in the head and not in the beard.

Swedish proverb

1561   A pseudo-sage is like a donkey that carries a load of books.   Zohar, Hadash, Tikkun

1562   Wisdom is not one word and then another,
Till words are like dry leaves under a tree;
Wisdom is like a dawn that comes up slowly
Out of an unknown ocean.

E. A. Robinson, Tristram 1927 Macmillan

1563   A wise man understands the common things which an ignorant one only sees.   From Starr King

1564   Men with little wisdom have much passion; men with much wisdom have little passion and great compassion.

From Nicholai Velimirovic,
Serbia in Light and Darkness 1916 Longmans

1565   It is not wisdom to close the eyes on the inward vision.

From Santayana

1566   Wisdom is the ability to respond, as a whole man and with some serenity, to the challenge of the previously unknown.

From Walter Kerr,
Decline of Pleasure 1962 243 Simon & Schuster

1567   Knowledge without justice ought to be called cunning rather than wisdom.   Plato

1568   There is no wisdom without goodness.   Unknown

1569   Wisdom is knowledge translated into proper action.

From William J. Mayo, in Eric Hoffer,
Passionate State of Mind 1955 97–99 Harper

1570   The wise only possess ideas; the greater part of mankind are possessed by them.

Coleridge, Miscellanies 1884 154

1571   Only more and wiser intelligence can make a happier world.

Bertrand Russell, Why I Am Not a Christian
1957 178 G. Allen; Simon & Schuster

1572   Brute force without wisdom falls by its own weight.

Horace, Odes III iv 65

1573   Science without wisdom is a poor thing, and technique without wisdom is poorer still.

G. Sarton,
in Anshen (ed.), Moral . . . 1952 446 Harper

1574   Wisdom lifteth the head of the lowly and filleth his heart with treasure.   Found by Mary Ellen Chase
in a British copybook.

1575   The heart of the wise, like a mirror, can reflect all objects without being sullied by any.   Confucius, Analects

1576   Of all the qualities of the sage, none is greater than that of being helper of men to right living.   Mencius

1577   Wisdom and games are to be pursued alike, each for its own sake.   Thomas Aquinus

1578   Many persons might have achieved wisdom had they not supposed that they already possessed it.   Seneca

1579   Wisdom does not grow with idleness, though the conceit of wisdom prospers nowhere more.

After Richard Baxter, Christian Politics

1580   Men who love wisdom should acquaint themselves with a great many particulars.

Heraclitus (Wheelwright tr.)
1959 Frag. 3 Princeton Univ. Press

1581   Who is a wise man? He who learns from all men.

The Talmud

1582   Knowledge includes others' thoughts; wisdom includes
also one's own.   After William Cowper

1583   The wisdom of a learned man comes through opportunity of leisure.   Ecclus. XXXVIII 24

1584   Wisdom brings freedom from dogmatism.
                        From Sharma and Raghavacharya (trs.),
                        Gems from Sanskrit ... 1959 77 Osmania

1585   Wisdom begets humility.
                                    Abraham ibn Ezra,
                    in Hertz (ed.), Book ... 1921 284 Oxford

1586   The wisest mind hath something yet to learn.
                        Santayana, Lucifer ... 1899 18

1587   A wise man neither deceives nor is deceived.
                    Wortabet (tr.), Arabian Wisdom 1910 38

MATURITY

1588   Does any one choose to live deceived, liable to mistake,
unjust, unrestrained, discontented, mean? No.
                    Epictetus, Discourses ... (Long, tr.) n.d. 301

1589   The eternal child dwells in fine natures.
                            De Quincey

1590   Men are but children of a larger growth.
                        Dryden, All For Love IV 1

1591   A person remains immature, whatever his age, as long as he thinks of himself as an exception to the human race.

H. A. Overstreet, Mature Mind 1949 51 Norton

1592   Maturity implies the capacity to fit into groups, in business, in home life, also in allegiances as well as in emancipation. It implies the capacity to accept illness, disappointments, bereavements, even death, and all that which is largely beyond our own control and influence; to accept our own makeup and individuality, the perfections and imperfections of self and others, success and failure, advice, criticism, and authority. Maturity assumes a philosophy of objectivity about the past and a vision of creative opportunity for the present and the future.

From Adolph Meyer, Child Study 1930 7:226–227

1593   Each is so far a complete man according as he possesses maturity.

Balthasar Gracian (Jacobs, tr.) Maxim 293

1594   Maturity may or may not accord with conventionality.

1595   He who is eternally more concerned with the symbols of successful living than with its realities, he who can be comfortable with his fellows only behind the armor of prestige and power, faces tragedy, for age gradually strips away this armor . . .

A contented old age is possible only for those who have achieved maturity in its broadest sense.

R. L. Jenkins,
Breaking Patterns . . . 1954 209 208 Lippincott

1596   A soul supreme, in each hard instance tried;
        Above all pain, all passion, and all pride,
        The rage of power, the blast of public breath,
        The lust of lucre, and the dread of death!
                                Pope, Epistle to ... Oxford ... 23–26

1597   It is in what we value, not in what we have, that the
test of us resides.   E. M. Forster

1598   Old wood inflamed doth yield the bravest fire,
        When younger doth in smoke his virtue spend.
                                        Philip Sidney, Acadia

1599   As soon as man begins to live rationally, any lack of
harmony between motive and deed, or between the believed
and the known, tends to become intolerable.
                                From Gerhard Szczesny,
                    in Brinton (ed.), Fate of Man 1961 25 Braziller

1600   It is the duty of society to evolve adults fit for children
to live with.
                                From Lillien J. Martin, in George Lawton,
                    How to be Happy though Young 1949 65 Vanguard

CHARM

1601   A quick responsiveness in word and deed,
        A dignity and stateliness at need,
        The will to follow or the art to lead.
                                L. C. Thomas, What is Charm?

1602   Elegant as simplicity, and warm
     As ecstasy.

        William Cowper, Table Talk 588

1603 Charming manners grow from habitual kindness.

1604 Honor and virtue are the ornaments of the mind, without which the fairest body cannot be beautiful.

        Cervantes, Don Quixote I XIV

1605 Goodness and love mould the form into their own image, and cause the joy and beauty of love to shine forth from the face.   From Swedenborg

1606 There is no beautifier of complexion, or form, or behavior, like the wish to scatter joy and not pain around us.

        Emerson, Behavior

1607 Charms strike the sight, but merit wins the soul.

        Pope, Rape of the Lock V 34

NOBILITY

1608 The pleasant life and the sensible, noble, and just life are one and the same.

       From Epicurus, Strodach (tr.),
   Philosophy . . . 1962 197 Northwestern Univ. Press

1609 A man's virtue must be measured not by his extraordinary efforts but by his ordinary life.

       After Pascal, Detached Thoughts XV

1610   Goodness does not consist in greatness, but greatness in goodness.   Atheneus, Deipnosophists XIV 46

1611   Great men are great even in little things.
Vauvenargues, Reflection 552

1612   The great man . . . never loses his child-like touch.
Mencius (Dobson, tr.)
1963 188 Univ. Toronto Press; Oxford

1613   True nobility is in being superior to one's previous self.   Hindu proverb

1614   The superior man understands what is right; the inferior man understands what will sell.   From Confucius

1615   It is easy in the world to live after the world's opinion; it is easy in solitude to live after our own; but the great man is he who in the midst of the crowd keeps with perfect sweetness the independence of solitude.

Emerson, Self-Reliance

1616   He who is not sure of himself may be less highly or more highly endowed than others. Often he strives to impress others, even by pretense, and is jealous of those who do impress others. He is liable to be too set up when praised, and too worked up when criticized. Often he is prejudiced for persons and policies that seem to forward him, and prejudiced against those that seem to hinder him. Thus he is essentially flimsy and perhaps mean.

One who *is* sure of himself may be likewise less highly or more highly endowed than others. He, however, is more likely to know his own abilities, and to understand himself in relation to the world. He therefore has many virtues.

1617   There are in all nine virtues . . .: Affability combined with dignity; mildness combined with firmness; bluntness combined with respectfulness; aptness for government combined with reverent caution; docility combined with boldness; straightforwardness combined with gentleness; an easy negligence combined with discrimination; boldness combined with sincerity; and valour combined with righteousness.

> Kao-Yao, in Lin-Yutang (ed.),
> Wisdom of China and India 1942 719 Random House

1618   The soul does violence to itself when it becomes an excrescence on the universe; when it turns from anyone, or opposes him, to his hurt, as happens in anger; when it is overcome by pleasure or pain; when it is not wholehearted or sincere; and when it is aimless.

> From Marcus Aurelius, Meditations II 16

1619   He who realizes that all things follow from the eternal laws of nature will not find anything worthy of hatred, derision, or contempt, nor will he bestow pity on anything, but will endeavor to do well and to live well . . . Yet he who is not moved to help others by reason or by compassion is rightly styled inhuman. [Pity is less constructive than sympathy or compassion.]   From Spinoza, Ethics IV l [fifty] Note

1620   All great minds sympathize.
    Great minds are stamped with expanded benevolence.

> Lavater, Aphorisms 600, 427 (1787 ed.)

1621   Purity can tolerate the unclean; benevolence can make sound judgments; cleverness need not pry so as to offend.

> From Hung, Chinese Garden . . .
> (Chao, tr.) 1959 48 Peter Pauper

1622   The true gentleman observes the rules of courtesy. No evil words leave his lips. With a benevolent mind he explains his ideas to others, with the mind of learning he listens to their words, and with a fair mind he makes his judgments. He is not moved by the censure or praise of the mob; he does not try to bewitch the ears and eyes of his observers; he does not cringe before the power and authority of eminent men; he does not feign delight in the words of the ruler's favorites. Therefore he can endure hardship without betraying his ideals, and can enjoy good fortune without overstepping the bounds of good conduct. He honors what is fair and upright and despises meanness and wrangling.

> From Hsün Tzu, Burton Watson (tr.),
> 1963 148–149 Columbia Univ. Press

1623   True merit is like a river: the deeper it is, the less noise it makes.   **From Savile, Some Cautions . . .**

1624   [A man's] true being lies in Humanity, Justice, Propriety, and Wisdom. These . . . appear on the face . . . in the set of the shoulders . . . in every movement of the arms and legs.   Mencius (Dobson, tr.),

> 1963 181 Univ. Toronto Press; Oxford

1625   Statesman, yet friend to truth! of soul sincere,
       In action faithful, and in honor clear;

Who broke no promise, served no private end,
Who gained no title, and who lost no friend.
>   Pope, Epistle to Mr. Addison, 67

1626   The climate of her nature was a clear steady sunshine.
There was no malice, no selfishness, no moodiness, in her;
neither was there any of that excessive pity which puts its re-
cipient at a disadvantage; she was a true comrade, loyal and
candid; she made everyone she talked to feel her equal. Ac-
cordingly she had innumerable friends.
>   Phyllis Bentley,
>   O Dreams, O Destinations 1962 250 Gollancz, © Peters

1627   I can conceive Socrates in the place of Alexander but
not Alexander in the place of Socrates.
>   From Montaigne, Of Repentance

1628   He is great who confers the most benefits.
>   Emerson, Compensation

1629   The nobler sort of man is firm but does not fight; he
mixes easily with others, but does not form cliques.
>   Confucius, in Lin-Yutang (ed.),
>   Wisdom of China and India 1942 833 Random House

1630   Softer than the flowers where kindness is concerned;
stronger than the thunder, where principles are at stake.
>   The Vedas

1631   Great people are not affected by each puff of wind that
blows ill. Like great ships, they sail serenely on, in a calm sea
or a great tempest.   G. Washington

1632   The strength of mind of the free man is his objectivity, his acquiescence in rationally ascertained truth, however personally disagreeable the truth may seem. Any other attitude to experience must seem to the free man merely stupid and childish, like the attitude of someone who kicks a chair because it causes him to stumble.

From Stuart Hampshire,
Spinoza [1951] 125–126 Barnes and Noble; Faber

1633   The point is not how long you live but how nobly you live; and sometimes this living nobly means that you cannot live long.   From Seneca

1634   He who knows himself is wise.
       He who conquers himself is strong.
       He who is contented is rich.
       He who dies, yet his power remains, has long
          life.

From Lao-tse

1635   Every land is open to a wise man; for the native land of the noble soul is the entire universe.   Democritus

1636   Who are the saints of humanity? Those whom perpetual habits have made nearly unconscious that what they do is good or grand—heroes with infantine simplicity.

From Lavater, Aphorism 333 (1787 ed.)

THE PERSONALITY

1637   A human personality is the peak of Nature's creations.
                                                 From Goethe

1638   Personality is the individual's total pattern of structure and functions, especially in relation to other people.

1639   Animal spirits are continually mistaken for wit and fancy; and the want of them, for sense and judgment.

One shining quality lends a lustre to another, or hides some glaring defect.

From Hazlitt, Characteristics CXLVII CLXII

1640   Good personality is to man what perfume is to a flower.

From C. M. Schwab

X

Economics, Social Life, and Self-Realization

1641   The belief that a man's ideas are wholly the product of his economic setting is of course as fatuous as the belief that they are wholly independent of it.

> William Empson,
> Some Versions . . . 1935 19 Chatto

1642   There are no wholly self-made men. All men are made largely by social inheritance. No man creates wealth by himself; and no business creates wealth by itself.

> From Arthur E. Morgan,
> Community . . . 1957 106 Community Service

1643   When mangers are empty, horses bite each other.

> Danish proverb

1644   For the starving poor, the economic is the spiritual.

> From Gandhi

1645   Unhappy are those who have more of money or time than they know how to use.   From Samuel Johnson

1646   In no man can spiritual disorder be resolved, or joy produced, by great wealth, by popular esteem, or by anything insofar as it causes unrestrained selfish desire.

> From Epicurus, Strodach (tr.),
> Philosophy . . . 1962 207 Northwestern Univ. Press

1647   Men have been slow to distinguish between the parasitic process of getting possession of wealth and the creative process of producing wealth.

> From Arthur E. Morgan,
> Observations 1968 74 Antioch Press

1648   The consumption-explosion is inherently self-defeating. Quantity of material production cannot be an end in itself. We must aim at qualitative satisfaction of human needs, material, physiological, mental, and spiritual.

From Julian Huxley,
Humanist Frame 1961 25 G. Allen

1649   Men can be said to be civilized no farther than economic needs can take a secondary place in our attention, as do air and water supply, while non-economic interests have the opportunity to determine the form and quality of social life.

From Arthur E. Morgan,
Observations 1968 68 Antioch Press

1650   It is a high thought for every man that his earthly influence will never end.   From Carlyle

WORK

1651   If any would not work, neither should he eat.

II Thessalonians III 10

1652   Lordlings and witlings not a few,
            Incapable of doing aught,
            Yet ill at ease with nought to do.

Walter Scott,
Bridal of Triermain ii 618–620

1653   By doing nothing we learn to do ill.   Proverb

1654   It is hard to say whether the increase of the unemployed poor, or that of the unemployed rich, is the greater social evil.

> Huxley, in Bibby, T. H. Huxley 1959 240 Horizon

1655   No thoroughly occupied man is very miserable.

> From L. E. London

1656   The labour we delight in relieves pain.

> Shakespeare, Macbeth II iii 56

1657   A free man feels more contented after heavy work than when he has done no work; for by work he has set his powers in motion, he feels them better, and his mind is more alive to pleasure.

When he earns his bread, he eats it with greater pleasure than when it is doled out to him.

Rest cannot be properly enjoyed except after occupation.

> From Kant, Lectures on Ethics
> (Infield, tr.) 1930 161–162 Methuen

1658   Work and health are friends.   Estonian proverb

1659   Work gives flavor to life.   Amiel, Journal

1660   No labor, however humble, is dishonoring . . .
Work gives man dignity.

> The Babylonian Talmud

1661   I long to accomplish a great and noble task, but it is my chief duty to accomplish humble tasks as though they were great and noble. The world is moved along not only by the mighty shoves of its heroes, but also by the tiny pushes of each honest worker.   From Helen Keller

1662   Even if you can do only a little, do what you can.
                                                From Sydney Smith

1663   . . . To climb steep hills
                    Requires slow pace at first.
                    Shakespeare, Henry VIII I i 131–132

1664   Though much drudgery can and should be reduced by machinery, man must work. He may, however, work grudgingly or gratefully, and as a machine or as a thinking man, one who understands his work and sees it in perspective. Within limits, there is no work so rude that a thinking man may not exalt it, and no work so dull that he may not enliven it.
                                                After Henry Giles

1665   Life without industry is guilt; industry without art is brutality.   Ruskin

1666   Things are not useful or necessary because they are unpleasant or tiresome, but in spite of these characteristics.
    The means by which we make a living must be transformed into ways of making a life that is worth the living.
                    From John Dewey, Schools of Tomorrow 1915 299–300;
                        J. L. Childs, in Schilpp (ed.), Philosophy
                    of John Dewey 1949 423 Northwestern Univ. Press

1667   The working man works more effectively, cheerfully, and honorably in proportion as he knows what he acts upon, knows the laws and forces of which he avails himself, and understands the reason of what he does. Labor becomes a new thing when thought is thrown into it, when the mind keeps pace with the hands.   From W. E. Channing

1668   When we take account of . . . ends, . . . we ask no longer: what have the producers produced, and what has consumption enabled the consumers in their turn to produce? We ask instead: what has there been in the lives of consumers and producers to make them glad to be alive? Have they experienced the glory of new knowledge? Have they known love and friendship? Have they rejoiced in sunshine and the spring and the smell of flowers? Have they felt the joy of life that simple communities express in dance and song?

Bertrand Russell,
Authority . . . 1949 115 G. Allen; Simon & Schuster

1669   There is endless merit in a man's knowing when to have done.   Carlyle

1670   [Even in the industrial age,] the use of man for work is turning, perhaps, to considerations of the use of work for man.

H. H. Perlman,
Persona 1968 62 Univ. Chicago Press

1671   I learned . . . what I think the best service that we can do for our country and for ourselves: To see so far as one may and to feel the great forces that are behind every detail . . . to hammer out as compact and solid a piece of work as one can, to try to make it first rate, and to leave it unadvertised.

(Justice) O. W. Holmes, in Irving Dilliard (ed.),
Spirit of Liberty 1952 1953 1960 © Knopf

1672   [Ultimately, as to the use of manpower,] the claims of economic efficiency and the claims of humanity tend to coincide.   John Spedan Lewis,
Partnership for All 1948 435 Kerr-Cros

BORROWING AND LENDING

1673   Neither a borrower nor a lender be;
For loan oft loses both itself and friend,
And borrowing dulls the edge of husbandry.
Shakespeare, Hamlet I iii 75–77

1674   Do not lend beyond your ability, nor refuse to lend according to your ability—especially when it will help others more than it will hurt yourself.   From William Penn

POVERTY

1675   Poverty consists in never being independent of poverty.
Sufism, S. G. Champion,
Eleven Religions 1945 195 Dutton

1676   Chill penury repressed their noble urge,
And froze the genial current of the soul.
From Thomas Gray, Elegy

1677   'Tis hard (but glorious) to be poor and honest: an empty sack can hardly stand upright; but if it does, 'tis a stout one.   Franklin

1678   Slow rises worth by poverty depressed.
Samuel Johnson, London 176

INDEPENDENCE

1679   With a constant livelihood the people have a constant mind. Without a constant livelihood the people will not have constant minds.   Mencius (Dobson, tr.)
1963 35 Univ. Toronto Press; Oxford

1680   When flies attach themselves to the tail of a galloping horse, they move at high speed; but they are an appendage. When vines entwine themselves around a tall pine, they reach an awesome height; but they are dependent.

  Those who depend upon the power of others are like the parasites on a tree: when the tree is chopped, the parasites are bereft of life.   From Hung, Chinese Garden . . .
(Chao, tr.) 1959 45 57 Peter Pauper

1681   Better enough in freedom than plenty at the table of another.   Benedict of Oxford,
in J. H. Hertz (ed.), Book . . . 1921 281 Oxford

1682   Let each man care well for himself lest he burden an-other.   From K. L. Patton, in Hymns for the
Celebration of Life 1964 381 Meeting House Press

MONEY

1683   By the whetstone gold is tried, and by gold the mind of good and evil men.   From Chilon, 6th Cent. B.C.

1684   One who thinks that money can do everything is likely to do anything for money.   Hasidic saying

1685   A man who knows the price of everything and the value of nothing.

Oscar Wilde, Lady Windermere's Fan III

1686   If money is not your servant it may be your master. The miser does not so much possess his wealth as it possesses him.   Charron

1687   Many receive profit; only the wise profit from it.

Publilius Syrus

1688   The use of money is all the advantage there is in having money.   Franklin

1689   To cut out useless expenditure is a great blessing to the world.   From Motse, Y.-P. Mei (tr.),

Ethical . . . 1929 119 Probsthain

1690   Those who know the true use of money, and measure wealth according to their needs, live content with no excess of things.   Spinoza, Ethics IV App. xxix

1691   Economy is a high humane office when it is practiced for freedom, or love, or devotion.

From Emerson, Man the Reformer

1692   If you throw money away idly, you lose your great support. If you hug it too closely, you lose it and yourself too.

Locke, in Maurice Cranston,
John Locke 1957 99 Macmillan

1693   The management of money is, in much, the management of the self.   E. G. Bulwer-Lytton, Caxtoniana

1694   Broadly, the more able the worker, the more important to him are considerations other than money.

> From John Spedan Lewis,
> Partnership for All 1948 169 189 Kerr-Cros

POSSESSIONS

1695   Man does not live by bread alone.

> Deuteronomy VIII 3

1696   Love tastes sweet, but only with bread.

> Yiddish proverb

1697   He that feasts every day feasts no day.

> From Jeremy Taylor, in Gest (ed.),
> House ... 1954 54 Univ. of Pa. Press

1698   We are all natural Jack Horners. If the plum comes when we put in and pull out our thumb we attribute the satisfactory result to personal virtue. It is not easy to distinguish obtaining from attaining.   From John Dewey,

> Human Nature ... 1922 253 Holt

1699   Better is a little with righteousness than great revenue without right.   Proverbs XVI 8

1700   Little with economy is better than much with waste.

> Wortabet (tr.), Arabian Wisdom 1910

1701   Waste not, want not.   Proverb

1702   Better unleavened cakes with kindliness of heart than riches with contentiousness.

> Amen-em-ope, G. A. Barton,
> Archeology . . . 1927 Am. S. S. Union

1703   Nothing is truly fine but what is fit for you; and that just so much as is proper for your circumstances of their several kinds.

Children and fools want everything because they lack wit to distinguish.

Remember that virtue is the greatest ornament, and good sense the best equipage.

> From Savile, . . . Advice to a Daughter, House . . .

1704   It's knowing what to do with things that counts.

> Poetry of Robert Frost (Lathem, ed.),
> At Woodward's Gardens, 1969 294 Holt

1705   The more a man possesses over and above what he uses, the more careworn he becomes.

> Bernard Shaw,
> Man and Superman, Maxims 1903 237

1706   It is a man's duty to provide moderately for his family, but anything beyond this may be a detriment to his descendants.

> W. J. Mayo,
> Proc. Mayo Clinic Aug. 31 1938 13:553–554

1707   It is better that great souls should dwell in small houses than for mere slaves of fortune to lurk in great houses.

> Epictetus,
> Discourses . . . (Long, tr.), n.d. 430

1708   Merely because a man regards wealth and power as fleeting as a cloud, it is not necessary for him to be a recluse living in a cliff or grotto.

From Hung, Chinese Garden . . .
(Chao, tr.) 1959 56 Peter Pauper

1709   When the well's dry we know the value of water.

Proverb

1710   For every talent that poverty has stimulated it has blighted a hundred. An abundant society need not be without challenge.   From John W. Gardner,
Excellence 1961 99 Harper

1711   The happiness of a community depends vastly more on the distribution than on the amount of its wealth.

W. E. Channing

1712   Men are disposed to live honestly, if the means of doing so are open to them.   Jefferson

1713   The real "haves" are they who can acquire freedom, self-confidence, and even riches without depriving others of them.   Eric Hoffer,
Passionate State of Mind 1955 73 Harper

1714   Do not be arrogant in prosperity; if you fall into poverty, do not humble yourself.

Cleobulus, Diogenes Laertius:
Lives . . . (Hicks, tr.) 1925 95 Putnam

1715   Wealth is not material for vainglory but opportunity for achievement. Poverty it is no disgrace to acknowledge, but it is a degradation to make no effort to overcome poverty.

From Pericles

1716   Riches adorn the dwelling; virtue adorns the person.

Seven Hundred Chinese Proverbs
(Hart, tr.) 1937 36 Stanford Univ. Press

1717   The question of bread for myself is a material question; but the question of bread for my neighbors, for everybody, is a spiritual and religious question.

Nikolai Berdyaev

1718   By *value* we mean not just the market price but the worth, the goodness, of a thing, process, quality, relation, to someone; as a rubber ball has value for a child, a painting for a connoisseur, a quiet mind for an anxious person, and health for everyone. We also apply the term value to something that has value; for example, we call health a value.

Values may be instrumental, intrinsic, or both.

Instrumental values are means to other values. Thus health is a value which is instrumental in part, in that health is a means to the values of earning a living, climbing mountains, and getting to an art exhibit.

Intrinsic values are good in themselves. Health, recreation, sociability, esthetic enjoyment, are intrinsic values, except insofar as they are used as means to other values.

A special kind of instrumental value is economic value expressed in market price. Strictly speaking, such economic values are purely instrumental, and are the only values that are purely instrumental.

After Everett,
Moral Values 1918 passim Holt

1719   Neither public nor private ownership is a guarantee of unselfishness.

From **D. K. Price**,
Science 1962 136:1105

1720   In the last analysis, the earth is for the life of all its people. The public good must come first.

After **G. Pinchot**,
Breaking New Ground 1947 322–326 Harcourt

1721   It is the business of society to bring about such discrimination and use of property as will result in the greatest total well-being. There is no natural right to property.

Arthur E. Morgan,
Observations 1970 67 Antioch Press

1722   The more one uses for the benefit of others, the more he possesses.

Mencius

1723   We can "possess" only what we can make part of us— the color of the emerald, for instance, but not the actual stone.

Georges Duhamel,
Possession du Monde 1919 . . . 1919 Mercure de France

1724   Not he who has but he who gives much is rich.

From Erich Fromm

1725   **Mark Antony**, when at an ebb of fortune, cried out that he had lost all except what he had given away.

From Rule of Life 1800 81

1726   Not what I have but what I do is my kingdom.

Carlyle, Sartor Resartus

1727   The wealthy man is the man who *is* much, not the one who *has* much.   Karl Marx, in Fromm,
Sane Society 1955 254 Rinehart; Routledge

1728   Ill fares the land, to hastening ills a prey,
Where wealth accumulates, and men decay.
Oliver Goldsmith, Deserted Village

ENVY AND JEALOUSY

1729   Envy flourishes between those who think of themselves as competing equals.   After Aristotle

1730   Many who are distrustful of themselves are envious of others; as many weak and cowardly persons are most resentful.
Some public favorites are impatient of any competition. Perhaps this may be accounted for by such intoxicating applause that they become jealous of popularity; or from a want of other resources so that they cannot rest on themselves without constant incense to their vanity.
Envy has, among other ingredients, some love of justice. We are more angry at undeserved than at deserved good fortune.
From Hazlitt,
Characteristics XXVII XXVIII XIX

1731   The envious are devoured by their disposition as iron by rust.   Antisthenes, Diogenes Laertius

1732   There are envious people so overwhelmed by your good fortune that they almost inspire you to pity them.
From Edmond et Jules de Goncourt

1733   The hate which we all bear with the most Christian patience is the hate from those who envy us.

C. C. Colton

1734   Envy can feed pride, anger, dejection, avarice, gluttony, lust, malice, and hypocrisy.

From W. F. May,
Christianity & Crisis 1963 22:241–242

1735   Jealousy may be even more dangerous than anger, because its workings are more subtle, and it is apt to recur oftener, and to last longer, until in the end it taints the whole life and thought.   I. W. Hart

1736   In jealousy there is more self-love than love.

La Rochefoucauld

1737   . . . Trifles light as air
Are to the jealous confirmations strong
As proofs of holy writ.

Shakespeare, Othello III iii 324–325

1738   Some people try to be tall by cutting off the heads of others.   Sri Yukteswar, in Paramhansa Yogananda, Autobiography . . . 1946 139 Philos. Lib.

CALUMNY

1739   Be thou chaste as ice, as pure as snow, thou shalt not escape calumny.   Shakespeare, Hamlet III i 142–143

1740   If they fear you in your presence, they speak ill of you in your absence.

> Walloon proverb, Champion (ed.), Racial . . .
> 1938 17 Macmillan, © Routledge; Barnes & Noble

1741   At every word a reputation dies.

> Pope, Rape of the Lock III 16

1742   Malicious reports harm him that makes them, and those they are made to, as well as those they are made of.

A good life does not silence calumny, but it disarms it.

> From Rule of Life 1800 30

BLAME, HATRED, RESENTMENT, AND REVENGE

1743   The superior man blames himself; the inferior man blames others.   Confucius

1744   Blame not before you have examined; interrupt not in the midst of speech; answer not before you have heard; understand first and then enlighten.

1745   Blaming is to be avoided. For people who never blame anyone, especially themselves, it is virtually impossible to become seriously upset.

This view does not mean that there should be no objective appraisal of wrongdoing, or that no one should be objectively penalized for his errors or wrongdoings. It does mean that no one should be punished blamefully. What one needs is to learn to do better.

> From Albert Ellis,
> Reason and Emotion in Psychotherapy
> 1962 138–146 Lyle Stuart

1746　　How should society treat the criminal?

Spinoza, Nietzsche, and many other students of human nature have held that society had best not blame and harm the criminal but should understand him individually and, if possible, bring him round to live as a self-directing and law-abiding citizen.

The more we understand the various criminals and learn how best they can develop into citizenhood, the more we can understand and overcome the causes of crime.

1747　　A man who lives, not by what he loves but what he hates, is a sick man.

A. MacLeish

1748　　We often hate that which we cannot be. We put up defenses against something we crave and cannot have.

Eric Hoffer,
Passionate State of Mind 1955 119 Harper

1749　　Hatred is like fire—it makes even light rubbish deadly.

George Eliot, Janet's Repentance

1750　　Hating people is like burning down your own house to get rid of a rat.　　　　H. E. Fosdick, Wages of Hate

1751　　Hatred places us beneath those we hate.

After La Rochefoucauld

1752　　Love thyself last: cherish those hearts that hate
　　　　thee;
　　　　Corruption wins not more than honesty.

Shakespeare, King Henry VIII III ii 444–445

1753   I was angry with my friend;
I told my wrath, my wrath did end.
I was angry with my foe;
I told it not, my wrath did grow.

William Blake, Poison Tree

1754   Hatred is increased by return of hatred, but may be destroyed by love.   Spinoza

1755   Resentment may spring more from a sense of weakness than from a sense of injustice.

After Eric Hoffer,
Passionate State of Mind 1955 74 Harper

1756   Life is too short to be spent in nursing animosity or registering wrong.   From Charlotte Brontë

1757   Let not the sun go down upon your wrath.

Ephesians IV 26

1758   Sulky men, having no outlet for their temper, keep the weight on their minds; because, as it does not show itself, no one attempts to reason it away, and digesting anger within oneself takes time. Such men are nuisances to themselves and to their friends.   From Aristotle,
Nicomachean Ethics (Chase, tr.) IV v

1759   He's truly valiant that can wisely suffer
The worst that man can breathe, and make his
     wrongs
His outsides, to wear them like his raiment,
     carelessly,

And ne'er prefer his injuries to his heart,
To bring it into danger.

                    Shakespeare, Timon of Athens III v 31–35

1760   Write injuries in dust, benefits in marble.

                                        Proverb

1761   Revenge is a kind of wild justice; which the more
man's nature runs to, the more ought law to weed it out.

                              Francis Bacon, Of Revenge

1762   The hand of Vengeance found the Bed
            To which the Purple Tyrant fled;
            The iron hand crush'd the Tyrant's head
            And became a Tyrant in his stead.

                        William Blake, Poems 1800–3

1763   Be not provoked by injuries to commit them.

                                    William Penn

1764   Revenge never repairs an injury.
  He that waits for an opportunity for revenge watches to do
himself a mischief.   From Rule of Life 1800 20 19

1765   Every chronically vindictive man or woman is partly
insane.   After David Lloyd George, in Ormont (ed.),
                    What Famous Men . . . 1935 State Law Rep. Co.

1766   When Mark Antony challenged Augustus, Augustus
sent back this answer: "If you are weary of life, Antony, there
are other ways of dispatch besides fighting me; and for my part,
I shall not trouble myself to be your executioner."

                            From Rule of Life 1800 19

1767   By taking revenge a man is but even with his enemy; but in passing it over he is superior.   Francis Bacon

1768   Retribution often means that we eventually do to ourselves what we have done unto others.

Eric Hoffer, Harper's Nov. 1966 91

1769   "Diogenes, how should one be revenged of his enemy?" "By being a virtuous and an honest man."

From Rule of Life 1800 30

DISPUTES, QUARRELS, AND FIGHTS

1770   Controversies, for the most part, leave truth in the middle and are factions at both ends.

Rule of Life 1800 66

1772   It is well for every man to experience opposition.
From J. G. Holland, Gold-Foil ... 1881 207

1773   Have you not learned great lessons from those who reject you, and brace themselves against you, or who treat you with contempt, or dispute the passage with you?

From Walt Whitman, Stronger Lessons

1774   He that hurts another hurts himself.
Marcus Aurelius, Meditations IX 4

1775   Insult can issue only from a debased mind and can injure only a weak mind.   C. Gessler,
Reasonable Life 1950 197 Day

1776   If you return an ass's kicks, most of the pain is yours.
                    Sardinian proverb, Champion (ed.), Racial . . .
            1938 213 Macmillan, © Routledge; Barnes & Noble

1777   "But what good came of it at last?"
            Quoth little Peterkin.
            "Why, that I cannot tell," said he,
            "But 'twas a famous victory."
                            Robert Southey, Battle of Blenheim

1778   Misunderstandings divide mankind more deeply than
disagreements.   Gustave Vapereau

1779   Abraham Myerson, a professor of psychiatry, observed
that many a quarrel between partners, between roommates,
between husband and wife, between associates, comes from
"the childishness of human beings." By this he meant the immature attitudes (such as expecting to be favored), manners
(interrupting instead of discussing), and stratagems ("illness"
for sympathy).

In some cases, this or that immaturity is so crippling as to
need professional help to learn, to grow up, to be normally
competent in the area of difficulty.

Adolf Meyer, often called "The Father of American Psychiatry," saw maturity as developed and developing ability to
meet situations, to maintain mental hygiene and ethics, and to
live reasonably successfully.

Such growing up may be demanding, but it is also rewarding to more than the person who achieves it.

                            Authors cited in
                        W. S. Taylor, Dynamic . . . 1954

1780   People generally quarrel because they cannot discuss.
From Chesterton

1781   When we are dissatisfied with ourselves, we are disposed to quarrel with others.
From Hazlitt, Characteristics CLXIII

1782   None more impatiently suffer injuries than those who are most forward in doing them.   Rule of Life 1800 18

1783   He who threatens is always afraid.
French proverb

1784   Thrice is he armed that hath his quarrel just.
Shakespeare, Henry VI II III ii 233

1785   Who overcomes by force has overcome but half his foe.
From Milton, Paradise Lost I 648–649

1786   It behooves a prudent person to make trial of everything before arms.   Terence, Eunuchus IV vii 19 (789)

1787   There is such a thing as a man being too proud to fight.
Woodrow Wilson, speech 1915

1788   A powerful member of the Convention during the French Revolution tried to wither an opponent of vulgar origin by asking him, "Is it true that the member from Arcis is a veterinary?" The man replied sweetly, "Yes, monsieur. Are you ill?"   From Edgar Johnson (ed.),
Treasury of Satire 1945 9–10 Simon & Schuster

1789   A soft answer turneth away wrath.   Proverbs XV 1

1790   If thine enemy hunger, feed him; if he thirst, give him drink: for in so doing thou shalt heap coals of fire on his head [which consume his ire].   Romans XII 20

1791   If one treat me unreasonably, I will say: "I must have been wanting in kindness or propriety"; then I will mend my ways. If the other continues perverse, I must have self-respect enough to say, "I must have failed to do my best." If all is vain, I say, "Why vex myself about a beast?"
                          From Mencius, n.d. 77 Peter Pauper

1792   Minds are conquered not by force but by love and high-mindedness.   Spinoza, Ethics IV App. xi

1793   [Of all who champion good causes,] the best soldiers are not warlike; the best fighters do not lose their temper; the greatest conquerors are those who overcome their enemies without strife.   Mencius, n.d. 93 Peter Pauper

1794   Most heroic is he who turns an enemy into a friend.
                          The Talmud

SHAME AND GUILT

1795   Shame may restrain.   Seneca

1796   So full of artless jealousy is guilt,
               It spills itself in fearing to be spilt.
                          Shakespeare, Hamlet IV v 19–20

1797   Only the dreamer venoms all his days,
          Bearing more woe than all his sins deserve.
                          Keats, Revision of Hyperion

1798   [Superficially,]
        There is a luxury in self-dispraise;
        And inward self-disparagement affords
        To meditative spleen a grateful feast.
                        Wordsworth, Excursion IV 477–479

1799   An intense feeling of guilt is often indistinguishable
from blind faith; it fosters the same ruthlessness and persistence.   Eric Hoffer,
                        Passionate State of Mind 1955 78 Harper

1800   Every church or government is involved in the flux
and relativity of human existence, and is subject to error and
sin.   From R. Niebuhr

1801   The most frightful idea that has ever corroded human
nature—the idea of eternal punishment.   Vauvenargues

1802   The doctrine of Original Sin often suggests a morbid
sense of humiliation.   From Herbert J. Muller,
                        Harper's Mag. Feb. 1964 85

1803   To erase the burden of Original Sin is to progress.
                Baudelaire, Oeuvres Posthumes 1952 2:109 Paris

1804   Why should it be thought any scandal to be a fool,
since the being so is one part of our nature?
                                    From Erasmus,
                In Praise of Folly 1910 112 Peter Eckler

REGRET AND REMORSE

1805   The mill cannot grind with the water that is past.
Proverbial

1806   . . . What's gone and what's past help
Should be past grief.
Shakespeare, Winter's Tale III ii 223–224

1807   The fountain in which sins are indeed to be washed away is that of love, not of agony.   Ruskin

1808   There is precious instruction to be got in finding we were wrong.
Carlyle, On the Choice of Books 1882

1809   Experience is not what happens to a man. It is what a man does with what happens to him.   Aldous Huxley

CONFESSION AND APOLOGY

1810   An occasional person repeats a crime to convince himself and others that it is not an enormity.
From Eric Hoffer,
Passionate State of Mind 1955 74 Harper

1811   . . . He that does one fault at first,
And lies to hide it, makes it two.
Isaac Watts, Song XV

1812   . . . Oftentimes excusing of a fault
Doth make the fault the worse by the excuse.
Shakespeare, King John IV ii 30–31

1813   What is concealed weighs heavily;
What is brought out into the open weighs
     lightly.

Buddhism

1814   One of the hardest things to do is to admit that you are wrong; and nothing is more helpful in resolving a situation than its frank admission.   From Disraeli

1815   A wrong confessed is half redressed.   Proverb

1816   A man should never be ashamed to own he has been wrong, which is but saying in other words that he is wiser today than he was yesterday.   Unknown

1817   An error gracefully acknowledged is a victory won.

W. Gascoigne

1818   The men who can be charged with the fewest failings are generally most ready to admit them.

From Samuel Johnson, Rambler XXXI

1819   A man who has made a mistake and does not correct it makes another mistake.   Confucius

REPENTANCE

1820   If you have done wrong, be not ashamed to make amends.   Confucius

1821   To do it no more is the truest repentance.

Martin Luther

FORGIVENESS

1822   The most wicked of men is he who overlooks no sin,
forgives no fault, and accepts no apology.

> From Wortabet (tr.), Arabian Wisdom 1910 18

1823   Pliny esteemed him the best man that forgave others
as if he were every day faulty himself; and who abstained from
faults as if he had pardoned nobody.

> From Rule of Life 1800 83

1824   The pleasure of forgiving is sweeter than the pleasure
of revenge.

> Wortabet (tr.), Arabian Wisdom 1910 17

1825   Forgiveness is the might of the mighty. Forgiveness
and gentleness are the qualities of the self-possessed. They represent eternal virtue.   From the Mahabharata

1826   Good sense makes a man slow to anger, and it is his
glory to overlook an offense.

> Proverbs XIX 11, Rev. Stan. Ver. 1952 Nelson

1827   Into the great account, which summeth a mor-
            tal's destiny,
        Add the forces from without, dragging him this
            way and that,
        And the secret qualities within, grafted on the
            soul from the womb,
        And the might of other men's example, among
            whom his lot is cast,

And the influence of want, or wealth, of kind-
    ness, or harsh ill-usage,
Of ignorance he cannot help, and knowledge
    found for him by others,
And first impressions, hard to be effaced, and
    leadings to right or to wrong,
And inheritance of likeness from a father, and
    natural human frailty,
And the habit of health or disease, and preju-
    dices poured into his mind,
And the myriad little matters none but Omnis-
    cience can know,
And accidents that steer the thoughts, where
    none but
Ubiquity can trace them.
. . . Count not a man more evil because he is
    more unfortunate.

From M. F. Tupper,
Proverbial Philosophy 1849 71 63

1829   To understand is to forgive.

Mme. de Staël, Corinne

1830   . . . Kneel not to me:
The power that I have on you, is to spare you;
The malice towards you, to forgive you: live,
And deal with others better.

Shakespeare, Cymbeline V v 418

1831   A forgiveness ought to be like a cancelled note, torn
in two and burned up, so that it can never be shown against
the man.   H. W. Beecher

PREJUDICE AND INTOLERANCE

1832   They condemn what they do not understand.

Cicero

1833   Prejudice is the child of ignorance.

Hazlitt, Sketches and Essays, On Prejudice

1834   Prejudice is strong when judgment is weak.

From K. O'Hara, Midas I iv

1835   We may not mind having our hair ruffled, but we will
not tolerate any familiarity with the toupee which hides our
baldness.   From Eric Hoffer,

Passionate State of Mind 1955 41 Harper

1836   We are never more discontented with others than
when we are discontented with ourselves. The heart quarrels
with what is outside it to deafen the clamor within.

From Amiel, Journal 1857

1837   Censoriousness is infectious.

From Richard Baxter,
Works 6 407 Christian Politics

1838   Prejudice is never easy unless it can pass itself off for
reason.   Hazlitt, Sketches and Essays 1839 90

1839   The elderly black woman told me about the whites
whose ability to look down upon her did not elevate their own

material or spiritual welfare. Oppressors, they knew little about the reasons for their own impoverishment.

From R. Coles,
Children of Crisis 1967 336 Atlantic-Little

1840   It is never too late to give up prejudices.

From Thoreau, Walden

1841   Intolerance and injustice can be alleviated by merciful deeds, but they can only be extirpated by the scientific spirit.

From G. Sarton,
in Anshen (ed.), Moral . . . 1952 445 Harper

TOLERANCE

1842   Each to his taste, as the woman said when she kissed her cow.   Rabelais, Pantagruel V XXIX

1843   Live and let live.   Proverbial

1844   Almost all men have learned the lesson of toleration with respect to *past* heresies and divisions.

John Dewey, Characters . . . 1929 567 Holt

1845   The first thing to learn in intercourse with others is noninterference with their own peculiar ways of being happy, provided those ways do not interfere by violence with ours. No one has insight into all the ideals. The pretension to dogmatize about them is the root of countless human injustices and cruelties.

From William James, Talks . . . 1900 265–266

1846   Virtuous and vicious every man must be,—
         Few in the extreme, but all in the degree.

                              Pope, Essay on Man, Virtue II 231

1847   The good nature of a heathen is more godlike than the
false zeal of a [so-called] Christian. Because I *may* be mistaken,
I *must* not be dogmatic and imperious; I *will* not break the
certain laws of charity.   From B. Whichcote,
                              in Gollancz (ed.), Man and God
                                            1951 176 Houghton

1848   How can I answer which is best
                 Of all the fires that burn?
                 I have been too often host or guest
                 At every fire in turn.

                 How can I turn from any fire,
                 On any man's hearthstone?
                 I know the wonder and desire
                 That went to build my own!

                                            Kipling

1849   Variety is spiritual richness; and variety and, indeed,
opposition are necessary for the highest achievements of individuals and of civilizations. We rightly admire the man of
manysided genius—Aristotle, da Vinci, Michelangelo, Goethe;
yet one-sidedness can attain great heights and intensities.

     Our tolerance must be active, springing from the knowledge
that any one human mind is too small to grasp more than a
little truth, to live more than a little reality. Out of diversity
alone comes advance.

                                            From Julian Huxley,
                    Religion Without Revelation 1957 175–176 Harper

1850   Tolerance is decency.   From Montaigne

1851   Time makes us generous, enlarges our minds each year, like the concentric circles in the trunk of a tree. Life also pacifies us as do the bearings of death; reconciles us with those who do not think and feel as we do. When you become indignant at some antique, absurd prejudice, remember that it has lived, so to speak, the life of humanity; one might well find a certain element of fraternity in every human thought.

From Guyau, Non-Religion ... 1897 19

1852   The idea that every human act results from causes keeps us from taking ourselves or others too seriously; it makes rather for a sense of humor.

From Einstein, Living Philosophies
1931 3–4 Simon & Schuster

1853   Knowledge about the limits of knowledge paves the way to tolerance ...
Those who know much about life are lenient judges.

H. Margolius,
Thoughts ... 1962 33 3 Lib. of Humane Lit.

1854   Pass not judgment upon your neighbor until you have put yourself in his place.

Hillel, Tract Aboth II Mishna E

1855   Would we hold liberty, we must have charity—charity to others, charity to ourselves.

Learned Hand, Dilliard (ed.),
Spirit of Liberty 1952 83 Knopf,
© Univ. Pa. Law Rev. 1930 79:1

1856   To agree to disagree is still a form of agreement and may provide a positive ground for community.

From H. W. Schneider,
Three Dimensions . . . 1956 138 Ind. Univ. Press

RESPECT FOR ONESELF AND OTHERS

1857   Excessive nationalist pride, like other variants of pride, can derive from lack of individual self-respect. The unattainability of individual self-respect is not the least factor behind the chauvinism of the populace in totalitarian regimes.

From Eric Hoffer,
Passionate State of Mind 1955 26 Harper

1858   Each human ability has its character. The most splendid talent cannot duplicate the effect of the homeliest skill.

From La Rochefoucauld

1859   There is a real kinship between great spirits and average men, and this . . . increases the dignity and worth of human life.   Radhakrishnan, East and West . . .
1933 121 G. Allen; Barnes & Noble

1860   A man is like a bit of Labrador spar, which has no lustre until you turn it to a particular angle; then it shows deep and beautiful colors.   From Emerson, Experience

1861   Every one should be respected but no one idolized.

From Einstein,
Living Philosophies 1931 5 Simon & Schuster

1862   One man is accommodating but not obsequious; another is obsequious but not accommodating.

From Confucius,
in Lionel Giles, Sayings . . . 1907 65

1863   Many who crouch to those above them are insolent to those below them. Both courses show meanness of spirit and want of conscious dignity.

From Hazlitt, Characteristics CXII

1864   Self-love . . . is not so vile a sin
As self-neglecting.

Shakespeare, Henry V II iv 74–75

1865   Of all our infirmities, the most savage is to despise our
being.   Montaigne, To Live Well

1866   A mentally healthy person is confident in his ability to comprehend and respond appropriately to other people and to engender appropriate responses in them. He knows that an interpersonal failure, though it may represent a limitation in himself, does not prove bankruptcy nor threaten disintegration of the self. He enjoys a comfortable sense of self in activities based upon realistic interpersonal expectations.

From W. Bonime,
Clinical Use of Dreams 1962 253 Basic Books

1867   The emotions of over-esteem and disparagement are always bad, whether applied to others or to the self. Extreme pride or dejection indicates extreme ignorance of self. The

proud and the dejected specially fall a prey to the emotions.
Worthy self-approval, however, may arise from reason.

Self-understanding makes for self-respect.

From Spinoza, Ethics IV xlviii-lv

1868   The man who gains his self-respect gains also the respect of those around him.   After A. P. de Seversky

1869   He who respects himself can respect others.

After Wortabet (tr.), Arabian Wisdom 1910 21

1870   Respect begets respect; suspicion begets suspicion;
hate begets hate. "The only way to have a friend is to be one."

From H. H. Lehman, Murrow (ed.),
This I Believe 1952 99 Simon & Schuster

1871   Never esteem anything as advantageous to you that
makes you break your word or lose your self-respect.

Marcus Aurelius, Meditations III 7

1872   Though all the governors in the world bid us to commit treason against man, and set the example, let us never
submit.   Theodore Parker

1873   How much respect has a noble person for his
          enemies!
          And such respect is already a bridge to love.

Nietzsche, Toward a Genealogy of Morals X

1874   It is surprising how much hardship and humiliation a
man will endure without bitterness when he has not the least

doubt about his worth or when he is so integrated with others that he is not aware of a separate self.

Eric Hoffer,
Passionate State of Mind 1955 1 Harper

1875   No soul is desolate as long as there is a human being for whom it can feel trust and reverence.

George Eliot, Romola

1876   It is difficult to respect someone when that is what he wishes.   Vauvenargues, Reflection 67

1877   Socrates has done human nature a great kindness in showing how much it can do of itself.

From Montaigne, Socrates

1878   Hardly compatible with happiness is the lessened respect which comes upon relinquishing useful work.

From A. Trollope, Rachel Ray

1879   Treat your inferior as you would be treated by your superior.   From Seneca, Ad Lucilium . . .
(Gummere, tr.) 1918 1:307 Putnam

1880   It is the duty of every person to respect himself as a vessel of truth to be conserved and used in any constructive way. No one should try to put the vessel of himself apart from the life he shares; and he should never be envious or discouraged because other vessels may seem larger, brighter, or stronger than his, for even a trickle of truth is precious.

From Henry White Taylor, letter 1943

PATIENCE WITH OTHERS

1881   Impatience relieves no ill; it is only an added pain.
              From Fénelon, Spiritual Letters to Men LXXXI

1882   Out of patience comes forth peace, the happiness of
the world. But let him that has no patience retire within himself, though even there he will have to put up with himself.
                          Balthasar Gracian (Jacobs, tr.) Maxim 159

1883   Men sin without intending it; and to be patient is a
part of justice.
                          From Marcus Aurelius, Meditations IV 3

1884   Let it be. Let it pass.   Traditional

1885   There is as much wisdom in bearing with other people's defects as in being sensible of their good qualities; and we
should make the follies of others rather a warning and instruction to ourselves than a subject of mirth and mockery or
undue concern.   After La Rochefoucauld

1886   Sometimes the remedy for an evil consists in disregard-
ing it; and at those times we commonly forget this remedy.
                          From Rule of Life 1800 128

1887   Patience may be a bitter plant, but it has sweet fruit.
                                                          Proverbial

1888   Where patience dwells what need of other
              shield?
        Why prate of foeman when to wrath we yield?

More warmth our kindred give than fires; and
   friends
Far more than soothing herbs our wounds have
   healed.

Paul Elmer More,
Century . . . 1898 XXXVII 59

1889   Men and nations have learned much when they practice patience . . .
   Faith, Love, and Hope together created patience.

From Goethe

1890   If you would bear your neighbor's faults, cast your eyes
upon your own.   Miguel de Molinos

1891   Consider the thousand things that made him all he is.

From M. F. Tupper,
Proverbial Philosophy 1849 346

1892   No soul wilfully misses truth nor justice nor wisdom
nor charity nor any other excellence. One must remember this
always, for it makes one gentler with everyone.

From Marcus Aurelius, Meditations VII 63

MAGNANIMITY

1893   Magnanimity is a rare virtue. There are more persons
of virtue than those who willingly acknowledge virtue in
others. Many persons have so little confidence in themselves
that they are crushed by the shadow of opposition, or stopped
by a whisper of rivalship.

From Hazlitt, Characteristics I V

1894   The anger of the magnanimous lasts only for a moment, that of the middling for an hour or two, of the mean for a day and night, and of the meanest for life.

The magnanimous, when wealthy, are not intoxicated; when young, they are not fickle; and when powerful, not irresponsible.

The magnanimous person regards all people as his own family.

The favors of the magnanimous one are wholly selfless.

> From Sharma and Raghavacharya (trs.),
> Gems from Sanskrit . . . 1959 15 33 9 13 Osmania

1896   The wise man anticipates neither deceit nor bad faith in others, yet detects them promptly when they appear.

> From Confucius

1897   A virtuous man ought to be like the sandal-tree, which perfumes the axe that destroys it.

> Niti Sastras, in Brian Brown (ed.),
> Wisdom of the Hindus 1921 210 Brentano

1898   With malice toward none, with charity for all, with firmness in the right, as God gives us to see the right.

> Lincoln, Address March 4 1865

1899   Magnanimity is not easily put out.

> Balthasar Gracian (Jacobs, tr.) Maxim 52

1900   Dignity is revered only when it is accompanied with magnanimity; enlightenment is respected only when it is accompanied with magnanimity.

> The Penal Code of Lü, in Y.-P. Mei (tr.),
> Ethical . . . 1929 45–46 Probsthain

SYMPATHY

1901   Does the sparrow know how the stork feels?

Goethe

1902   ... Two may journey hand in hand,
         Yet utterly alone,
         And heart may lie on throbbing heart
         As far as pole and pole apart.

J. S. Holme,
I Have Been a Pilgrim 1935 17 Henry Harrison

1903   A sound man's heart is not shut within itself
         But is open to other people's hearts.
         I feel the heart-beats of others
         Above my own
         If I am enough of a father,
         Enough of a son.

Witter Bynner,
Way of Life according to Laotzu 1944 56 Day

1904   Surely, surely the only true knowledge of our fellow-
man is that which enables us to feel with him—which gives us
a fine ear for the heart-pulses that are beating under the mere
clothes of circumstance and opinion.

George Eliot, Janet's Repentance

1905   One pain is lessened by another's anguish.

Shakespeare, Romeo and Juliet I ii 48

1906   Sorrow tends to be diminished by the knowledge that
another sorrows with us.

From A. F. Shand, Foundations ... 1914 341

1907   Shared joy is doubled joy.

> Danish proverb

1908   As the spring sun revives plants, a friendly heart warms people.

1909   Our sympathy is limited by our sensibility.

> From Hazlitt, Characteristics CCCCX

1910   The wretched have no compassion.

> Samuel Johnson,
> in G. B. Hill (ed.), Letters . . . 1892 2:215

1911   He jests at scars that never felt a wound.

> Shakespeare, Romeo and Juliet II ii 1

1912   He that is sated believes not the hungry.

> Yiddish proverb

1913   The man who has come through sorrow and trouble is apt to be more of a man than he who has had none.

> From Pestalozzi,
> Education . . . 1953 51 Philos. Lib.

1914   With higher development comes sympathy.

> From Marcus Aurelius, Meditations IX 9

1915   If we could read the secret history of our enemies we should find in each man's life sorrow and suffering enough to disarm all hostility.   Longfellow

KINDNESS, MERCY

1916   It is more blessed to give than to receive.   Acts XX 35

1917   In giving we receive.   From Francis of Assisi, Prayer

1918   Better do kindness near home than to go far to burn
incense.   Chinese proverb

1919   A righteous man regardeth the life of his beast.
                                             Proverbs XII 10

1920   Many people come to praise the cherry trees in bloom,
but they are truly kind who visit them after the blossoms are
fallen.   Japanese poem

1921   [Yet] not always actions show the man: we find
        Who does a kindness is not therefore kind.
                                 Pope, Moral Essays I 109–110

1922   The bane of a generous action is to mention it . . .
   When you do a kindness hide it, and when a kindness is done
to you proclaim it . . .
   Inopportune kindness is injustice.
                    Wortabet (tr.), Arabian Wisdom 1910 25 26 23

1923   Rich gifts wax poor when givers prove unkind.
                                 Shakespeare, Hamlet III i 101

1924   Charity knows neither race nor creed.   Gittin

1925   The quality of mercy is not strained,
        It droppeth as the gentle rain from heaven

Upon the place beneath. It is twice blest;
It blesseth him that gives and him that takes.
                    Shakespeare, Merchant of Venice IV i 184–187

1926   A kindly man benefits himself; a cruel man hurts himself.   Proverbs XI xvii

1927   Gentleness is one of the noblest traits in a man's character.
                    Wortabet (tr.), Arabian Wisdom 1910 18

1928   Sweet mercy is nobility's true badge.
                    Shakespeare, Titus Andronicus I i 119

1929   To share a heavy burden to ease another is noble; to do it cheerfully is sublime.
                    Lavater, Aphorism 554 (1787 ed.)

1930   Beauty, reason, and even genius are outshone by kindness of the heart.   From Schopenhauer

1931   Potent among men is a gift timely bestowed.
                    M. F. Tupper, Proverbial Philosophy 1849 136

1932   Let a benefit be ever so considerable, the noblest part is the manner of conferring it.   Rule of Life 1800 81

1933   The kindly word that falls today may bear its fruit tomorrow.   Gandhi

1934   Because you bestowed, you seem to yourself greater than he upon whom it was bestowed. Wish him to be your equal.   Augustine

1935   Let your kindness be your final self-conquest.
                              Nietzsche, in Walter Kaufmann,
                              From Shakespeare to Existentialism
                              1960 5 Doubleday

1936   Kindness can become its own motive.
                                        Eric Hoffer,
                        Passionate State of Mind 1955 77 Harper

1937   Kindness begets kindness.   Sophocles, Ajax

1938   Kindnesses, like grain, increase by sowing.   Proverb

1939   Do unto others as you would have them do unto you.
                        From Matthew VII 12, Luke VI 31

1940   Fear is stronger than death, and love, than fear, and
kindness is the greatest endearment of love.
                              From Jeremy Taylor, in Gest (ed.),
                              House . . . 1954 76 Univ. Pa. Press

1941   Beauty lives with kindness.
                   Shakespeare, Two Gentlemen of Verona IV ii 46

LOVE, TENDER AND BENEVOLENT

1942   Though I speak with the tongues of men and of angels,
and have not love, I am become as sounding brass or a tinkling
cymbal.
    Love is not boastful, or conceited, or rude; love is patient,
kind, and without envy.   From I Corinthians XIII 1 4

1943   Love is active, sincere, courageous, patient, faithful, prudent, and manly.

From Thomas à Kempis, Imitation of Christ III v

1944   I am in love with this green earth; the face of town and country, the ineffable rural solitudes, and the sweet security of streets.   From Charles Lamb, Essays of Elia

1945   The tenderness children need . . .
            . . . is in the way mothers look at tired children;
            . . . in the half-voice fathers use
            Feeling some surprise and gladness
            To see their children there at all.

Hilda Conkling,
Shoes of the Wind 1922 161 Frederick A. Stokes

1946   Teach us delight in simple things,
                And mirth that has no bitter springs;
                Forgiveness free of evil done,
                And love to all men 'neath the sun.

Kipling

1947   When love is a disease, it can be cured; when it is a pleasure, it can be refined; when it is an inspiration, its full powers can be released.

Albert Guérard,
Fossils . . . 1957 76 Stanford Univ. Press

1948   The emotions of love and fear are contraries: at any single moment, given love, it shuts out fear; or fear, love.

After Sifre

1949   We do not trust a brain without a heart, and we cannot respect a heart without a brain.   Mark Van Doren,
Liberal Education 1959 162 Beacon

1950   To love and win is the best thing; to love and lose the next best.   Thackeray

1951   Damnation is the sorrow that one cannot love.
Dostoevsky

1952   A present is cheap, but love is dear.   Russian proverb

1953   Where love is there riches be.
Keep us all from poverty.
Medieval prayer

1954   Who loves, gives.

1955   Happiness finds no entrance when love is gone.
Thomas Paine

1956   Love is its own enjoyment.
From G. C. Anderson,
Man's Right . . . 1959 181 Morrow

1957   Love makes those young whom age doth chill,
And whom he finds young keeps young still.
William Cartwright, To Chloe

1958   Love is a true renovator.   Unknown

1959   To love abundantly is to live abundantly.

Mary E. Taylor Bishop, MS 1888

1960   Hatred ceases not by hatred but by love.

From The Dhammapada I

1961   He that strives to conquer hatred with love (as through kindly enlightenment, or resolving differences toward friendliness) fights his battle in joy and confidence. Those whom he vanquishes yield gladly, not through failure but through increase of strength.

From Spinoza, Ethics IV xlvi Note and passim

1962   So long as we love, we serve. So long as we are loved by others I would almost say we are indispensable; and no man is useless while he has a friend.   R. L. Stevenson

1963   Love will accomplish that by imperceptible methods which force could never achieve.

From Emerson, Man the Reformer

1964   Love is not a higher power which descends upon man nor a duty which is imposed upon him; it is his own power by which he participates in the world.

From Erich Fromm,
Man for Himself 1947 14 Rinehart; Routledge

1965   We are born with the need to be loved and to love.

From Ashley Montagu,
Meaning of Love 1953 18 Julian

1966   Tenderness, kindness, and gentleness: these are the seeds from which love is born, and which makes us lovable.

From G. C. Anderson,
Man's Right . . . 1959 181 Morrow

1967   Tenderness grows out of the heart, but it matures in the mind, which ennobles its course.

Max Roden,
Spiegelungen 1951 19 Johannes-Presse

1968   The love of an object, whatever it is, is child of knowledge of it. The ardor of the love corresponds with the certainty of the knowledge; and that certainty proceeds from the integrating knowledge of all the parts which, reconstructed together, produce the unity of the object which is to be loved.

Leonardo da Vinci,
Notebooks, Polemics—Speculation

1969   Some people feel that one whose motive is love can make no mistake; yet even this precious motive, without which society could scarcely endure, is fallible, and may go far wrong without the guidance and discipline of free, critical inquiry.

From Arthur E. Morgan,
Community . . . 1957 37 Community Service

1970   Love is union with something outside oneself while keeping one's integrity.   From Erich Fromm,
Sane Society 1955 31 Rinehart

1971   The tragic mistake is to assume that any treasure, person or object, must be possessed to be loved.

Ethel Sabin Smith,
Dynamics of Aging 1956 178 Norton

1972   To feed a person without loving him is to treat him like a pig. To love without respecting him is to treat him like a domestic pet.

> Mencius, in Cranmer-Byng and Watts (eds.),
> Book ... (Giles, tr.) 1942 116 Murray

1973   ... Pity melts the mind to love.

> Dryden, Alexander's Feast 96

1974   Seek Love in the Pity of others' Woe,
In the gentle relief of another's care,
In the darkness of night and the winter's snow,
In the naked and outcast, Seek Love there!

> William Blake, Poems 1800–3

1975   Lavish love upon the poor, where it is easy; especially upon the rich, who often need it most; and most of all upon our equals, where it is difficult.   From H. Drummond

1976   Love evokes love: unending increase.

> H. Margolius,
> Thoughts ... 1962 13 Lib. of Humane Lit.

1977   If you love others but are not loved in return examine your own feeling of benevolence.

> Mencius, in Cranmer-Byng and
> Watts (eds.), Book ... (Giles, tr.) 1942 71 Murray

1978   Love is not a thing of enthusiastic emotion. It is a rich, vigorous expression of the whole character.

> Mary E. Taylor Bishop, MS 1888

1979   Love is an art, and like any art requires discipline and cultivation.   Editorial, Life Dec. 24, 1956, © Time

1980   Love means . . . seeing with the other man's eyes, feeling with his heart and understanding with his mind.

Radhakrishnan, East and West . . .

1933 83 G. Allen; Barnes & Noble

1981   Every one who is guided by reason desires for others the good which he seeks for himself.

From Spinoza, Ethics IV lxxiii Note

1982   That which is to be loved long must be loved more with reason than with passion.   From Samuel Johnson

1983   After you have been kind, after Love has stolen forth into the world and done its beautiful work, say nothing about it. Love hides even from itself.

Mary E. Taylor Bishop, MS 1888

1984   In moral life we cannot wait to respond to others till we have experienced their treatment of us. Often the very waiting causes a change in the treatment. The principle of universal love as taught by Motse in China and Jesus in the west is unsurpassed.   From Y.P. Mei, Matse . . .

1934 193–194 Probsthain

GRATITUDE

1985   Blow, blow, thou winter wind!
Thou are not so unkind
As man's ingratitude.

Shakespeare, As You Like It II vii 174

1986   Gratitude is the memory of the heart.

J. B. Massieu

1987   Gratitude takes three forms—a feeling in the heart, an expression in words, and a giving in return.

Wortabet (tr.), Arabian Wisdom 1910 24

1988   Many times a day I realize how much my own outer and inner life is built upon the labors of my fellow-men, both living and dead, and how earnestly I must exert myself in order to give in return as much as I have received.

Einstein, Living Philosophies 1933 Simon & Schuster

1989   No one is so poor or powerless that he cannot return a good deed.   Aesop

1990   Without good-nature and gratitude, men had as well live in a wilderness as in a civil society.

Rule of Life 1800 85

1991   He who receives a good turn should never forget it; he who does one should never remember it.   Charron

1992   He is ungrateful who makes returns of obligations to free himself from owing thanks.   From Joseph Butler

1993   There is a princely manner of giving and accepting.

Lavater

1994   To receive a present handsomely and in a right spirit, even when you have none to give in return, is to give one in return.   Leigh Hunt

1995   Gratitude preserves old friendship and procures new.
Rule of Life 1800 61

1996   Do not forget an old act of kindness because of a re-
cent dispute.   Tut-Tut, in Lin-Yutang (ed.),
Wisdom of China and India 1942 1095
Random House

1997   Cherish life and bounty from the earth,
Ever mindful of mercy and grace among men.
Grace before a meal

FRIENDSHIP

1998   Friendship dances around the world, summoning every
one of us to awaken to the gospel of the happy life.
Epicurus, Strodach (tr.),
Philosophy . . . 1962 206 Northwestern Univ. Press

1999   A friend loveth at all times.   Proverbs XVII 17

2000   You must act in your friend's interest whether it
pleases him or not; the object of love is to serve, not to win.
Woodrow Wilson

2001   A man may be the friend of my spiritual life while he
seems the enemy of my corporeal; but if a man is the enemy of
my spiritual life while he pretends to be the friend of my corporeal, he is a real enemy.
From William Blake,
Letter to Thomas Butts Apr. 25 1803

2002   Friendship is essentially a social virtue, and is not confined to one object.

Justus Lipsius,
Seneca . . . (Gummere, tr.), 1918 1:434 Putnam

2003   There is no greater wilderness than to be without true friends. Without friendship society is but a meeting and acquaintance ceremony.   From Richard Brathwait,
English Gentleman 1630 243

2004   A friend in need is a friend indeed.   Proverb

2005   It is not so much friends' services that we find serviceable as the assurance of their services.

Epicurus, Strodach (tr.),
Philosophy . . . 1962 205 Northwestern Univ. Press

2006   Friendship doubles joys and halves griefs.
From Francis Bacon, Of Friendship

2007   Our want is somebody who can make us do what we can; by whom we can measure ourselves, and who will hold us to good sense and virtue.   From Emerson, Social Aims

2008   It is strange what gross errors and absurdities, damaging to fame and fortune, many (especially of the greater sort) commit for want of a friend to tell them of them.
From Francis Bacon

2009   A friend must be free to advise, and even to upbraid, without feeling embarrassed. Our satisfaction in him and our trust in his steadfast faith give him that power.
Balthasar Gracian (Jacobs, tr.) Maxim 147

2010   A faithful friend is a medicine of life.   Ecclus. VI 16

2011   Hecato wrote: "I have begun to be a friend to myself."
Such a man is a friend to all mankind.

From Seneca,
Ad Lucilium . . . (Gummere, tr.) 1918 1:29 Putnam

2012   That friendship which is begun for an end will hardly
continue to the end.   From Francis Quarles

2013   If men share false and vain things, their friendship
will be false and vain; if that which is good and true, their
friendship will be good and true.

Francis de Sales, Devout Life III XVII

2014   Our friendships are short and poor because we have
made them of wine and dreams instead of the tough fibre of
the human heart.   After Emerson, Friendship

2015   High-mindedness is the bond of true friendship.
Stanton Coit, Message of Man 1902 206

2016   No man can be provident of his time that is not prudent in his choice of company.
From Jeremy Taylor, Holy Living I i 5

2017   Be not easily acquainted, lest, finding reason to cool,
you make an enemy instead of a good neighbor.
Be intimate with very few, and upon very good grounds.
From William Penn

2018   The world gives back to every man the reflection of his own face. Frown at it, and it in turn will look sourly upon you; laugh at it and with it, and it is a jolly, kind companion.

From Thackeray

2019   The condition which high friendship demands is ability to do without it.   Emerson, Friendship

2020   One does not approach another human being as a potential friend if one does not bring something of value to the relationship.

From Ethel Sabin Smith,
Dynamics of Aging 1956 71 Norton

2021   The only way to have a friend is to be one.

Emerson, Friendship

2022   Friendship is equality.

Pythagoras, in Diogenes Laertius:
Lives . . . (Hicks, tr.) 1925 2 329 Putnam

2023   There can be no friendship where there is no freedom.

Rule of Life 1800 65

2024   True friendship speaks a simple, honest language.

Francis de Sales, Devout Life III XX

2025   The true gentleman is friendly but not familiar; the inferior man is familiar but not friendly.

Confucius, Analects XIII XXIII

2026   Friendship cannot live without civility.

From Savile, Complete Works . . . 1912 243

2027   One must let one's friends have their peculiarities.
From David Grayson

2028   None of us is perfect. All we can do is to make the best of our friends, love and cherish what is good in them, and keep out of the way of what is bad; but no more think of rejecting them for it than of throwing away a piece of music for a flat passage or two.   From Jefferson, Letter 1790

2028a   To accept a favor from a friend is to confer one.
Churton Collins,
Some Maxims ... Eng. Rev. Apr. 1914 98

BROTHERHOOD

2028b   To be a man means to be a fellow man.
Leo Baeck,
Essence of Judaism 1948 193 Schocken

2028c   Brotherhood is neither sold nor bought.
Moroccan proverb, Westermarck (ed.),
Wit and Wisdom ... 1931 211 H. Liveright,
© Routledge

2028d   Your neighbor's gain is your gain, and your neighbor's loss is your loss.   Taoism

2028e   The deeds of men are the deeds of our kin; wherefore we love them, and sometimes pity, in that they know not the better and the worse.   Marcus Aurelius, Thoughts II 13

2028f   Use of jungle logic instead of human reason in settling disputes will restore the earth to a jungle. If brothers not in life, then brothers in violent death.

> Paramhansa Yogananda,
> Autobiography . . . 1946 447 Philos. Lib.

2028g   Those things, which beget harmony, are such as are attributable to justice, equity, and honorable living.

> Spinoza, Ethics IV App. 15

2028h   To this event the ages ran:
Make way for Brotherhood—make way for Man!

> Edwin Markham, Brotherhood

2028i   It is an evil thing to expect too much either from ourselves or from others. One does not really love mankind when one expects too much from them.

> From Eric Hoffer,
> Passionate State of Mind 1955 65 Harper

2028j   The brotherhood of man must be watched and cared for at home . . . Once it has safely sprouted there, you may undertake to transplant it.

> After Pestalozzi,
> Education . . . 1953 24 Philos. Lib.

2029   Impart as much as you can of your spiritual being to those who are on the road with you, and accept as something precious what comes back to you from them.

> Schweitzer, Memoirs . . . 1931 92 Macmillan

HUMANITY, BENEVOLENCE

2030   He who is indifferent to the welfare of others does not
deserve to be called a man.

Persian Scriptures,
M. K. Schermerhorn, Sacred . . . 1883 287

2031   If one has identified his life with the life of mankind,
his own waning powers are only incidental. His interest in the
future is keen.   From Arthur E. Morgan,
Observations 1968 22 Antioch Press

2032   Let a man glory not that he loves his country but that
he loves his fellow men.   From a Persian proverb

2033   Never elated, while one man's oppressed;
            Never dejected, while another's blessed.
Pope, Essay on Man IV 323

2034   The supposition that pain is somehow a good in itself,
and that its sufferance, if not its infliction, is a duty, is one of
man's major crimes against himself. That crime is negated now
by the mastery of anesthesia.

After T. V. Smith,
Non-existent Man 1962 266 Univ. Tex. Press

2035   The hurts we inflict on others really strike at ourselves,
and the good things we do to others benefit us, since our lives
are interdependent.   After Ben Zion Bokser,
Wisdom . . . 1951 124 Philos Lib.

2036   Parental and sexual instincts, social life and cooperation carry . . . the very faculty to recognize a fellow-being.

Santayana, Reason in Science 1905 259 Scribner

2037   A fellow-feeling makes one kind.

2038   There are times when it is easier to make peace with
the darker sides of life: when someone lends a hand.

From H. Margolius,
Thoughts . . . 1962 7 Lib. of Humane Lit.

2039   Requite injury with kindness.

Lao-tse, in Lionel Giles (ed.), Sayings . . . 1907 51

2040   Some who are fond of setting things to rights have no
great objection to seeing them wrong. There can be malice at
the bottom of what appears to be benevolence.

After Hazlitt, Characteristics CCCCXXII

2041   To justify themselves, the weak appeal to necessity, the
strong to destiny. The humane assume responsibility.

Unknown

HELPFULNESS

2042   We have no more right to consume happiness without
producing it than to consume wealth without producing it.

Bernard Shaw

2043   Our duty is to be useful according to our powers.

From Amiel

2044   It is every man's duty to make himself profitable to mankind: if he can, to many; if not, to fewer; at least to himself.
From Seneca,
Roger L'Estrange, . . . Morals 1756 132

2045   To foster conditions that widen the horizon of others and give them command of their own powers, so that they can find their own happiness in their own fashion, is the way of social action.
From John Dewey,
Human Nature . . . 1922 293–294 Holt

2046   Our task is to change every human potential for good into good actually realized.
From J. A. C. F. Auer, in Auer and Hartt,
Humanism . . . 1951 65 Antioch Press

2047   That man may last, but never lives,
Who much receives, but nothing gives.
T. Gibbons, When Jesus Dwelt

2048   A useless life is an early death.   From Goethe

2049   To help others expands one's life.

2050   Sow good services: sweet remembrances will grow from them.
Mme. de Staël

2051   Happiness is a perfume you cannot pour on others without getting a few drops on yourself.   Emerson

2052   Unity of life requires unity of aim: aim for the common good.

Whenever one furthers the common good, he acts according to his complete nature and therein has his reward.

From Marcus Aurelius, Meditations XI 21 IX 42

2053   Anyone who proposes to do good must not expect people to roll stones out of his way, but must accept his lot calmly if they even roll a few more upon it.

Schweitzer, Out of My Life . . .
(Campion, tr.) 1933 112 Holt; G. Allen

2054   Do as you would be done by.

Persian Scriptures,
M. K. Schermerhorn, Sacred . . . 1883 286

2056   Give, looking for nothing again.

Jeremy Taylor, in Gest (ed.),
House . . . 1954 77 Univ. Pa. Press

2057   The function of the physician is to cure a few, help many, and comfort all.

Percival Bailey, Perspectives . . . 1961 4:254

2058   He added to the sum of human joy, and if every one for whom he did some loving service were to bring a blossom to his grave, he would sleep tonight beneath a wilderness of flowers.   Ingersoll, Address

2059   He plants his trees to serve a race to come.

Statius, in Cicero, Essay . . . (Schuckburgh, tr.)

2060   The great use of life is to spend it for something which outlasts it.   William James

2061   I have to make one person good: myself. My neighbor I am to make happy—if I may.

From R. L. Stevenson, Christmas Sermon

2062   It is not enough to do good; one must do it the right way.

John Morley, On Compromise

2063   The good we do to others is spoilt unless we efface ourselves so completely that those we help have no sense of inferiority.

Balzac

2064   Be parent, not possessor,
Attendant, not master,
Be concerned not with obedience but with
benefit,
And you are at the core of living.

Witter Bynner,
Way of Life according to Laotzu 1944 57 Day

2065   It has been often said that power corrupts. But weakness, too, corrupts. Power corrupts the few, while weakness corrupts the many. Our healing gift to the weak is the encouragement to self-help.

After Eric Hoffer,
Ordeal of Change 1963 12 Harper

CRITICISM AND PRAISE

2066   Trust him little who praises all, him less who censures all, and him least who is indifferent about all.

Lavater, Aphorism 481 (1787 ed.)

2067   The most censorious and the indifferent are generally the least secure in themselves.

2068   O'er my Sins thou sit and moan:
             Hast thou no sins of thy own?
             O'er my Sins thou sit and weep,
             And lull thy own Sins fast asleep.
                              William Blake, Poems 1800–3

2069   With a friend, praise him when you can; for
             many a friendship has decayed,
        Like a plant in a crowded corner, for want of
             sunshine on its leaves.
                M. F. Tupper, Proverbial Philosophy 1849 135

2070   Raillery is a mode of speaking in favor of one's wit and against one's good nature.   From Montesquieu

2071   The truest liberality is appreciation.   Goethe

2072   Scolding begets fear; praise nourishes love; and not only are human hearts, as a general rule, more easily governed by love than by fear, but fear often leads less to the correction of faults and the struggle for merits than toward the concealment of the one and discouragement of the other. But by praise I do not mean flattery; I mean nothing insincere. Insincerity alienates love, and rots away authority. Praise is worth nothing if it be not founded on truth.
                From E. G. Bulwer-Lytton, Caxtoniana . . . 1864 199

2073   It is hard to praise those who are dispraised by others. He is little short of a hero who perseveres in thinking well of a worthy friend who has become a butt for slander and a byword.

After Hazlitt, Characteristics XVI

2074   To praise is to characterize [and so encourage] . . .
    It is important to recognize both the human frailty in even the greatest, and the greatness in the little and frail.

From H. Margolius,
Thoughts . . . 1962 5 6 Lib. Humane Lit.

2075   The readiness to praise others indicates a desire for excellence and perhaps an ability to realize it.

Eric Hoffer,
Passionate State of Mind 1955 81 Harper

2076   Praise a fool and you may make him useful.

Danish proverb

2077   It is better to overestimate than to underestimate a man's virtue; for many a one, by being thought better than he was, has become better, while many a one, by being thought worse, has become worse.   From B. Jowett

2078   To dwell on the shortcomings of friends yields no gain.
    To pay attention to the merits of adversaries gives advantages.   From Goethe

2079   Who observes his own faults and the perfections of another, without either envying him or despairing of himself, is blessed.   From Lavater, Aphorism 269 (1787 ed.)

2080　Those who speak or listen to unpalatable but salutary words are rare.　　　　　Sharma and Raghavacharya (trs.),
Gems from Sanskrit . . . 1959 63 Osmania

2081　To be receptive to criticism means to erase half of every deficiency and fault.　H. Margolius, Thoughts . . . 1962
6 Lib. of Humane Lit.

2082　I frequent the company more of those who find fault with me than those that flatter me; and am more proud of a conquest gained over myself when I submit to the force of my adversary's reason than I am pleased with a victory obtained over him by reason of his weakness.　　　　　Montaigne

2083　When we commend good and noble actions, we make them in some measure our own.　　　Rule of Life 1800 130

2084　A mean person can discern others' flaws though they are as small as mustard seeds, while he shuts his eyes to his own flaws though they are as big as elephant-apples.
　A mean person vilifies every virtue in good persons. One who is modest he condemns as a dullard; one devoted to religion, a hypocrite; pure in mind and body, fraudulent; valiant, cruel; contemplative, witless; speaking agreeably, timid; dignified, haughty; and eloquent, garrulous.
From Sharma and Raghavacharya (trs.),
Gems from Sanskrit . . . 1959 23 27 Osmania

2085　To find fault is easy; to do better may be difficult.
Plutarch

2086　Faults are thick where love is thin.　English proverb

2087   We always like those who admire us; we do not always like those whom we admire . . .

Flattery is like false money, and if it were not for the vanity of the flattered, could never pass in payment.

La Rochefoucauld, former from Maxim 294

2088   He that reviles me (it may be) calls me fool; but he that flatters me, if I take not heed, will make me one.

Rule of Life 1800 97

2089   Why do you behold the speck that is in your brother's eye, but do not consider the plank that is in your own eye?

First cast the plank out of your own eye, then you will see clearly to cast the speck out of your brother's eye.

From Matthew VII 3 5

2090   It is better to correct your own faults than those of another.   Democritus, Frag. 60

2091   Our intelligence is misapplied if it is wholly directed to discern the faults of others, when it is so often needed to mend and prevent our own.

The triumph of intelligence is to make your good nature subdue your censure; to be quick in seeing faults, and slow in exposing them.

Nothing softens the arrogance of our nature like awareness of some frailties of our own. They pull our rage by the sleeve, and whisper gentleness to our censures, even when they are rightly applied.

Do not dwell too long upon a weak side, touch and go away; take pleasure to stay longer where you can commend, like bees

that fix only upon those herbs out of which they may extract
the juice of which their honey is composed.

From Savile,
. . . Advice to a Daughter, Censure, Husband

2092   We should speak of the shortcomings of others only
when their shortcomings are likely to have disastrous consequences.   Mencius (Dobson, tr.)
1963 188 Univ. Toronto Press; Oxford

2093   For right judgment of any man, it is essential to see his
good qualities before pronouncing on his bad.

From Carlyle

2094   Great Spirit, help me never to judge another until I
have walked in his moccasins for two weeks.

Sioux Indian prayer

2095   They have a right to censure that have a heart to help.
From William Penn

2096   Criticism without suggestion is like trying to stop flood
with flood and put out fire with fire.

Motse, Y.-P. Mei (tr.),
Ethical . . . 1929 88 Probsthain

2097   We do not have the right to make miserable those
whom we cannot make good.

Vauvenargues, Reflection 27

2098   I gain my point if I reach my companion with any
statement which teaches him his own worth.

From Emerson, Success

COMMUNICATION

2099   Often we remain impenetrable to each other out of self-defensive shyness, neither having the courage to break through.   Bernard Berenson Treasury
(Kiel, ed.) 1962 192 Simon & Schuster

2100   None preaches better than the ant, and she says nothing.   Franklin

2101   In many ways doth the full heart reveal
            The presence of the love it would conceal.
                Coleridge, Poems Written in Later Life, Motto

2102   ...A kind
            Of excellent dumb discourse.
                    Shakespeare, Tempest III 3 38–39

2103   The language of the eyes is much the most significant and the most observed.
                                    From Savile,
                ...Advice to a Daughter, Behaviour...

2104   The silence often of pure innocence
            Persuades, when speaking fails.
                    Shakespeare, Winter's Tale II ii 41

2105   Silence is the perfectest herald of joy:
        I were but little happy, if I could say how much.
                                    Shakespeare,
                Much Ado About Nothing II i 319–320

2106   Things are not made for words, but words for things.

Myson, in Diogenes Laertius . . . III

2107   Words are but the images of matter, and except they have the life of reason and invention, to fall in love with them is all one as to fall in love with a picture.

Francis Bacon,
Advancement of Learning I IV iii

2108   We would have far fewer disputes in the world if people remembered that many a word means different things to different people.

After John Locke,
Essay Concerning Human Understanding

2109   The ability to communicate depends, I think, not so much on the field as on the level of competence. It is almost as hard for a linguist to speak to a historian, or for a practising engineer to speak to a new Ph.D. in some kinds of physics, as it is for a scientist to talk to a humanist about his work. But I believe communication is easier at the top of the pyramid of competence, where people are likely to be capable of the highest level of generalization.

From B. C. Keeney, Science 1970 169:26

2110   Language is public property that must not be rough-hewn to private ends.   Unknown

2111   In language, perspicuity is everything.
He who does not know the force of words can-
not know men.   Confucius, Analects
(Soothill, tr.) XV XL XX III

2112   Pleasant words are as a honeycomb, sweet to the soul, and health to the bones.

A word fitly spoken is like apples of gold in pictures of silver.   Proverbs XVI 24 XXV 11

2113   A word in season spoken
            May calm the troubled breast.
                                        C. Jefferys

2114   Wit . . . contracts an essay to an aphorism; bottles an argument in a jest.   E. A. Duyckinck

2115   The word once spoken can never be recalled.
                                        Traditional

2116   He only speaks safely who is silent willingly.
                        Thomas à Kempis, Imitation of Christ I XX

2117   Not every question deserves an answer.
                                Publilius Syrus, Maxim 581

2118   Let thy speech be better than silence, or be silent.
                                Dionysius the Elder, Frag. 6

2119   Speak concisely; say much in a few words.
                                        Ecclus. XXXII 8

2120   If men would only say what they have to say in plain terms, how much more eloquent they would be!
                                        Coleridge

2121   Against gossip, neither believe all you hear, nor report all you believe.   After Rule of Life, 1800 138

2122   Evil communications corrupt good manners.

I Corinthians XV 33

2123   ... Good, the more
Communicated, more abundant grows.

Milton, Paradise Lost V 71–72

2124   The newspaper's duty is to its readers and to the public at large, and not to the private interests of its owner.

In the pursuit of truth, the newspaper shall be prepared to sacrifice its material fortunes for the public good.

The newspaper shall be fair and free and wholesome in its outlook on public affairs and public men.

E. Meyer, Washington Post 1935

2125   But all the fun's in how you say a thing.

Poetry of Robert Frost
(Lathem, ed.), The Mountain 1969 44 Holt

CONVERSATION

2126   The torment of solitary confinement is that it deprives one not of information but of conversation, however uninformative.

Michael Polanyi,
Personal Knowledge 1958 210 Univ. Chicago Press

2127   Talking with a friend is thinking aloud.

From Addison

2128   The world is adorned only here and there by persons who are poor in unpleasant words and rich in pleasant words.

From Sharma and Raghavacharya (trs.),
Gems from Sanskrit ... 1959 7 Osmania

2129   A wholesome tongue is a tree of life; but perverseness therein is a breach in the spirit.   Proverbs XV 4

2130   Believe nothing against another but upon good author- ity, nor report what may hurt another, unless it be a greater hurt to others to conceal it.

It is wise not to seek a secret and honest not to reveal one.

William Penn

2131   Contradiction and gross flattery are poor materials for good conversation. That society is the most pleasant in which the persons composing it have a cheerful respect for one an- other.   Goethe

2132   The soul of conversation is sympathy.

Hazlitt, On the Conversation of Authors

2133   The art of conversation is the art of sharing the inter- ests of others.   From H. Margolius,

Aphorisms . . . n.d. 9 Black Mt. News

2134   Have the art of conversation. That is where the real personality shows itself. No act in life requires more attention, though it be the commonest thing in life . . . Do not be a critic of words, or you will be taken for a pedant; nor a taxgatherer of ideas, or men will avoid you, or at least sell their thought dear. In conversation discretion is more important than elo- quence.

Balthasar Gracian (Jacobs, tr.) Maxim 148

2135   There is a time to speak and a time to be still.

Traditional

2136   Silence is often more eloquent than words.

> Wortabet (tr.), Arabian Wisdom 1910 33

2137   He had occasional flashes of silence, that made his conversation perfectly delightful.

> Sydney Smith, referring to Macaulay

2138   The art of conversation is the art of hearing as well as of being heard.

> Hazlitt, On the Conversation of Authors

2139   There are people who, instead of listening to what is being said to them, are listening already to what they are going to say.

> Albert Guinon

2140   Blessed is the man who, having nothing to say, abstains from giving us wordy evidence of the fact.

> George Eliot,
> Impressions of Theophrastus Such IV

2141   We should always accommodate ourselves to the capacity of those with whom we converse. The discourse of some men is as the stars, which give little light because they are so high.

> Rule of Life 1800 67

2142   In speech, not quantity but ingenuity, not eloquence but insight, should be cultivated.

> Motse, Y.-P. Mei (tr.),
> Ethical ... 1929 8 Probsthain

2143   The worst part of an eminent man's conversation is, nine times out of ten, that in which he means to be clever.

> From E. G. Bulwer-Lytton,
> Caxtoniana 1864 25

2144   Part of the art of conversation is to be prompt without being refractory, to refute without argument, and to clothe great matters in a motley garb.   After Disraeli

2145   Wit is the salt of conversation, not the food.
                    Hazlitt, Lectures on English Comic Writers I

2146   Let your speech be always with grace, seasoned with salt.   Colossians IV 6

DISCUSSION

2147   Let us reason together.   Isaiah I 18

2148   We will, and should, continue to have debates; but we can conduct them as the honest differences of honest men in quest of a consensus. We can recognize that those who disagree with us are not necessarily attacking us but only our opinions and ideas. Above all, we must recognize that there may be truth or merit in the views of those who disagree with us.
                    From J. W. Fulbright, Address . . . Dec. 5 1963

2149   Often by silence error is approved, the lustre of virtue is darkened and wholesome precepts are suppressed.
                    From Pythagoras

2150   Truth leaps from the clash between conflicting opinions.
                    From J. Proskauer, in Ormont (ed.),
                    What Famous Men . . . 1935 State Law Rep. Co.

2151   Truth often suffers more by the heat of its defenders than from the arguments of its opposers.   William Penn

2152 From controversy often comes exaggeration; and exaggeration often does the work of falsehood unawares.

From Peter Mere Latham

2152a When discussion heats to controversy, the discussants shrivel to partisans.

2153 Often in the wrong are those who cannot endure to be so.

La Rochefoucauld

2154 That was excellently observed, say I, when an author's opinion agrees with mine.

From Swift

2155 None but a fool is always right.   A. J. C. Hare

2156 Where two humble men meet together, their conference is sweet and profitable; where one is humble, it is profitable; where neither, it is pernicious.

From Richard Brathwait,
English Gentleman 1630 13

2157 Where two discourse, if the one's anger rise,
    The man who lets the contest fall is wise.

Euripides, Frag. 656 Protesilaus

2158 In all debates, let truth be your aim, not victory or an unjust interest, and endeavor to gain rather than to expose your antagonist.

William Penn

2159 To be listened to, one must be a good listener.

2160   Be quick to hear; interrupt not in the midst of speech; answer not until you have heard; and answer with patience.

From Ecclus. V 11 XI 8

2161   He approaches the gods who knows how to restrain his tongue even when he is in the right.   From Cato

2162   The more you say, the less people remember.

Fénelon

2163   If you think twice before you speak once, you will speak twice the better for it.   William Penn

2164   He ceased; but left so pleasing on the ear
His voice, that listening still they seemed to
hear.

Homer, Odyssey (Pope, tr.) XIII 1

2165   Men should speak with rational awareness and thereby hold to that which they have in common.

Heraclitus, Frag. 110

COMPETITION

2166   Many are called, but few are chosen.

Matthew XXII 14

2167   The stairway of time is ever echoing with the wooden shoe going up, the polished boot coming down.

A French writer

2168   Homer was wrong in wishing that emulation might cease to be, for if that were to happen then all things would perish.

From Heraclitus

2169   We should not, therefore, attempt to abolish competition but only to see to it that it takes forms which are not too injurious.

Bertrand Russell,
Authority . . . 1949 22 G. Allen; Simon & Schuster

2170   There is something very deep, perhaps in the inborn traits of men, and at least in the cultural tradition, which, when conditions are favorable, will respond to good will and confidence. Quite commonly in such cases the practice of competition is tempered and humanized, though not eliminated.

Arthur E. Morgan,
Community . . . 1957 12 Community Service

2171   If a man has good corn, or wood, or boards, or pigs, to sell, or can make better chairs or knives, crucibles or church organs, than anybody else, you will find a broad hard-beaten road to his house, though it be in the woods.

Emerson, Journals Feb. 1855

2172   Competition with oneself leaves unimpaired one's benevolence toward his fellow men.

From Eric Hoffer,
Passionate State of Mind 1955 108 Harper

2173   Our great duty, as social beings, is to derive constant aid from society without becoming subservient; to open our minds to the thoughts and persuasions of others, and yet to hold fast the sacred right of private judgment; to sympathise with others, and yet to determine our own feelings; to act with others, and yet to follow our own consciences.

From W. E. Channing, Works 1875 1:138

2174   Competition continues necessary so that men shall not be cumbered by mediocrity.

When opportunity has been so equalized throughout the world that merit can rise to its natural place, there will be little danger of domestic disorder or of foreign war.

From Arthur E. Morgan,
Observations 1968 290 Antioch Press

COOPERATION

2175   A threefold cord is not easily broken.

Ecclesiastes IV 12

2176   A dwarf standing on the shoulders of a giant sees farther than the giant himself.   Traditional

2177   When Crew and Captain understand each
         other to the core,
   It takes a gale and more than a gale to put their
         ship ashore;
   For the one will do what the other commands,
         although they are chilled to the bone,
   And both together can live through weather
         that neither can face alone.

Kipling

2178   As many hands make light work, so several purses make cheap experiments.   William Penn

2179　What is not good for the swarm is not good for the bee.　　　　　　　　　Marcus Aurelius, Meditations VI 54

2180　Generally speaking, you cannot, even if you would, separate your life from that of humanity; you live in it, by it, for it.　　　　　　　　　Mazzini, Duties of Man

2181　Cooperation is not a sentiment—it is a necessity.
　　　　　　　　　From C. Steinmetz

2182　So far as men live according to reason, they agree essentially, so live in harmony with one another.
　Although men are generally governed in everything by their own lusts, yet association brings with it many more advantages than drawbacks; wherefore it is better to bear patiently the wrongs our fellows may do us, and to strive to promote whatsoever serves to bring about harmony and friendship.
　　　　　　　　　Spinoza, Ethics IV xxxv xl App. 14

2183　The child tries to solve many a problem by fighting or fleeing; the adult, by understanding and cooperation.
　　　　　　　　　From L. J. Saul, in Murrow (ed.),
　　　　　　　　　This I Believe 1952 Simon & Schuster

2184　Men who differ in principles cannot help each other in plans.　　　　　　　　　Confucius

2185　Given common interest, space, and time, two heads are better than one. The heads give solution and lift: Eureka!

2186　Much practice of comradeship is necessary before society can organize itself in accordance with reason.
　　　　　　　From William Kingdon Clifford, Lectures . . . 1886 417

2187   In overcoming prejudice, working together is even more effective than talking together.   R. W. Sockman

2188   Men are used as they use others.

Fables of Pilpay IX

2189   The law of service is mutual considerateness.

Stanton Coit, Message of Man 1902 130

2190   I take it that all those things are to be held performable which may be done by some though not all persons; by many together though not by one alone; in the succession of ages though not in one man's life; and by public though not private designation and expense.   From Francis Bacon

LEADERSHIP

2191   If the blind lead the blind, both shall fall into the ditch.   Matthew XV 14

2192   Divide and rule, the politician cries;
          Unite and lead is the watchword of the wise.

Goethe

2193   So far in the history of the world there have never been enough mature people in the right places.

G. B. Chisholm, Psychiatry 1946 9:6

2194   You have lost a good captain to make him a poor general.   Saturninus

2195   One good head is better than a great many hands.

Charron

2196   . . . Few sometimes may know, when thousands err.

Milton, Paradise Lost VI 148

2197   An intellectual elite formed the concept of democracy, kept it alive, and is responsible for nearly every progression in science, art, and human relations.

From an editorial, Boston Herald, in
Brand Blanshard (ed.), Education . . .
1959 181 Basic Books

2198   When the true gentleman directs men at their work, he considers their capacities. The inferior man expects his workers to be fit for everything.

Confucius, Analects XIII XXIV

2199   He is the rich man in whom the people are rich, and he is the poor man in whom the people are poor.

Emerson, Wealth

2200   Great concerns of men are these, to make him who is an enemy a friend, to make him who is wicked righteous, and to make him who is ignorant learned.

Shayast-La-Shayast XX 6

2201   I do not know how to make men equal; but if I can make good men able, or able men good, their example will raise the people to integrity and civilization.

Will Durant, from Confucius, in Murrow (ed.),
This I Believe 1954 166 Simon & Schuster

2202   Good leadership consists in waking the decency dormant in most if not all persons.

> After Eric Hoffer,
> Passionate State of Mind 1955 86 Harper

2203   One of the great functions of leaders is to help a society to achieve the best that is in it.

> John W. Gardner, Excellence 1961 126 Harper

2204   People seldom improve when they have no model but themselves.   From Goldsmith

2205   When the shepherd strays, the sheep stray after him.

> The Talmud, in Bokser,
> Wisdom . . . 1951 166 Philos. Lib.

2206   You are not only good yourself, but the cause of goodness in others.   From Socrates, in Plato, Protagoras

2207   Great mistakes are retrieved by keeping others from making them, and great triumphs perfected by spurring others beyond them.   From F. L. Wells

2208   We are influenced by those we influence.

> Eric Hoffer,
> Passionate State of Mind 1955 78 Harper

2209   A brave man will yield to a brave man.   Unknown

2210   Those members of mankind who see, think, and move forward are always obliged to drag a long train of those who neither see, nor think, nor wish to move forward. They do move forward, however, in the long run.

> From Guyau, Non-Religion ... 1897 374

2211 Many a man who is ahead of his fellows is misunderstood, criticized, even villified. Every great man understands this; and understands, too, that it is no proof of greatness. The great man endures contumely without resentment.

> After E. Hubbard,
> Get Out or Get in Line

2212 Only great natures grow greater through possessing power.

> From Balzac

2213 He that makes others fear him has reason to fear them.

> From Rule of Life 1800 124

2214 He who sets himself up as his brother's keeper may end by being his jailkeeper.

> From Eric Hoffer,
> Passionate State of Mind 1955 69 Harper

2215 Those he commands move only on command,
Nothing in love...
... None serve with him but constrained things
Whose hearts are absent too.

> Shakespeare, Macbeth V ii 19–20 iii 14–15

2216 Allegiance which is gained by ... force is not an allegiance of the heart—it ... comes from imposing upon weakness.

Allegiance which is gained by the exercise of virtue is true allegiance . . . the response of joy.

Mencius (Dobson, tr.)
1963 136 Univ. Toronto Press; Oxford

2217   No respect is lasting but that which is produced by our being in some degree useful to those that pay it. Not even the greatest prince can at once preserve respect and neglect his people. No age ever erected altars to insignificant gods; they all had some quality applied to them to draw worship from mankind.

From Savile, . . . Advice to a Daughter, House . . .

2218   In courts nobility holds first place, in villages age; and for usefulness to one's generation, and controlling the people, neither is equal to virtue.   Mencius

2219   Say what you please of your humanity, no wise man will ever believe a syllable while I and MINE are the only two gates at which you sally forth and enter, and through which alone all must pass who seek admittance.

Lavater, Aphorism 434 (1787 ed.)

2220   A man may have authority over others; but he can never have their heart but by giving his own.

Thomas Wilson, Maxims . . . 1898

2221   He who has the truth in his heart need never fear the want of persuasion on his tongue.   J. Ruskin

2222   One who has confidence in himself gains the confidence of others.   Hasidic saying, in Lewis Browne (ed.),
Wisdom . . . Random House 1945 596

2223   The nobler sort of man composes himself before he moves others.   From Confucius

2224   If you love men and they are unfriendly, look into your love; if you rule men and they are unruly, look into your wisdom.   Mencius

2225   He who reforms himself does more to reform the public than does a crowd of noisy impotent patriots.
                            Lavater, Aphorism 511 (1787 ed.)

2226   Humanity extinguishes Inhumanity just as water extinguishes fire . . . The people turn in allegiance to Humanity . . .   Mencius (Dobson, tr.)
                    1963 137 166 Univ. Toronto Press; Oxford

2227   Minds at once logical and capacious are sure to be followed, provided one gives the people time enough.
                            Guyau, Non-Religion . . . 1897 20

2228   Caligula made himself ridiculous by the softness and fanaticalness of his habit; and Augustus was as much admired for the modesty and gravity of his.   Rule of Life 1800 104

2229   Civility is a kind of charm that attracts the love of all men.   Rule of Life 1800 133

2230   A gentle hand can lead even an elephant by a hair.
                                    Persian Scriptures,
                in M. K. Schermerhorn, Sacred . . . 1883 286

2231   Let it be not the intelligent man who rules, but intelligence; not the wise man, but wisdom.   After Goethe

2232   A leader is best when people barely know he exists.

Lao-tse

2233   We owe it to our fellows to keep upright, to encourage them to keep their feet.   From George Sand,
Letter to Flaubert Jan. 12, 1876

2234   The worthy man, by being enlightened, enlightens others.   Mencius (Dobson, tr.)
1963 187 Univ. Toronto Press; Oxford

2235   The world follows example.

From the Bhagavad-Gita, III

2236   Example is the softest and least invidious way of com-manding.   Pliny

2237   To have loyal, efficient employees be a loyal, efficient employer.   A. W. Newcomb

2238   Let a man overcome anger by love, let him overcome evil by good; let him overcome the greedy by liberality, the liar by truth.   The Dhammapada CCXXIII

2239   Suppose you've no direction in you,
I don't see but you must continue
To use the gift you do possess,
And sway with reason more or less.

Poetry of Robert Frost
(Lathem, ed.) To a Thinker 1969 226 Holt

2240   He who endeavors to lead men by reason acts not by impulse but courteously and kindly, and his intention is always consistent.   Spinoza, Ethics IV xxxvii Note 1

2241   One can properly attempt to influence another by encouraging him to think for himself, instead of endeavoring to instil ready-made opinions into his head.

From Leslie Stephen 1904

2242   No one—not I—would give them up for lost
        Simply because they don't know where they
            are . . .
        If the day ever comes when they know who
        They are, they may know better where they
            are.

From Poetry of Robert Frost (Lathem, ed.),
A Cabin In the Clearing 1969 414 Holt

2243   To manage men one ought to have a sharp mind in a velvet sheath.   George Eliot

2244   Confidence placed in another often compels confidence in return.   Livy

2245   I have believed the best of every man,
        And find that to believe it is enough
        To make a bad man show him at his best,
        Or even a good man swing his lantern higher.

Yeats

2246   What is really "unlucky" is to keep worthy men in obscurity.   Mencius (Dobson, tr.)
1963 187 Univ. Toronto Press; Oxford

2247   The proper leader for mankind is not a man but a cause.   From J. A. Rice

2248   The men who stir the world most are not always those who lift it most. To lift a little is better than to stir much.
                                        Arthur E. Morgan,
                        Observations 1968 322 Antioch Press

POPULARITY

2249   Woe to him whom nobody likes; but beware of him whom everybody likes.
                            Hasidic saying, in Lewis Browne (ed.),
                            Wisdom . . . 1945 596 Random House

2250   Anyone who becomes a good power in the world is liable to make enemies . . .
    Praise is sweet, but the soul cannot thrive upon honey alone.
                        From J. G. Holland, Gold-Foil . . . 1881 206 207

2251   Common men are cowards, and dread a mocking laugh; but ridicule is a weak weapon, when levelled at a strong mind.
                    From M. F. Tupper, Proverbial Philosophy 1849 133

2252   As a solid rock is not shaken by the wind, wise people falter not amidst blame and praise.
                                        The Dhammapada VI

2253   Improvements . . . in religion, in art, and in science, . . . also . . . in the sense of social obligation, as in everything else, have been largely due to solitary men whose thoughts and emotions were not subject to the dominion of the herd. Although ... they are often persecuted in their own day, they are apt to be, of all men, those to whom posterity pays the highest honor. Bertrand Russell, Authority ...

1949 113 G. Allen; Simon & Schuster

REPUTATION AND FAME

2254　I would much rather have men ask why I have no statue than why I have one. Cato, in Plutarch

2255　The excesses of popular applause never satisfy the sensible. Balthasar Gracian (Jacobs, tr.) Maxim 28

2256　Character is like a tree and reputation like its shadow; the tree is the real thing. From Lincoln

2257　Many people are willing to be estimated by what they possess instead of what they are.

From Hazlitt, Characteristics CLXXXII

2258　Fortune gives, to some, honor without deserving; to others, deserving without honor.

From George Chapman, All Fools V i

2259　A slave is twice enslaved, once by his chains and once again by the glances that fall upon him and say "Thou slave."

Thornton Wilder

2260　Fame is the scentless sunflower, with gaudy crown of gold;

but friendship is the breathing rose, with sweets in every fold.

(Doctor) O. W. Holmes,
No Time Like the Old Time

2261　Who does evil and is afraid lest it be known has still a seed of good in his evil; who does good and is anxious to have it known has still a root of evil in his good.

Confucius, in Lin-Yutang (ed.),
Wisdom of China and India 1942 1096 Random House

2262　Though nothing is so vain as the eager pursuit of empty applause, to be well thought of, and to be kindly used by the world, is a charm against ill will.

From Savile, . . . Advice to a Daughter, Censure

2263　To be blamed by an idiot may be equivalent to being praised by a good man.　　G. Sarton, Science 1960 131:1187

2264　It is better to be believed than admired.

From Richard Brathwait,
English Gentleman 1630 84

2265　The True Gentleman . . . would be ashamed of a reputation that exceeded his deserts.

Mencius (Dobson, tr.)
1963 172 Univ. Toronto Press; Oxford

2266　Fame compels its devotees to shape their lives to the opinions of men, shunning what they shun and seeking what they seek.　　　　　　　　From Spinoza,
On the Improvement of the Understanding

2267   Who pants for glory finds but short repose:
       A breath revives him, or a breath o'erthrows.
                          Horace, Epistle (Pope, tr.) II i 300

2268   Virtue must be in oneself, and praise left to others.
                          From Balthasar Gracian, El Heroe

2269   Men are too apt to be concerned for their credit more
than tor the cause.   William Penn

2270   Honor is better than honors.
                   Flemish proverb, Champion (ed.), Racial . . .
              1938 17 Macmillan, © Routledge; Barnes & Noble

2271   I look on that man as happy, who, when there is a question of success, looks into his work for a reply, not into the
market, not into opinion, not into patronage.
                          Emerson, Worship

2272   Integrity is its own reward.   Bernardino Telesio

2273   Have little care that Life is brief,
               And less that Art is long.
               Success is in the silences
               Though Fame is in the song.
                          Bliss Carman, Envoi

2274   Do not worry about people not knowing you, but endeavor to be worth knowing.   Confucius

2275   The desire to appear clever often prevents becoming
so.   La Rochefoucauld

2276   It is not he that searches for praise that finds it.

Antoine de Rivarol

2277   The way to gain a good reputation is to endeavor to be what you desire to appear.   Socrates

2278   Approval by others must come **voluntarily**; our business is to get on with our development.

From Epicurus, Strodach (tr.),
Philosophy . . . 1962 207 Northwestern Univ. Press

2279   Does any man contemn me? That is his concern. Mine is to see that no deed or word of mine merits contempt.

Marcus Aurelius, Meditations XI 13

2280   When the world blames and slanders us, our business is not to be vexed but to consider whether there is any foundation for it.   John Henry Newman

2281   And is thine aim so low that the breath of those
         around thee
      Can speed thy arrow, or retard its flight?

M. F. Tupper,
Proverbial Philosophy 1849 135

2282   If you are standing upright, do not worry if your shadow is crooked.

Seven Hundred Chinese Proverbs
(Hart, tr.), 1937 37 Stanford Univ. Press

2283   Whether in favor or in humiliation, be not dismayed. Let your eyes leisurely look at the flowers blooming and falling in your courtyard.   Hung, Chinese Garden . . .
                                   (Chao, tr.) 1959 32 Peter Pauper

2284   Do not lace your boots in a neighbor's melon field, nor adjust your hat under his plum tree; thus avoid suspicion.
                                             Armenian proverb

2285   I shall not be sorry that men do not know me; I shall be sorry that I do not know men.   Confucius

2286   Fame is the inheritance not of the dead, but of the living. It is we who look back with lofty pride to the great names of antiquity, who drink of that flood of glory as of a river, and refresh our wings in it for future flight.
                                   Hazlitt, Characteristics CCCLXXXIX

EGOISM

2287   Egoism is interest in one's selfish good.
    Many an egoist wants to be admired. He may think that he is more important than other people, and that he is a finer or greater person than he is. In so thinking, he is an egotist.
    If he is preoccupied with himself, whether he thinks of himself as superior or inferior, egotistic or modest, egoistic or altruistic, he is egocentric.

2288   I find no sweeter fat than sticks to my own bones.
                                   Walt Whitman, Song of Myself

2289   Extreme individualism is the youth of the mind, the fanaticism of liberty.   A. B. Alcott, Table-Talk 1877 53

2290   Some persons who wish to be vitally individual become merely competitive.   From M. M. duPont,
Definitions . . . 1965 Swallow

2291   Selfish people think their own discomforts are more important than anything else in the world.
George Eliot, Middlemarch

2292   It is a sad failing in a person who makes heavy demands upon others and only light ones on himself.
From Mencius, in Cranmer-Byng and Watts (eds.),
Book . . . (Giles, tr.) 1942 126 Murray

2293   The possessor of a self-fantasy tries to make the world serve him, while the objective person tries to serve the world.
From F. Künkel, Let's Be Normal
(Jensen, tr.) 1929 31–32 Washburn

2294   Men of proud and passionate tempers cause all the world to fly from them.   From Balzac

2295   A man wrapped up in himself makes a very small bundle.   B. Franklin

2296   He who serves none but himself is a slave to a slave of egoism.   After Rule of Life 1800 24

2297   When your neighbor's wall is on fire, it becomes your business.   Horace, Epistles I xviii 84

2298   If I am not for myself, who is for me? And when I am for myself only, of what use am I? And if not now, when?
Hillel, Abot I 14

ALTRUISM

2299   Egoism is excessive interest in one's own welfare; it is wanting good for the self without regard for others.

Altruism is wanting good for others; it is interest in their welfare.

Every interest that one has is one's own; but that does not make it self-interest. Many of the interests are in behalf of the self, which is always at hand. Some interests, however, may be in behalf of others, who are not so at hand.

As compared with egoism, altruism requires more learning and thought. The egoist has learned to care for good for himself. The altruist has learned further to care for good for others —parents, family, friends, community, nation, humanity—according to his development. Many people become largely altruistic.

2300   A man has at least started to discover the meaning of human life when he plants shade trees under which he knows he will never sit.   From D. E. Trueblood

2301   Altruistic love develops the lover and his object.

2302   He who wishes to secure the good of others has already secured his own.   Confucius

2303   Men who are free, who are enlightened, and who reason well, desire nothing for themselves but what they desire in effect for every man; wherefore they are just and honorable.
                                   From Spinoza, Ethics IV xviii Note

2304   Ample psychological evidence is available to indicate that man is neither wholly selfish nor wholly altruistic. People not only help others but find it rewarding as well.

From R. F. Weiss and others,
Science 1971 171:1263

2305   Glory not in thyself, but rather in thy neighbor.

Siamese Buddhist maxim

2306   Do not force upon your neighbor a hat that hurts your own head.   Brahmanic Scriptures,

M. K. Schermerhorn, Sacred . . . 1883 297

SELF-RENUNCIATION AND SELF-SACRIFICE

2307   Great actors give themselves not to their egos but to enriching human life.

2308   The great day comes when a man begins to get out of himself, to be a free man in a world where persons, causes, truths and values exist, worthful for their own sakes.

From H. E. Fosdick,
On Being a Real Person 1943 84 Harper

2309   In every moment of [what some call] pure consciousness the self ceases to be separate and unites with the world.

After H. l'A Fausset,
in D. B. Phillips and others,
Choice . . . 1948 102 R. R. Smith

2310   A vital person grows from a limited self to become a more inclusive self.

2311   A sound man . . .
              By not confining himself to himself
              Sustains himself outside himself:
              By never being an end in himself
              He endlessly becomes himself.

Witter Bynner,
Way of Life according to Laotzu 1944 28 Day

2312   The ultimate unification of the self depends upon one's integration of the shifting scenes of the world into that totality we call the universe.

From John Dewey,
Common Faith 1934 19 Yale Univ. Press

2313   A complete life may be one ending in so full an identification with the notself that there is no self left to die.

B. Berenson,
Sketch . . . 1941 21 Ind. Univ. Press

2314   Creative dedication of the individual self to the wider good is integral to every great religion.

2315   Perhaps the final test of human freedom and dignity is the freedom to choose self-sacrifice for greater ends; yet supposed sacrifice of self can be a masquerade for the sacrifice of others.   From P. B. Sears,

Am. Scholar 1957 26:451

2316   Freedom is the child of intelligence.   Ingersoll

2317   One who controls the ego has the strength of ten, for then, truly, his heart is pure.

From Dean Acheson,
Homage to Gen. Marshall, Reporter Nov. 26 1959 25

2318   Thinking about one's self can become a habit.

From James T. Fisher and Lowell,
Diary . . . 1952 37 Hutchinson

2319   The attention you pay to yourself you probably owe to others. To speak to them and at the same time listen to yourself cannot turn out well.

Balthasar Gracian (Jacobs, tr.) Maxim 141

2320   The renunciation of individual for larger ends is immediately compensated by a richer life.

From E. Carpenter, Civilisation . . . 1889 126

2321   If one can, so to speak, have lost the self during a whole existence, it is also possible to find a whole life in one moment of love and sacrifice.   From Guyau, Sketch . . . 1898 213

2322   Disinterestedness is entire surrender of self; nothing less. Any such disinterested effort must increase the sum of good will in the world.   From G. Sarton,

History . . . 1937 117 Harvard Univ. Press

SELF-REALIZATION

2323   The great object of living is to attain more of the good life—more in quality as well as quantity.

Julian Huxley,
Religion Without Revelation 1927 357 Harper

2324　The only way to live long is to live sufficiently.

From Seneca, Ad Marciam XXI

2325　We can strike bargains and make contracts by proxy, but all men must work out their salvation in person.

Rule of Life 1800 173

2326　No bird soars too high, if he soars with his own wings.

William Blake, Marriage of Heaven and Hell

2327　Were I a nightingale, I would act the part of a nightingale; were I a swan, the part of a swan.

Epictetus, Discourses XVI

2328　A man's happiness is to do the things proper to man.

Marcus Aurelius, Meditations VIII 26

2329　The primary yes is self-affirmation; the primary no, resentment of oneself.

Walter Kaufman, From
Shakespeare to Existentialism, 1960 30 Doubleday

2330　No one doubts that an ordinary man can get on with this world; but we demand not strength enough to get on with it, but strength enough to get it on.

Chesterton, Orthodoxy 1908 130

2331　Always, we can do what we can with what we have.

2332　What shall it profit a man if he gain the whole world in fancy and lose his own soul from reality?

Learned Hand, Irving Dilliard (ed.),
Spirit of Liberty 1952 10 Knopf

2333   Resolve to be thyself; and know that he who finds himself loses his misery.   Matthew Arnold

2334   To be wholly alive is to be completely engaged with the world with all one's passions and faculties.
From W. Lippmann,
Preface to Morals 1929 8 Macmillan

2335   To thy best self be true.   R. Devereux

2336   He that is a true friend to himself is also a friend to mankind.   Seneca

2337   If he does not know what is good, a man cannot be true to his best self.   Confucius, in Lin-Yutang (ed.),
Wisdom of Confucius 1938 121 Modern Lib.

2338   Every man is the son of his works.   Spanish proverb

2339   Mountains culminate in peaks, and nations in men.
Martí, America of José Martí (de Onís, tr.)
1953 6 Noonday, © 1954 Farrar

2340   Man's most sacred duty is to realize his possibilities of knowing, feeling, and willing, in the development of individuals, societies, and the whole human species.
From Julian Huxley,
BBC Woman's Hour, Mar. 15, 1960

2341   What must a man do to gratify his deepest wish, his wish to grow, in the modest sense, more powerful? He must use all his power, as one of a world of men, to make that world most likely to produce the scientist, the moralist, the artist.

From E. A. Singer, Jr., Am. Scholar 1934 3:318

2342   The goal of the American educational system is to enable every young person to fulfill his potentialities, regardless of his race, creed, social standing, or economic position.

A professor of education, in
John W. Gardner, Excellence 1961 75 Harper

2343   Individuals collectively form communities. The communities of the earth are interknit.

Evolutionary values are not merely those restricted to the survival of individuals. That is less important, in the end, than survival of the communities and of humanity.

From Bentley Glass, Science and Ethical Values
1965 11–12 26 Univ. N.C. Press

XI

Society, Government, and Peace

MANKIND

2344   Each of us is but a leaf from the human tree. Though individuals are vital to the race, the race is vital to the individual.
After G. Sarton,
History . . . 1937 xviii Harvard Univ. Press

2345   The human race is never old, or middle-aged, or young, but moves on through perpetual decay, fall, renovation, and progression.
From Edmund Burke

2346   The whole human race is composed of various members who play different parts in the total life of mankind.
After Pietro Pomponazzi, in Kristeller, Studies . . .
1956 276 Edizioni di Storia e Letteratura

2347   What a piece of work is man! How noble in reason! how infinite in faculty! in form, in moving, how express and admirable! in action, how like an angel! in apprehension, how like a god! the beauty of the world! the paragon of animals!
From Shakespeare, Hamlet II ii 309–313

2348   Besides the women who take the place of muses and of Delphic Sibyls, are there not those who fill our vases with wine to the brim, and with roses that fill the house with perfume; who inspire us with courtesy; who unloose our tongues, and we speak; who anoint our eyes, and we see? Once our walls of habitual reserve vanish, and leave us at large, we are children playing with children in a wide field of flowers.
From Emerson, Manners

2349   Man can not degrade woman without himself falling into degradation; he can not elevate her without at the same time elevating himself.   Alexander Walker

2350   Wherever a man sets his foot he treads a hundred paths.
East Indian lore

2351   Nothing is more useful to man than man. Men can wish for nothing more excellent for their own being than that all together should seek what is useful to all.
From Spinoza, Ethics IV xviii Note

2352   I am a man, and whatever concerns humanity is of interest to me.   Terence

LONELINESS

2353   There's too much beauty upon this earth
For lonely men to bear.

Richard Le Gallienne,
Ballad of Too Much Beauty 1913 147

2354   People are lonely because they build walls instead of bridges.   A. Edward Newton

2355   Art thou lonely, O my brother?
Share thy little with another!
Stretch a hand to one unfriended,
And thy loneliness is ended.

John Oxenham, in Wallis (ed.),
Selected Poems . . . Lonely Brother
1948 Harper, © Dunkerley

2356   If a man does not make new acquaintances as he advances through life, he will soon find himself left alone.

From Samuel Johnson

2357   They are never alone that are accompanied by noble thoughts.   Philip Sidney, Acadia I

2358   Religion offers man a language which makes real loneliness impossible.   Walter Kaufmann,
Critique of Religion and Philosophy
1958 249 Harper, © Kaufmann

CUSTOM AND FASHION

2359   Custom is almost second nature.

Plutarch, Preservation of Health

2360   Custom sanctions things both just and unjust.

From Terence, Heaut. IV vii 11

2361   Custom, here and there, robs many joys of their finest lustre; but, in turn, it creates new joys which only custom knows how to create.

From H. Margolius,
Thoughts . . . 1962 7 Lib. of Humane Lit.

2362   The simplicity and informality of the modern beau form a striking contrast to the dazzling finery and ceremony of the old-fashioned courtier; yet both are studied devices and symbols of distinction. It would be interesting to trace the influences of Newton's Principia and Rousseau's Émile and the like on the march of fashion from the age of Elizabeth to the present time.   From Hazlitt, Characteristics CLV

2363   Custom, without reason, is no better than **ancient** error.
                                                          Jeremy Collier

2364   The fashion wears out more apparel than the man.
                        Shakespeare, Much Ado About Nothing III iii 148

2365   Most men live according to opinion or fashion, which varies and changes, and therefore is disturbing; forgetting the direct rule of wisdom, which renders us calm and serene.
                                            From Rule of Life 1800 9

2366   Imitation is the sincerest of flattery.
                                    C. C. Colton, Lacon 1852 123

2367   Any idea or custom that crushes and enslaves the human spirit, that takes the zest and gaiety out of life, is a foe.
                                            From George Lawton,
                            How to Be Happy . . . 1949 275 Vanguard

INDIVIDUALITY

2368   We ought to belong to society, to have our place in it, and yet be capable of a sound individual existence.
                                            From P. G. Hamerton

2369   Be what you virtuously are, and let not the ocean wash away your tincture.
                        From Thomas Browne, Christian Morals I ix

2370   Whatever crushes individuality is despotism, by whatever name it may be called.
                                    John Stuart Mill, On Liberty III

2371   We want a state of things which allows every man the largest liberty compatible with the liberty of every other man.

Emerson

2372   What is food to one may be poison to another.

Traditional

2373   'Tis better to be alone than in bad company.

George Washington, Rules of Civility

2374   Whatever my neighbor does or says, my duty is to be good.

Marcus Aurelius, Meditations VII 15

2375   Be thine own palace,
                Or the world's thy gaol.

John Donne, To Sir Henry Wotton 52

2376   Let us keep in mind each his own uniqueness, his integrity, and that of his fellow men.

C. Gessler,
Reasonable Life 1950 204 Day

2377   Nature forms us to be, not to seem.

From Montaigne, Of the
Remembrance of Children to Their Brothers

THE RICH AND THE GREAT

2378   Many people court the rich and great not merely for what they can obtain from them, but because external rank and splendor gratify the imagination; just as we prefer the company of those who are in good health and spirits to that of the sickly and hypochondriacal, or as we would rather converse with a beautiful woman than with an ugly one.

From Hazlitt, Characteristics CCCLXII

2379   Be not afraid of greatness: some are born great, some achieve greatness, and some have greatness thrust upon them.

Shakespeare, Twelfth Night II v 158–160

2380   Uneasy lies the head that wears a crown.   **Proverb**

2381   Great men are not always wise.   Job XXXII 9

2382   The Sages are of the same species as ourselves.

Mencius, in Lin-Yutang (ed.),
Wisdom of China and India 1942 743 Random House

2383   For hundreds of years society has been a battleground between two great principles—the principle of selection by family and the principle of selection by merit . . .
    The soil grows castes. The machine makes classes.

Michael Young, Rise of the
Meritocracy . . . 1958 24 21 Thames; Random House

2384   Exclusive is no synonym of *select* and still less of *elect*.

Bernard Berenson Treasury
(Kiel, ed.), 1962 190 Simon & Schuster

2385   The aristocracy of today is the aristocracy of wealth; the aristocracy of tomorrow will be the aristocracy of intellect and virtue.   From Mazzini

2386   I believe in an aristocracy of the sensitive, the considerate, and the plucky. Its members are to be found in all nations and classes, and all through the ages, and there is a secret understanding between them when they meet. They represent the true human tradition.

From E. M. Forster,
Two Cheers for Democracy 1951 73 Harcourt

2387   We may not be able to eliminate class but we can avoid the development of caste.

L. F. Carter and J. B. Margolin,
Am. Psychologist 1964 19:359

2388   It is better to be humble with the lowly than to share spoil with the proud.   Proverbs XVI 19

2389   One's own rank and precedence, which the vulgar prize, the sage stolidly ignores.

After Chuang Tzu n.d. 102 Peter Pauper

2390   For anyone who feels hurt because of the true superiority of another, there is the remedy of understanding.

SOCIETY, STATE, AND NATION

2391   As much as man is a whole, so is he also a part; and it were partial not to see it.

Emerson, Nominalist and Realist

2392   Society is a partnership in animal existence, science, art, virtue and perfection; a partnership between those who are living, those who are dead, and those who are to be born.

From Edmund Burke

2393 If a woman could turn her back altogether on the cul·
ture she lives in, she would cut herself off, and her children,
from the heroes and causes that embody its ideals (St. Francis,
Thomas Jefferson), from the intricate pattern of human relationships that it sponsors (marriage, family), and finally and
fatally, from the multiplicity of experiences in love and loyalty
that are bread and wine to the soul.　　　From C. P. Seton,
Special and Curious Blessing 1968 18–19 Norton

2394 Society is a chain of obligations, and its links must
support each other.
M. F. Tupper, Proverbial Philosophy 1849 44

2395 But rarely will it be true that what is good for one or
another pressure-group must be good for the country as well.
From H. G. Rickover,
Address, Ind. Univ. March 20 1960

2396 ... The ship of State, that ship on whose seaworthiness
the lives even of the mutineers depend.
Walter Raleigh,
Complete Works of George Savile ... 1912 vii

2397 A state well administered is our greatest safeguard.
Democritus, Frag. 252

2398 If you ask me whether a country with no highly developed sense of national purpose, with the overwhelming accent
of life on personal comfort, with a dearth of public services
and a surfeit of privately sold gadgetry, with insufficient social
discipline even to keep its major industries functioning without
grievous interruption, has, over the long run, good chances of

competing with a purposeful, serious and disciplined society,
I must say that the answer is no.   From G. Kennan

2399   It can never be well with any state unless it is well with
the nation; and now it can never be well with any nation unless
it is well with the world.
                    From H. E. Fosdick, Living . . . 1956 306 Harper

2400   The worth of a State, in the long run, is the worth of
the individuals composing it.   John Stuart Mill, On Liberty

2401   I believe there is no permanent greatness to a nation
unless it be based upon morality.   John Bright

2402   A society does not, or at least should not, exist to satisfy
an external survey, but to bring a good life to the individuals
who compose it.   Bertrand Russell, Authority . . .
                    1949 116 G. Allen; Simon & Schuster

2403   No institution can be good that does not tend to improve the individual.   Margaret Fuller

2404   Loyalty to country, like love, cannot be created by
legislation or compulsion. Loyalty must arise spontaneously
from the hearts of people who love their country and respect
their government because it offers freedom, justice, and opportunity for all.   From A. A. Morris, AAUP Bull. 1964 50:224

2405   A nation is a community in so far as it is a community
of communities.   From M. Buber,
                    Paths in Utopia 1949 136 Macmillan; Routledge

2406   No human society can continue to exist without some mutual confidence, good will, and responsible brotherhood. The more fully these social qualities are developed the stronger and better the society will be. By and large these qualities are not inborn but are acquired. The most favorable environment for such development is the intimate, face-to-face social group that we call the small community.

Characteristically, indigenous small communities have been too conservative to consider old ways and possible new ways in the light of new conditions. Cities, where widely different cultures, loyalties, and ideas meet, engender tolerance and intellectual stimulation which sometimes brings about great cultural advances. On the other hand, the city commonly fails to keep alive and strong those elemental traits without which society cannot exist. Social disintegration is characteristic of city life, and but for the fact that most city dwellers are but one or two generations removed from the small community this disintegration would be more marked.

The small community of the future will be neither a replica of the village of the past nor a surrender to the city. It will be a new creation, uniting the values of both, and largely avoiding their limitations.

From Arthur E. Morgan, Community . . . 1957 10 11 25
51 54 Community Service

2407   A liberal social order is a society of men who are diverse and various and love different things but have elbow room to live cheerfully together.

Diversity of preferences is not only pleasant; it is a social necessity.   From C. Frankel, Case for Modern Man
1956 84 149 Harper

2408   There is no room for authoritarian dogma in the field of human relations.   G. B. Chisholm, Psychiatry 1946 9:19

2409   The social order has nothing to do with our thoughts; but our actions must be accommodated to its ways.

Montaigne, Custom

2410   A good citizen pulls his oar.

2411   The patriot . . . must learn that to bear revilings and persecutions is a part of his duty.   Jefferson

2412   Our country, right or wrong! When right, to be kept right; when wrong, to be put right!   Carl Schurz

GOVERNMENT

2413   When men live in isolation and do not cooperate there will be insufficiency; when they live in community without order there will be conflict.

Hsüntse, in Y.-P. Mei, Motse 1934 124 Probsthain

2414   Man has given up his share of the natural right of defence into that of the state in order to be protected by it.

From Edmund Burke

2415   There is more strength in union than in number.
A people cannot stand without government. As old and as big as a nation is, it cannot go by itself; it must be led.

From Savile, Political Thoughts . . . , Of the People

2416 All history shows that the more widely and completely religion and government are separated, the better it is for both.
From Ohio Supreme Ct., Bd. of Educ.
Cincinnati vs. Minor 1872

2417 The powers of government are but a trust, and they cannot be lawfully exercised but for the good of the community. Daniel Webster, Address 1825

2418 As the happiness of the people is the sole end of government, so the consent of the people is the only foundation of it. John Adams

2419 A general discontent works several ways: sometimes like a slow poison that has its effects at a great distance from the time it was given, and sometimes like dry flax prepared to catch at the first fire, or like seed in the ground ready to sprout upon the first shower.

No government is perfect unless it has a kind of omnipotence to exercise upon great occasions. This cannot be obtained by force alone, be it never so great; there must be the consent of the people, too, or else a nation moves only by being driven, a sluggish and constrained motion, void of that life and vigor which is necessary to produce great things. All power exercised without consent is like wounding and gashing a tree, and tapping it at unseasonable times, which soon must destroy it. When the virtual consent of the whole people is included in their representatives, these execute whatever is so enjoined as their own wills; and whatever sap or juice there is in the nation may be produced to the last drop, whilst it rises naturally from the root.
From Savile,
Character of a Trimmer, Conclusion; id., . . . Laws . . .

2420   Order cannot be secured merely through fear of punishment; it is hazardous to discourage thought, hope, and
imagination. Fear breeds repression; repression breeds hate;
and hate menaces stable government. The fitting remedy for
evil counsels is good ones. Safety lies in the opportunity to
discuss freely grievances and proposed remedies.

From Brandeis

2421   Few are those rulers who, neglecting the virtuous and
slighting the learned, could still maintain the existence of
their countries.

The state and the people are to be governed by exalting
the virtuous, so that those in the state that do good will be
encouraged and those that do evil will be obstructed.

When the virtuous are not at the side of the rulers, the
vicious will be on their right and left.

When the honorable and wise run the government, the ignorant and humble remain orderly; but when the ignorant and
humble run the government, the honorable and wise become
rebellious.   From Motse, Y.-P. Mei (tr.),
Ethical . . . 1929 1 48 40 1 36 Probsthain

2422   The legitimate object of government is to do for a
community of people whatever they need to have done but
cannot do at all, or cannot do so well, for themselves in their
separate and individual capacities.

From Lincoln, Collected Works . . .
1953 2: July 1 1854 Rutgers Univ. Press

2423   That which is everybody's business is nobody's business.   Izaak Walton, Compleat Angler I II

2424   The danger is not that a particular social class is unfit to govern. Every social class, as such, is unfit to govern.

After J. E. E. D. Acton, Letters

2425   There are as good hearts to serve men in palaces as in cottages.   Robert Owen

2426   Raise to office men of virtue and talents.

Confucius, in Y.-P. Mei, Motse . . .

1934 119 Probsthain

2427   A ruler who appoints any man to an office when there is in his dominions another man better qualified for it sins against God and against the State.   The Koran

2428   Great actions speak great minds, and such should govern.   John Fletcher, The Prophetess II iii

2429   A man who cannot manage his own business is not to be trusted with the people's business.

From Savile, Maxim 29

2430   Public men must have public minds as well as salaries, or they will serve private ends at the public cost.

From William Penn

2431   If members of the parliament stay away out of laziness, let them be gratified by taking their ease at home without interruption.   From Savile, Some Cautions . . .

2432   Those who govern us are much beneath us if they are not far above us: having promised more, they must do more.

From Montaigne, in Lowenthal (ed.),
Autobiography . . . 1935 217 Houghton

2433   A political representative ought always to prefer the people's interest to his own; but he owes the people not only his industry but his judgment.   From Edmund Burke

2434   One in authority who follows his own opinion too soon is in danger of repenting it too late.

From Savile, Maxim 18

2435   The lack of spontaneity from which our highly organized societies tend to suffer is connected with excessive control over large areas by remote authorities.

Bertrand Russell, Authority . . .
1949 119 G. Allen; Simon & Schuster

2436   Every country where begging is a professions, is ill-governed.   Voltaire

CIVIC LAW

2437   As the fish die when they are out of water, so do people die without law and order.

Abodah Zarah, Gemara, in Newman and Spitz
(eds.), Talmudic Anthology 1945 247 Behrman

2438   A good conscience is a great help in sleeping soundly, but it is no substitute for law.

Walter Kaufmann, Critique of
Religion and Philosophy 1958 213 Harper

2439   The purpose of all law is to enhance human life.
The ultimate sanction of all law is the consent of the people who are to be governed by it.

> From The Talmud, in Bokser,
> Wisdom . . . 1951 13 108 Philos. Lib.

2440   The civilized world has always paid a willing subjection to laws. Even conquerors have done homage to them; as the Romans, who took patterns of good laws even from those they had subdued, and by this wise method arrived at such an admirable constitution of laws that this excellency of theirs triumphs still.

Laws secure men not only against one another, but against themselves too. They are to mankind what the sun is to plants: where they have their force and are not clouded or suppressed, everything smiles and flourishes; but where they are darkened, and not allowed to shine out, everything withers and decays. Without laws the world would become a wilderness, and men little less than beasts.

It would be too great partiality to say that the laws are perfect or liable to no objection; such things are not of this world; but if they have more excellences and fewer faults than any other that we know, it is enough to recommend them to our esteem.

But with all this, the best things may come to be the worst, if they are not in good hands. If it be true that the wisest men generally make the laws, it is as true that the strongest do often interpret them; and, as rivers belong as much to the channels where they run as to the springs from which they rise, so the laws depend as much upon the pipes through which they pass as upon the fountains from whence they flow.

To see the laws mangled, disguised, speak quite another language than their own; to see them thrown from the dignity of protecting mankind to the disgraceful office of destroying the people, will infuriate men and tempt them to follow the evil examples given them of judging without hearing.

> From Savile, Character of a Trimmer, . . . Laws . . .

2442　Laws are dumb in the midst of arms.

> Cicero, Pro Milone IV 11

2443　Every free people holds that only the law shall govern; the military must yield to the law.　　　From H. L. Black

2444　Reason is the life of the law.

> Edward Coke (1552–1634)

2445　In the long run, respect for law can be maintained only by maintaining respectable laws.

> H. W. Schneider, Three Dimensions . . .
> 1956 89 Ind. Univ. Press

2446　The law ought to prohibit only actions hurtful to society.

> Decl. . . . Rights
> of Man . . . 1789 V

2447　It does not follow that a man is more free where there is least law and more restricted where there is most law. A general prohibition in a state may increase the sum of liberty, and a general permission may diminish it.

> From H. G. Wells, Modern Utopia 1905 33

2448　Laws and institutions must progress as new discoveries are made, new truths disclosed, and manners and opinions change with the change of circumstances.　　From Jefferson

2449   Of all injustice, that is the greatest which goes under the name of law; and of all sorts of tyranny, the forcing of the letter of the law against the equity is the most insupportable.

Roger L'Estrange

2450   For so long as a law meets the needs of human society it is a just law.

From Epicurus, Strodach (tr.),
Philosophy . . . 1962 202–203 Northwestern Univ. Press

2451   Whoever draws his sword against the laws threatens the best of us with the whip and the noose.

Montaigne, in Lowenthal,
Autobiography . . . 1935 26 Houghton

2452   The people should fight for their law as for their city wall.   Heraclitus (Wheelwright, tr.)
1959 Frag. 111 Princeton Univ. Press

2453   He that hinders not a mischief when it is in his power is guilty of it.   Rule of Life 1800 134

2454   More states have perished from the violation of morality than from the violation of law.   Montesquieu

CIVIL EQUALITY

2455   Where privilege reigns,
        The hungry judges soon the sentence sign,
        And wretches hang that jurymen may dine.

Pope, Rape of the Lock III 21

2456   . . . Think ye that building shall endure
        Which shelters the noble and crushes the poor?
                        From Emerson, Man the Reformer

2457   The only stable state is the one in which all men are
equal before the law.   Unknown

2458   That is the most perfect government under which a
wrong to the humblest is an affront to all.   Solon

2459   The law forbids the rich as well as the poor to steal
from pushcarts and to sleep under bridges.
                                        From Anatole France

2460   The history of freedom in our country has been the
history of knocking down the barriers to equal rights.
                                        Adlai E. Stevenson

2461   That government is most perfect in which . . . the
supreme and constant aim is to secure the rights of every human being.   W. E. Channing, Works 1848 2:38

INJUSTICE

2462   To do injustice is more disgraceful than to suffer it.
                            Plato, Gorgias cccclxxxix

2463   Injustice to strangers does not breed justice to our
friends.   W. E. Channing, Works 1875 2:93

2464   Nations fall where judges are unjust, because then there is nothing which the multitude think worth defending.

From Sydney Smith,
Judge that Smites Contrary to the Law

JUSTICE

2465   In the early modes of thinking, justice is defined by the express appointment of law. The notion of a higher justice, to which laws themselves are amenable, and by which the conscience is bound, is a later extension of the idea.

From John Stuart Mill, Three Essays . . . 1885 52

2466   The law is no more than the formal expression of that tolerable compromise that we call justice, without which the rule of tooth and claw must prevail.

Learned Hand, Irving Dilliard (ed.),
Spirit . . . 1952 87 Knopf

2467   Justice is justly represented blind because she sees no difference in the parties concerned.   William Penn

2468   Abraham Lincoln was as just and generous to the rich and well-born as to the poor and humble—a thing rare among politicians.   John Hay

2469   His way of dealing with those whom it is easy to wrong shows whether a man really loves justice.

From Plato (Bury, tr.)

2470   How should a husband treat his wife, or a friend a friend? The basic answer is the same as to the question, How should they treat one another justly?

After Aristotle,
Nicomachean Ethics (Welldon, tr.) VIII XIV

2471   Justice is a greater good than property.

W. E. Channing, Works 1848 2:40

2472   I care about life, but . . . there are things I care about more than life . . . I do not like death, but . . . there are things I dislike more than death. I care about life, but too I care about Justice. If I cannot have both, then I choose Justice.

Mencius (Dobson, tr.)
1963 142 Univ. Toronto Press; Oxford

2473   Ideal justice and perfect altruism alike intend the best possible for everyone.

After Stanton Coit, Message of Man 1902 177

2474   The ideal of penal justice is the maximum of social defense with the minimum of individual suffering.

From J. M. Guyau, Sketch . . . 1898 180–181

2475   To be objective and fair is to be strong, and the world is at the feet of him whom it cannot tempt.

From Amiel, Journal

2476   When the world begins to look unreal, in any action of justice or charity things look solid again.

From Emerson, Journal

2477   For justice in a controversy, one man's word is no man's word; we should hear both sides.   From Goethe

2478   If the Court does not remain true to principles, the workmen will not keep true to standards. If the ruler contravenes Justice, lesser men will contravene the penal code.

Mencius (Dobson, tr.)
1963 151–152 Univ. Toronto Press; Oxford

POLITICAL LIBERTY

2479   For untold generations man has sought liberty—liberty to live his life, subject only to the right of other men to live their lives; liberty to worship or not worship according to his own conscience; liberty to adapt customs to whatever new environment he may choose for himself; liberty to express his own thoughts; liberty to find in the social order the niche for which he is best adapted, regardless of race, or creed, or color; liberty to work at any available task, suitable to his abilities and taste, for a sufficient wage to support himself and his family in reasonable comfort; liberty to follow his own political convictions; liberty to keep his children in school until they are equipped to put their abilities into service.

After Harold L. Ickes, Autobiography . . .
1943 326 Reynal, © Harcourt

2480   Liberty in the concrete means release from something once taken as normal but now experienced as bondage. At one time, liberty signified release from serfdom; at another time, emancipation from chattel slavery. During the late Seventeenth and early Eighteenth Centuries it meant liberation from despotic dynastic rule. A century later it meant release of industrialists from legal customs that hampered the new forces of production. Now it signifies liberation from material insecurity and from the coercions and repressions that keep multitudes from participation in the vast cultural resources that are at hand.

From John Dewey, Liberalism ... 1935 48 Putnam

2481   As authors, our first professional duty is to watch over the freedom of our art; as citizens, our first civic duty is to watch over the liberty of our fellow citizens; as men, our first human duty is to watch over liberty [within fairness to all].

Salvador de Madariaga,
Essays with a Purpose 1954 42 Hollis

2482   The most certain test by which we judge whether a country is really free is the amount of security enjoyed by minorities.

J. E. E. D. Acton, Address, History of Freedom ...

2483   Without the freedom to be wrong in the face of a majority that is right, there can be no freedom to be right when the majority is wrong.

G. S. Stanford, AAUP Bull. 1963 49:285

2484   The majority must not abrogate the fundamental rights in virtue of which the minority is free to become the majority.   J. Middleton Murry, Love ...

1957 210–211 Cape, © Soc. of Authors

2485   Like the course of the heavenly bodies, harmony in national life is a resultant of the struggle between contending forces. In frank expression of conflicting opinion lies the greatest promise of wisdom in governmental action; and in suppression lies ordinarily the greatest peril.

Brandeis, Gilbert v. Minnesota 254 U.S. 325 (1920)

2486   Free men have found no alternative to tolerance for opposing political ideas. There is the beginning of the end of liberty when a difference of opinion becomes confused with treason or disloyalty. The strength of the parliamentary method is in the contest for men's hearts and minds, with both majority and minority content to abide the result.

William O. Douglas,
Almanac of Liberty 1954 258 Doubleday; Lantz

2487   We would rather die on our feet than live on our knees.   F. D. Roosevelt, Address 1939

2488   Liberty is both a privilege and a test.

From Lecomte de Noüy,
Human Destiny 1947 118 Longmans

2489   Freedom is an atmosphere which makes the sun brighter, and the air clearer, and the honey sweeter.

Nicholai Velimirovic,
Serbia in Light and Darkness 1916 Longmans

2490   When Liberty is gone,
          Life grows insipid and has lost its relish.

Addison, Cato II 3

2491   True liberty makes us modest and high-minded.

Pestalozzi, Education . . . 1953 63 Philos. Lib.

2492   Lean liberty is better than fat slavery.

Thomas Fuller

2493   I prefer dangerous liberty rather than quiet servitude.

Jefferson

2494   Though the laziness of a slavish subjection has its charms for the more gross and earthy part of mankind, to men made of a better clay all that the world can give without liberty has no taste. Liberty has powerful charms which so dazzle us that we find beauties in it which perhaps are not there; yet since the reasonable desire of it ought not to be restrained, and even the unreasonable desire of it cannot be entirely suppressed, those who would take it away from a people are likely to fail in the attempting, or be very unquiet in the keeping of it.

From Savile, Character of a Trimmer . . . Laws . . .

2495   In the long run, the free have triumphed over the enslaved.   A. Barth, Loyalty . . . 1951 238 Viking

2496   What light is to the eyes, what love is to the heart, liberty is to the soul of man. Liberty is the condition of progress. Without liberty there can be no true civilization.

From Ingersoll

2497   If the people of a nation value anything more than freedom, they will lose their freedom; and if it is comfort or money that they value more, they will lose that too.

From Maugham

2498   Freedom without moral commitment is aimless and self-destructive.

Free men must be competent men.

From John W. Gardner,
Excellence 1961 137 159 Harper

2499   When words lose their meaning, the people will lose their liberty.   Confucius

2500   There is only one cure for evils which newly acquired freedom produces, and that cure is freedom.   Macaulay

2501   Eternal vigilance is the price of liberty.

Traditional

2502   We must remember that vigilance without knowledge is blindfold.   From W. R. Brain, Science 1965 148:194

2503   As with a man, that state will be the best in which liberty and order fuse.

From E. G. Bulwer-Lytton, Caxtoniana 1864 433

2504   The cause of civil liberty must not be surrendered at the end of one or even one hundred defeats.

Lincoln, Letter Nov. 19 1858

CIVIL RIGHTS

2505   Chains are but an ill wearing, how much soever we gild or polish them.

From John Locke, Works ... 1812 I V 212

2506   It is no light thing to have secured a livelihood on condition of going through life masked and gagged.

John Morley, On Compromise 1913 III 92

2507   The first-recorded judicial murder of a scientific thinker was composed and effected, not by a despot, not by priests, but by eloquent demagogues.

From Huxley, in Bibby,
T. H. Huxley 1959 257 Horizon Press

2508   No man was ever endowed with a civil right without a responsibility.   From Gerald W. Johnson

2509   Our civil rights have no dependence on our religious opinions, any more than our opinions in physics or geometry.
Jefferson, Bill for disestablishing church

2510   In the religious beliefs of individuals, government effort to force compliance leads only to hypocrisy. The civil authority should allow orthodox and heterodox, for the common good.   Themistius, in J. B. Bury, History . . . 1913 55

2511   Compulsory unification of opinion would achieve only the unanimity of the graveyard.

From F. Frankfurter,
Public . . . 1930 Yale Univ. Press

2512   Due process of law is guaranteed specifically because situations might arise in which society or its authorities might be inclined to deny it. Freedom of speech is granted for the sake of those situations in which someone might believe curtailment necessary, warranted, or even patriotic.
From M. S. Arnoni, Minority of One Feb. 1960 3

2513   The First Amendment protects two kinds of interests in free speech. There is an individual interest, the need of many men to express their opinions on matters vital to them if life is to be worth living, and a social interest that the country may find the wisest course of action and carry it out in the wisest way.

Nevertheless, there are other purposes of government, such

as order, the training of the young, protection against external aggression. Unlimited discussion sometimes interferes with these purposes, which must then be balanced against freedom of speech, but freedom of speech ought to weigh very heavily in the scale.

In wartime, speech should be unrestricted by the censorship or by punishment, unless it is clearly liable to cause direct and dangerous interference with the conduct of the war.

The real value of freedom of speech is not to the minority that wants to talk, but to the majority that does not want to listen.

"We are especially called upon to maintain free discussion for unpopular sentiments or persons, as in no other case will any effort to maintain it be needed." (From a friend of Lovejoy, the Abolitionist printer killed in the Alton riots.)

From Z. Chafee, Jr.,
Free Speech in the United States
1941 33 31 35 ix 4 Harvard Univ. Press

2514   To help the slave to be free supports freedom for all.

2515   He that would make his own liberty secure must guard even his enemy from oppression.   Thomas Paine

2516   I disagree entirely with what you say, and I shall defend to the death your right to say it.   From Voltaire

2517   Freedom is not something one can own by prescriptive right, but a boon which every day must be fought for anew.

Alf Ross, Why Democracy?
1952 4 Harvard Univ. Press

2518   Freedom of opinion, of speech, and of the press is our most valuable privilege, the safeguard of all other rights.
From W. E. Channing, Duties of the Citizen . . .

2519   For all its excesses and inconveniences, societies that tolerate criticism unconditionally tend to be stronger and more stable than those that do not.
Alan Barth, Loyalty of Free Men 1951 236 Viking

2520   True security will be ours only as we keep each of the freedoms intact.   J. W. Caughey, In Clear and Present
Danger 1958 18 Univ. Chicago Press

INTELLECTUAL FREEDOM

2521   To put chains upon the body is as nothing compared to putting shackles on the brain.   Ingersoll

2522   Where all think alike, no one thinks very much.
Walter Lippmann

2523   When things are "unthinkable," thinking stops and action becomes mindless.   From J. W. Fulbright,
"Old Myths . . ." Senate speech 1964

2524   Isolation from opposed views encourages narrow sectarianism, which makes for political paranoia.
From Irving Kristol, Reporter 1959 21:9 48

2525   A morality that is pushed upon the people through dogmatic indoctrination, not developed in them through education, proves more halfhearted or fanatical than genuine.
Santayana, Reason in Society 1905 134

2526   The real disturbers of the peace are those who seek to curtail the liberty of judgment which they are unable to tyrannize over.

From Spinoza, Theologico-political Treatise XX

2527   The opinions of men are not the object of civil government, nor under its jurisdiction. It is time enough for the rightful purposes of civil government for its officers to interfere when principles break out into overt acts against peace and good order.

Truth will prevail unless disarmed of her natural weapons, free argument and debate.

From Jefferson, Virginia Act
for Establishing Religious Freedom 1779

2528   Truth is not taught by laws, nor has she any need of force to procure her entrance into the minds of men. Errors indeed prevail by the assistance of coercive "authorities." But if truth makes not her way into the understanding by her own light, she will be but weaker for any borrowed force violence can add to her.

From John Locke, Concerning Toleration

2529   I believe that that community is already in process of dissolution where each man begins to eye his neighbor as a possible enemy, where non-conformity with the accepted creed, political as well as religious, is a mark of disaffection; where denunciation, without specification or backing, takes the place of evidence; where orthodoxy chokes freedom of dissent; where faith in the eventual supremacy of reason has become so timid that we dare not enter our convictions in the open lists, to win or lose. The mutual confidence on which all else depends can be maintained only by an open mind and a brave reliance upon free discussion. We must not yield a foot upon demanding a fair field and an honest race to all ideas.

From Learned Hand, Address 1952

2530   Forcing a person cannot make him sincere.

2531   To restrict free thought is to make men think one thing and say another, to the corruption of good faith, that mainstay of government, and to the fostering of hateful flattery and perfidy, whence spring stratagems, and the corruption of every good art.

From Spinoza, Theologico-political Treatise XX

2532   Truth is compared in Scripture to a streaming fountain; if her waters flow not in a perpetual progression, they sicken into a muddy pool of conformity and tradition . . .

That which purifies us is trial, and trial is by what is contrary . . .

Where there is much desire to learn, there of necessity will be much arguing, much writing, many opinions; for opinion in good men is but knowledge in the making.

Milton, Areopagitica 1951 37 18 45

2533   Most philosophical and scientific doctrines emphasize only one aspect of the truth; conflicting theories are often complementary; the successful doctrine may therefore have to go back to its defeated rivals and learn from them.

From Lancelot Law Whyte,
Unconscious . . . 1960 7 Basic Books

2534   Shallow streams are soon exhausted.
A river does not come from a single source.

> From Motse, Y.-P. Mei (tr.),
> Ethical . . . 1929 5 Probsthain

2535   It often happens that the saints are wrong and the
children of this world right.   Gilbert Murray

2536   The price of freedom of religion or of speech or of the
press is that we must put up with a good deal of rubbish.

> From Robert H. Jackson

2537   Error of opinion may be tolerated where reason is left
free to combat it.   Jefferson

2538   You cannot think right without running the risk of
thinking wrong; but for any evils that may come from thinking, the cure is more thinking.

> Elmer Davis, in Murrow (ed.),
> This I Believe 1952 37 Simon & Schuster

2539   If ideas when aroused cannot be communicated, they
may fade away or become warped and morbid.

> After John Dewey, Philosophy . . . 1931 297 Minton

2540   It is always probable that dissentients have something
worth hearing, and that truth would lose something by their
silence.

If all mankind minus one were of one opinion, and only one
person were of the contrary opinion, mankind would be no
more justified in silencing that one person than he, if he had

the power, would be justified in silencing mankind. The peculiar evil of silencing the expression of an opinion is that, if the opinion is right, mankind are deprived of the opportunity of exchanging error for truth; if wrong, they lose, what is almost as great a benefit, the clearer perception and livelier impression of truth produced by its collision with error.

From John Stuart Mill, On Liberty 1892 II 28 10

2541   No faith can live today in anything but a fool's paradise unless it ventures out into the open air of critical reason as science does.   From Morris R. Cohen,
Reason and Nature 1931 x
Harcourt, © Rosenfield

2542   There can be no wisdom without freedom of thought, and no public liberty without freedom of speech.

From Franklin,
New England Courant 1722

2543   If there is anything that cannot bear free speech, let it crack.   Wendell Phillips, Speech 1861

2544   The best test of truth is the power of the thought to get itself accepted in the competition of the market.

(Justice) O. W. Holmes, . . .
Abrams et al v. U.S. 250 U.S. 616 1919

2545   Academic freedom is not a privilege of a few; it is a right of the people to learn what scholars may find if they are left free and secure.

From F. Machlup, AAUP Bull. 1955 41:757

2546   The society which subordinates academic freedom to public-security precautions faces many more problems than it solves.   From Academic Freedom Com.,
Am. Civil Lib. Union, School and Soc. Oct. 7 1961

2547   A good book is the precious life-blood of a master spirit, embalmed and treasured up on purpose to a life beyond life.

Why should we abridge or scant those means, which books freely permitted are, both to the trial of virtue and the exercise of truth?

For the want of a rejected truth, whole nations fare the worse.

From Milton, Areopagitica 1951 6 26 6

2548   Public libraries should be open to all—except the censor. The Bill of Rights is the guardian of our security as well as our liberty.   J. F. Kennedy, Sat. Rev. Oct. 29, 1960

2549   In the long run of history, the censor and the inquisitor have always lost. The only sure weapon against bad ideas is better ideas.   From A. W. Griswold

2550   We must give liberty to art. If she strays from the way, she will reach it again. Not Shakespeare himself can prescribe to art her roads and aims.   Dostoevsky

2551   Culture will always be in peril where criticism cannot be freely practised.

André Gide, in Richard Crossman (ed.),
God That Failed 1940 190 Harper

2552   No man who in his heart limits freedom to those who think as he thinks is a true lover of freedom.

> J. Frank Dobie,
> Wild and Free 1952 privately printed

2553   To a man intellectually free, truth is not a foreign substance, dormant, lifeless, fruitless; but penetrating, prolific, full of vitality, and ministering to the health and expansion of the soul.   From W. E. Channing, Napoleon Bonaparte

2554   Freedom of thinking is required not only to form great thinkers but, even more, to enable average human beings to attain the mental stature which they are capable of.

> From John Stuart Mill, On Liberty 1892 II 20

2555   The mark of a truly civilized man is confidence in the inquiring mind.   From F. Frankfurter,
> Concurrence, Smith Act case 1951

2556   Without free speech no wholehearted search for truth is possible, no discovery of truth is most useful. Any abuse of free speech dies in a day, but the denial of free speech entombs the hope of the race.

> From Charles Bradlaugh

2557   Give me the liberty to know, to utter, and to argue freely according to conscience, above all liberties.

> Milton, Areopagitica 1951 49

2558   The spirit of liberty, taught nearly two thousand years ago, is that the least shall be heard and considered side by side with the greatest.

> From Learned Hand, N. Y. Times Aug. 20 1957 4–5

2559   Equality of opportunity among opinions is essential
if there is to be real freedom of thought.

> Bertrand Russell, Free Thought . . . 1922 41 Huebsch

2560   Let us freely hear both sides.   Jefferson

2561   There is such a thing as passionate intelligence, as
ardor in behalf of light shining into the murky places of social
existence, and as zeal for its refreshing and purifying effect.
Mankind has not tried devotion to intelligence as a force in
social action.   From John Dewey,

> Common Faith 1934 79 Yale Univ. Press

2562   As mankind progresses towards freedom from want
and from fear, freedom of religion and of speech will more and
more become a living reality.

> Sumner Welles, World of The
> Four Freedoms 1943 Columbia Univ. Press

2563   When a man has the talent to attack with effect falsehood, prejudice, and imposture, it is his duty to use it. Knowledge, and therefore civilization, are advanced by criticism and
negation as well as by construction and positive discovery.

> From J. B. Bury, History . . . 1913 156

2564   Clear and honest thinking can almost always be expressed in simple words which are understandable by the people who matter in a democracy . . . everyone who can be
reached and given help toward intellectual freedom and honesty for themselves and for the children whose future depends
on them.   G. B. Chisholm, Psychiatry 1946 9:9

2565   I have sworn upon the altar of God eternal hostility against every form of tyranny over the mind of man.

Jefferson, Letter Sept. 23 1800

2566   The state must guarantee freedom of spirit to every citizen lest it become a house of slaves; for no man is free unless his spirit be free.   Winthrop S. Dakin,
Amherst (Mass.) Rec. May 15 1958

2567   Free inquiry makes for constantly renewed effort to see life as it is, and to see it whole.

From Arthur E. Morgan,
Observations 1968 249 Antioch Press

ANARCHY, DESPOTISM, AND DEMOCRACY

2568   Men have very different tempers and capacities from one another, naturally; have very different educations; do improve themselves very differently by study, according to their different capacities, application, and opportunities; have different interests, passions, and infirmities, by which they are influenced and actuated; and are all fallible.

Anthony Collins,
Discourse of the Grounds . . . 1724 xxxviii

2569   "America isn't a democracy. I can't drive my car down the left side of Main Street without getting arrested." So spoke a Nazi who was teaching in an American college. He was intelligent, but, as a devotee of a despotic system, he failed to distinguish democracy from anarchy. Perhaps most persons who say "I don't believe in democracy" take the word to mean unlimited individualism, chaos with no well-structured government and order.

Anarchy means, of course, without government; anarchists want no person, group, or institution to govern them. All anarchists want to do as they please.

Roughly speaking, there are three kinds of anarchists: the simple, the violent, and those who call themselves philosophical anarchists.

Simple anarchists seek to do as they please without concern for obstacles. The first simple anarchists were Adam and Eve. "Genesis," plus Mark Twain's authoritative "Adam's Diary" and "Eve's Diary," and our knowledge of human nature, when combined, create the following history:

Naturally, at first, Adam was a simple anarchist. So was Eve. Their satisfaction in living together increased from day to day, but only as their simple anarchy waned. Neither one, however, took on either violent anarchy or philosophical anarchy. Before their simple anarchy was far-gone, it encouraged them to eat of the forbidden tree. Consequently, when they were driven out of the Garden of Eden into the world of men, they renounced their anarchy and fitted in, more or less, to whatever system was then in vogue. Their children labored for anarchy anew; but Adam and Eve and their neighbors forbade.

Simple anarchy cannot survive in the world of men.

Violent anarchists are concerned about obstacles, especially human and institutional obstacles; so concerned that they attack and even destroy whatever persons and institutions get in their way. Consequently, all nonanarchists try to keep the violent anarchists down, if necessary by locking them up.

Human obstacles limit violent anarchy.

Philosophical anarchists seem to assume that every person is good so long as he neither governs nor is governed by another, and that for any one to govern another is bad for both the governor and the governed. At the same time, these anarchists look to "voluntary associations" to take care of the people's banking, health services, and so on. Such associations would seem to require their own controls of any wayward members;—but are not any such controls really anti-anarchistic?

Philosophical anarchy might have been workable for Adam and Eve and all their descendants if every one had been either a solitary islander, or a saint, or a ghost. This is because the solitary islander cannot get in anybody's way; the true saint would not; and if the ghost got in the way, it wouldn't matter. Since the usual human being is unwilling to become either a solitary islander, a saint, or a ghost, the future of philosophical anarchy, like the future of the other kinds, seems unfruitful.

Anarchists get very much in other people's way; so much that some of the other people who want to do as they please become despots.

Despotism means rule by and for the interests of the despot, without fair regard for the interests of the ruled. The compulsion may be physical, as through beating; economic, through poverty; psychological, through brainwashing; or any combination of such devices.

The despot may be an individual, or, in effect, a group, even a minority or a majority.

The despot's interests may be largely if not wholly benevolent; but he is likely tyrannical and certainly narrow. He is narrow as a man as he fails to understand, learn from, and share his subjects' interests. He is narrow also as an executive as he fails to deal fairly with all his subjects' interests, especially their interests to be self-directing.

For example: The inhabitants of a small island are ruled

by a despot. Rumblings from their long-dormant volcano make the despot and all his subjects plan to flee. Two ships, the *Ark* and the *Dart,* are at hand. Either ship is large enough to carry all the people. As there are only enough crewmen and fuel for one ship, one ship must be chosen. The *Ark* is a plain craft. The *Dart* is elegant. It had been made historic by the despot's ancestors, and he pictures himself as well framed on that ship. He therefore chooses the *Dart.*

The majority of his subjects raise no question; but a minority, including the crew, judge that ship to be unseaworthy. The despot silences the minority. He herds all his subjects aboard the *Dart,* and forth they go.

A storm sinks the ship with all on board, but not until everyone except the despot believes that he had been unfair to everyone's interests, including his own.

If the despot had come to understand and appreciate his people's general need for self-direction, he might have found himself not an overlord but a democratically chosen umpire for emergency decisions. He might even have proved to be a leader and fellow of free men, so far as men can be free.

Perhaps every person who says he does not believe in democracy believes that "the people" are continually wrong, and supposes that a "true leader" (here a euphemism for despot) can be found who will be continually right. "Right" means, naturally, what the one who favors the despot takes to be right.

An occasional proponent of despotism would like to be the despot, or at least to own and operate a despot—that is, to be the real despot but behind the scenes.

Of course, authoritative but kind direction is necessary for infants, juveniles of any age, and abnormal persons, and, in emergencies, for seriously uninformed persons; necessary to protect them and the public. Such direction, however, often can be reduced systematically by developing every subject's cooperation and self-direction so far as possible. Even psychotics in mental institutions benefit more or less from meeting together and working out some self-government.

From the point of view of mental hygiene, any one who favors despotism as the best way to manage all the people is markedly obtuse or obsessed. In enlightened countries, many would-be despots reside in mental hospitals.

Despots are against anarchists, as they find them bad for the despots. Real democrats are against anarchists and despots, as they find them bad for all the people.

Some persons think that democracy is only a daydream of "liberty, equality, and fraternity"; a daydream because it is contrary to human nature. In their view, man is really self-seeking; all the animals, including man, have evolved through individual struggle for survival; and thus each man, in order to survive, must look out for himself. From that point of view, "justice for all" is unnatural; "dog eat dog" is the natural way; and any society that fails to recognize this truth is too anemic to survive.

Those who hold this view need to know that species have evolved through selection of variations that preserve not only the individual but also the group. These variations enable the individual to keep fit under ordinary circumstances; to be congenial with at least some of his fellows; to summon help from them, and to help them; to cooperate, and develop common purposes; to enjoy associates' individual differences and contributions to the group life; and to learn and communicate the ways to keep fit and to live as an individual member of the group.

Some persons take democracy to mean that everybody must decide everything; and, since that is impossible, there can be no real democracy. Such persons are thinking of a fictitious realm called "absolute or pure democracy" as distinguished from "representative democracy." That "pure" kind is possible only for small groups, or for large groups on clear issues with full communication. Ordinarily, for large groups the democracy must be largely representative.

What, then, is democracy?

Democracy is "government of the people, by the people, for the people." All the people are the sovereign.

Ideally, in a democracy every person is free to choose associates; to think, discuss, and learn; to have individual interests and jobs, so far as available, according to abilities; and to be equal before the law; all so far as best for all the people. (The immature, the ignorant, and the abnormal must be protected and controlled, by force if necessary.) All normally qualified persons have the right to vote. The voters choose, directly or indirectly, their political representatives, executives, and laws, including any constitution or other "law above the laws."

Every enlightened citizen realizes that intellectual freedom is a great good in itself, that it is supported by every other good of democracy, and that it is a necessary support for all those other goods.

Thus the people develop their own government and community, and, through these, they develop the individual citizens.

Consequently, for example, it is not undemocratic to place school children in sectioned classes and let each section, or even each child, advance at its own speed. To hold every child to the same schedule would be regimentation unfair to every pupil whose ability is either above or below the conventional pace. (The children's need to know children of different kinds can be taken care of otherwise, as in sports and arts.) Ideally, all the children should be equal in *doing their best with what genes and opportunities they have.* On this individual *ratio of performance to personal equipment* many a less-favored person is superior to a more-favored one.

To quote Arthur E. Morgan, the democratic hope is that "there shall no longer be a gulf between those who think, and those who have their thinking done for them; between those whose lives count, and those whose lives do not count. . . . Yet it is fundamental that competence, wisdom, insight and skill shall be respected by those who do not have them." (*Observations,* 1968, 90–91, Antioch Press.)

Democracy assumes that, *under favorable living conditions,* whatever is *really* best for the individual is best for the group, and whatever is *really* best for the group is best for the individual.

This does not mean that a particular social order, such as the one Plato envisioned for *his* ideal state, or whatever order Hitler might have approved for *his* master-race, could be really best for any group and its members. Neither does it mean that whatever particular way of life a person espouses must be really best for the group or even for him. Any stereotyped scheme for living, whether for the group or for a person, is too constricting and contrary to evolution to be the best way. The group thrives best not when it sacrifices unnecessarily, but when it conserves, the physical lives and the mental powers, spontaneity, and joy of living of its members. In turn, every member lives most fully when he is as free as he can be, while letting others be as free as they can be, considering the good of all.

As Ernst and Lindey observed, "Liberty is not a luxury. It is a basic necessity without which man declines. This is a biologic fact, not a philosophic concept." (Hold Your Tongue, 1932, 341, Morrow.) Spinoza noted that a conquered group is guided more by fear than hope; a free group, more by hope than fear; in that the former aims to escape death, but the latter, to secure life.

Democracy seeks not the most rigid but the soundest organization of the group. The soundest organization is that which makes for the best life for the individual and the group. Thus democracy aspires to what Ralph Barton Perry called "harmonious happiness."

Whenever either individuals or groups must compete to survive, the democratic way has some disadvantages. Especially in its early stages, a democracy may suffer from public unawareness of issues and from divided counsels. On the other hand, a democratic society best enables its members to understand, so far as they can, themselves, each other, and their opponents, and to withstand unreasonable opposition. These abilities to understand and withstand develop through the intellectual freedom that is integral to democracy: the essentially scientific freedom to question, examine, infer, invent, and test.

The anarchist and the despot alike fail to appreciate democracy as more highly evolved than either anarchy or despotism. In contrast, the democrat has observed anarchy and despotism, sometimes in himself, and often at the zoo, in barnyards, among immature persons, and in abnormal persons; and he understands how anarchy and despotism fall short of the responsibilities and satisfactions of democracy.

Democrats undertake to replace physical struggle with ideational struggle, the free competition of ideas.

Darwin pointed out that island species are less robust than continental species, because an island cannot support the large number of individuals that are needed to allow many favorable variations to occur. In that vein, if there were an anarchistic society, intellectually it would be like a lot of one-man islands:

the men would be so out of touch with each other that all their ideas could not struggle as they would in a democratic community. A despotism, intellectually, is all one island; yet it allows only the ruler's ideas to grow up, and so eliminates struggle between ideas. In this respect, any despotism, from the despotism of "only one party and only one policy within the party" to the despotism of the toughest dictator, is on a level with an authoritarian seminary in which immature minds are protected from tabooed ideas. A democracy, on the other hand, is an intellectual continent which allows ideas to burgeon and compete freely, that the best may come to survive and help the democracy to survive. Thus democracy is the most realistic, robust, and adaptable way.

Democracy itself tends to survive through its propensity to inherit the earth, not for special individuals or a favored group but for all individuals, the world group. This does not mean that democracy is a word which can dissolve all problems of overpopulation, ambition, and other individual and group conflicts. It means that the democrat is more fitted than the anarchist or the despotist to understand that a human enemy represents failure to discover common interest; and that, in Spinoza's phrase, "nothing is so useful to man as man." It means, too, that other nations are far more willing to join a democracy than to be taken over by a despotism.

True democracy defends itself by brute force when it must. Otherwise it conquers aggressors by persuasion such that the conquered yield "not through weakness but through increase of strength."

Democracy is, as Franklin Delano Roosevelt observed, "the most humane, the most advanced, and in the end the most unconquerable of all forms of human society." Third Inaugural Address.

Partly from W. S. Taylor, J. Soc. Psychol. 1945

2570   Slavery and knavery go as seldom asunder as tyranny and cruelty.

Nathaniel Ward, Simple Cobbler . . . 1647 49

2571   Oppression makes a poor country, and a desperate people who always wait an opportunity to change.

William Penn

2572   Man's capacity for justice makes democracy possible; but man's inclination to injustice makes democracy necessary.

Reinhold Niebuhr, Children . . . 1953 xi Scribner

2573   What is the best government? That which teaches us to govern ourselves.   Goethe

2574   To be afraid of ideas, any idea, is to be unfit for self-government.   A. Meiklejohn,
Free Speech . . . 1956 27 Harper

2575   Change is inherent in democracy. Thus democracy is inimical to all systems of authority, whether professedly Christian or Muslim, Capitalist or Communist, which believe themselves to be possessed of absolute and final truths. This conflict between democracy and authoritarianism remains even if the authoritarian systems themselves contain, as all these do, important democratic elements.

From Francis Williams, in Julian Huxley (ed.),
Humanist Frame 1961 99–102 G. Allen

2576   No personal habit more surely degrades the conscience and the intellect than blind and unhesitating obedience to unlimited authority.

Huxley, in Bibby, T. H. Huxley 1959 257 Horizon

2577   The people can and do make grave mistakes; but compared with the mistakes that have been made by every kind of autocracy they are unimportant.

From Calvin Coolidge, Address 1923

2578   Democracy is bigger than the demagogue and can survive his onslaughts, as history has many times demonstrated.

From C. R. Adrian, AAUP Bull. 1958 44:573–574

2579   Leadership is as necessary in a democratic as in a totalitarian state. When leadership is inept or misguided, free men have a means of correcting mistakes by a change of leadership.

From Alan Barth,
Loyalty of Free Men 1951 232–233 Viking

2580   Caste and class societies thwart and squander the assets of human diversity. Equality of opportunity makes for utilization of diversity.

From T. Dobzhansky,
Science 1962 137:112–113

2581   The democratic idea has fostered societies in which the individual is left free to pursue truth and virtue as he imperfectly perceives them, with due regard for the right of every other individual to pursue a different, and quite possibly superior, set of values. When we acknowledge our own fallibility, tolerance and compromise become possible and fanaticism becomes absurd.

"Democratic" nations are susceptible to dogmatism, but this susceptibility is a denial of the democratic spirit.

From J. W. Fulbright, Address Dec. 5 1963

2582   The tolerant mind is not as inefficient or paralyzed as it may look. The greater the freedom of thought, the more

concentrated and disciplined the power of action, because freedom of thought tends to eliminate impulsive, premature, or panic-stricken action.   From N. Frye,
By Liberal Things 1959 21 Clarke Irwin

2583   Tolerance of diversity may threaten national unity, but intolerance will destroy it.   From Alan Barth

2584   Only those reasoned convictions which emerge from diversity of opinion can lead to unity.
From J. B. Conant,
Education . . . 1949 179 Harvard Univ. Press

2585   The final decision of the group is usually superior to that of the individual.
Friends' Book of Discipline

2586   Often the public rises to meet its problems when it sees clearly what they are.   From J. S. Bixler,
Harvard Foundation . . .
Newsletter Dec. 30 1961 2

2587   In practically every major war for the past two hundred and fifty years the more democratic side, the side giving more weight to the popular will, has been victorious (the only possible exception is the Franco-Prussian War, if that can be regarded as a major war).
From Francis Williams, in Julian Huxley
(ed.), Humanist Frame 1961 97 G. Allen

2588   In a democracy, the price of freedom is eternal vigilance to make certain a strong and viable nation will remain at all times superior to the demands of selfish groups for increased power, wealth or special privilege.

H. G. Rickover,
Address Ind. Univ. March 20 1960

2589 When a man is drowned in a political party, plunged in it beyond his depth, he can hardly be called a free agent and one to be trusted with the people's liberty.

From Savile, Some Cautions . . .

2590 Democracy depends on competence for self-government. The competence is learned by actual participation in government. The best school for competence is the local community where people may know the facts they are dealing with, and can observe the results of their actions and policies. A nation with a broad foundation of local self-government will have a reservoir of ability which can be drawn upon for larger fields, and will be relatively secure from dictatorships and from wild fluctuations of policy.

From Arthur E. Morgan,
Community . . . 1957 97 Community Service

2591 A free society that refuses to exert itself will not last long. Freedom alone will not save it.

From John W. Gardner,
Life, June 13 1960 100, © Time

2592 How to give all access to the masterpieces of art and nature is the problem of civilization.

From Emerson, Wealth

2593   Creative activity flourishes best when ordinary men have a sense of freedom and responsibility, and extraordinary men work in free association with their fellows.

Walter R. Agard,
What Democracy Meant to the Greeks
1942 4 Univ. N. C. Press

2594   If a democracy is healthy, it produces its own antidotes to whatever disease it suffers.

The maxim "Nothing avails but perfection" may be spelt: "Paralysis."   From Winston Churchill

2595   You can fool some of the people all of the time, and all of the people some of the time, but you cannot fool all of the people all the time.

Why should there not be a patient confidence in the ultimate justice of the people? Is there any better or equal hope in the world?   From Lincoln

2596   Word or sword?   Hal Koch, in Alf Ross,
Why Democracy? 1952 96 Harvard Univ. Press

2597   Liberty, equality, fraternity: no one of these can be maintained as an ideal without involving all three.

From H. W. Schneider,
Three Dimensions . . . 1956 43 Ind. Univ. Press

2598   The democrat has some reason to believe that western civilization is moving from the fight for liberty, through the quest for equality, and towards human fraternity.

From David Thomson,
Equality 1949 154 Cambridge

2599   In the ever-renewing society what matures is a system or framework within which continuous innovation, renewal and rebirth can occur.
John W. Gardner,
Self-Renewal . . . 1964 5 Harper

2600   We must understand the significance of laws and institutions, perform our duties as well as insist on our rights, consider minority opinion, and by peaceful and lawful means try to develop a democratic society of all mankind.
From Japanese Ministry of Educ.,
Moral Education 1959

2601   The ideal of the Athenian dramatists, like that of Pericles, would seem to be the well-rounded man of sound judgment, master of his impulses, ready to discuss, eager to come to a reasoned agreement with any honest opponent; in short, the democratic man.
From W. R. Agard,
What Democracy Meant to the Greeks
1942 151 Univ. N. C. Press

POLITICS

2602   The principles of true politics are those of morality enlarged.
Edmund Burke

2603   The aim of politics should be to make the will of the people effective in compassing the people's good.
From E. E. Harris, Ethics 1957 68:10

2604   The *boys* in politics want position in order to *be* something; the *men* want position in order to *do* something.
From Eric Sevareid

2605   Those who believe that [as private citizens] making things happen in politics is beneath their dignity or not worth their time are likely to be hurt.

H. D. Babbidge, Jr., and Rosenzweig,
Federal Interest ... 1962 203 McGraw

DEFENSE

2606   The defense of nations sometimes causes a just war against the injustice of other nations.

Daniel Webster, Constitution and the Union 1850

2607   What stronger breastplate than a heart un-
            tainted!
        Thrice is he armed that hath his quarrel just,
        And he but naked, though locked up in steel,
        Whose conscience with injustice is corrupted.

Shakespeare, King Henry VI II III ii 232–235

2608   I love peace; but I hope I shall never be such a coward as to mistake oppression for peace.   Kossuth

2609   Peace is kept not by force but by understanding.

CIVIL AND INTERNATIONAL PEACE

2610   The wolf also shall dwell with the lamb, and the leopard shall lie down with the kid; and the calf and the young lion and the fatling together; and a little child shall lead them.

They shall beat their swords into plowshares, and their spears into pruning hooks; nation shall not lift up sword against nation, neither shall they learn war any more.

From Isaiah XI 6 II 4

2611   . . . Peace hath her victories
            No less renowned than war.
                    Milton, To the Lord General Cromwell

2612   The world has become the victim of dogmatic political
creeds, of which, in our day, the most powerful are capitalism
and communism.   Bertrand Russell, Authority . . .
                    1949 120 G. Allen; Simon & Schuster

2613   Any nation whose peace depends on subjects that are
led about like sheep may more properly be called a wilderness
than a nation.   From Spinoza, Political Treatise V iv

2614   Peace has higher tests of manhood than battle ever
knew.   Whittier

2615   There is harmony between the good of the state and
the moral freedom and dignity of the individual.
                                    From W. E. Channing

2616   Life is given to the peaceful.
            Memphite Drama (ca. 3400 B.C.), Homer W. Smith,
                    Man and His Gods 1952 46 Little

2617   The world stands on justice, truth, and peace.
                    From Simeon ben Gamaliel, Aboth I 18

2618   A federation of all humanity, together with sufficient
social justice to ensure health, education, and a rough equality
of opportunity, would mean such a release and increase of
human energy as to open a new phase in human history.
                                    From H. G. Wells,
                    Outline of History 1920 Macmillan

2619   Blessed are the peacemakers.   Matthew V 9

2620   The same reason that makes us wrangle with a neighbor causes a war betwixt princes.

Montaigne, Apology for Raimond Sebond

2621   Stealing a dog or a pig is called wicked; but stealing a city is regarded as righteous. This is like calling a little blackness black, but much blackness white.

From Motse, Y.-P. Mei (tr.),
Ethical . . . 1929 246 158 Probsthain

2622   War will disappear, like the dinosaur, when changes in world conditions have destroyed its survival value.

R. A. Millikan,
Living Philosophies 1931 48 Simon & Schuster

2623   A people, a nation, is but an individual of the society at large. A war is a duel between two such individuals; whereupon it is the duty of the society of the world to reconcile or repress the combatants.   From Volney

2624   No myth is necessary to arouse ardor for the good and the emotion of universal brotherhood. That which is great and beautiful bears in itself its light and flame.

From Guyau, L'irréligion . . . 1889 III II 358

2625   Science is of its very essence international and interracial; it is thus a strong bond of union between the peoples of the earth.   From G. Sarton,

in Anshen (ed.), Moral . . . 1952 445 Harper

2626   Our scientific genius has made the world a neighborhood; our moral genius must make it a brotherhood.

> From Martin Luther King, Jr.

2627   The family and the small, face-to-face community are the birthplaces of good will. Normally there is more of it within the family than in the community, more in the community than in the state or nation, and more within the nation than between nations. Local community government is a training ground for the growth of good will. "Peace on earth" will come, not primarily because of treaties or world governments, but because the quality of good will has had such vigorous growth in the more intimate relationships that it has become a way of life which overflows its bounds and gives character to human relations on a larger scale.

> From Arthur E. Morgan,
> Community . . . 1957 92–93 Community Service

2628   Peace is not mere absence of war, but is a virtue that springs from force of character.

> Spinoza, Political Treatise V iv

2629   Our work for peace must begin within the private world of each one of us.   Dag Hammarskjold

2630   Give every other human being every right you claim for yourself.   Ingersoll

2631   A nation is able to lead other nations not through bigness but through greatness.

> From Adlai Stevenson, Address 1962

2632   International coexistence really means living *with* each other. This coexistence is based on mutual tolerance and respect for the special characteristics and attitudes of others. It has become the only way to live together and for the continued progress of mankind.   From Willy Brandt,
Ordeal of Coexistence
1963 2 Harvard Univ. Press

2633   [Against war,] seize every pretext, however small, for arbitration methods, and multiply the precedents; foster rival excitements, and invent new outlets for heroic energy; and from one generation to another the chances are that irritation will grow less acute and states of strain less dangerous among the nations.

William James, Memories . . . 1911 305–306

2634   We ought to wage war not against men but against vices, which are our real enemies.   From Juan Luis Vives

2635   There must be, not a balance of power, but a community of power; not organized rivalries, but an organized common peace.   Woodrow Wilson, Speech 1917

2636   With international government, business organization, and birth control, men could devote themselves to the progress of science, the diminution of disease, the postponement of death, and the liberation of the impulses that make for joy.

From Bertrand Russell,
Living Philosophies 1931 17 Simon & Schuster

2637   The earth is but one country and mankind are its citizens.   Bahaism

2638   The claims of men have passed far beyond the claims of nations.   J. E. Woodbridge, Am. Scholar 1932 1:95

2639   As we become more enlightened, we perceive that it is with the whole human population as it was with the primeval clan; the welfare of every individual depends on the welfare of the community, and the welfare of the community, on the welfare of every individual.   From W. Reade,
Martyrdom of Man 1926
475 Dutton; Routledge

2640   When people learn to think of themselves as members of a single world society, they can agree on a single ethical system.   From R. Linton,
in Anshen (ed.), Moral . . . 1952 660 Harper

2641   Realized in one man, fitness has its rise;
Realized in a family, fitness multiplies;
Realized in a village, fitness gathers weight;
Realized in a country, fitness becomes great;
Realized in the world, fitness fills the skies.
Witter Bynner (tr.), Way of Life
according to Laotzu 1944 57 Day

XII

History and Progress

2642 Bear not the burthen of a world outworn,
   Nor to the future bow;
   With every hour thy joy be newly born,
   And earth be new-created every morn,—
   Thy life is here and now.

          Indian epigram,
      Paul Elmer More, Century . . . 1898 104

2643 When I was young . . .
   I went to school to age to learn the past.
   Now I am old . . .
   I go to school to youth to learn the future.

       Poetry of Robert Frost (Lathem, ed.),
        What Fifty Said, 1969 267 Holt

THE PAST

2644 . . . What's past is prologue.
       Shakespeare, Tempest II 1 261

2645 The Moving Finger writes; and having writ,
   Moves on: nor all your Piety nor Wit,
   Shall lure it back to cancel half a Line,
   Nor all your Tears wash out a Word of it.
       Omar Khayyám, Rubáiyát lxxi

2646 Those who cannot remember the past are condemned
to repeat it.   Santayana,
    Reason in Common Sense 1905 284 Scribner

2647   In America, indifference to the past in Europe relieved men of both cultural liabilities and cultural assets.

From Arthur E. Morgan,
Observations 1968 41 Antioch Press

2648   Life can only be understood backwards, but it must be lived forwards.   Kierkegaard

2649   Instead of asking first, "How did such a thing happen?" men ought to ask, "Did it happen?"

From Montaigne, in Lowenthal (ed.),
Autobiography... 1935 234 Houghton

2650   Among the deficiencies of hindsight is that, while we know the consequences of what was done, we do not know the consequences of some other course which was not followed.

From Winston Churchill

2651   If the past to a man is nothing but a dead hand, then in common honesty he must be an advocate of revolution. But if it is regarded as the matrix of present and future, he will labor to read its lessons and shun the heady short-cuts which end only in blank walls.   From John Buchan,
Pilgrim's Way 1940 283 Houghton

HISTORY

2652   All things are engaged in writing their history. The planet, the pebble, goes attended by its shadow. The rolling rock leaves its scratches on the mountain; the river, its channel in the soil; the animal, its bones in the stratum; the fern and leaf, their modest epitaph in the coal. The falling drop makes its sculpture in the sand or the stone. Every act of the man inscribes itself in memories, manners and face. Every object is covered with hints which speak to the intelligent.

Emerson

2653   If a person would understand either the Odyssey or any other ancient work, he must never look at the dead without seeing the living in them, nor at the living without thinking of the dead. We are too fond of seeing the ancients as one thing and the moderns as another.

Samuel Butler,
in H. F. Jones (ed.), Notebooks 1912 193

2654   Far from me and from my friends be such frigid philosophy as may conduct us indifferent and unmoved over any ground which has been dignified by wisdom, bravery, or virtue. That man is little to be envied whose patriotism would not gain force upon the plain of Marathon, or whose piety would not grow warmer among the ruins of Iona!

Samuel Johnson

2655   The world rewards discovery. The first man to climb a mountain or discover a planet, a cure or a natural law is a hero. It is not always certain, to be sure, that the discoverer made the discovery. In the realm of ideas especially, the true inventors are apt to be unknown . . . But the hunger for heroes is as great as the hunger for scapegoats; and as some innocent men are hanged lest murder go unpunished, some undeserving men are rewarded lest discovery remain anonymous.

James R. Newman,
Science and Sensibility 1961 2:142 Simon & Schuster

2656   History is written by the survivors.   Unknown

2657   When a man writes his autobiography he is expected to show a certain modesty; but [traditionally] when a nation writes its autobiography there is no limit to its boasting and vainglory.   Bertrand Russell,
Free Thought ... 1922 21 Huebsch

2658   A good historian is timeless; although he is a patriot, he will never flatter his country.   Fénelon

2659   The history of thought is a great mixture of vibrant disclosure and deadening closure.
After Whitehead,
Modes of Thought 1938 81 Macmillan; Cambridge

2660   He who is ignorant of what happened before his birth is always a child.   Cicero

2661   If history is falsified, the people will have lost their guidance.   Anna Ella Carroll, in Sydney Greenbie,
Suit ... 1958 92 Traversity Press, © Greenbie

2662   Lack of the historical sense may make the present seem more intolerable than an imagined past. This supposed contrast may discourage people and make for evasion of the responsibilities of the present.
From Herbert J. Muller, Harper's Feb. 1964 85

THE PRESENT

2663   NOW is the constant syllable ticking from the clock of time.   M. F. Tupper, Proverbial Philosophy 1849 198

2664   All that which is past is as a Dream; and he that hopes or depends upon Time coming, dreams waking.

Unknown

2665   **The present hour alone is man's.**   Samuel Johnson

2666   We are always getting ready to live, but never living.
Emerson, Journals ... 1910–1914 3:276

2667   We must be satisfied to catch our triumphs on the wing.   Santayana, Last Puritan 1936 584 Scribner

2668   **All the flowers of all the tomorrows are in the seeds of today.**   Chinese proverb

CONSERVATISM

2669   A sound man is good at salvage,
At seeing that nothing is lost.

Witter Bynner,
Way of Life according to Laotzu 1944 41 Day

2670   Be cautious lest you be over-cautious.
From W. E. Channing, Works 1875 2:299

2671   Is there anything so dangerous as being absolutely safe?
Thurman B. Rice

2672   **The man's the true conservative who lops the moldered branch away.**   Tennyson

EVOLUTION

2673   Evolution is progress from an indefinite, incoherent homogeneity toward a definite, coherent heterogeneity.

From Herbert Spencer, First Principles 1896 380

2674   Throughout organic evolution, single-celled organisms have conflicted with one another for food and space. Some individual cells, however, specialized and became combined into multicellular organisms.

The multicellular organisms have conflicted with one another likewise; but many have developed special roles and have combined as members of groups.

The groups have conflicted at their meeting points. Some, however, have come together to be larger groups.

Each constituent, whether it be a cell, a multicellular organism, or a group, tends to fit within its larger unit so long as the constituent lives well enough there. Still, each constituent tends somewhat to go its own way; and it goes its own way, if it can, whenever the larger organization fails the constituent's needs or interests.

Most human individuals want to express both their individual and their social interests. In organizations of groups, the several groups have their own-group and their whole-organization interests.

In every case, from the simplest symbiosis to international cooperation, the larger organization thrives so far as its constituents find, under the circumstances, their best life as members of the larger organization.

2675   Who are the fittest to survive depends upon conditions. The conditions with respect to which the term "fit" must *now* be used include the existing social structure with all the habits, demands, and ideals which are found in it.

Fiske observed that civilization is a product of the long dependence of the human child. We must add that not only the long dependence, but the multiplication of its forms, physical and cultural, has increased intelligent foresight and planning and the bonds of social unity. Such qualities are positive instruments in the struggle for existence, and those who develop them are fit to survive.

The struggle for existence is constantly modifying itself, because, as the conditions of life change, the modes of living must change also.

Our animal inheritance is not an enemy to the moral life; without it no life is possible. These impulses and tendencies become good when trained in one way, and become bad when trained in another way. What are courage, persistence, patience, enterprise, initiation, temperance, chastity, benevolence, self-sacrifice itself, but developments of those impulses which are basic to the life process?

Impulse and ideal are mutually necessary for the ethical process. It is well for the ideal that it meet the opposition of the impulse, and for the animal prompting to be held to functioning as suggested by the ideal.

Not only is one species or form of life selected at the expense of other forms, but one mode of action in the same individual is constantly selected at the expense of other modes.

Education and social approval and disapproval in modifying behavior mark a more economical form of selection than had ruled previously. The modification of any structure is certainly not an end in itself; it is simply one device for changing function, what that structure is to do.

"Adjustment" does not mean that the life-form passively accepts or submits to the conditions as they are, but that it subordinates these natural circumstances to its own needs.

The difference between man and animal is not that selection of the fittest in man has ceased, but that selection of human functions which enhance man's environment is active as never before.

The basic conditions of righteousness and unrighteousness alike are implicit in the natural order. Man is a part of this order. In his conscious struggles, in his doubts, temptations, and defeats, in his aspirations and successes, he is moved on and buoyed up by the divers forces which have developed all nature; and in this moral struggle he acts not as a mere individual but as an organ in maintaining and carrying forward the universal process.

From John Dewey,
Monist 1898 8:326–330 336–338 340–341

2676   We have come to the point in biological history where we are largely responsible for our own evolution. Evolution means selecting, and this means valuing.

From A. H. Maslow, Am. Psychologist 1969 24:727

2677   We may doubt the just proportion of good to
           ill.
       There is much in nature against us. But we
           forget:
       Take nature altogether since time began,
       Including human nature, in peace and war,
       And it must be a little more in favor of man,
       Say a fraction of one per cent at the very least,
       Or our number living wouldn't be steadily
           more,

Our hold on the planet wouldn't have so increased.

> Poetry of Robert Frost (Lathem, ed.),
> Our Hold on the Planet, 1969 349 Holt

2678   If we are the result of an evolutionary process beginning with brute matter, how cheering, how comforting, how
marvelous that we have got so far with such possibilities of
happiness, goodness and beauty.

> Bernard Berenson Treasury
> (Kiel, ed.), 1962 192 Simon & Schuster

2679   It cannot lessen the dignity of our race to gain such
victories over Time.   Charles Lyell

REFORM

2680   The intellectual ignominy of believing what we believe simply because of the time and place of our birth escapes
many evolutionists.

> Santayana, Egotism ... 1916 129–130 Scribner

2681   Would man but wake from out his haunted
    sleep,
Earth might be fair and all men glad and wise.

> Genevan Psalter, Turn Back, O Man

2682   Only when you light a candle can you show what the
night was like, and only when you lance a cataract can you
show what blindness meant.

> Pestalozzi, Education ... 1953 55 Philos. Lib.

2683   The world must be known before it can be reformed pertinently, and happiness, to be attained, must be placed in reason.   Santayana, Reason in Science 1905 91 Scribner

2684   Let us accept what we cannot change, enjoy what we should not change, and change what we can and should.

2685   Mere change without conservation is a passage from nothing to nothing . . . Mere conservation without change cannot conserve.   Whitehead, Science . . .
1925 289 Macmillan; Cambridge

2686   The problem is the reconciliation of unbridled radicalism and inert conservatism in reasonable reform.
From John Dewey, Monist 1898 8:335

2687   Unless there is power behind the expression of grievances, the grievances are apt to be neglected.
Alexander D. Lindsay,
Modern Democratic State 1943 19 Oxford

2688   It is better to work on institutions by the sun than by the wind.   Emerson, Man the Reformer

2689   They are slaves who fear to speak
For the fallen and the weak;
They are slaves who will not choose
Hatred, scoffing and abuse,
Rather than in silence shrink
From the truth they needs must think:

They are slaves who dare not be
In the right with two or three.

J. R. Lowell,
Stanzas on Freedom, Complete . . . 1911 55

2690   Love your fellow beings, destroy errors, fight for the truth without any cruelty.

Johannes Weyer (Ioannes Wierus)

PROGRESS

2691   Thoughts that great hearts once broke for
         We breathe cheaply in the common air.
         The dust we trample heedlessly
         Throbbed once in saints and heroes rare,
         Who perished, opening for their race
         New pathways to the commonplace.

From unknown

2692   A worthy idea can be blocked by contrary custom, dogma, or preoccupation. Sometimes it wins like a growing tree that slowly pushes rocks out of its way. Sometimes it takes over like a day that follows night.

2693   Man may be an entirely fortuitous by-product of blind energies. Yet once here, it is his best to build a world of his own where his mind and heart work together to help produce individuals who will enjoy exercising functions that are good for the community.   From B. Berenson,
Sunset and Twilight 1963 332 Harcourt

2694   We think our civilization near its meridian, but we are yet only at the cock-crowing and the morning star.

Emerson, Politics

2695   Men are prone to laugh at every proposed deviation from practice as impossible—then, when it is carried into effect, to be astonished that it did not take place before.

From Sydney Smith

2696   Human attitudes and actions have been guided by biologically inherited drives, cultural tradition, and, appearing last in evolution, critical and creative thinking.

From Arthur E. Morgan,
Community . . . 1957 14 Community Service

2697   Commonly, new truths begin as heresies.

From Thomas Huxley,
Science and Culture 1871 312

2698   The history of civilization is strewn with creeds and institutions which were invaluable at first and deadly afterwards.   From W. Bagehot,
Physics and Politics n.d. 74

2699   We might as well require a man to wear the coat that fitted him as a boy, as civilized society to remain ever under the regime of their ancestors.   Jefferson

2700   Everything that enlarges the sphere of human powers is valuable.   From Samuel Johnson

2701   Progress, for the most part, only substitutes one partial and incomplete truth for another; the new fragment of truth being more wanted, more adapted to the needs of the time, than that which it displaces.

From John Stuart Mill, On Liberty 1892 II 27

2702   Progress means the advance toward the fullest development of forces of which any given human organization, whether it be a man or a society, is capable.

From E. G. Bulwer-Lytton, Caxtoniana 435

2703   'Tis Use alone that sanctifies Expense,
And Splendor borrows all her rays from Sense.

Pope, Moral Essays IV 179–180

2704   The present state of the world calls for a moral and spiritual revolution to place human personality above production, techniques, the collective, the state, the race.

From N. Berdyaev, in Victor Gollancz (ed.),
Man and God 1951 10 Houghton

2705   Be not overcome of evil, but overcome evil with good.

Romans XII 21

2706   If the two billion years of life are represented by the 200-foot height of, say, the Rockefeller Chapel at Chicago, the million years of man make a one-inch block on the top of the chapel. The 20,000 years of agriculture make a thick postage stamp on top of that, and the 400 years of science make the ink on top of the postage stamp.

Now, suddenly, we see what is about to come within a single generation or two—that is, in the thickness of the film of moisture on top of the ink on the postage stamp. In that short time we shall move, if we survive the strain, to a wealthy and powerful and coordinated world society; a society that might find out how to keep itself alive and evolving for thousands or millions or billions of years.

From J. R. Platt, Science 1965 149:613

2707 Often we ourselves become discouraged as we see the gap between our technological skills and our economic and political machinery. We must, of course, improve our knowledge and competence in social, economic, and political areas; but, as we do so, we will need more than ever a strong science and technology to provide the tools to move toward our goals.

From L. A. DuBridge, Science 1969 164:1138

2708 As long as dogmatism, fanaticism, and intolerance are kept out, various modes of leverage may be employed to raise life to a higher level. J. Tyndall, Address 1874 61

2709 Our comfort and the delight of the religious imagination are no better than forms of self-indulgence when they are secured at the cost of that love of truth on which, more than on anything else, the increase of light and happiness among men must depend. J. Morley, On Compromise 1874 116

2710 As belief in the transcendent importance of salvation in the next world has dimmed, so belief in the transcendent importance of realizing a society of justice and freedom has grown. J. Middleton Murry,
Love . . . 1957 212 Cape, © Soc. of Authors

2711 But for their divine discontent men would not have been men, and there would have been no progress in human affairs. Humayan Kabir, Am. Scholar 1957 26:417

2712 By nature, man is greedy for novelty.

From Pliny the Elder

2713 Most of man's thoughts and actions are not thoroughly rational, and his impulses are not consistently social. Nevertheless, the evolution of culture has its chief biological bases in man's superior intelligence and his exceptional tendency to pursue, by rational means, the common good of his group.

From H. J. Muller, in Julian Huxley (ed.),
Humanist Frame 1961 404 G. Allen

2714 It is the intellectual itching stimulated by disparate experiences, concepts or conceptual systems which drives man forward. To exclude all systems but one is to clip the wings of the mind. R. L. Jenkins

Breaking Patterns . . . 1954 257 Lippincott

2715 Often some of those who are willing or forced to be different advance society.

2716 The progress of the world is the history of men who would not permit defeat to speak the final word.

J. R. Sizoo, On Guard 1941 20 Macmillan

2717 By changing what man knows about the world, he changes the world he knows; and by changing the world in which he lives, he changes himself.

T. Dobzhansky,
Am. Scientist 1961 49:285

2718   If individuality has no elbowroom, society does not advance; if individuality breaks out of all bounds, society perishes.   Huxley, in Bibby,
T. H. Huxley 1959 256 Horizon

2719   Freedom of individuals to express and develop many ideas is necessary for progress in social evolution.
From H. Hoagland, Science 1964 143:111–112

2720   Life in this world has advanced because new things were tried, of which the majority failed but the small minority succeeded in a relative sense.

Humanity is too undeveloped to see more than about one step ahead. That step, however, can be discerned by enough people to give rise to a salutary trend and enable us to see more advance ahead.

From Hermann J. Muller,
Sci. Mo. 1956 83:285; Science 1961 134:649

2721   Things done *for* people may not be progressive, but things done *with* people are likely to promote progress.
Eduard C. Lindeman, in Robert Gessner (ed.),
Democratic Man 1956 135 Beacon

2722   Progress in science and its applications furthers progress in all fields of human endeavor.

After George Sarton,
History . . . 1937 19–20 Harvard Univ. Press

2723   Make the time to come the disciple and not the servant of the time past.   Francis Bacon

2724   There is no civilization where there is no satisfaction.
Will Rogers, Autobiography 1949 221 Houghton

2725   Civilization is something more than social justice, something more than security; it is also the enhancement of pleasure, the love of loveliness, the refinement of relationships, and the embellishment of life.

From Harold Nicolson,
Good Behaviour 1956 285 Doubleday

2726   Ethical thinking is hard to change, but history teaches us that it does change. Slavery, infanticide, burning of witches, gladiatorial circuses, and human religious sacrifices were supported by the best men of their times, yet have been abolished. In this nuclear age, war must be abolished.

From Hudson Hoagland, Science 1964 143:114

2727   We may take as the essential element in civilization the ethical perfecting of the individual and of society as well.

Schweitzer

2728   Those who speak most of progress measure it by quantity and not by quality; how many people read and write, or how many people there are, or what is the annual value of their trade; whereas true progress would rather lie in reading or writing fewer and better things, and being fewer and better men, and enjoying life more.

Santayana, Winds of Doctrine 1913 5 Scribner

2729   The wonders, mysteries, truths, of the stellar universe and the world about us, the arts, fellowship, affection of wife and husband, activities for humanity—all these will possess the intellect and heart of future generations.

From W. M. W. Call, Final Causes 1891 160–161

2730 Our purpose is . . . to build, here and everywhere, the beloved community in which justice, liberty, and peace are universal; . . . holding that the human spirit is most truly guided when guided from within; . . . keeping our purpose always open that we may be free to grow.

From Our Statement of Purpose, 1944,
Unitarian Church of Northampton and
Florence (Mass.)

2731 Wisdom makes for genetic and cultural evolutionary advance. The general direction of such evolution is toward richness of experience.

From C. H. Waddington, Ethical Animal 1961
102 176 204 Atheneum, ⓒ G. Allen

2732   Oh places I have passed!
       That journey's done.
       And what will come at last?
       The road leads on.

Quoted from Collected Poems by Edwin Muir, p. 166, ⓒ 1960 by Willa Muir. Reprinted by permission of Oxford University Press, Inc., and of Faber and Faber Ltd.

2733 When our use of this world is over and we make room for others, may we hand on our common heritage fairer and sweeter through our part in it.   After W. Rauschenbusch

2733a   Pessimism about man serves to maintain the status quo. It is a luxury for the affluent, a sop to the guilt of the politically inactive, a comfort to those who continue to enjoy the amenities of privilege. Pessimism is too costly for the disfranchised; they give way to it at the price of their salvation. No less clearly, the false "optimism" of the unsubstantiated claims made for behavioral engineering, claims that ignore biological variation and individual creativity, foreclose man's humanity.

What is known about the power of the social-psychological determinants of human behavior compels the conclusion that the set of axioms for a theory of human nature must include a Kantian imperative: men and women must believe that mankind can become fully human in order for our species to attain its humanity. Restated, a soberly optimistic view of man's potential (based on recognition of man's attainments, but tempered by knowledge of its frailties) is a precondition for social action to make actual that which is possible.

Leon Eisenberg, Science 1972 176:124

XIII

Family Life

2734   An intelligent, cooperative family is the best school for citizenship.   Arthur E. Morgan,
Observations 1968 80 Antioch Press

2735   The Empire lies rooted in the state, the state . . . in the family, and the family . . . in the individual.
Mencius (Dobson, tr.)
1963 188 Univ. Toronto Press; Oxford

2736   Abhorred is the face that smiles abroad and flashes fury when it returns to a tender and helpless family.
From Lavater, Aphorism 241

2737   . . . Love's contentment more than wealth.
Whittier

SEXUAL LOVE

2738   Yonder a maid and her wight
Come whispering by:
War's annals will fade into night
Ere their story die.
Thomas Hardy, In Time of "The Breaking of
Nations," Collected . . . 1925 511 Macmillan

2739   Eros is not without language, but for this language there is no verbal translation.
From H. Cleckley,
Caricature . . . 1957 298 Ronald

2740   Love's mysteries in souls do grow,
But yet the body is his book.
John Donne, Extasie 71–72

2741   Are we not beasts to call what begets us beastly?
                                              From Montaigne

2742   The sexually satisfied individual can feel love-starved.
Sex concerns the choice of a body; love, the choice of a personality. The one relaxes muscles; the other opens the floodgates
of personality. The object of sex is desired only during the
short time of excitement; the beloved person is the object of
continued tenderness.
                                              From Theodor Reik,
                        Psychology ... 1945 17–18 Rinehart; Routledge

2743   When beauty fires the blood, how love exalts the mind!
                                    Dryden, Cymon and Iphigenia 41

2744   But love is blind, and lovers cannot see
        The pretty follies that themselves commit.
                            Shakespeare, Merchant of Venice II vi 36–37

2745   My heart is like a singing bird
        Whose nest is in a watered shoot;
        My heart is like an apple-tree
        Whose boughs are bent with thick-set fruit;
        My heart is like a rainbow shell
        That paddles in a halcyon sea;
        My heart is gladder than all these
        Because my love is come to me.
                                    Christina Rossetti, Birthday

2746   You, Hector, are father and mother and brother to me,
as well as my beloved husband.
                                    Andromache, in Iliad VI

2747   Human sexual love, in its higher forms at least, is some blend of the mating urge with tender emotion, esthetic appreciation, admiration, altruism, and further interests.

Ordinarily, the most delightful physical emotion occurs in the fulfilment of sexual love. Thus nature safeguards the continuation of life, its immortality. To be able so to love, however, we must be worthy of being loved. Human sexual love must be generous; as must any human love. Whether or not a person has sexual love, in whatever love he has, filial, fraternal, parental, friendly, humane, to give freely and willingly maintains the exchange of warmth and energy without which we cannot live and grow.   From Hume and from M. Gumpert,
Anatomy of Happiness 1951 208 McGraw

2748   Yet beauty . . . hath strange power,
              After offence returning, to regain
              Love once possessed.
                                   Milton, Samson Agonistes 1003–1005

2749   I could not love thee, dear, so much,
              Loved I not honor more.
                                   Richard Lovelace, To Lucasta,
                                   Going to the Warres 11–12

2750   All true love is founded on esteem.
                                   George Villiers Buckingham

2751   Love does not consist only in gazing at each other, but in looking outward in the same direction.
                                   Antoine de Saint-Exupéry

2752   The emotion of love endures when the lovers love many things together, and not merely each other.

From W. Lippmann,
Preface to Morals 1929 308–309 Macmillan

2753   That love must be blind is romantic pessimism.

2754   Married in haste, we may repent at leisure.
William Congreve, Old Bachelor V i

2755   Love itself dreams of more than mere possession; to conceive happiness, it must conceive a life to be shared in a varied world, full of events and activities, which shall be new and ideal bonds between the lovers. But unlawful love cannot pass out into this public fulfilment. It is condemned to be mere possession—possession in the dark, without an environment, without a future. It is love among the ruins.

From Santayana,
Three Philosophical Poets 1910 110

2756   Deceive not thyself by overexpecting happiness in the marriage estate. Remember the nightingales which sing only some months in the spring, but commonly are silent when they have hatched their eggs.

Thomas Fuller, Of Marriage

2757   Healthy love includes full trust, commitment, and independence with neither insulation nor domination.

From W. Bonime,
Clinical Use of Dreams 1962 252 Basic Books

MARRIAGE

2758   Marriage is not an end in itself. It is a means: a means
for the expression of love.

Jessamyn West,
Love Is Not What You Think, 1959 6 Harcourt

2759   Never marry but for love; but see that you love what
is lovely. Prefer the person before money, virtue before beauty,
the mind before the body. Then you have a wife, a friend, a
companion, a second self.   William Penn

2760   Better is a marriage portion in a wife than with a wife.
From Rule of Life 1800 111

2761   Neither her out-side formed so fair, nor aught
In procreation common to all kinds
(Though higher of the genial Bed by far,
And with mysterious reverence I deem)
So much delights me, as those graceful acts,
Those thousand decencies that daily flow
From all her words and actions, mixt with Love
And sweet compliance, which declare unfeign'd
Union of Mind, or in us both one Soul:
Harmony to behold in wedded pair
More grateful than harmonious sound to the
    ear.

Milton, Paradise Lost VIII 596–606

2762   Two persons who have chosen each other to be each
other's mutual comfort and entertainment have, in that action,
bound themselves to be good-humored, affable, discreet, for-

giving, patient, and joyful, with respect to each other's frailties
and perfections, to the end of their lives.   From Addison

2763   Let me not to the marriage of true minds
           Admit impediments. Love is not love
           Which alters when it alteration finds.
                              Shakespeare, Sonnet CXVI

2764   Marriage without good faith is like a teapot without a
tray.   Moorish proverb, Champion (ed.), Racial . . .
            1938 561 Macmillan, © Routledge; Barnes & Noble

2765   Give thine ear to all, thy hand to thy friends, but thy
lips only to thy wife.   Yiddish proverb

2766   When there's marriage without love, there will be love
without marriage.   Franklin

2767   In marriage, sexual happiness contributes to love, but
not more than love contributes to sexual happiness. If a sexually inhibited or even perverted spouse can become free of fear,
anger, guilt, disgust, or other frustration of the pleasant emotions, and can love, normally the sexual problem is soon solved.
            After Erich Fromm, Art of Loving 1956 89 Harper

2768   In love as in all other things, nature provides only the
rough materials: there is an art of loving. The art is trans-
forming a fugitive desire into a lasting emotion, a unique
mingling of tender emotion, friendship, sensuality, and respect,
without which there is no true marriage.

Perfection can never be achieved; we can only try patiently and continually to approximate perfection.

> From André Maurois, Art of Living
> (Whitall, tr.) 1940 1–2 37 75 70–71 Harper

2769   However great a man or his contribution, and whether or not he does marry, he is less than a complete man so far as he is physically, mentally, or spiritually not fit for the married state.   After Samuel Johnson

2770   Every man who is happily married is a successful man.
                                                    W. L. Phelps

2771   He is the half part of a blessed man,
            Left to be finished by such as she;
            And she a fair divided excellence,
            Whose fulness of perfection lies in him.
                        Shakespeare, King John II i 437–440

2772   He who beats his wife beats his left hand with his right.
                                                    Danish proverb

2773   Marriage is in harmony with reason if the love of the man and the woman is caused not only by bodily beauty but also by freedom of soul.

> From Spinoza, Ethics IV App. xx

2774   We must be our own before we can be another's.
                                                    Emerson, Friendship

2775   To the lazy mind the perfect soul-mate is Echo.
                                                    Elizabeth Drew,
                        Discovering Poetry 1933 60 Norton

2776   The "right person" doesn't exist. Those who change mates with every infatuation miss the greatest happiness in love: learning to be the right person for each other. So to live and experience much together is deeply rewarding.

From Georg [sic] Brochmann,
Humanity . . . 1950 153–156 Viking

2777   To live, let live. Hear, see, and be silent. A day without dispute brings sleep without dreams. Long life and a pleasant one is the fruit of peace. There is equal folly in troubling our heart about what does not concern us and in not taking to heart what does.

From Balthasar Gracian (Jacobs, tr.), Maxim 192

2778   . . . Venus smiles not in a house of tears.

Shakespeare, Romeo and Juliet IV i 8

2779   The institution of marriage is a failure only to the extent that the human race is a failure.   From Ingersoll

HOME

2780   A net to snare the moonlight,
                A sod spread to the sun,
                A place of toil by daytime,
                Of dreams when toil is done.

Vachel Lindsay, General William Booth
1917 106 Macmillan

2781   "Home is the place where, when you have to
                go there,
            They have to take you in."

"I should have called it
Something you somehow haven't to deserve."
From Poetry of Robert Frost (Lathem, ed.),
Death of the Hired Man 1969 38 Holt

2782   For its members, almost every family yields boredom,
irritation, conflicts, retreat, help, affection and communion.
From André Maurois,
Art of Living (Whitall, tr.) 1940 77 Harper

2783   . . . How few actual families are examples of what we
think of as a family at its best! The family is subject to every
kind of distortion, perversion, impoverishment, neglect, dis-
harmony, coldness, disloyalty, stress and suspicion. Its very
possibilities of excellence make it the more susceptible to injury
and distortion, just as many more things can go wrong with
an airplane than with an oxcart.
Arthur E. Morgan,
Community . . . 1957 13 Community Service

2784   Have ye leisure, comfort, calm,
                Shelter, food, love's gentle balm?
                                    Shelley

2785   He is the happiest, be he king or peasant, who finds
peace in his home.   Goethe

2786   Anger in a home is like rottenness in fruit. Immorality
in a home is like a worm in fruit.   Sotah

2787   A hundred men make an encampment, but one woman
makes a home.   Armenian proverb

PARENTHOOD

2788   "Therefore shall a man leave his father and his mother, and shall cleave unto his wife: and they shall be one flesh." Their child, which for the Quakers is "their pledge of affection," needs room to grow to become self-reliant. The parents too, however harmonious, need room to keep on growing as self-directing persons. The parents and their offspring can grow best and enjoyably through learning, mutual respect, and continued affection.   Quoting Genesis II 24

2789   The most excellent wife is able to take the place of her children's father, should he be taken from them.

                                                    From Goethe

2790   Unhappy the man for whom his own mother has not made other mothers venerable.   Jean Paul Richter

2791   The place to take the true measure of a man is by his own fireside. I can forgive much to that fellow mortal who would rather make men swear than women weep; who would rather have the hate of the whole world than the contempt of his wife; who would rather call anger to the eyes of a king than fear to the face of a child.   From W. C. Brann

2792   Cornelia kept her in talk till her children came from school; and these, said she, are my jewels.

                    Robert Burton, Anatomy of Melancholy III

2793   The joy of parents in their children prolongs life.
                    Wortabet (tr.), Arabian Wisdom 1910 54

2794   Children are the anchors that hold a mother to life.

Sophocles, Phaedra Frag. 619

2795   Sweet childish days, that were as long
As twenty days are now.

Wordsworth, To a Butterfly

2796   The youths, the people's spring.   Demades

2797   The force of motherhood—its vitality turns timidity into fierce courage, and dreadless defiance into tremulous submission; thoughtlessness into foresight, yet stills all anxiety into calm content; makes selfishness become self-denial, and gives even to hard vanity the glance of admiring love.

From George Eliot

2798   O the blessing of a home, where old and young mix kindly, the young unawed, the old unchilled, in unreserved communion!

M. F. Tupper, Proverbial Philosophy 1849 349

2799   Time and the flow of life are differently experienced by the young and the old. Each rate of time has its own rules, its advantages and its disadvantages. If these different levels of existence cooperate, life can be richer for everyone; if they oppose each other, conflict must result.

M. Gumpert,
Anatomy of Happiness 1951 149 McGraw

2800   When the generations are in conflict, what each needs is the knowledge of when "to let go," as important in human relations as when "to take hold."

From George Lawton,
Aging Successfully 1946 166 Columbia Univ. Press

2801   Between a man and his wife nothing ought to rule but love. Authority is for children and servants; yet not without sweetness.

A husband and wife that love and value one another show their children and servants that they should do so too. Others visibly lose their authority in their families by their contempt of one another, and teach their children to be unkind by their own example.

If we would amend the world, we should mend ourselves, and teach our children to be not what we are, but what they should be.   From William Penn

2802   There is a vast difference between being parents *of* our children and parents *to* them. There is a realm of sympathy, comradeship and *understanding*.   From G. H. Betts,
Fathers and Mothers 1915 9

2803   Unless truth, strength, and happiness dwell in the homes of the people, the people will not be truly civilized.
Pestalozzi, Education . . . 1953 24 Philos. Lib.

XIV

Completion of the Life Cycle

2804 Sweet day, so cool, so calm, so bright,
The bridal of the earth and sky,
The dew shall weep thy fall tonight,
For thou must die.

Sweet rose, whose hue, angry and brave,
Bids the rash gazer wipe his eye,
Thy root is ever in its grave,
And thou must die.

Sweet spring, full of sweet days and roses,
A box where sweets compacted lie,
My music shows ye have your closes,
And all must die.

Only a sweet and virtuous soul,
Like seasoned timber, never gives . . .

From George Herbert, Virtue iv

2805 Be at one with all these living things which,
   having arisen and flourished,
Return to the quiet whence they came,
Like a healthy growth of vegetation
Falling back upon the root.

Witter Bynner,
Way of Life according to Laotzu 1944 34 Day

RETIREMENT

2806 Life is a fragment, a moment, influenced by all that has preceded, and to influence all that follows. The only way to illumine it is by extent of view. From W. E. Channing

2807   There is no life that is not short.

> Seneca, Ad Lucilium . . .
> (Gummere, tr.) 1918 2:181 Putnam

2808   Not till time has torn out half the leaves from the Book of Human Life to light the fires of passion from day to day, man begins to see that the leaves which remain are few.

> From Longfellow, Hyperion IV VIII

2809   Why, then, all this impatience with the ills of life?

> From Wortabet (tr.), Arabian Wisdom 1910 61

2810   The pale leaf falls in pallor, but the green leaf
>   turns to gold;
> We that have found it good to be young shall
>   find it good to be old.

> Chesterton, To M. E. W.

2811   As people grow older, often they feel less inclined to enter upon any new work. To grow old, however, is in itself to enter upon a new business.   From Goethe

2812   To be retired invites idleness; to retire creates leisure. Time, like money, has to be spent in order to be saved; and age is as wasteful as youth of what it has much less to spare.

> From T. V. Smith,
> Non-Existent Man 1962 244 Univ. Tex.

2813   Like the Kingdom of Heaven, the Fountain of
>   Youth is within us;
> If we seek it elsewhere, old shall we grow in the
>   search.

> Longfellow, Elegiac Verse X

2814   The good are always young in spirit, no matter when they die.

> M. Hilliard,
> Woman Doctor . . . 1957 175 Doubleday

2815   For him in vain the envious seasons roll
Who bears eternal summer in his soul.

> (Doctor) O. W. Holmes, Old Player

2816   Say I'm weary, say I'm sad;
Say that health and wealth have missed me;
Say I'm growing old, but add—
Jenny kissed me.

> Leigh Hunt, Jenny Kissed Me

2817   Love, whether sexual, parental, or fraternal, is essentially sacrificial, and prompts a man to give his life for his friends. In thus losing his life gladly he in a sense finds it anew . . . Nature, in denying us perennial youth, has at least invited us to become unselfish and noble.

> Santayana,
> Reason in Religion 1905 254–255 Scribner

2818   I've enjoyed boyhood and youth and manhood; but the disciplines of the years bring, or ought to bring, more appreciative judgments, release from prejudices, ability to be patient with small annoyances, readiness to give the oncoming generation a chance. Let's assume that our children and our children's children are able and sincere.

Let's be eager to add not just years to our life, but life to our years.

> From Samuel A. Eliot

AGING

2819   Autumn woods are calling, warm and fragrant;
        Autumn woods are calling, bright with gold.
        A lazy wind is rustling through the branches.
        This is nature's way of growing old.
                        Ruth T. Abbott, The Humanist 1942 1:101

2820   The tragedy of King Lear was that he grew old before
he grew wise.   From H. Silverman,
                        Contemporary Psychol. 1969 14:672

2821   One equal temper of heroic hearts,
        Made weak by time and fate, but strong in will
        To strive, to seek, to find, and not to yield.
                                        Tennyson, Ulysses

2822   The old age of an eagle is better than the youth of a
sparrow.   Greek proverb

2823   At the end, one has the face that one has earned.
                                        Max Roden,
                        Spiegelungen 1951 39 Johannes-Presse

2824   As a white candle
                    In a holy place,
                    So is the beauty
                    Of an agèd face.
        Joseph Campbell, after Ecclus. XXVI 17, in Church
        and Bozman (eds.), Poems . . . 1900–1942 1945 22
        Dent

2825   Is it so small a thing
         To have enjoyed the sun,
         To have lived light in the spring,
         To have loved, to have thought, to have done;
               . . .
         That we must feign a bliss
         Of doubtful future date,
         And, while we dream on this,
         Lose all our present state . . .?

                     Matthew Arnold, Empedocles on Etna I ii

2826   The greatest compensation of old age is its freedom of
spirit . . .[This freedom] is accompanied by a certain indifference to many of the things that men in their prime think important. Another compensation is that it liberates one from
envy, hatred, and malice.

     I can still read with pleasure the poets that I read in my
youth and with interest the poets of today . . . I can still occupy
myself with my old excitement . . . [with] the philosophy that
treats the problems that confront us all. Plato, Aristotle . . .
Plotinus and Spinoza, with sundry moderns, . . . and the Greek
tragedians deal with things that are important to man. They
exalt and tranquilize. To read them is to sail with a gentle
breeze in an inland sea studded with a thousand isles.

                     Maugham, Writer's Notebook
                1949 353–354 359–360 Doubleday; Heinemann

2827   If it has any provender, so to speak, of study and learning, nothing is more enjoyable than a leisured old age.

                                                     Cato

2828   What seems to grow fairer to me as life goes by is the
love and peace and tenderness of it; not its wit and cleverness

and grandeur of knowledge, grand as knowledge is, but just
the laughter of little children and the friendship of friends and
the cosy talk by the fireside and the sight of flowers and the
sound of music.

J. R. Green, in
Leslie Stephen (ed.), Letters . . . 1901 241

2829   In the later years, at their best, diminished physical
vitality is more than offset by the values of wisdom and mel-
lowed experience; the contribution to society may reach its
peak and yet the tempo of life need not be hurried. This is the
Indian summer of life.

From R. L. Jenkins,
Breaking Patterns . . . 1954 207 Lippincott

2830   Something remains for us to do or dare;
Even the oldest tree some fruit may bear; . . .
For age is opportunity no less
Than youth itself, though in another dress,
And as the evening twilight fades away
The sky is filled with stars, invisible by day.

Longfellow, Morituri Salutamus

2831   A man is not old so long as he is seeking something.

Jean Rostand,
Substance of Man 1962 178 Doubleday

2832   As living grows briefer, I must make it grow deeper.

Montaigne, in Lowenthal (ed.),
Autobiography . . . 1935 379 Houghton

2833   As time moves me along:
Let me not be the authority on all subjects,

nor the umpire for every discussion.
Let me be thoughtful but not moody,
and not over-wise lest I lose my friends.

Let me have grace to not recite endless details,
but make only cogent remarks.
Let me be adorned with silence on my aches
     and pains,
and endurance for others' accounts.

May I rein in my memory,
be sporting about my errors,
and be hospitable to the tales that are told,
and be reasonable whenever I can.

May I keep sweet, neither saint nor devil.
May I see good things here and there,
and talents in unexpected places;
and have heart to speak in praise.

After unknown

2833a   Nobody loves life like an old man.

Sophocles, Frag. 63

2834   Against the disappointments of ambition, the decline of one's faculties of living, loving, and acting, I place the capacity for contemplative enjoyment of excellence of every kind ...

The older I get, the more I feel my unity and identity in substance with the rest of nature: . . . even inanimate things.

Bernard Berenson Treasury
(Kiel, ed.), 1962 192 285 Simon & Schuster

2835   Ripe age gives tone to violins,
        Wine, and good fellows.
                John Townsend Trowbridge, Three Worlds

2836 The day becomes more solemn and serene
      When noon is past—there is a harmony
      In autumn, and a luster in its sky,
      Which through the summer is not heard or
          seen,
      As if it could not be, as if it had not been! . . .
                Shelley, Hymn To Intellectual Beauty

BEREAVEMENT

2837   How sleep the brave who sink to rest
        By all their country's wishes blest!
        When Spring, with dewy fingers cold,
        Returns to deck their hallowed mold,
        She there shall dress a sweeter sod
        Than Fancy's feet have ever trod.

        By fairy hands their knell is rung,
        By forms unseen their dirge is sung;
        There Honour comes, a pilgrim grey,
        To bless the turf that wraps their clay,
        And Freedom shall awhile repair,
        To dwell a weeping hermit, there!
                William Collins, Ode 1746

2838   If it were possible to heal sorrow by weeping and to
raise the dead with tears, gold were less prized than grief.
                Sophocles, Frag. 510

2839   Moderate lamentation is the right of the dead, excessive grief the enemy to the living.

> Shakespeare, All's Well That Ends Well I i 65–66

2840
> Beware the vain lament,
> The hunger for what's spent.
> . . . What is past is past.

> Melville Cane,
> And Pastures New 1956 Harcourt

2841   Give sorrow words.
> The grief that does not speak
> Whispers the o'er-fraught heart and bids it
>   break.

> Shakespeare, Macbeth IV iii 209–210

2842   Stay but till tomorrow, and your present sorrow will be weary, and will lie down to rest.

> From Jeremy Taylor,
> Course of Sermons 1653 I 237

2843   If we still love those we lose, can we altogether lose those we love?   Thackeray

2844   Let us call to mind the years before our little child was born. We are now in the same condition as then, except that the time she was with us is to be counted an added blessing.

> Plutarch, in Corliss Lamont,
> Illusion . . . 1935 237 Putnam

2845   Patch grief with proverbs.
                 Shakespeare, Much Ado About Nothing V i 17

2846   The mind has greater power over the emotions and is
less subject thereto in so far as it understands that all things
happen according to natural law. Thus the pain arising from
the loss of any good is mitigated as soon as the one who has lost
it perceives that it could not have continued.
                                             From Spinoza, Ethics V vi

2847   The busy bee has no time for sorrow.
                 William Blake, Marriage of Heaven and Hell

2848   The best thing for being sad is to learn something.
That is the only thing which the mind can never exhaust,
never alienate, never be tortured by, never fear or distrust, and
never dream of regretting.
                                             From T. H. White,
                 Once and Future King 1958 185–186 Putnam

2849   Make for the departed a memorial in your life.
                                 F. Adler, Creed and Deed 1890

2850   Fame, as a noble mind conceives and desires it, is not
embodied in a monument, a biography, or the repetition of a
strange name by strangers; it consists in the immortality of a
man's work, his spirit, his efficacy, in the perpetual rejuvena-
tion of his soul in the world . . .
     Those will substantially remember and honor us who keep

our ideals, and we shall live on in those ages whose experience
we have anticipated.

Santayana,
Reason in Society 1905 144 146 Scribner

2851   . . . Lasting is the song, though he,
             The singer, passes . . .

Meredith, Thrush in February,
Poetical . . . 1928 328 Scribner

2852   As I stood behind the coffin of my little son the other
day, with my mind bent on anything but disputation, the offi-
ciating minister read, as a part of his duty, the words, "If the
dead rise not again, let us eat and drink, for tomorrow we die."
I cannot tell you how inexpressibly they shocked me. [The
apostle] Paul had neither wife nor child, or he must have
known that his alternative involved a blasphemy against all
that was best and noblest in human nature. I could have
laughed with scorn. What! because I am face to face with irre-
parable loss, because I have given back to the source from
whence it came, the cause of a great happiness, still retaining
through all my life the blessings which have sprung and will
spring from that cause, I am to renounce my manhood, and,
howling, grovel in bestiality?

. . . *Sartor Resartus* led me to know that a deep sense of
religion was compatible with the entire absence of theology.
Secondly, science and her methods gave me a resting-place independent of authority and tradition. Thirdly, love opened
up to me a view of the sanctity of human nature, and im-
pressed me with a deep sense of responsibility.

T. H. Huxley, in
Leonard Huxley, Life . . . 1902 1:237

DEATH

2853　In spite of the advances which man has made over his biological predecessors, death remains an essential part of his nature.　　　　　　　　　　　　　　　　　C. H. Waddington,
Ethical Animal 1960 213 Atheneum, © G. Allen

2854　Protozoa, germ cells, and various somatic cells and even tissues can be immortal. The somata of multicellular organisms die because such organisms are made up largely of cells too specialized and interdependent to exist by themselves. As the various cells wear out at different rates, the organism becomes unable to function.

Thus death is a by-product of progressive evolution—the price we pay for differentiation and specialization of structure and function.

Death also makes room for new variations, new specimens, that may be better than those that have gone before.
After R. Pearl, Sci. Mo. 1921 12:15–16,
Biology of Death 1922 224 Lippincott

2855　All men have one entrance into life, and one way out of it.　　　　　　　　　　　　　　　　Wisdom of Solomon VII 6

2856　Protection is possible against other things, but as to death all of us live in a city without walls.
From Epicurus, Strodach (tr.),
Philosophy ... 1962 205 Northwestern Univ. Press

2857　... Death,
The undiscovered country, from whose bourn
No traveller returns.
Shakespeare, Hamlet III i 78–80

2858   Even if a man has clenched the past and the present in his two fists, he has finally to release them; and if he has shouldered the wind and the moon with a bamboo cane, he has eventually to unload them.

> From Hung, Chinese Garden . . .
> (Chao, tr.) 1959 25 Peter Pauper

2859   When death, the great Reconciler, has come, it is never our tenderness that we repent of, but our severity.

> George Eliot, Adam Bede

2860   Death seems hard to him who dies well known to all the world yet knowing not himself.

> From Seneca, Thyestes II 438–440

2861   . . . Men must endure
Their going hence, even as their coming hither:
Ripeness is all.

> Shakespeare, King Lear V ii 9–11

2862   To live in hearts we leave behind
Is not to die.

> Thomas Campbell, "Hallowed Ground"

2863   On parent knee, a naked new-born child,
Weeping thou lay while all around thee smiled;
So live that, sinking in thy last long sleep,
Calm thou mayst smile, while all around thee
    weep.

> From William Jones, From the Persian

2864   So may'st thou live, till like ripe Fruit thou
            drop
        Into thy Mother's lap.

                        Milton, Paradise Lost XI 535

2865   It is not growing like a tree
        In bulk, doth make man better be;
        Or standing long an oak, three hundred year,
        To fall a log at last, dry, bald, and sere:
        A lily of a day
        Is fairer far in May,
        Although it fall and die that night;
        It was the plant and flower of light.

                        Ben Jonson, Pindaric Ode . . . III

2866   We must try to make the latter part of the journey
better than the first; and when we reach the end, we must keep
an even keel and remain cheerful.

                        From Epicurus, Strodach (tr.),
                    Philosophy . . . 1962 206 Northwestern Univ. Press

2867   . . . Nature . . . takes away
        Our playthings one by one, and by the hand
        Leads us to rest so gently that we go
        Scarce knowing if we wished to go or stay.

                        From Longfellow, Nature

2868   Let a man once overcome his personal terror at his
own finitude, and his finitude is, in one sense, overcome.

                        From Santayana
                    (Boyle, tr.), Ethics of Spinoza 1910 viii

2869   In death, pain, and a vanished past there is a sacredness, an awe, which accounts for moments of insight when trivialities vanish.   From Bertrand Russell,
Philosophical Essays 1910 67

2870   I often feel that death is not the enemy of life, but its friend, for the knowledge that our years are limited makes them precious.   From J. L. Liebman,
Peace of Mind 1946 135 Simon & Schuster

2871   Not a single man or woman has ever existed whom I should wish to engage to play forever, rather than fill my theater from age to age with fresh faces and new accents of nature.   From Santayana, J. of Philos. 1909 6:415

2872   There are things that are mightier than death. Honor, justice, and love: many men and women will die for the sake of one or more of these.

From F. J. Gould, Funeral . . . 1906 12

2873   He that dies in earnest pursuit is like one that is wounded in hot blood; who, for the time, scarce feels the hurt; and therefore a mind fixed upon somewhat that is good doth avert the dolours of death.   From Francis Bacon

2874   Let death take me while I am setting my cabbages, caring less of her than of my imperfect garden.

Montaigne, Reflections on Death

2875   If our sickness permits it, let our last breath expire with an act of love.

From Jeremy Taylor, in
Gest (ed.), House . . . 1954 98 Univ. Pa. Press

2876 A man dies nobly when . . . he is interested to the last in what will continue to be the interests and joys of others . . .
One who lives the life of the universe cannot be much concerned for his own.

> Santayana, Reason in Religion 1905 185 Scribner,
> Three Philosophical Poets 1910 56

2877 Into dying, there is reason to believe, great bodily anguish does not often enter.

> From Peter Mere Latham

2878 I have no sympathy with the man who would shorten the death agony of a dog but prolong that of a human being.

> S. B. Woodward, in
> R. E. Osgood, New Eng. J. Med. 1930 202:846

2879 The growing good of the world is half owing to the number who lived faithfully a hidden life and rest in unvisited tombs. From George Eliot, Middlemarch

2880   The sweet remembrance of the just
          Shall flourish when he sleeps in dust.

> N. Tate and N. Brady,
> New Version . . . CXII 6

2881 Not on sad Stygian shore, nor in clear sheen
Of far Elysian plain, shall we meet those
Among the dead whose pupils we have been,
Nor those great shades whom we have held as
    foes;
No meadow of asphodel our feet shall tread,
Nor shall we look each other in the face
To love or hate each other being dead,

Hoping some praise, or fearing some disgrace.
We shall not argue, saying " 'Twas thus" or
  "thus,"
Our argument's whole drift we shall forget;
Who's right, who's wrong, 'twill be all one to us;
We shall not even know that we have met.
  Yet meet we shall, and part, and meet again,
  Where dead men meet, on lips of living men.

Samuel Butler (1612–1680)

2882 The splendors of the firmament of time
May be eclipsed, but are extinguished not;
Like stars to their appointed height they climb,
And death is a low mist which cannot blot
The brightness it may veil.

Shelley, Adonais 388–392

XV

Nature, the Universe, Space, and Time

2883   O, mickle* is the powerful grace that lies
In herbs, plants, stones, and their true qualities;
For nought so vile that on the earth doth live
But to the earth some special good doth give,
Nor aught so good but strained from that fair
     use
Revolts from true birth, stumbling on abuse.
Shakespeare, Romeo and Juliet II iii 15–20

*large

THE SEASONS

2884   Behold, in yon stripped Autumn, shivering
     grey,
Earth knows no desolation.
She smells generation
In the moist breath of decay.

G. Meredith, Ode . . . ,
Poetical . . . 1928 177 Scribner

2885   At Christmas I no more desire a rose
Than wish a snow in May's new-fangled mirth;
But like of each thing that in season grows.
Shakespeare, Love's Labour's Lost I i 105–106

2886   To be interested in the changing seasons is a happier state of mind than to be hopelessly in love with spring.
Santayana, Reason in Art 1905 189 Scribner

2887   While I enjoy the friendship of the seasons, I trust that nothing can make life a burden to me.
From Thoreau

NATURE

2888   One generation passes away, and another generation comes; but the earth abides forever.   Ecclesiastes I 4

2889   Nature recks not, and cares
              No more for what befalls
              Mankind than for the ant.
                        Giacomo Leopardi, Poems . . .
                        (Bickerstrath, tr.) 1923 351 Cambridge

2890   All growth is integration within itself, and is natural. All decay is disintegration, and is natural.
                                              After Ingersoll

2891   Nature often produces the most graceful and pleasant things out of the decay and corruption of others.
                                  From Rule of Life 1800 128

2892   Nature is as adapted to the life of man as it is to animals, plants, and atoms.
                        F. J. E. Woodbridge, Am. Scholar 1932 1:92

2893   Natural law is the true basis of morality and religion.
                                              From Volney

2894   Man, as he is a part of nature, is a part of the power of nature.   Spinoza, Theologico-political Treatise IV

2895   . . . To man, nature is colorful, animated, rhythmic to the ear, varied to the eye, solid to the touch, and stable underfoot; it is edible, drinkable, sittable, swimmable, and full of surprising fragrances, tastes, events, processes and companions.

That nature contains other less pleasant things does not change or destroy what nature proffers.

J. Barzun, Science . . . 1964 108 Harper

2896   To him who in the love of nature holds
Communion with her visible forms, she speaks
A various language: for his gayer hours
She has a voice of gladness, and a smile
And eloquence of beauty; and she glides
Into his darker musings, with a mild
And healing sympathy, that steals away
Their sharpness, ere he is aware.

William Cullen Bryant, Thanatopsis

2897   . . . This our life exempt from public haunt
Finds tongues in trees, books in the running
    brooks,
Sermons in stones, and good in every thing.

Shakespeare, As You Like It II i 15–17

2898   Nature nourishes spirit as the soil sustains flowers.

I. Edman, in Baron and others,
Freedom and Reason 1951 127 Free Press

2899   You never enjoy the world aright till the sea itself floweth in your veins, till you are clothed with the heavens, and crowned with the stars: and perceive yourself to be the sole heir of the whole world, and *more* than so, because men are in it who are every one sole heirs as well as you. Till you can sing and rejoice and delight in it, as misers do in gold, and kings in scepters, you never enjoy the world.

Traherne, First Centuries XXIX XXXI

2900   Mortal though I be, yea ephemeral, if but a
         moment
       I gaze up to the night's starry domain of
         heaven,
       Then no longer on earth I stand . . .
                          Robert S. Bridges, Spirit of Man,
                     Ptolemy the Astronomer 1916 160 Longmans;
                          Poetical Works . . . 1936 Clarendon

2901   I turned and looked back up at the sky,
          Where we still look to ask the why
          Of everything below.
                              Poetry of Robert Frost
                          (Lathem, ed.), Afterflakes 1969 303 Holt

2902   The sky is the daily bread of the eyes.   Emerson

2903   The Crickets sang
            And set the Sun
            And Workmen finished one by one
            Their Seam the Day upon.

            The low Grass loaded with the Dew
            The Twilight stood, as Strangers do
            With Hat in Hand, polite and new
            To stay as if, or go.

            A Vastness, as a Neighbor, came,
            A Wisdom, without Face, or Name,
            A Peace, as Hemispheres at Home
            And so the Night became.
                    Emily Dickinson, in Thomas H. Johnson (ed.),
                          Complete Poems . . . 1960 498 Little

2904   The poetry of earth is never dead.
                    Keats, On the Grasshopper and Cricket

2905   Great things are done when men and moun-
            tains meet;
        This is not done by jostling in the street.
                    William Blake, Gnomic Verses I

2906   Who will prefer the jingle of jade pendants if
        He once has heard jade growing in a cliff!
                    Witter Bynner,
            Way of Life according to Laotzu 1944 51 Day

2907   The rainbow, which hangs a splendid circle in the
heights of heaven, is also formed by the same sun in the dewdrop of the lowly flower.   Jean Paul Richter

2908   There's music in the sighing of a reed;
        There's music in the gushing of a rill;
        There's music in all things, if men had ears.
                    Byron, Don Juan XV 5

2909   Tomorrow to fresh woods and pastures new.
                    Milton, Lycidas 193

2910   . . . I my languid limbs will fling
        Beneath the plane, where the brook's murmur-
            ing
        Moves the calm spirit, but disturbs it not.
                    Moschus (Shelley, tr.)

2911   . . . When the melancholy fit shall fall
        Sudden from heaven like a weeping cloud,

That fosters the droop-headed flowers all,
And hides the green hill in an April shroud:
Then glut thy sorrow on a morning rose,
Or on the rainbow of a salt sandwave . . .

> Keats, Ode on Melancholy

2912
When a breeze blows lightly
And lilac scent floats near,
The earth, speaking gently,
Breathes reverie—
Dispells intensity.

2913   A butterfly? What lovelier thought
Has nature's hand of beauty wrought
Than your gay wing?—delightful notion,
A flower petal kissed to motion.

> Henrik Wergeland, The First Butterfly, Stork (tr.)
> Anthology of Norwegian Lyrics 1942 29 Princeton
> Univ. Press, ⓒ Am.-Scand. Found.

2914   Full many a flower is born to blush unseen,
And waste its sweetness on the desert air.

> Thomas Gray, Elegy 55–56

2915   My garden, with its silence and the pulses of fragrance
that come and go on the airy undulations, affects me like sweet
music. Care stops at the gates, and gazes at me wistfully through
the bars.   Alexander Smith

2916   What is a weed? A plant whose virtues have not yet
been discovered.

> Emerson, Fortune of the Republic

2917   True, a plant may not think; neither will the profoundest of men ever put forth a flower.

D. C. Peattie

2918   How did these beautiful rainbow-tints get into the shell of the fresh-water clam, buried in the mud at the bottom of our dark river?   Thoreau

2919   Glory be to God for dappled things—
           For skies of couple-color as a brinded cow;
           For rose-moles all in stipple upon trout that
                swim . . .

Gerard Manley Hopkins,
Pied Beauty, Poems 1967 69 Oxford

2920   The birds are machines, if we will; but they are singing machines, and he who forgets the singing has not discovered what birds are.

From F. J. E. Woodbridge, Am. Scholar 1932 1:93

2921   The birds are to be envied:
           They avoid
           Thinking about the trees and the roots.
           Agile, self contented, all day long they swing
           And sing, perched on ultimate end.

Paul Klee, Inward Vision
(Guterman, tr.) 1958 Abrams

2922   What scene is commonplace to the eye that is filled with serene gladness, and brightens all things with its own joy?

George Eliot, Janet's Repentance

2923   Nature is never so admirable or so admired as when she is understood.   Fontenelle (Marsak, tr.), Am. Philos. Soc. 1959 49: Part 7 44

2924   A people that obliterates many natural habitats, and exterminates many valuable animals and plants, suffers in health and enjoyment from polluted air, rivers and beaches, poisoned and tasteless foods; from soil erosion, deforestation, flooding, and loss of pure-water supplies; and from growing congestion, all through lack of sense about the right relation of people to the earth.

A slum is a neighborhood where too many people, through crowding or ignorance, misuse their living space. A pest is an organism which becomes a nuisance or a menace to others. Why is modern man rapidly turning the earth into a slum and himself into its most serious pest? Why does he not see that an ill-placed technological project can destroy, irrevocably, precious goods which it has taken millenia to create?

Civilization is challenged when greed, irresponsibility, ignorance, prevent conservation. Societies which have an esthetic and moral sense, and are scientifically enlightened, conserve.

After E. M. Nicholson, in Julian Huxley (ed.), Humanist Frame 1961 390–396 G. Allen

2925   Nature is man's partner rather than his servant.

W. Temple, Hope of a New World 1943 67 Macmillan

2926   Man's destiny is not just to live in nature, but to create a new nature.   From Francis Bacon

2927   The supreme critic of all our deeds and plans is that
great nature in which we rest.

> After Emerson, Over-Soul

CHANCE

2928   When I was writing the chorus in G Minor, I suddenly
dipped my pen into the medicine bottle instead of the ink; I
made a blot, and when I dried it it took the form of a natural,
which instantly gave me the idea of the effect which the change
from G minor to G major would make, and to this blot all the
effect—if any—is due.   From Rossini

2929   Not always is the race to the swift, the battle to the
strong, bread to the wise, riches to men of understanding, nor
favour to men of skill; time and chance happen to them all.

> From Ecclesiastes IX 11

Chance favors the prepared mind.   Pasteur

2930   All nature is but art, unknown to thee;
          All chance, direction, which thou canst not see.

> Pope, Essay on Man I x

CERTAINTY

2931   The one certainty in this world is that nothing is certain.   John Drinkwater

2932   The fixed arithmic of the universe,
          Which meteth good for good and ill for ill,
          Measure for measure, unto deeds, words,
             thoughts;

Watchful, aware, implacable, unmoved;
Making all futures fruits of all the pasts.
                              Buddha, Light of Asia (Arnold, tr.) V

2933   Any one who can at all catch the drift of experience—
moral no less than physical—must feel that mechanism [orderly
cause-and-effect] rules the whole world.

Intelligence is most at home in the ultimate [the elemental,
universal] . . . Those realities which it can trust and continually
recover are its familiar and beloved companions.

                                                   Santayana,
                        Reason in Common Sense 1905 130 Scribner

CHANGE

2934   No single thing abides, but all things flow. Even the
systems and their suns shall go back slowly to the eternal drift.
                                             From Lucretius

2935   Life is a river into which you cannot step twice, for
other and yet other waters are ever flowing on.
                                             Heraclitus

2936   What we love is animation. What we hate is corruption. But corruption in its turn becomes animation, and animation once more becomes corruption.   Chuang Tzu

2937   Manners with fortunes, humors turn with
           climes,
        Tenets with books, and principles with times.
                        Pope, Moral Essays I 172–173

2938   All things change, and we change with them.

Matthias Borbonius,
Deliciae Poetarum Germanorum I 685

THE UNIVERSE

2939   The morning stars sang together.
Canst thou bind the sweet influence of Pleiades, or loose the
bands of Orion?   From Job XXXVIII 7 31

2940   Man has only begun to understand, not the vastness,
but that such vastness exists, and that it dwarfs all previous
calculations.

From Whitehead, in
Lucien Price, Dialogues ... 1954 368 Little

2941   It is a conceit that the world owes any one of us anything; not even deference does it owe. "It is enough for us that
the universe has produced us and has within it all that we
love."   From (Justice) O. W. Holmes

2942   Is there not transcendent beauty in suns that blaze
and fade as they roll onward in their orbits, in a world taking
form, in the combining of molecules, in the microcosmos of the
atom, in growth, reproduction, and death, in evolution?

From E. M. East

2943   The spiritual and the material, though we call them
by different names, in their origin are one and the same. This
sameness is . . . the mystery of mysteries. It is the gate of all
spirituality.   Mencius

2944   There is far more mystery in the universe for the learned than for the ignorant. Knowledge, mystery, and beauty grow up together.

After G. Sarton,
History . . . 1937 45 Harvard Univ. Press

2945   Man's aspiration for and creation of the good and the true and the beautiful, and his consciousness of the universe, he has added to the cosmic reality.

After C. H. Vessey, God and Man, n.d.
mimeographed Community Church, White Plains, N.Y.

2946   Why should we not look on the universe with piety? Is it not our substance? Are we made of other clay? All our possibilities lie . . . hidden in its bosom. It is the dispenser of all our joys. We may address it without superstitious terrors; it is not wicked. It follows its own habits abstractedly; it can be trusted to be true to its word . . . Shall we not cling to it and praise it, seeing . . . that it is not for us to blame it for what, doubtless, it never knew that it did? Where there is such infinite and laborious potency there is room for every hope.

Santayana,
Reason in Religion 1905 191–192 Scribner

2947   Whatever is harmonious to thee is harmonious to me,
O Universe.   Marcus Aurelius, Meditations IV 23

2948   The Earth, the Universe, belongs to Everyone.
Confucius

SPACE, TIME AND ETERNITY

2949   They cannot scare me with their empty spaces
Between stars—on stars where no human race is.
I have it in me so much nearer home
To scare myself with my own desert places.
Poetry of Robert Frost
(Lathem, ed.), Desert Places 1969 296 Holt

2950   The . . . noiseless foot of Time.
Shakespeare, All's Well that Ends Well IV 3

2951   One life—a little gleam of time between two eternities.
Carlyle, Hero as a Man of Letters

2952   As if we could kill time without injuring eternity!
Thoreau

2953   To every thing there is a season: a time to be born, and
a time to die; a time to plant, and a time to pluck up that
which is planted.
Every man should eat and drink, and enjoy the good of all
his labor.   From Ecclesiastes III 1–2 13

2954   Heaven is under our feet as well as over our
heads . . .
Time is but the stream I go a-fishing in.
Thoreau

2955   We plead, Hasten! Time stands still. We cry, Stay! It
flies like a swallow. We attend to it; it tarries. We forget it;
it (usually) forgets us.
Time . . . is the bars of our cage or aviary which vanish away

the moment we begin to sing, or to listen to a fellow-captive engaged in the same inexplicable pursuit.

Walter de la Mare, Behold This Dreamer

1939 4 5 Knopf, © his Lit. Trustees

2956   The perfect moment is fadeless in the lapse of time.

Whitehead,

Process and Reality 1929 479 Cambridge

2957   Yet one who is aware of the course of existence
Is master of every moment,
Feels no break since time beyond time
In the way life flows.

From Witter Bynner,

Way of Life according to Laotzu 1944 32 Day

2958   Time is the root of all this earth;
These creatures, who from Time had birth,
Within his bosom at the end
Shall sleep; Time hath nor enemy nor friend.

All we in one long caravan
Are journeying since the world began;
We know not whither, but we know
Time guideth at the front, and all must go.

Like as the wind upon the field
Bows every herb, and all must yield,
So we beneath Time's passing breath
Bow each in turn,—why tears for birth or death?

From Sanskrit,

Paul Elmer More, Century ... 1898 90

2959   Time is the image of eternity.

                            Plato, Diogenes Laertius XLI

2960   I saw eternity the other night
        Like a great ring of pure and endless light.

                             Henry Vaughan, World

2961   Time, the ever-disappearing, is the opposite of eternity, the steadfast and unchanging, but, looked at steadily, as when man tries to grasp it in its entirety, time becomes one with eternity.   Ethel Sabin Smith,
                 Furrow Deep and True 1964 221 Norton

XVI

Art, Literature, Science, Philosophy, and Religion

2962   An attempt to understand man need not proceed by way of a study of rats. One can also proceed by considering man's most distinctive endeavors: art, religion, philosophy, morality, and science.

Walter Kaufmann,
Critique of Religion and Philosophy 1958 3 Harper

2963   All the arts are brothers: each is a light to the others.
Voltaire

2964   Man wants to understand the milieu in which he finds himself. He wants to engineer and control his environment to sustain and enrich his life.

From W. A. Tiller, Science 1969 165:469

2965   To confront a blank wall may be the first step toward seeing around it.   J. S. Bixler,
Mass. Rev. 1969 10:410, after Camus

2966   Art clarifies complexity, relieves the pressure of the living event, and substitutes the cleaner pressures of liberated feeling and thought.

From J. Kroll, Newsweek Mar. 17 1969 133

2967   Both the man of art and the man of science live at the edge of mystery; both struggle to harmonize the new with the familiar, to make order in chaos. They can make the paths that connect arts and sciences with each other and with the world at large the bonds of a world-wide community.

From J. Robert Oppenheimer,
Open Mind 1955 145–146 Simon & Schuster

2968   If anyone objects to the arts and sciences because they can be misused for wickedness, luxury, and the like, the same may be said of all earthly goods—of wit, courage, strength, beauty, wealth, light itself.   From Francis Bacon

2969   It is the common fate of knowledge to begin as heresy and end as orthodoxy.   Thomas Huxley

2970   A doctrine lives on for a long time, even when wounded, even when its soul has fled.   Paul Hazard

2971   I can imagine love without physical caresses, religion without ritual, and art without material tokens. I do not deny that the spirit may dwell, and may live more intensely, in the forms which have been specially prepared to receive it. There is religion in the churches, and most of all in the cloisters. There is art in the museums and the libraries, and most of all in the studies and the studios. What I deny is that the mechanical standardized forms are identical with the spirit.

Albert Guérard,
Bottle in the Sea 1954 72 Harvard Univ. Press

2972   The most beautiful thing we can experience is the mysterious. It is the source of all true art and science. He to whom this emotion is a stranger, who can no longer pause to wonder and stand rapt in awe, is as good as dead; his eyes are closed.   Einstein

2973   The essentially unclear is not surely profound. Great art, literature, science, philosophy, and religion are not essentially unclear.

2974   One of the tragedies in the arts is that many individuals say not what they think but what they think they should think.   From B. L. Burman,
Sat. Rev. Nov. 1, 1952 35:9

2975   Science is the finest instrument yet developed for the physical adaptation of man to his environment and the adjustment of his environment to man. For the evolutionist, it is *right* to utilize science to develop and regulate technological and social progress.   After Bentley Glass,
Science and Ethical Values 1965
Univ. N. C. Press

2976   If we look at the various levels of science—atomic physics, chemistry, physiology, psychology, sociology—we can say that each is a science of the "composition effects" of the elements of the next lower level interacting among themselves and with their "environment." Thus, the interaction of a number of atoms in an environment of a certain pressure and temperature might organize them to the "chemical" level; a number of molecules in a particular biological environment might organize to the "physiological" level; a number of physiological (for example, neural) processes interacting in an external environment might organize into "psychological" events; and a number of psyches interacting in a social environment might organize to the "sociocultural," or group, level.
Walter Buckley, Sociology and Modern
Systems Theory 1967 111–112 Prentice-Hall

2977   How much stronger in youth the urge to shine was than the urge to see by the light one had!   R. Musil,
Man Without Qualities 1965 61 Capricorn

2978   Every single poem written regular is a symbol small or great of the way the will has to pitch into commitments deeper and deeper to a rounded conclusion and then be judged for whether any original intention it had has been strongly spent or weakly lost; be it in art, politics, school, business, love, or marriage—in a piece of work or in a career. Strongly spent is synonymous with kept.   Selected Prose of Robert Frost
(Cox and Lathem, eds.) 1956 24 Holt

DOGMA, CREED, AND RITUAL

2979   Man cannot make a worm, and yet he makes gods by dozens.

From Montaigne, Apology for Raimond Sebond

2980   Dogma is for those who need to be governed; thought is for men who can rule themselves and others.

Giordano Bruno

2981   The partisans of dogma go through life like horses with blinders that keep them from looking to the right or the left.

From J. M. Guyau,
L'irréligion de l'avenir II I 112

2982   The doctrinal method is limited and private. The method of intelligence is open and public.

From John Dewey,
Common Faith 1934 39 Yale Univ. Press

2983   Mythology attributes many natural phenomena to hidden dramatic causes. For mythology, disease is a punishment for sin, or a disciplinary means to virtue. Disease can be cured by holy relics, religious ritual, or pious thoughts. The natural world, its inhabitants, and cultures came from a superhuman creator, and all will turn out as he ordains or permits.

In Santayana's view, myths and parables express reality in metaphor, and so justify themselves. Dogma, however, calls for an apology. Thus "a thing born of fancy, moulded to express universal experience and its veritable issues, has to be hedged about by misrepresentation, sophistry, and party spirit."

When a myth has become the center or sanction for habits and institutions, these habits and institutions oppose any conception incompatible with that myth. Thus, the mythological explanations of disease delayed and embarrassed the discovery of scientific treatment, such as immunization. The Biblical and like stories of creation have hindered the masses and many leaders from understanding and using the evolutionary explanation of the natural world, organisms, and cultures.

"To confuse intelligence and dislocate sentiment by gratuitous fictions is a short-sighted way of pursuing happiness. Nature is soon avenged."

Many myths express values like self-control, human brotherhood, and constructive outlook. All these values could stand on more solid intellectual ground; but traditional views and mental inertia have been too congenial for many persons to tolerate this change.

As unreasonable beliefs and practices fade, candor, justice, and progress can grow.

> Quoting Santayana,
> Reason in Religion 1905 53 10 Scribner

2984   Mythic thought has brought boundless suffering upon man.   From Einstein

2985   Why were witches tortured even to death?
Apparently because myth-bound men feared and hated espe-

cially witches; the witches made good scapegoats; and the men wanted to punish the witches, drive out their devils, convert the witches, and save their souls.

2986   Theology is a misguided attempt to make poetry scientific, and the result is neither science nor poetry.
Walter Kaufmann, Critique of Religion
and Philosophy 1958 170 Harper, © Kaufmann

2987   I know the enormous stream of elaborate thinking that has been poured into Christian theology: I respect the magnitude of the effort, and I deplore the waste.
Albert Guérard,
Bottle in the Sea 1954 141 Harvard Univ. Press

2988   Wherever there is a creed, there is a heretic around the corner or in his grave.   Whitehead, Adventures . . .
1933 66 Macmillan; Cambridge

2989   The greatest dangers to liberty lurk in insidious encroachment by men of zeal, well-meaning but without understanding.   Brandeis, Dissenting opinion June 4 1928

2990   It is because they have mistaken the dawn of new truth for a conflagration of old truth that theologians have often been foes of light.   After an Anglican divine
quoted by Andrew Dickson White

2991   Though reason is broad and open to all men, many a person seems to feel that his present knowledge is all-sufficient.
From Heraclitus, Sextus Empiricus,
Against the Logicians I 133 circa

2992   Men who converse with but one sort of men and read but one sort of books will not venture out to survey other riches no less genuine, solid, useful than what has fallen to them in their own little spot, which to them contains whatever is good in the universe.

From Locke, in
Cranston, John Locke 1957 419 Macmillan

2993   When we believe ourselves in possession of the only truth, we are likely to be indifferent to common everyday truths.

Self-deception, credulity and charlatanism are somehow linked together.   Eric Hoffer,
Passionate State of Mind 1955 53 Harper

2994   Sacred Books are an obstacle to moral and intellectual progress because they consecrate the ideas and customs of a given epoch as divinely appointed.

From J. B. Bury, History . . . 1913 54

2995   Religions are necessarily rivals, but sciences are necessarily allies . . .

Supernatural machinery is either symbolic of natural conditions and moral aims or else is worthless . . .

The margin of ineptitude is much broader in religious myth than in religious ethics.

Santayana, Reason in Science 1905 24;
Reason in Religion 1905 276–277;
Reason in Art 1905 5 Scribner

2996   Religions are undernourished when they find their inspirations in their dogmas.

After Whitehead, Religion
in the Making 1926 144 Macmillan; Cambridge

2997   The greatest faith is that which looks at life and the world without shrinking or evasion.

Arthur E. Morgan,
Observations 1968 8 Antioch Press

2998   If instead of making decisions we have but to obey and do our duty, we feel it as a sort of salvation.

Eric Hoffer,
Passionate State of Mind 1955 53 Harper

2999   This is man's way: So long as he thinks that something he does not like is not true, he will scoff at it; but when he comes to think that it might be true after all, he begins to think up reasons why it cannot be true.

Pestalozzi, Education . . . 1953 69 Philos. Lib.

3000   The prejudice of unfounded belief becomes at last rank hypocrisy.   Thomas Paine

3001   [However unwittingly,] the more these self-indulgent minds fear and hate a truth, the more insistently they give the name of truth to the mask that hides it.

Santayana, Realm of Truth 1937 107 Scribner

3002 Those who thirst before everything for certitude do not understand and really love truth.

> After M. Bonaparte, in
> Ernest Jones, Sigmund Freud 1955 2:466 Hogarth

3003 We are most credulous where we know least.

> From Eric Hoffer,
> Passionate State of Mind 1955 80 Harper

3004 When native zeal and integrity, either in nations or persons, has given way to fatigue or contagion, a supernatural assurance needing no test may take possession of the mind.

> Santayana,
> Genteel Tradition . . . 1931 43–44 Scribner

3005 Dogmatism and assertiveness are the express signs of stupidity.

> From Montaigne, in Lowenthal
> (ed.), Autobiography . . . 1935 376 Houghton

3006 As weighty as the word *Fundamental* appears, no feather has been more blown about in the world than this word.

> From Savile,
> Political Thoughts . . . , Of Fundamentals

3007 Ritual was made for man, and not man for ritual.

> After Mark II 27

3008 When the heart is uneasy we support it with ritual.

> Li Chi XXV, Waley,
> Three Ways . . . 1939 181 G. Allen

3009   Ritual has a place in life. The deference may not be for a personality, or even for an institution; but it can be for the ideas embodied in the ceremony.

R. W. Livingstone, in
Lucien Price, Dialogues . . . 1954 360 Little

3010   Not the liturgy or the chapel is sacred, but what they should stand for: justice and humility, and the loving heart and serving hand.   After Emerson, Preacher

3011   It was one of the greatest insights of the founders of the American republic that untrue religious beliefs need not prevent men of good will from working together for the common good.   Walter Kaufmann, Critique
of Religion and Philosophy 1958 215 Harper

3012   Ah! Brothers! Sisters! seek
    Nought from the helpless gods by gift and
        hymn,
    Nor bribe with blood, nor feed with fruit and
        cakes;
    Within yourselves deliverance must be sought.
                    Buddha, Light of Asia (Arnold, tr.) VIII

3013   Men are better than their theology.
                    Emerson, Compensation

3014   Whether in shop, laboratory, library, or society, the open-minded, the fact-finding, the scientific attitude is developed common sense.

To quote Newman: "Though the scientific attitude considers every dogma to be a source of evil, it cannot fail to notice that the certainty offered by orthodox religion is much less of an 'intellectual and moral drug' than the certainties of racism, nationalism, religio-fascism and their kin. These are the wellsprings of tyranny, sustenance for seekers of power in the social, political and economic spheres. We are familiar also with the critics, for whatever purpose, of centralization, social planning and of every aspect of the welfare state, who, in their arguments, invoke the certainties most destructive of freedom as allegedly the sole means of preserving it."

The scientific attitude supports enlightened moral convictions and ideals, found in religion and elsewhere, which lead men to better ways. It must, on the other hand, expose any effort, religious or secular, to maintain authority by fear, superstition, intolerance, or alliance with despotism, and must maintain and promote intellectual freedom.

Newman cites Waddington, who shows that the scientific attitude is " 'on the side of democracy'; but only a democracy that is prepared to make social experiments and to abide by their results."

> Quoting J. R. Newman, Science
> and Sensibility 1961 2:109–110 Simon & Schuster

3015   A liberal and relativistic philosophy is capable of giving men guidance in a more objective and public way than any absolutism.
> From C. Frankel,
> Case for Modern Man 1956 73 Harper

ERROR

3016   Errors, like straws, upon the surface flow;
     He who would search for pearls must dive below.

> Dryden, All for Love, Prologue

3017   To free a man from error is to give him truth. Knowledge that a thing is false is a truth. Error always does harm: sooner or later it will bring mischief to the man who harbors it.   Schopenhauer, Religion:

A Dialogue (Saunders, tr.) 1890 29

3018   When disillusion comes, while it may bring a momentary shock, it ends by producing a settled satisfaction unknown before.   Santayana, Reason in Society 1905 195 Scribner

3019   Nothing is so harmful to a new truth as an old error. Some persons, on being aroused from error, turn to truth with renewed vigor.   From Goethe

TRUTH

3020   Truth and understanding are not such wares as are to be monopolized and traded in by tickets and statutes and standards.   Milton, Areopagitica 1951 32

3021   He who loves Christianity more than what he feels is true loves his own sect more than Christianity, and his supposed self more than all.

After Coleridge,
Moral and Religious Aphorisms xxv

3022   The dogmatist uses his "truth" to distinguish "the sheep" from "the goats." The humane seeker for truth wants to find and share what knowledge he can.

3023   Truth is as impossible to be soiled by any outward touch as the sunbeam.   Milton, Doctrine and
Discipline of Divorce, Introduction

3024   Truth is often drowned in rhetoric.   B. Zawadzki

3025   Some have thought that truth will defeat error regard-less of conditions. This is an idle sentimentality. Truth, merely as truth, has no more power than error to prevail against the dungeon and the stake. The real advantage which truth has is that, when an opinion is true, it may be extinguished once, twice, or many times, until it escapes persecution enough to make such head as to withstand all subsequent attempts to suppress it.   From John Stuart Mill, On Liberty II

3026   Truth is not a wax flower in a glass case guarded with-in an institution. Truth is a growing plant that draws its strength from all outdoors; and in growing it has to slough off some parts that seemed good in the past.

3027   There can be no peace in delusion.
                        Santayana, Realm of Truth 1937 107 Scribner

3028   No discovery of fact, however trivial, can be wholly useless to the race, and no trumpeting of falsehood, however virtuous in intent, can be anything but vicious.
                                        From H. L. Mencken,
                Living Philosophies 1931 192 Simon & Schuster

3029   The truth is always the strongest argument.
                                        Sophocles, Frag. 737

3030   Truth is the secret of eloquence and of virtue.
                                        Amiel, Journal

3031   Truth is a medicine that takes hold.
                        Pestalozzi, Education . . . 1953 69 Philos. Lib.

3032   When all treasures are tried, truth is the best.
Vision of Piers Plowman

3033   It is noble to seek truth, and it is beautiful to find it.
Sidney Smith

3034   Though we follow the truth for itself, we feel that it
will make us free and glad.   From F. Adler

3035   Every day in the mountains of truth, either you climb
further or you exercise your strength to climb further.
After Nietzsche, Thus Spake Zarathustra

3036   If truth acquired does not compensate for every pet
illusion dispelled, the path is thorny indeed, although it must
still be faithfully trodden.   [W. R. Cassels],
Supernatural Religion 1879 xcviii

3037   [Often] the truth is cruel, but it can be loved, and it
makes free those who have loved it.
Santayana, in Boyle (tr.),
Ethics of Spinoza 1910 xix

3038   In politics and jurisprudence, a precious wreath awaits
science if it will wage a candid fight against superstition,
factual errors, poor thinking, and lies. The triumph of truth
will carry the triumph of justice.
From A. Brecht,
Political Theory 1959 416 Princeton Univ. Press

3039   Mortals may never agree on "universal truth," on "the
most important truth," or even that any such truth is possible.

Many do agree, however, on many truths, and many can learn to agree on more truths.

3040   No one can master truth fully or miss it wholly. Each adds a little to our knowledge of nature, and from all the facts assembled there arises grandeur.   Aristotle

3041   To be pleasing to us, even truth requires at different times a different raiment.

G. C. Lichtenberg, in
Stern, Lichtenberg 1959 316 Ind. Univ. Press

3042   Unless you expect the unexpected you may fail to find truth.   After Heraclitus (Wheelwright, tr.)
1959 Frag. 19 Princeton Univ. Press

3043   Truth has failed, will fail again,
If not backed by truthful men.
A. J. Ellis

3044   The fewer the voices on the side of truth, the more distinct and strong must be your own.

W. E. Channing, Works 1875 2:319

BEAUTY

3045   The beautiful is where all the right parts are in the right balance.   From E. Delacroix, Journal Feb. 14 1847

3046   Perfect grace consists not in exterior ornamentation of the substance, but in the simple fitness of its form.

I Ching (Wilhelm, tr., Baynes, tr.) 1967 93
Princeton Univ. Press; Routledge

3047   Beauty contains truth, and truth, beauty.

After Keats, Ode on a Grecian Urn

3048   What is beautiful is good, and who is good will be beautiful.

Sappho, Frag. 101

3049   A thing of beauty is a joy for ever.   Keats, Endymion

3050   There is a high breathlessness about beauty that cancels lust and superstition.

Santayana, Reason in Art 1905 171 Scribner

3051   There is culture in the hearts of a people when the very utensils in the kitchen are beautiful as well as useful.

From Yeats

3052   It would surprise any of us if we realized how much store we unconsciously set by beauty, and how little savor there would be left in life if it were withdrawn. It is the smile on the earth's face, open to all, and needs but the eyes to see, the mood to understand.

Galsworthy, Candelabra 1933 Scribner

3053   If the mind is calm and at ease, then even beauties that are mediocre will gratify the eye, sounds that are mediocre will gratify the ear. Thus one may not be able to enjoy all the most beautiful things in the world, and yet he can increase his joy.

From Hsün Tzu, Burton Watson (tr.)
1963 155 Columbia Univ. Press

3054   Beauty is Nature's coin, must not be hoarded,
        But must be current, and the good thereof
        Consists in mutual and partaken bliss.

                            Milton, Mask (Comus) 739–741

3055   To a classic Greek, good actions bring beauty into the
world and for that reason are valuable for their own sake.

                            From R. W. Livingstone, Lecture 1956

EVIL AND GOOD

3056   Evil is that which is against our well-being, and good
is that which promotes it.

                                            John Burroughs,
                        Accepting the Universe 1920 120 Houghton

3057   A good, absolute in the sense of being divorced from
all natural demand and all possible satisfaction, would be as
remote as possible from goodness.

    Evil would seem to be a sort of friction, capable of being
diminished indefinitely as the world is better known and the
will is better educated.

                                            Santayana,
                Reason in Common Sense 1905 222–223 Scribner;
                    and from Three Philosophical Poets 1910 210

3058   If you pursue evil with pleasure, the pleasure passes
away, but the evil remains; if you pursue good with labor, the
labor passes away, but the good remains.   Proverb

PERFECTION

3059   Nothing makes the soul so pure, so religious, as the endeavor to create something perfect.   Michelangelo

3060   Man forever seeks the perfect, though he never becomes perfect.

3061   Whoever thinks a faultless piece to see,
Thinks what ne'er was, nor is, nor e'er shall be.
Pope, Essay on Criticism II 253

3062   In small proportions we just beauties see,
And in short measures life may perfect be.
Ben Jonson, Pindaric Ode . . . III

ORDER

3063   Order is the sanity of the mind, the health of the body, the peace of the city, the security of the state. As the beams to a house, as the bones to the body, so is order to all things.
Robert Southey

3064   The mind voyaging through chaos and reducing it to clarity and order is the symbol of all the quests which lend glory to our dust.
From J. L. Lowes, Road to Xanadu 1927 Houghton

HARMONY WITH ONESELF AND THE WORLD

3065   He that strives against essential nature will for ever strive in vain.   After Samuel Johnson, Idler No. 51

3066   There is mystical happiness in accepting existence
without understanding it.

> Santayana, Soliloquies . . . 1922 201 Scribner

3067   To have attained to the human form must be always a
source of joy.   Chuang Tzu

3068   As I look back on fully seventy years of awareness . . .
the moments of greatest happiness . . . were, for the most part,
moments when I lost myself all but completely in some instant
of perfect harmony.

> B. Berenson, Sketch . . . 1949 18 Pantheon

3069   When man thinks of himself not as a little god outside
of nature, but as a ganglion within nature, he is a creative part
of the infinite.   After (Justice) O. W. Holmes,
> Collected Legal Papers 1920 Harcourt

HAPPINESS

3070   Man's happiness, his flaunting honey'd flower of soul,
is his loving response to the wealth of Nature.

> Robert Bridges,
> Testament of Beauty 1929 14 120–121 Oxford

3071   Often what appears to be unhappiness is hap-
        piness
        And what appears to be happiness is unhappi-
        ness.

> Witter Bynner,
> Way of Life according to Laotzu 1944 62 Day

3072   Potential happiness surrounds us. We can be blinded to it by anxiety, by suppression of happy emotions, or just by ignorance of what happiness is, so that the happy incident all too often passes us by.

From M. Gumpert,
Anatomy of Happiness 1951 226 McGraw

3073   Much happiness is overlooked because it does not cost anything.   **Proverb**

3074   Among the most harmful, irrational ideas in our culture are these:

Any danger, failure, or other stress is catastrophic.

Whatever has affected one markedly must continue to affect one in that same way.

Every person should have some one stronger than himself on whom to rely.

It is better to avoid than to face difficulties and responsibilities.

Unhappiness comes from without and is wholly beyond one's control.

Happiness can be gained by sheer inertia.

From Albert Ellis,
J. Individual Psychol. 1957 13:39–40

3075   To believe that if only we had this or that we would be happy, or to pursue any excessive desire, diverts us from seeing that happiness depends on an adequate self.

After Eric Hoffer,
Passionate State of Mind 1955 3 Harper

3076   I sent my soul through the Invisible,
Some letter of that After-life to spell;

> And by and by my Soul returned to me,
> And answer'd: "I myself am Heav'n and Hell."
>
> Omar Khayyám, Rubáiyát lxvi

3077   Happiness makes up in height for what it lacks in length.

> Poetry of Robert Frost (Lathem, ed.) 1969 333 Holt

3078   Happiness is generally as fine-grained as life itself, and so intimately intermixed with living that it can be extracted from breathing, eating, sleeping, waking, from the humblest labor, from all achievement and creation and understanding.

> From Homer W. Smith,
> Man and His Gods 1952 444 Little

3079   The direct pursuit of Happiness is folly.

> Bernard Shaw,
> Maxims . . . Man and Superman 1903 236

3080   There is no intelligent pursuit of happiness where there is not at least an attempt at moral self-government.

> H. W. Schneider,
> Three Dimensions . . . 1956 123 Ind. Univ. Press

3081   Cultivate the thoughts of an immortal by being lofty of soul, but of a mortal by enjoying in due measure the good things you possess.   Isocrates, Oration to Demonicus

3082   There are two ways of being happy: We may either diminish our wants or augment our means.

If you are idle or sick or poor, however hard it may be to diminish your wants, it will be harder to augment your means.

If you are active and prosperous or young or in good health, it may be easier for you to augment your means than to diminish your wants.

But if you are wise, you will do both; and if you are very wise you will do both in such a way as to augment the general happiness of society.   From Franklin

3083   No one is happy who thinks he is unhappy.
                              After Publilius Syrus, Maxim 584

3084   A great obstacle to happiness is to expect a too-great happiness.   Fontenelle, Du bonheur

3085   He who joy of life would store,
                       Heart of his be widely open.
                                        James Stephens

3086   Happiness and unhappiness are not like snow or wind; they can be ruled according to the laws of human nature.
                                                 Paracelsus

3087   Happiness, whether for ourselves or for others, we cannot buy; we must create it.   Unknown

3088   Happiness depends, as Nature shows
        Less on exterior things than most suppose.
                          William Cowper, Table Talk 246

3089   The happy life depends upon the attainment of reason.
                              Seneca, Ad Lucilium . . .

                          (Gummere, tr.) 1918 2:447 Putnam

3090   To finish the moment, to find the journey's end in every step of the road, to live the greatest number of good hours, is wisdom.   Emerson, Experience

3091   Beatitude consists in the noblest action of man in reference to the most excellent objectives.   After Aristotle

3092   Love directed towards the timeless and universal feeds the mind with joy.   From Spinoza

3093   Happiness is a habit.
                                   L. B. McCue, in Murrow (ed.),
                        This I Believe 1952 106 Simon & Schuster

3094   Human happiness seems to consist of three ingredients: action, pleasure, and ease.   From Hume

3095   Virtue itself makes man happy.
                            From Pomponazzi, in Kristeller,
                Studies ... 1956 274 Edizioni di Storia e Letteratura

3096   Happiness is activity in accordance with virtue.
                    From Aristotle, Nicomachean Ethics I viii

3097   Happiness is soundness and perfection of mind.
                                      From Marcus Aurelius

3098   Happiness is a roadside flower, growing on the highways of usefulness.
                    M. F. Tupper, Proverbial Philosophy 1849 87

3099   Goodness does not more certainly make men happy than happiness makes them good.

> W. S. Landor, Imaginary Conversations:
> Lord Brooke and Sir Philip Sidney

3100   True happiness renders men kind and sensible; and that happiness is always shared with others.

> Montesquieu

3101   For the sons of men there is nothing better than to rejoice, and to do good, so long as they live.

> From Ecclesiastes III 10–12

THE EXPLORATORY URGE

3102   He knew a path that wanted walking;
He knew a spring that wanted drinking;
A thought that wanted further thinking.

What comes over a man, is it soul or mind—
That to no limits and bounds he can stay confined?

> Poetry of Robert Frost (Lathem, ed.),
> A Lone Striker 1969 274 Holt

3103   All men desire to know, often with no utilitarian end.

> From Aristotle, Metaphysics 980 982

3104   Curiosity is, in great and generous minds, the first passion and the last.

> Samuel Johnson, Rambler No. 50

3105   The thirst to know and understand is an essential test of human freedom and dignity.

From P. B. Sears, Am. Scholar 1957 26:451

3106   Material for art is always at hand.

Marcus Aurelius, Meditations VII 68

3107   The very beholding of the light is a fairer thing than all the uses of it.   Francis Bacon

3108   Even perfection will not bear the tedium of indefinite repetition. Adventure is essential—the search for new perfections.   From Whitehead,

Adventures . . . 1933 332 Macmillan; Cambridge

3109   Hills peep o'er hills, and Alps on Alps arise!

Pope, Essay on Criticism II 232

FURTHER MOTIVES

3110   The main cause of progress in science is curiosity. Other causes include practical necessity, humanitarian interests, and love of glory, power, wealth, and escape. Nevertheless, as a man continues his research, he may reach that complete self-forgetfulness which is perhaps our nearest approach to heaven.   After G. Sarton,

History . . . 1937 34–36 Harvard Univ. Press

3111   Thought product and food product are to me
Nothing compared to the producing of them.
I sent you once a song with the refrain:

Let me be the one
To do what is done—
My share at least, lest I be empty-idle.

> Poetry of Robert Frost (Lathem, ed.),
> Build Soil 1969 324 Holt

3112   Devotion is the master of all arts.   Proverbial

3113   'Tis to create, and in creating live
A being more intense, that we endow
With form our fancy, gaining as we give
The life we image.

> Byron, Childe Harold III 28–31

3114   Every man who possesses real vitality can be seen as the resultant of two forces. He is first the child of a particular age, society, convention; of what we may call in one word a tradition. He is secondly, in one degree or another, a rebel against that tradition. And the best traditions make the best rebels.   Gilbert Murray

3115   Of old, men wrought strange gods for mystery,
Implored miraculous tokens in the skies,
And lips that most were strange in prophecy
Were most accounted wise.

And so they built them altars of retreat,
Where life's familiar use was overthrown,
And left the shining world about their feet,
To travel worlds unknown.

We hunger still. But wonder has come down
From alien skies upon the midst of us;

The sparkling hedgerow and the clamorous
    town
Have grown miraculous.

And man from his far traveling returns,
To find yet stranger wisdom than he sought,
Where in the habit of his threshold burns
Unfathomable thought.

John Drinkwater,
Poems 1908–1919, New Miracle 1919 Houghton

INSPIRATION

3116   I hearing get, who had but ears,
    And sight, who had but eyes before;
    I moments live, who lived but years,
    And truth discern, who knew but learning's
      lore.

From Thoreau, Inspiration

3117   Inspiration may be specific or general. It occurs during sleep, half sleep, recreation, solitude, sociability, related or unrelated work, and intense experience.

3118   Like wind for a sailboat, inspiration for creative work is vital but undependable.

3119   Whether inspiration or hope makes a person try to do creative work, the very working may bring inspiration. Bach, Mozart, Beethoven, and Wagner settled down day after day to the job in hand.   After Ernest Newman

CREATION

3120   Seldom do men really create. They inherit, imitate, or adopt, often usefully. They also merely innovate, not always usefully.   After Arthur E. Morgan,
Observations 1968 45 Antioch Press

3121   Talent and training, spontaneity and discipline, creativity and proportion, make for best contribution.

3122   Genius begins great works; labor alone finishes them.
Joubert

3123   Arts and sciences are formed and perfected by often handling and polishing.
From Montaigne, Apology for Raimond Sebond

3124   In the creating artist, the highest ecstasy and the deepest peace come together.

Max Roden,
Spiegelungen 1951 17 Johannes-Presse

3125   During thousands of years, men have imagined worlds more reasonable, more generous, and more interesting than their own. These acts of imagination have had an enormous influence on history.

From René Dubos,
Dreams of Reason 1961 100 Columbia Univ. Press

3126   That society prospers best which can provide the freest scope for art.   From Whitehead, in
Lucien Price, Dialogues . . . 1954 162 Little

3127   The creative impulses must not be thought of as limited to the liberal arts; one can be a creative clerk, craftsman, teacher, or housewife.

> From L. M. Brammer and Shostrom,
> Therapeutic Psychology 1960 109 Prentice-Hall

3128   Not only the creation of a concrete end-product but also a creative handling of one's human relationships furthers a person's self-realization and self-transcendent dedication.

> From C. Buhler,
> Am. Psychologist 1971 26:385

3129   If a bird sing among your branches be not too ready to tame it.   Amiel

3130   The wind of creative spirit bloweth whither it listeth.

> From Whitehead, in
> Lucien Price, Dialogues . . . 1954 118 Little

3131   The artist creates through his sensitiveness and his power to impose form.   From E. M. Forster,

> Two Cheers . . . 1951 94 Harcourt

3132   For what reason would grope for in vain, spontaneous impulse
Ofttimes achieves at a stroke with light and
pleasureful guidance.

> Goethe

3133   A scientific hunch springs from a wide knowledge of facts but goes beyond a mere necessary conclusion from available data. It is a process of creative thought.

From W. Platt and R. Baker,
J. Chemical Ed. 1931 8:1969

3134   In his selection of limits for his work the master is revealed.   From Goethe

3135   Imagination deserted by reason creates monstrosities. United with reason, imagination gives birth to great marvels and true art.   Goya,
Caption for the etching, The Dreams of Reason

3136   All serious thinking combines in some proportion and perspective the actual and the possible. Actuality supplies contact and solidity; and possibility, the ideal from which criticism and creative effort spring.

From John Dewey, Characters ... 1929 437 Holt

3137   He who would write well in laudable things ought himself to be a true poem, a composition and pattern of the best and most honorable things.

From Milton, Apology for Smectymnuus

EXPRESSION

3138   Whether the charmer sinner it or saint it,
If folly grow romantic, I must paint it.
Pope, Moral Essays II 15

3139   If you mean to please everybody you will
Set to work both ignorance and skill;

For a great multitude are ignorant,
And skill to them seems raving and rant;
Like putting oil and water into a lamp,
'Twill make a great splutter with smoke and
   damp;
For there is no use, as it seems to me,
Of lighting a lamp when you don't wish to see.

William Blake, Note-Book,
English Encouragement of Art

3140   Good expression requires something worthwhile to express.   After Phyllis Bentley,
O Dreams . . . 1962 127 Gollancz, © Peters

3141   A genuine craftsman will not adulterate his product.
W. Lippmann

3142   The style is the man.

Leclerc, Comte de Buffon

AN OVERVIEW OF ART

3143   Nature often does not give us the best; for that we must
have recourse to art.

After Balthasar Gracian (Jacobs, tr.) 12

3144   The smallest thing, well done, becomes artistic.
William Mathews

3145   The Chinese artist who would draw a fish studies fish
until he feels its shape and movement in his own body, I suppose with an empathy which gets somehow into the hand and
fingers that hold the brush. All irrelevant details have been

eliminated, and what he swiftly puts down on the paper or silk
is the essence of the fish—what one might call its essential fish-
ness.   O. W. Larkin, letter 1965

3146   The work of art enables us to see more deeply into
Nature around and within us.

From Albert Guérard,
Bottle in the Sea 1954 71 Harvard Univ. Press

3147   Art discovers, selects, synthesizes, and presents spiritually enriching experience.

3148   The world embraces not only a Newton, but a Shakespeare—not only a Boyle, but a Raphael—not only a Kant, but
a Beethoven—not only a Darwin, but a Carlyle. Not in each
of these, but in all, is human nature whole.

From John Tyndall, Address 1874 64

3149   All honor to the beauty of form! Let us cultivate it in
men, women, and children—in our gardens and in our houses.
But let us love that other beauty too, which lies in human sympathy. Paint us an angel, if you can, with a floating violet robe,
and a face paled by the celestial light; paint us yet oftener a
Madonna turning her mild face upward and opening her arms
to welcome the divine glory; but do not impose on us any
aesthetic rules which shall banish from the region of Art those
old women scraping carrots with their work-worn hands, those
heavy clowns taking holiday in a dingy pot-house, those
rounded backs and stupid weather-beaten faces that have bent
over the spade and done the rough work of the world—those
homes with their tin pans, their brown pitchers, their rough
curs, and their clusters of onions. In this world there are so
many of these common coarse people, who have no picturesque

sentimental wretchedness, we should remember their existence,
else we may frame lofty theories which only fit a world of extremes.   George Eliot, Adam Bede

3150   Great art deals even with simple subjects freshly.
                                        From Whitehead, in
                        Lucien Price, Dialogues . . . 1954 181 Little

3151   Clothing the palpable and familiar
            With golden exhalations of the dawn.
                            Coleridge, Death of Wallenstein I i

3152   And of course there must be something wrong
        In wanting to silence any song.
                                    Poetry of Robert Frost
                        (Lathem, ed.), A Minor Bird 1969 251 Holt

3153   Pure and subtle music is something keener and more
intense than the howling of storms or the rumble of cities.
    Poetry is an extraction, a rehandling, an epitome of crude
experience; it is a theoretic vision of things at arm's length.
    Constructive study or experience in any art, science, philos-
ophy, or religion is a more intense sort of experience than most
of common life is.
            After Santayana, Three Philosophical Poets 1910 124

3154   Children choose bread formed in the image of a bird
or man rather than a loaf plucked rudely from the baker's
lump because it entertains more faculties and pleases on more
sides.   From Jeremy Taylor, in Gest (ed.),
                            House . . . 1954 78 Univ. Pa. Press

3155   All art appeals primarily to the senses.

> Joseph Conrad, Nigger of the Narcissus, Preface

3156   It is vain to charm the ears or gratify the eyes if the mind be not satisfied.   Rule of Life 1800 135

3157   In fine art, the heart, the head, and the hand go together.   From Ruskin

3158   Nature contains the elements, in color and form, of all pictures, as the keyboard contains the notes of all music.

> Whistler

3159   Painting, like poetry, selects from the universe what it considers best for its own end. In a single created figure it is able to concentrate circumstances which nature scatters among a crowd of individuals.   Goya

3160   The difference between detailedness and refinement seems to be this—that the one relates to the parts, and the other to the whole. Thus, the accumulation of distinct particulars in a work, as the threads of a gold-laced buttonhole, or the hairs on the chin in a portrait of Denner's, is minute finishing; the giving the gradations of tone in a sky of Claude's from azure to gold, where the distinction at each step is imperceptible, but the whole effect is striking and grand, is true refinement and delicacy.

> After Hazlitt, Characteristics CCCXXVII

3161   I had it from one of the youngest lately: "Surely art can be considered good only as it prompts to action." How soon, I asked him. But there is danger of undue levity in teasing the young.

> From Robert Frost,
> E. A. Robinson, King Jasper, Intro. 1935 Macmillan

3162   To be an artist is to be a person in whom knowledge passes into feeling, and feeling comes forth as knowledge.

> After George Eliot

3163   Art rests upon a kind of religious sense, a deep, immutable earnestness.   Goethe

3164   The greatest artists are men of distinguished mind and character.   After a Chinese saying

3165   In the aesthetic domain as well as in the purely intellectual, our dignity should prevent us from accepting slavishly any authority or tradition.   Albert Guérard

3166   If people did not confuse intelligence with cleverness, they would value simplicity more than they do.

> Max Roden, Spiegelungen 1951 39 Johannes-Presse

3167   Simplicity is an exact medium between too little and too much.   Joshua Reynolds

3168   Once refinement exists for its own sake, it becomes mannerism.   A. Temko,
> Columbia Univ. Forum 1958 1: No. 2 21

3169   Art conceals technique.   From Ovid, Art of Love

3170   The hidden harmony is better than the obvious.

> Heraclitus (Wheelwright, tr.),
> 1959 Frag. 116 Princeton Univ. Press

3171   As long as art is the beauty parlor of civilization, neither art nor civilization is secure.

> John Dewey, Art as Experience 1934 344 Minton

3172   At all times, even in moments of the highest happiness, we need the perspective that works of art give.

> After Goethe

3173   Only when the past ceases to trouble and anticipations of the future are not perturbing is a being wholly united with his environment and therefore fully alive. Art celebrates with peculiar intensity the moments in which the past reenforces the present and in which the future is a quickening of what now is.

> John Dewey, Art as Experience 1934 18 Minton

3174   The conscious artist hopes to arrest, for the space of a breath, the hands busy about the work of the earth, and compel men entranced by the sight of distant goals to glance for a moment at the surrounding vision of form and color, of sunshine and shadows; to make them pause for a look, for a sigh, for a smile.

> From Joseph Conrad, Nigger of the Narcissus, Preface

3175   This is the priesthood of art—not to bestow upon the universe a new aspect, but upon the beholder a new enthusiasm. We are born sleeping and few of us ever awake, unless it is when death startles us and we learn what bit of Olympian fire our humid forms enwrapped. But we could open our eyes to joy also. The artist cries "Awake!" and sings the song of the morning.   From Max Eastman

3176   It is only in some works of art that ecstasy endures.
                                        Walter Kaufmann, From
             Shakespeare to Existentialism 1960 261 Doubleday

3177   Art is a hermitage to which man may withdraw to gather fresh strength. Art teaches man humility, tolerance, wisdom and magnanimity.

                                            From Maugham,
                   Summing Up 1938 302–303 Literary Guild

3178   The imagination, by means of art, uses the materials of sense to suggest ideal truth. Art is thus a way of having the substantial cake of reason while also enjoying the sensuous pleasure of eating it.   From John Dewey,
                        Art as Experience 1934 258 Minton

3179   Art makes that understood and felt which, in the form of an argument, might be incomprehensible and inaccessible. Art transmits men's best feelings and insights.

                                            After Tolstoy

3180   If the spirit of art be absolute disinterestedness and honesty, it may point the way out of our tragic confusions, social and spiritual.

                                     From Albert Guérard,
                   Bottle in the Sea 1954 64 Harvard Univ. Press

3181   The perfect in art suggests the perfect in conduct.
                                            Ingersoll

3182 Having beheld a poem or a painting with appreciation helps you turn in like spirit toward man.

After Max Roden,
Spiegelungen 1951 19 Johannes-Presse

3183 We shape our dwellings, and afterwards our dwellings shape us. Winston Churchill, Speech Oct. 1944

3184 Art sanctions, justifies, and unifies sensation, feeling and reason.

From Hegel, Vorlesungen über die Aesthetik

3185 A living art does not produce curiosities to be collected but spiritual necessaries to be diffused.

Santayana, Reason in Art 1905 209 Scribner

3186 The quality of greatness in music—in literature—in art —is that the work contains you, sustains you, carries you forward as on a rising wave and, however far your perception goes, indicates a farther horizon.

M. M. duPont, Definitions . . . 1965 Swallow

3187 We live by symbols, and what shall be symbolized by any image depends upon the mind that perceives it.

After (Justice) O. W. Holmes,
Collected Legal Papers 1920 270 Harcourt

DANCE

3188 The poetry of the foot.
Dryden

3189   For the good are always the merry,
Save by an evil chance,
And the merry love the fiddle,
And the merry love to dance.

Yeats, Fiddler of Dooney

3190   Without dancing you can never attain a perfectly graceful carriage, which is highly important in life.

Disraeli, Vivian Grey

3191   Dancing is no mere translation or abstraction from life; it is life itself.

Havelock Ellis, Dance of Life 1923 65 Houghton

MUSIC

3192   O music, sphere-descended maid,
Friend of pleasure, wisdom's aid.

William Collins, Passions 95

3193   . . . Sweet compulsion doth in music lie,
To lull the daughters of Necessity.

Milton, Arcades 68

3194   Music produces a kind of pleasure which human nature cannot do without.   Confucius

3195   Music fathoms the sky.   Baudelaire

3196   Music is a higher revelation than philosophy.

Beethoven

3197   After silence, that which comes nearest to expressing the inexpressible is music.   Aldous Huxley

VISUAL ARTS

3198   Architecture is frozen music.

> Schelling, Philosophie der Kunst II IV cvii

3199   . . . To seize some shape that we see,
That others may keep
Its moment of mystery.

> Lord Dunsany, Fifty Poems 1929 2 Putnam

3200   To know that a painting is good, we must look and look and look till we live in the painting and for a fleeting moment become identified with it. If then we do not love what through the ages has been loved, a rough test is whether we feel that it is reconciling us with life.

> From B. Berenson,
> Italian Painters . . . 1952 xiii and passim Phaidon

THEATRE

3201   A good play stirs the deep layers of thought with bold and broad insights and observations. It fertilizes our minds, and enables us to know ourselves better than we did. It offers real ideas or illuminations.

> From M. Mannes, Reporter Apr. 25, 1963 49–50

3202   Tragedy makes man a partaker with his kind. It considers what can affect our common nature. It exhibits the passions, and corrects their excesses in ourselves by pointing to the sufferings and crimes to which they have led others. Tragedy creates a balance of the affections.

By painting the extremes of human calamity, tragedy kindles the affections and raises the most intense imagination and desire of the contrary good.

From Hazlitt, Characters . . .
1906 32, Characteristics CCLXXXVIII

POETRY

3203   "Poetry," said Emilia, "seems like talking on tiptoe."
Meredith

3204   . . . A Poet . . .
Distills amazing sense
From ordinary Meanings—
And Attar so immense

. . .

The Poets light but Lamps—
Themselves—go out—
The Wicks they stimulate—
If vital Light

Inhere as do the Suns—
Each Age a Lens
Disseminating their
Circumference—
Emily Dickinson, Thomas H. Johnson (ed.),
Complete Poems 1960 215 419 Little

3205   . . . Versification is only the carved vase which holds the precious wine of poetry . . .

Brander Matthews, Study of Versification 1911 6

3206   Poetry is the achievement of the synthesis of hyacinths
and biscuits.   Carl Sandburg,
                        Good Morning, America 1928 X Harcourt

3207   No man was ever yet a great poet without being at the
same time a profound philosopher; for poetry is the blossom
and the fragrancy of all human knowledge, human thoughts,
human passions, emotions, language.   Coleridge

3208   A poem . . . begins in delight and ends in wisdom.
                        Selected prose of Robert Frost
                        (Cox and Lathem, eds.) 1956 18 Holt

3209   Bards of Passion and of Mirth,
            Ye have left your souls on earth!

            . . .

            Never slumbered, never cloying.
            Here, your earth-born souls still speak
            To mortals, of their little week;

            . . .

            Of their glory and their shame;
            What doth strengthen and what maim.
            Thus ye teach us, every day,
            Wisdom, though fled far away . . .
                                    Keats, Ode

3210   Man has a spirit capable of compassion and sacrifice
and endurance. The poet's, the writer's, duty is to write about
these things. It is his privilege to help man endure by lifting
his heart, by reminding him of the courage and honor and
hope and pride and compassion and pity and sacrifice which

have been the glory of his past. The poet's voice need not merely be the record of man, it can be one of the props, the pillars to help him endure and prevail.

From William Faulkner, Speech Dec. 10 1950

3211   The poet does not restore the life that was there in childhood or in the childhood of the race: he creates new life, more than life—that for which human life is a reach and aspiration.   Walter Kaufmann, From
Shakespeare to Existentialism 1960 260 Doubleday

3212   Poetry is the most direct way of saying anything. While we are arguing through pages of prose, a poem has given us the essence of the idea in two perfect lines.

From M. L. Becker, in
Emily Dickinson, Poems for Youth 1934 Little

3213   Poetry must be as new as foam, and as old as the rock.
Emerson, Journal Mar. 1845

3214   Your lay, heavenly bard, is to me even as sleep on the grass to the weary, as in summer heat the slaking of thirst in a dancing rill of sweet water.   Vergil

3215   A verse may find him who a sermon flies,
     And turn delight into a sacrifice.

George Herbert, Church Porch

3216   A Poet without love were a physical and metaphysical impossibility.   Carlyle

3217   It is easier to write an indifferent poem than to understand a good one. Montaigne

3218   A line will take us hours maybe;
        Yet if it does not seem a moment's thought,
        Our stitching and unstitching has been naught.
                                    Yeats, Adam's Curse

3219   Poetry has given me the habit of wishing to discover the good and beautiful in all that surrounds me.
                                    From Coleridge

LITERATURE

3220   . . . Books . . .
        I thank these Kinsmen of the Shelf—
            Emily Dickinson, Thomas H. Johnson (ed.),
                Complete Poems . . . 1960 296 Little

3221   A book is like a garden carried in the pocket.
                                    Arabian proverb

3222   There is first the literature of knowledge, and second the literature of power. The first is a rudder, the second an oar or a sail. From De Quincey

3223   Fiction, imaginative work, is like a spider's web, attached ever so lightly perhaps, but still attached to life at all four corners. Often the attachment is scarcely perceptible; Shakespeare's plays, for instance, seem to hang there complete by themselves. But when the web is pulled askew, hooked up at the edge, torn in the middle, one remembers that these webs are not spun in mid-air by incorporeal creatures, but are the work of human beings, and are attached to material things like health and money and the houses we live in.

From V. Woolf,
Room of One's Own 1929 62–63 Harcourt

3224   We have more faith in well-written fiction, while we are reading it, than in ordinary history. The vividness of the representations outweighs the mere facts.

From Hazlitt, Characteristics CCXC

3225   True wit is nature to advantage dressed,
        What oft was thought, but ne'er so well ex-
            pressed.

Pope, Essay on Criticism II 297–298

3226   The spirit of literature is unifying; it joins the candle and the star, and by the magic of an image shows that the beauty of the greater is in the less. And, not content with the disclosure of beauty and the bringing together of all things whatever within its focus, it enforces a moral wisdom by the tracing everywhere of cause and effect.   Arnold Bennett

3227   All great literature is, in one aspect, a criticism . . . of the society in which the author lives.

T. S. Eliot, radio address 1944

3228   The great writers, pagan, Christian, agnostic, are the imagination and the conscience of mankind.

From D. Bush, in Brand
Blanshard (ed.), Education . . . 1959 187 Basic Books

3229   Homer is new this morning, and will be newer tomor-row than today's newspaper.

3230   The classics are always modern.

3231   A book that inspires you with noble and courageous sentiments is a good book by a good author.

From Jean de La Bruyère

3232   Read in order to live.

Flaubert, Letters 1950 115 Weidenfeld

3233   Book love, my friends, will make your hours pleasant to you as long as you live.   From A. Trollope

3234   There is no Frigate like a book
             To take us Lands away . . .

Emily Dickinson, Thomas
H. Johnson (ed.), Complete Poems . . . 1960 553

3235   From other men's writings you can gain easily what others have labored for.   From Socrates

3236   The great books exist, not to hem us in, but to help us break our bonds.

Albert Guérard,
Bottle in the Sea 1954 78 Harvard Univ. Press

3237   He who loves a book will need so much the less a wholesome counsellor, companion, or comforter.

From Isaac Barrow

3238   As, by exercise, bodily health is preserved and strengthened; by reading, virtue, the health of the mind, is kept alive and confirmed.   From Addison, Tatler

3239   Medicine for the soul.
            Inscription over the door of the Library at Thebes

3240   There can be no literary genius without freedom of opinion.   Tocqueville

3241   To convince, one must be convinced and sincere.

3242   The man who does not read good books has no advantage over the man who can't read them.   Mark Twain

3243   Books which no hand opens and no glance caresses die on the shelf.
            Max Roden, Spiegelungen 1951 18 Johannes-Presse

SCIENCE

3244   Those who are more given to abstract discussions than to observations are prone to dogmatize on the basis of a few observations.
            Aristotle, Generation and Corruption I ii

3245   The empiricists are like the ant; they only collect and use. The rationalists resemble spiders, who make cobwebs out of their own substance. The scientist is like the bee; it takes a middle course; it gathers its material from the flowers, but adapts it by a power of its own.
            From Francis Bacon, Novum Organum XCV

3246   The scientific attitude differs from any other approach to human action only in what it is trying to do. Instead of try-

ing to earn more money, or to improve the condition of the working class, or to create visual beauty, a scientist tries to find how things work.   From C. H. Waddington,
Scientific Attitude 1941 33 Hutchinson

3247   Science cannot let man's development be checked by the barriers which dogma and myth try to keep around territory that science has not yet effectually occupied.
After K. Pearson, Grammar of Science 1900 25

3248   Science is teaching the world that the ultimate court of appeal is not authority but evidence.
From Thomas Huxley, Lay Sermons 1901 118

3249   In science, compromise has no place.
A. T. Waterman, Science 1965 147:18

3250   To think scientifically, one must have, first, intimate, habitual, intuitive familiarity with things; secondly, systematic knowledge of things; and thirdly, an effective way of thinking about things.   From L. J. Henderson, in Barnard,
Organization . . . 1948 54 Harvard Univ. Press

3251   Everybody uses scientific method about many things, and only ceases to use it when he does not wish or know how to apply it.   From C. S. Peirce

3252   Science seeks answers to questions which men hold important; but, unlike all other systems of thought, science seeks answers which are reducible to everyone's experience. Thus it is shared by all participants, irrespective of creed, color, class, or nationality.

Science assumes that the quest for truth is a major end in itself, not only for the individual but for society as a whole, even though we know that ultimate, final truth with a capital T is not to be found.

From H. Hoagland, Science 1964 143:112

3253   Science is too broad to be national.

From W. J. Mayo,
St. Paul Med. J. 1914 16:601–605

3254   Science, properly interpreted, is not dependent on or concerned with any sort of metaphysics. It merely attempts to cover a maximum of facts by a minimum of laws.

After H. Feigl, Am. Q. 1949 1:148

3255   Science must concern itself with determining both the means and the ultimate ends of life.

Arthur E. Morgan,
Observations 1968 8 Antioch Press

3256   Nature's powers can be reached only through understanding the laws of nature. This view cuts the taproot of all superstitions.

From J. Bronowski, in Julian Huxley (ed.),
Humanist Frame 1961 87–88 G. Allen

3257   Science is the getting of knowledge from experience on the assumption of dependable order.

From William Kingdon Clifford,
Lectures . . . 1886 289

3258   Science discovers the predictable.

From F. Fremont-Smith

3259   Every scientific procedure assumes and every success of science confirms the belief that no effect is without its cause, and no cause is without its effect.

From H. Sidgwick, Methods of Ethics 1874 47, and Everett, Moral Values 1918 369 Holt

3260   Necessity, cause-and-effect, is blind only so far as it is not understood.   From Hegel

3261   Science enriches and broadens human life, especially mental life.

After A. M. Weinberg, Science 1961 134:161

3262   Principles, rightly uncovered, carry whole troops of works along with them.   From Francis Bacon

3263   A little key may open a box where lies a bunch of keys.

Roger Williams,
Key into the Language of America London 1643

3264   It is only the worn-out cynic, the devitalized sensualist, and the fanatical dogmatist who interpret the continuous change of science as providing that . . . the whole record is error and folly.

John Dewey, Essays in Experimental
Logic 1916 101–102 Univ. Chicago Press

3265   Wonder is the seed of science.   From Emerson

3266   [In part,] the scientist studies nature because he delights in it, and he delights in it because it is beautiful.

From Poincaré, Value of Science 1907 8

3267 "Authorities," "disciples," and "schools" greatly hamper the scientific spirit. From Thomas Huxley

3268 Science increases our power in proportion as it lowers our pride. Claude Bernard

3269 If we require really epoch-making, basic, discoveries we must see that all fields of science are investigated without thought of the use but only of the knowledge.

From F. Sherwood Taylor,
Short History . . . 1949 354 Norton

3270 Science is willing to reckon in any terms and to study any subject-matter; where it cannot see precise cause-and-effect it will notice law; where laws cannot be stated it will describe habits; where habits fail it will classify types; and where types even are indiscernible, it will not despise statistics.

From Santayana,
Reason in Science 1905 98 Scribner

3271 There is but one sure road to truth: patient, cooperative inquiry through observation, experiment, record, and controlled reflection. From John Dewey,
Common Faith 1934 32 Yale Univ. Press

3272 Experiments that yield Light are more worth while than experiments that yield Fruit.

Francis Bacon, Novum Organum XCIX

3273 It is an oversimplification to compare the impersonal aspect of science with the impersonal aspects of industrial society, and to deplore both in one breath. The two things have quite different roots. The former is an achievement of self-forgetful concentration upon truths about nature. The latter are deplorable to the extent that they exhibit crude power of men over men. By contrast, the selflessness of the scientific calling does silent honor to personal existence.

From R. Hocking, in T. J. J. Altizer and
others (eds.), Truth, Myth, and Symbol
1962 5 Prentice-Hall

SCIENCE AND OTHER INTERESTS

3274   In the ultimate analysis science is born of myth and religion, all three being expressions of the ordering spirit of the human mind.

Lancelot Law Whyte,
Unconscious Before Freud 1960 82–83 Basic Books

3275   Only maladjusted individuals are unable to combine the detachment necessary for the pursuit of truth with an ardent interest in the improvement of the condition of humanity.   H. Feigl, Am. Q. 1949 1:146

3276   We welcome "the kind of experience in which science and the arts are brought unitedly to bear upon industry, politics, religion, domestic life, and human relations in general."

Lin-Yutang, On the Wisdom of America 1950 20 Day

3277   More than ever before, despite its dangers, science is providing mankind with devices and discipline for humane living.

3278   It is well that we recognize the social usefulness of science before we go into it as a career. It is not well that we hold the test of social usefulness too immediately before us in the very difficult task of extending science.

Norbert Wiener, Science 1962 138:651

3279   For the true scientist, the enormous utilitarian and financial treasures which science yields are incidental; its main reward is the discovery of truth. As in the discovery or creation of beauty, the reward is that of contemplating something which pleases the soul.   From G. Sarton,

History . . . 1937 14 Harvard Univ. Press

3280   Science, in obeying the law of humanity, will always labor to enlarge the frontiers of life.   Pasteur

3281   Science, truly assimilated, is a great cleanser of the human spirit; it makes impossible any religion but the highest.

After B. H. Streeter, Reality 1926 272 Macmillan

3282   Science is larger than all systems, and nature larger than all science.

Jean Rostand, Substance of Man 1962 95 Doubleday

ETHICS

3283   The unexamined life is not worth living.   Socrates

3284   Nature is innocent, and so are all her impulses and moods when taken in isolation; it is only on meeting that they blush.

Santayana, Reason in Art 1905 168–169 Scribner

3285   We are all of us born in moral stupidity, taking the world as an udder to feed our supreme selves.

George Eliot, Middlemarch XXI

3286   In the art of living, man is both the artist and the object of his art.

From Erich Fromm,
Man For Himself 1947 17–18 Rinehart; Routledge

3287   Preeminent is the study of what man is and of what life he should live.   Plato

3288   What is your vocation? To be a good human being. And how can one achieve this but by understanding cosmic and human nature?

Should the architect and the doctor have more respect for the principles of their art than man for his?

From Marcus Aurelius, Meditations XI 5 VI 35

3289   Though custom reflects, morality transcends geography, period, and race.

After Herbert Spencer, Evanescence of Evil

3290   With maturity comes the recognition that the authorized precepts of morality were essentially not arbitrary . . . that their alleged alien and supernatural basis was . . . but a mythical cover for their forgotten natural springs. Virtue is then seen to be admirable essentially.

Santayana, Reason in Science 1905 218 Scribner

3291   Social life wins out over isolation because it can better hold its own in a hostile world. Integrity and honor win be-

cause they conserve life. Love combines such conservation with beauty.   From Arthur E. Morgan,
Observations 1968 186 Antioch Press

3292   Morality, which has ever changed its injunctions according to social requirements, will necessarily be enforced as part of human evolution, and is not dependent upon religious terrorism or superstitious persuasion.

[W. R. Cassels]
Supernatural Religion 1879 583

3293   To have courage, to inquire honestly, to do justice, to have mercy, to walk humbly, to share the common lot of men— these traits are not the monopoly of any religious faith.
Arthur E. Morgan, Observations 1968 4 Antioch Press

3294   It is the understanding of human nature and its true needs, the clear perception of moral relations and moral laws, that sets men free.   From Everett,
Moral Values 1918 359 Holt

3295   Some students take the right, the moral, to be merely the customary. Thus they point to one culture in which custom makes it "right" for marriage to be dissolved only by death, while in another culture custom makes divorce "right" under certain conditions. For those students, what is moral in one culture is immoral in another, and, apart from custom, there is no real right or wrong.

Ethics, as a systematic study, acknowledges that many customs differ from culture to culture, that different customs are often useful for different conditions, and that authoritarian so-called morality is often harmful. Ethics seeks, however, to find and define essential morality. Ethics would weigh every traditional claim, every radical doubt, and the available evidence as to which customs, innovations, ways of living, are really moral: moral as making for the abundant life.

> From Ralph Barton Perry, Realms of Value 1954
> 88 and passim Harvard Univ. Press.

3296   In the end, all ethical issues are concrete.

> Joseph Fletcher, Morals and Medicine 1954 214
> Princeton Univ. Press

3297   Look to this day for it is life.   Oriental saying

3298   Conduct is three-fourths of our life.

> Matthew Arnold, Literature and Dogma, Preface

3299   In Shakespeare, the morally sound people are the majority; and, except in a few scenes, there are few sizable passages that do not relate in some way to standards of right and wrong.   From A. Harbage, in

> R. E. Fitch, Decline ... 1951 111 Harcourt

3300   The world at any time is good or bad according to what its ruling values are.

> From R. W. Livingstone, Some Thoughts ...
> 1948 27 Nat. Book League

3301   Right action is better than knowledge; but in order to do what is right, we must know what is right.

> Charlemagne, Capitular on founding schools

3302   The punishments which religious fables threaten the dead with are, for the most part, symbols for the actual degradation which evil-doing brings upon the living.

From Santayana, Three Philosophical Poets 1910 46

3303   Foolish is a person who supposes that, if he did not believe in eternal reward and punishment, he would simply indulge himself without altruism, idealism, or any morality. Such a course might seem to enliven, but really would deaden his whole human life, in that it would end his higher human living. Therein his assertion is as foolish as though a fish were to say, "If no eternal life is to follow this life in the water, then I shall leave the water for the land."

After Spinoza,
in Leon Roth, Spinoza 1929 161 Little

3304   Qualities which some call divine—love, mercy, justice, goodness—developed first in men, and later were ascribed to deity.

3305   The mental conflicts that we experience when education and science compel an inventory of traditional faiths are, in my observation, due to the grafting of practical ethics on the stem of ancient dogma. When you have worked your way out of that confusion the meadows are still green, the sunset as charming as ever, and you look on man with a new and saner interest. Justice, now, may assume an added significance.

When the shadow lengthens toward the east, I am content to call it a day and leave the arena forever. This dismissal of the traditional tomorrow seems to have added interest to my work today, greater interest in my students, in my fellow men, in other things that seem worth-while human efforts.

From Anton J. Carlson,
Univ. Chicago Mag. 1930 23:14–15

3306   Moral and ethical systems are necessary for normal human functioning and, in various religions, are major adaptive elements, elements that adjust us to living in this world and make for human survival. Examples are the Ten Commandments. (At the same time, various religions contain non-adaptive elements such as irrational taboos and magical practices.) The disposition to develop moral precepts, and the precepts themselves, are vital adaptations gained through biological and social evolution.

After G. G. Simpson,
This View . . . 1964 23 Harcourt

3307   The popular philosophy that inverts the natural order of ideas thinks piety to the gods the source of morality. But piety, when genuine, is rather an incidental expression of morality.

Santayana, Reason in Religion 1905 187 Scribner

3308   Morality is in essence the higher biological laws of nature.   From J. A. Hadfield,
Psychology . . . 1923 136–140 Methuen

3309   "Only a morality frankly relative to man's nature is . . . at once vital and rational, martial and generous"; whereas any morality believed to come from outside man's nature "smells of fustiness as well as of faggots" [burnings at the stake].

Blindness to the truth that morality is rooted and flowers in human nature "kills charity, humility, and humour."

"The attempt to subsume the natural order under the moral is like attempts to establish a government of the parent by a child—something children are not averse to."

Quoting Santayana,
Genteel Tradition . . . 1931 73–74 51,
Reason in Religion 1905 24 Scribner

3310   Naturally and rightly, the allegiance of conscience is to man.

Those religions which undermine this truth are especially apt to teach wrong precepts [e.g., Do not read Darwin], and even when they command men to do the right things they put the command upon wrong motives [Monogamy was sanctified by Adam and Eve] and do not get the things done.

From William Kingdon Clifford,
Lectures . . . 1886 385–386

3311   The adherents of any faith would be no worse for having at the back of their beliefs a system of natural morals.

From R. W. Livingstone, Education . . . 1952 40 Oxford

3312   Morality should embody those rules which are most useful and beneficial.

From Hume, Enquiry Concerning . . . Morals III ii

3313   Moral principles that exalt themselves by degrading human nature (for example, treating fleshly appetites as always despicable) are self-defeating.

After John Dewey, Human Nature . . . 1922 2 Holt

3314 Moral progress occurs as men emerge from the tribal group and become individuals, develop personal integrity, and choose values intelligently.

After Joseph Fletcher,
Morals and Medicine 1954 26 Princeton Univ. Press

3315 Our confidence in our fellows assumes no fragment of conduct to be without its cause.

The theory that all events follow necessarily from preceding events offers hope to every one who can learn to avoid the evil and enjoy the good in life.

From Everett,
Moral Values 1918 354–355, 368 Holt

3316 It follows that indeterminism, the view that "the will" can be free without cause-and-effect, would undermine learning from experience and would make human behavior, mental life, and morality forever unpredictable.

3317 Values, individual and social, are phenomena and therefore can be studied by the methods of science.

From Julian Huxley,
Humanist Frame 1961 37 G. Allen

3318 Controlled moral progress requires sifting and communication of the results of all relevant experiences.

From John Dewey,
Living Philosophies 1931 32 Simon & Schuster

3319 I bid him look into the lives of men as though into a mirror, and to take an example for himself.

Terence, Adelphoe III iii 61 (415)

3320   Within the limits set by each society's needs, its system of ethics seeks to provide for the physical and mental needs of individuals.   From R. Linton

3321   To deny that pleasure is good and pain an evil is a grotesque affectation.

Santayana,
Reason in Common Sense 1905 54–55 Scribner

3322   Freedom, knowledge, choice, responsibility—all these things of personal or moral stature are in us, not *out there.*

Joseph Fletcher,
Morals and Medicine 1954 211 Princeton Univ. Press

3323   A moral good can delight innumerable human noses without losing a trace of its fragrance.

Edmond Cahn,
Moral Decision 1955 299 Ind. Univ. Press

3324   A feeling for order, harmony, beauty and peace is a main source of morality.

Pestalozzi, Education . . . 1953 78 Philos. Lib.

3325   A great secret of morals is identification of ourselves with the beautiful which exists in thought, action, or person, not our own.   Shelley, Defense of Poetry

3326   The moral sense arises in all men's minds from their necessary intercourse and united labor.

From William Kingdon Clifford,
Lectures . . . 1886 375

3327   Men are punished by their sins.

From E. Hubbard

3328   Personal merit consists in qualities useful or agreeable to the person himself or to others.

From Hume, Enquiry Concerning . . . Morals IX i

3329   Acts are good or bad only as they affect the actor and others.   From Ingersoll

3330   The highest good for man, what is for him the ultimate value, reduces not to any concrete object or activity but to the sum and harmony of those specific goods upon which his nature is directed.   After Santayana

3331   A virtue is not essentially the mean between extremes but a way of living that carries the most good.

From Aristotle, Nicomachean Ethics II vi

3332   Virtue (for mere good nature is a fool)
        Is sense and spirit with humanity.

John Armstrong,
Art of Preserving Health 1744 IV

3333   My actions are good that tend to improve me as an organism, to make me move upward from those intermediate forms through which my race has passed; or bad that make me go down again.   From William Kingdon Clifford,
Lectures . . . 1886 410

3334   Virtue is to play one's part in evolutionary develop-ment.   From Ashley Montague,
On Being Human 1951 83 Schuman

3335   Vice is deformity.

3336   Vice is like a part of the ship trying to go its own way without the rest, yet looking for an enjoyable voyage.

3337   A free man is not the slave of ignorance, destructive impulse, negative emotion, or inadequate thinking. On the contrary, affective in all his impulses, affective life, learning, thought, and action, the free man lives in accordance with reason. Thus he knows and wants to do what is worth while, whether as a means to good or as good in itself.

From Spinoza, Ethics IV lxvi and passim

3338   Let a man avoid evil deeds . . . as a man who loves life avoids poison.   From The Dhammapada IX

3339   He who does good to escape evil is not most enlightened. It is most reasonable to seek good directly, and so shun evil indirectly.

From Spinoza, Ethics IV lxiii Proof of Corollary

3340   The cost of a thing is the amount of life that must be exchanged for it, immediately or in the long run.

From Thoreau

3341   Ends pre-exist in the means.   Emerson

3342   A person of open mind, independent judgment, and moral courage, only concerned to be right and not afraid to be singular, is most valuable; a nation of such would leaven and regenerate the world.

From James Ward, Psychology
Applied to Education 1926 182–183 Cambridge

3343   Let us suppose that Peter is both hungry and sleepy, and, at the moment, has no other interest. Which shall he do first, eat or sleep?

Peter and Paul want the same apple. Which shall have it?

From a psychological point of view, eating, sleeping, possessing, likewise the food, the bed, and the apple, are *values*.

When any value gets a person to try or think of trying to gain that value, it and his nature create in him an *interest*—an interest to eat, or to sleep, or to have that apple.

If mankind had never experienced any *conflict between interests,* like between eating and sleeping, or between the apple as Peter's and the same apple as Paul's, there would be no vices: gluttony, laziness, rapacity, and the rest would be impossible and unnamed. There would likewise be no virtues: temperance, industry, justice, would not even be empty sounds. A person's every eating, sleeping, taking, would occur simply unhindered.

Morality, as considered in ethics, is man's endeavor to harmonize conflicting interests; to prevent such conflict when it threatens, to remove it when it occurs, and to promote cooperation of interests within a person and between persons.

Morality derives not from regimentation of a person's interests by a higher power either within or without him. Morality derives from *organization* of each person's own interests. Personal morality derives from personal organization. Social morality derives from social organization.

Peter's personal morality is his organization of his interests to have each one express itself as fully as it can given all his other interests. Often this means that a particular or short-range interest must be modified or denied to make way for a general or long-range interest or constellation of interests that is more important in Peter's life. Such organization is necessary, both for the several interests whose life is in Peter, and for the best life for Peter; especially in a world that includes Paul.

Peter and Paul are a group, of some sort, at least for so long as they want the same apple. Their social morality is the way they work out the conflict about the apple—to divide it between them, or give it to the poor, or perhaps plant the seeds, according to their lights. Thus Peter and Paul become a more organized group in which each satisfies his interests, so far as *all* his interests permit; and he shares in the life of this group which is greater, in some ways, than either Peter or Paul.

One's interests are organized through reflection: a thinking over, in which the several interests are reviewed and invited to present their claims. Reflection calls up overlooked considerations, further interests. It takes account of the interests not only of the present situation but also those of further time and place. It brings to light the causal relations between one interest and another. From reflection there emerge plans, schedules, quotas, substitutions, and other arrangements with which the conflicts evolve unto harmony.

Peter's personal morality inheres in Peter, and would be his even apart from all society. Peter and Paul's social morality inheres in Peter and Paul, respectively and perhaps in different degrees; yet, in either of them, it comprehends more than merely personal interests.

In any case, the moral interest is greater than any of the particular interests that gave rise to it. It is greater in that, so far as seems workable, the moral interest includes and represents all the particular interests from which it came; its voice is their organized voice.

The personal will that emerges from reflection is analogous to a resultant of forces. Its accumulated decisions form a character, an unwritten personal constitution.

As the personal will emerges from reflection, so the social

will emerges from communication and discussion. In both cases the emergent will represents a totality of interests, and through organization reduces conflict and increases harmony. The difference is that the personal will is composed of sub-personal interests, whereas the social will is composed of persons.

The height of any claim in the moral scale is proportional to the breadth of its representation. What suits all of a person's interests is exalted above what merely suits a fraction; what suits everybody is exalted above what merely suits somebody.

> After Ralph Barton Perry, Realms of
> Value 1954 90–93 and passim Harvard Univ. Press

3344   Three values have had a predominant role, at least in the West: freedom, justice, and security-survival.

> D. Callahan, Science 1972 175:488

PHILOSOPHY

3345   Philosophy begins in wonder.   Socrates

3346   Philosophy expresses the need to feel at home in the universe.   From Novalis

3347   To reflect on life is not simply to clarify and order it. Reflection is itself a special kind of human living.

> From H. Margolius,
> Aphorisms . . . n.d. 7–8 Black Mt. News

3348   In surveying the forms and places of many things at once and conceiving their movement, the intellect . . . locks flying existence, as it were, in its arms, and stands, all eyes and breathless, at the top of life.

Santayana, Genteel Tradition ... 1931 67 Scribner

3349   A great philosophy does not establish final truths; it stirs one to think.   From Péguy

3350   Very much of what has been presented as philosophical reflection is in effect simply an idealization, for the sake of emotional satisfaction, of the brutely given state of affairs.

John Dewey, German Philosophy ... 1915 7 Holt

3351   Often, what epithets you apply to the whole of things are merely judgments of yourself.

Your business as thinkers is to make plainer the way from some thing to the whole of things; to show the rational connection between your fact and the frame of the universe.

After (Justice) O. W. Holmes,
Collected Legal Papers 1920 246 30 Harcourt

3352   Philosophy must battle to keep language from bewitching our intelligence.

After L. Wittgenstein,
Philosophical Investigations 1953 cix Blackwell

3353   Words are but the shadow of actions.

Democritus, in Plutarch,
On the Training of Children

3354   Metaphysicians, confounding dialectic with physics and thereby corrupting both, will discuss forever the difference it makes to substance whether you call it matter or God.

Santayana, Reason in Science 1905 202–203 Scribner

3355   Chief errors in philosophy are over-statement and the supposition that language is an exact medium.

From Whitehead

3356   Thy task is first to learn WHAT IS, and in pursuant knowledge pure intellect will find pure pleasure and the only ground for a philosophy conformable to truth.

From Robert Bridges,
Testament of Beauty 1929 14 129–133 Oxford

3357   As long as we worship science and are afraid of philosophy we shall have no great science.

The naturalistic method destroys many things once cherished. But its main purport is not destructive; empirical naturalism is rather a winnowing fan.

When philosophy cooperates with the course of events and makes clear the meaning of the daily detail, emotion and science will interpenetrate, imagination and practice will embrace.

From John Dewey, Philosophy and Civilization 1931 12 Minton; A. H. Johnson (ed.), Wit and Wisdom of John Dewey 1949 67 Beacon; Reconstruction . . . 1920 212–213 Holt

3358   Philosophy maintains an active novelty of fundamental ideas illuminating the social system.

From Whitehead,
Modes of Thought 1938 237 Macmillan; Cambridge

3359   The true medicine of the mind is philosophy.

Cicero

3360   Often the dream of the philosopher becomes the creed of the minority, then the faith of the majority.

3361   Posterity is for the humanistic philosopher what the other world is for the other-worldly religious.

After Diderot

3362   Mankind can flourish in the lower stages of life with merely barbaric flashes of thought. But when civilization culminates, the absence of a coordinating philosophy of life, spread throughout the community, spells decadence, boredom, and the slackening of effort. There can be no successful democratic society till general education conveys a philosophic outlook.

From Whitehead,
Adventures . . . 1933 125 Macmillan; Cambridge

3363   Heard philosophies are sweet, but those unheard may be sweeter. They may be more unmixed and more profound for being adopted unconsciously, for being lived rather than taught.

Santayana, Three Philosophical Poets 1910 142

3364   Intellectual activity at its best is an intense kind of living; it has its own throbs of emotion; and in its white light may be found healing for the passions and sufferings that afflict our earth-bound spirits.

From Everett,
Honors Day Address Brown Univ. 1923

3365   In wonder all philosophy began; in wonder it ends. But the first wonder is the offspring of ignorance; the last is the parent of adoration.

From Coleridge

3366   Any restraint put upon philosophers' reasonings must be dangerous to the sciences and even to the state. Philosophy requires entire liberty above all other privileges.

From Hume,
Enquiry Concerning Human Understanding, XI

RELIGION

3367   It is well said that a man's religion is the chief fact with regard to him. By religion I do not mean the church creed he professes, but what a man does practically believe, does practically lay to heart, concerning his vital relations to the universe.   Carlyle

3367a   Religion is a total response to life's meaning.

H. E. Fosdick

3368   Degrading customs, sensual orgies, cannibalism, human sacrifice, abject superstition, hysteria, hatred, bigotry, savagery, were characteristic of primitive religion.

The notion that that conduct is right which will lead some god to protect you reflects bargaining, neither ethics nor religion.   After Whitehead,
Religion . . . 1926 37 Macmillan; Cambridge

3369   My . . . piety toward the universe . . . denies only gods fashioned by men in their own image, to be servants of their human interests.

Santayana, Soliloquies . . . 1922 246 Scribner

3370 There may be little or much beyond the grave,
But the strong are saying nothing until they
see.

Poetry of Robert Frost (Lathem, ed.),
The Strong Are Saying Nothing 1969 299 Holt

3371 In the third millenium B.C. the Sumerians developed
rites and ceremonies to please the gods as well as provide for
man's love of pageantry and spectacle.

From S. N. Kramer,
Sumerians 1963 112 Univ. Chicago Press

3372 As Santayana observed, "There must needs be something humane and necessary in an influence that has become
the most general sanction of virtue, the chief occasion for art
and philosophy, and the source, perhaps, of the best human
happiness . . . 'Depth in philosophy bringeth men's minds
about to religion.' In every age the most comprehensive thinkers have found in the religion of their time and country something they could accept, interpreting and illustrating that religion so as to give it depth and universal application . . .

"We have need . . . to remember how slowly and reluctantly
religion has gained spiritualization, how imperfectly as yet its
superstitious origin has been outgrown . . .

"Superstitions come of haste to understand . . .

"Primitive thought has the form of poetry and the function
of prose . . .

"People seldom take a myth in the same sense in which they
would take an empirical truth. All the doctrines that have
flourished in the world about immortality have hardly affected
men's natural sentiment in the face of death, a sentiment

which those doctrines, if taken seriously, ought wholly to re-
verse . . . Prayer, among sane people, has never superseded
practical efforts to secure the desired end . . .

"The poetic value of religion would initially be greater
than that of poetry itself, because religion deals with . . . sides
of life which are in greater need of some imaginative touch
and ideal interpretation . . . But this initial advantage is
neutralized in part by the abuse to which religion is subject,
whenever its symbolic rightness is taken for scientific truth
. . . This deception . . . can work indefinite harm in the world
and in the conscience."

For an area for which there is no adequate vocabulary, when
the mind must use symbols, it pours into those symbols "a part
of its own life and makes them beautiful. Their loss is a real
blow, while the incapacity that called for them endures; and
the soul seems to be crippled by losing its crutches. For this
reason religions do not disappear when they are discredited;
it is requisite that they should be replaced."

> Quoting Santayana, Reason in Religion 1905 4 3
> 68 24 49 52 11–12; in L. P. Smith (ed.), Little Essays
> 1920 53 Scribner

3373   The ideal of human life is not to conquer other men
or even nature. It is to honor both.

> From J. E. Woodbridge, Am. Scholar 1932 1:96

3374   Man lives by his devotions. He places his confidence in
something, whether it be in human nature, reason, scientific
method, church, nation, Bible, or God.

> From James Luther Adams, in
> Montagu (ed.), Meaning of Love 1953 236 Julian

3375   It furthers one to abide in what endures.

> I Ching (Wilhelm, tr., Baynes, tr.),
> 1967 25 Princeton Univ. Press; Routledge

3376   The solid meaning of life is always the marriage of some ideal with some fidelity, courage, and endurance; and whatever or wherever life may be, there will always be the chance for that marriage to take place.

> From William James, Talks ... 1900 298–299

3377   Once man has discerned that he *is* a real child of earth, he will find himself falling naturally into a feeling of at-homeness in the universe.

> B. E. Meland,
> Modern Man's Worship 1934 143 Harper

3378   We have inherited the world. Why should we go crying beyond it? The present is amazingly ours.

There is a Heaven in Time, now and forever, ending for each, staying for all, a Heaven of Laughter and Bodies and Flowers and Love and People and Sun and Wind.

> Rupert Brooke, in Hassall,
> Rupert Brooke 1964 208 207 Harcourt

3379   The meaning of life lies in the chance it gives us to produce, or to contribute to, something greater than ourselves.

> Will Durant, On the Meaning of
> Life 1932 128 R. Long & R. R. Smith

3380   In the service of the highest values he knows, man is most significantly religious.   From Ethel Sabin Smith,

> Dynamics of Aging 1956 188 Norton

3381   The kernel of the religious life is the feeling that certain things are sacred. Those things primarily concern human destiny and the forces with which it comes in contact.

The situations which arouse the religious feeling are not the same for all persons, and for a developing person they change with experience and education.

With progress, the religious feeling is purged of cruder elements such as fear, and becomes attached to ever larger, nobler, and more rational objects and situations.

From Julian Huxley,
Religion Without Revelation 1957 9–14 Harper

3382   Nature, including humanity, with all its defects and imperfections, may evoke heartfelt piety as the source of ideals, of possibilities, of aspiration in their behalf, and as the eventual abode of all attained goods and excellencies.

John Dewey, Quest for Certainty 1929 306 Minton

3383   The astonishment with which we gaze upon the starry heavens and the microscopic life in a drop of water, the awe with which we trace the marvellous working of energy in the motion of matter, the reverence with which we grasp the universal dominance of the law of substance throughout the universe—all these are part of our emotional life, falling under the heading of "natural religion."

E. Haeckel,
Riddle of the Universe (McCabe, tr.) 1913 344

3384   Is not life genuinely lived a long and roundabout pilgrimage back to the sources of our being and the rudiments of our universe, to which we return with an appreciation, a comprehension, a penetration that could not have been felt at the start?   B. Berenson, Sketch . . . 1949 153 Pantheon

3385   Why may not a goose say thus: "All the parts of the universe I have an interest in: the earth serves me to walk upon, the sun to light me; the stars have their influence upon me; I have such an advantage by the winds and such by the waters; there is nothing that yon heavenly roof looks upon so favourably as me. I am the darling of Nature! Is it not man that keeps and serves me?"

Montaigne, Apology for Raimond Sebond II XII

3386   For modern man, the sacred is born when he accepts the present world and wants to improve it.

After T. J. J. Altizer, in Altizer and
Hamilton, Radical Theology . . . 1966 29 Bobbs-Merrill

3387   Suppose there is a cosmic purpose and plan. Does not all the evidence indicate that if there is such it calls for men to work out their own salvation?

I feel that the greatest loyalty I can have is to the great human adventure—is to do all I can to help it succeed.

From Arthur E. Morgan,
Observations 1968 214 49 Antioch Press

3388   There is a conceit fostered by perversion of religion which assimilates the universe to our personal desires; but there is also a conceit of carrying the load of the universe from which religion liberates us. Within the flickering inconsequential acts of our separate selves dwells a sense of the whole which claims and dignifies each person. In its presence we put off mortality and live in the universal. The life of the community in which we live is the fit symbol of this relationship.

From John Dewey,
Human Nature . . . 1922 331–332 Holt

3389   With all beings and all things we shall be as relatives.
Sioux saying

3390   True religion shows man his unimportance as an ego
and his importance as an individual part of a larger whole.
After F. Künkel, Allg. ärzt. Zsch.
f. Psychotherap. u. psych. Hyg. 1929 2: [sic]

3391   Religion has to do directly with the conscience, at one
time to rouse it from lethargy, at another time to soothe it
when fretted.   From Goethe

3392   When we have used our thought and our puny strength
to their utmost, we feel that our lot is one with whatever is
good in existence.
After Dewey, in Ratner (ed.),
Philosophy of John Dewey 1928 553 Holt, © Ratner

3393   Futile—the Winds—
To a Heart in port—
Emily Dickinson (Thomas H. Johnson, ed.)
Complete Poems . . . 1960 114 Little

3394   There are men who believe that they have spanned the
chasm: the mystics. In ecstasy they feel the oneness between
their own life and the life universal. The rationalist has no
right to deny *a priori* the possibility and the validity of such
an experience, which by definition is beyond his scope.
Albert Guérard,
Bottle in the Sea 1954 152 Harvard Univ. Press

3395   The mystical attitude is the esthetic attitude extended to cosmic proportions.

> B. E. Meland,
> Modern Man's Worship 1934 292 Harper

3396   Mysticism that exists for its own sake is the salt which has lost its savor.

> Schweitzer, Civilization . . . 1929 241 Black

3397   Human living calls for fusion of the finite and the infinite. The cry, "Let us eat and drink, for tomorrow we die," expresses the triviality of the merely finite. The mystical, ineffective drowse expresses the vacuity of the merely infinite.

> From Whitehead,
> Modes . . . 1938 108 Macmillan; Cambridge

3398   Religion is an emotional attitude inseparably bound up with the search for truth.   From J. S. Bixler,

> Bull. IX Nat. Coun. on Rel. 1935 18

3399   Religion, in its fullest form, combines the quest of truth, beauty, and moral good.

Our real religion is whatever we feel to be most worth while in life, the dominant object of our reverence and aspiration, and the response that this provokes in the conduct of our lives.

> From J. H. Badley,
> Form and Spirit 1951 23 24 Routledge

3400
> I heard the hymn of being sound
> From every well of honor found
> In human sense and soul.

> Ralph Hodgson, Song of Honor 1913 9

3401   Whatever in religion cannot stand up to criticism is not worth having—and that means a great deal, but it does not mean everything. Among the things that remain is the aspiration which is the soul of religion.

Religion is rooted in man's aspiration to transcend himself.
Walter Kaufmann, Critique of
Religion and Philosophy . . . 1958 308 253 Harper

3402   We must see heaven in the midst of earth, just above it, accompanying earth as beauty accompanies it. We must not try to get heaven pure, afterwards, or instead. Christ is *essentially* a spirit of the earth.

Santayana, in Daniel Cory,
Santayana: The Later Years 1963 249 Braziller

3403   To be always consciously religious is as intolerable as to be always laughing, or always working, or always playing golf. To give each faculty and each approach its due place in life is to live not only richly but truly. The biologist or engineer who would deny all value to religious meditation and the religious life, the missionary who suppresses all native activities of which he disapproves, the administrator who would lock up as a vagrant every one who is not constantly at work—all are limited in their outlook, and because limited are wrong.

From Julian Huxley,
Religion Without Revelation 1957 175–176 Harper

3404   True religion is a cheerful thing, so far from being always at blows with good humor that it is inseparably united to it. Nothing unpleasant belongs to it, though spiritual cooks have done their unskilful part to give an ill relish to it. No other thing is the better for our being sour; and it would be hard that religion should be so, which is the best of things. This surly kind of devotion has perhaps done little less hurt in the world, by frightening it, than the most scandalous examples have done by infecting it.

Unskilful daubers have laid on such ill colors, and drawn such harsh lines, that the beauty of religion is not easily to be discerned; they have put in all the forbidding features that can be thought of.

They have even made it an irreconcilable enemy to nature; when, in reality, they are not only friends, but twins, born together at the same time; and it is doing violence to them both, to go about to have them separated.

Nothing is so kind and so inviting as true, unspoiled religion. Instead of imposing unnecessary burdens upon our nature, it eases us of the greater weight of our passions and mistakes; instead of subduing us with rigor, it redeems us from slavery to our appetites let loose and not restrained; it raises us above little vexations, and brings us to a temper, not of stupid indifference, but such that we may live in the world so that it may hang about us like a loose garment, and not tied too close to us.

Religion is exalted reason, refined and sifted from the grosser parts of it; it dwells in the upper region of the mind, where there are fewest clouds or mists to darken or offend it; it is both the foundation and the crown of all virtues.

Since this is so, it is worth our pains to make religion our choice, and not make use of it only as a refuge.

From Savile . . . ,
Advice to a Daughter, Religion, 1687

3405   A religious society to encourage or propagate vice is not possible.

Voltaire, Essay on the Manners and Spirit of Nations

3406   There are now more significant differences between the philosophic and the naïve forms of a single religion than between any two major religions.

> From L. Elvin, in Julian Huxley (ed.),
> Humanist Frame 1961 272 G. Allen

3407   Religion speaks to us in many dialects. It has diverse complexions. And yet it has one true voice, the voice of human ... compassion, of mercy, of patient love.

> Radhakrishnan, East and West ...
> 1933 140 G. Allen; Barnes & Noble

3408   A man must free himself from making too much of "I" and "mine."   From the Bhagavad-Gita XII

3409   A man is truly religious when he is truly good.

> Arabian saying

3410   He that loves make his own the grandeur he loves.

> Emerson, Compensation

3411   All great happiness has holiness.

> H. Margolius,
> Gedanken—Thoughts 1964 14 Pandanus

3412   The soul's salvation is a development to be attained. It is an inner richness and ripeness, a sensitiveness to truth, to beauty, to the dignity of life.

> From M. C. Otto, Things and Ideals 1924 246 Holt

3413   Though we may object to seeking help from an unseen world, we may often withdraw from the crowd and commune with ourselves until the agitations of the moment have calmed down, the distorting mirage of a worldly atmosphere has subsided, and the greater objects and more enduring affections of our life have reappeared in their due proportions.

From F. Galton, Inquiries . . . 1883 298

3414   Grace will still be found in the lure of the ideal and its amazing power to transform.

J. S. Bixler,
Bull. IX Nat. Coun. on Rel. 1935 19

3415   True piety is the desire to do well according to the guidance of reason.

From Spinoza, Ethics IV xxxvii Note 1

3416   In religion, the ends of moral conviction are so inclusive that they unify the self.

From John Dewey,
Common Faith 1934 22 Yale Univ. Press

3417   Religion at its fullest would be nothing less than the harmonious response of the whole of our personality to the whole of experience.   After J. H. Badley,
Form and Spirit 1951 23 Routledge

3418   He who sows good corn sows religion. He who builds a good bridge builds religion. He who helps mankind helps religion.   From Zoroaster

3419   Apart from some religious aspiration, expressed in ways generally intelligible, populations sink into the apathetic task of daily survival, with minor alleviations.

From Whitehead, Atlantic Mo. 1939 163:318

3420   He who is devoted and enlightened so lives as to give the thing he lives for the best chance of outliving him.

> After E. A. Singer, Jr., Am. Scholar 1934 3:323

3421   What impresses us about the religious man is his serenity, his courage, his loyalty, his conviction that life has a deep meaning and that whatever happens to him as an individual is relatively unimportant compared with that which is greater than himself.

> From R. B. MacLeod, in Fairchild and others (eds.), College Teaching . . . 1952 iii 272 Ronald

3422   Concerning the gods, I know neither whether they exist nor what they are like. The subject is obscure and our life is short.   From Protagoras

3423   When myth meets myth, the collision is very real.

> S. J. Lec,
> Unkempt Thoughts 1962 41 St. Martin's

3424   Ignorance created miracles; knowledge reduces them.

> From [W. R. Cassels]
> Supernatural Religion 1879 3:571

3425   We do not need the hope of heaven or fear of hell.

> Stanton Coit, Message of Man 1902 311

3426   Heav'n but the Vision of fulfilled Desire,
And Hell the Shadow of a Soul on fire.

> Omar Khayyám, Rubáiyát lxvii

3427 Heaven is where one's heart lives.

From Sharma and Raghavacharya (trs.),
Gems from Sanskrit . . . 1959 73 Osmania

3428 It looks like want of health in a church when, instead of depending upon the power of that truth which it holds, and the good examples of them that teach it, to support itself and suppress errors it resorts to the secular authority.

From Savile,
Character of a Trimmer, . . . Religion, 1684

3429 The best guarantee of religious freedom is to keep the political government out of religious affairs.

From Supreme Court U.S.,
42nd Ann. Rep. Am. Civil Lib. U. 1962 22

3430 Fish (fly-replete, in depth of June,
Dawdling away their wat'ry noon)
Ponder deep wisdom, dark or clear,
Each secret fishy hope or fear.
Fish say, they have their Stream and Pond;
But is there anything Beyond?
This life cannot be All, they swear,
For how unpleasant, if it were!
One may not doubt that, somehow, Good
Shall come of Water and of Mud;
And, sure, the reverent eye must see
A Purpose in Liquidity.
We darkly know, by Faith we cry,
The future is not Wholly Dry,
Mud unto mud!—Death eddies near—
Not here the appointed End, not here!

But somewhere, beyond Space and Time,
Is wetter water, slimier slime!
And there (they trust) there swimmeth One
Who swam ere rivers were begun,
Immense, of fishy form and mind,
Squamous, omnipotent, and kind;
And under that Almighty Fin,
The littlest fish may enter in.
Oh, never fly conceals a hook,
Fish say, in the Eternal Brook,
But more than mundane weeds are there,
And mud, celestially fair;
Fat caterpillars drift around,
And paradisal grubs are found;
Unfading moths, immortal flies,
And the worm that never dies.
And in that Heaven of all their wish,
There shall be no more land, say fish.

Rupert Brooke, Heaven, Collected Poems,
1915 127–128 Dodd; Sidgwick; McClelland

3431   If thinking men would have the courage to think for themselves, and to speak what they think, it would be found they do not differ in religious opinions as much as is supposed.

Jefferson, Letter to John Adams 1813

3432   Organized religion becomes increasingly helpful to mankind when it faces change in the same spirit as does science.

After Whitehead,
Science . . . 1925 270 Macmillan; Cambridge

3433   There is no alleviation for the sufferings of mankind except in facing the world as it is when the make-believe, by

which pious hands have hidden its uglier features, is stripped
off.   From Thomas Huxley, **Lay Sermons** . . . 1871

3434   High speculations are as barren as the tops of cedars;
but the fundamentals of religion are fruitful as the valleys or
the creeping vine.

> After Jeremy Taylor, in
> Gest (ed.), House . . . 1954 106 Univ. of Pa. Press

3435   The world needs less faith and more love and nobility.
   Nobility means being hard with oneself, making demands on
oneself, devotion.
   People confound devotion with devoutness.

> Walter Kaufmann, From Shakespeare
> to Existentialism 1960 xii xiv Doubleday

3436   If our nominally religious institutions learn how to use
their symbols and rites to express and enhance a faith in experience itself, they may become useful allies of a conception
of life that is in harmony with knowledge and social needs.

> From John Dewey,
> Living Philosophies 1931 29 Simon & Schuster

3437   By religious action, I mean with Jesus the deeds of the
good Samaritan: relieving human suffering, and curbing the
evils which are its sources. In definite terms, this implies today
working for peace, social welfare, and social justice. The sects
do more than lip-service to this ideal: they do attempt to alle-
viate human distress. But their professed purpose is to ex-
pound and maintain a doctrine. If it were not so, they would
disappear as sects, and merge into the Church Universal, the
fighting conscience of mankind.

Universal religion, slowly evolving, transcends all particular creeds.

From Albert Guérard, Bottle in the Sea 1954 143
Harvard Univ. Press, Fossils and Presences 1957 264
Stanford Univ. Press

3438   The new church will be founded on moral science. Poets, artists, musicians, philosophers, will be its prophet-teachers. The noblest literature of the world will be its Bible—love and labor its holy sacraments—and instead of worshiping one savior, we will gladly build an altar in the heart for every one who has given to humanity.

From Emerson

3439   Live in the present but as part of the whole.

W. E. Leonard

3440   Slave to no sect.   Pope, Essay on Man IV 33

3441   The demand of our day is for a religion within which virtuous actions, heroic character, the practice of the Golden Rule, are seen to be their own reward, and the security of the future is in well-doing and well-being in the present.

Such a religion develops a human brotherhood that is more inclusive than sectarian.

After John Burroughs,
Accepting the Universe 1920 314 Houghton

3442   "The goal and character of the religious life," Schleiermacher tells us, "is not the immortality desired and believed in by many . . . In the midst of finitude to be one with the Infinite, and in every moment to be eternal, is the immortality of religion."

Where more often than in art do we have this sense of the timeless meaning of our temporal experiences? The Taj Mahal is an expression of deathless love; the interior of Santa Sophia has intimations of an extra-temporal infinity; the lines of Chartres converge at a point where the human struggle is transcended. Merely to see some earthenware jars as Picasso saw them is to have a glimpse of the timelessness of pattern. In drama and music the unity of the time structure speaks of a harmony that is above temporal life.

Does not truth also belong to the world of timeless things?

Finally, the demands of righteousness lift us as far above the biological level as do those of beauty and truth. Devotion to the good rises above lower nature and places itself in the time-less world of freedom.

Perhaps immortality should stand not for an unending exist-ence but for the realization in mortal life of that by which mortality is itself transcended.   From J. S. Bixler,
Immortality . . . 1931 46 48 50 54 Harvard Univ. Press

3443   Religion has two main goals, personal and racial. The personal goal is the raising of the soul to levels on which it experiences peace, illumination, and communion, and knows that it has attained the utmost of which it is capable. The racial goal is work for humanity, including future humanity.
From Julian Huxley,
Religion Without Revelation 1927 370 Harper

3444   Consideration of the language of theology and of phi-losophy of religion brings us to questions about the nature of reality and the ways in which men come to know that reality.

I think we should start with experience: from experience as it flows, experience with its color, with its sound and fury, with its eddies and its flats, with its patterns, halts, and resistances.

Within experience so conceived many realities can be, and are, constructed. Each such reality is formulated and transmitted in some language or other.

The one great sin against the human spirit is closure against the diversity and variety of experience—a narrow dogmatism that insists on the absolute and exclusive validity of some particular language and the particular version of reality that this language articulates. And the central virtue, therefore, is openness to experience, *caritas* for the differences and diversities to be found within experience. Religion at its best is perhaps the supreme example of openness to experience.

A democratically organized state is possible only if different people with widely different outlooks, skills, and goals understand, tolerate, and openly accept each other's differences. Otherwise coordination is achieved only in the ant heap of the monolithic state, at the cost of individuality, variety, and plurality. All of this applies even more when we pass, as we must hope eventually to do, beyond the democratically organized state to a democratically organized world society, a universal city.

> From W. T. Jones, The Sciences and the
> Humanities 1965 273 275 280 281 Univ. Calif. Press
> © The Regents

3445   Rational religion is "piety, or loyalty to necessary conditions, and spirituality, or devotion to ideal ends."

> Quoting Santayana,
> Reason in Religion 1905 276 Scribner

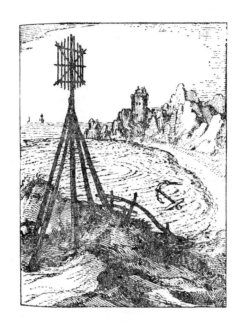

XVII

A Philosophic View

3446   The basic philosophy for this collection derives from many sources. It is briefly as follows.

Every philosophic view, including this one, is a product of the individual's native capacities, experience, and reflection, and may well change with further experience and reflection. Indeed, every bit of knowledge, even "This is a tree," is shaped likewise by one's native capacities, experience and reflection.

What we call facts are items which we accept either without question or as hypotheses which seem well supported by evidence. Our physical, emotional, and intellectual interests require always that we set up and proceed upon further hypotheses; hypotheses that go beyond the facts that "This is a tree" and "That is a tree" to, for example, "We can grow more trees"; often with good results. Out of such human nature and knowledge, such givens and probabilities, we build our survival together with our further knowledge, aspirations, creations, and satisfactions; in a word, our lives.

So far as we know now, the universe is continuous in stuffs, at least in practical effect. This means that the universe is not a composite of disparate provinces such as material vs. immaterial, matter vs. mind, natural vs. supernatural, each with its separate nature and laws which can be known only by a special mental approach. On the contrary, whether we call everything matter, or mind, or natural, or supernatural, or by any other term or combination of terms, we find the universe to consist of countless qualities and quantities, every one of them unique at least in its setting; yet they all seem, in the last analysis, so akin as to be equally open to study, though not equally easy to study.

Further, the universe seems dependable, orderly in processes. The more we study each constituent, the more we find that each one behaves always the same, or behaves as we should expect when other dependable items affect it; each one functions according to cause-and-effect.

By "cause-and-effect" we do not mean "creator and created," no matter whether "cause" be supposed to work from before, during, or after "effect" (a statement inserted for technical theorists). By "cause-and-effect" we mean merely a dependable sequence of events. When we say that a cause precedes its effect, or that an effect is caused by something that came before it, we are only citing the order in which we noticed "the cause" and "the effect" in what we take to be the time flow; the order in which we experienced the events that occurred in an apparently dependable sequence.

Given such an orderly universe, we assume with Montaigne that "whoever has sufficiently considered the present state of things might certainly conclude as to both the past and the future." (Works II XII)

These generalizations that the universe is continuous in stuffs and dependable in processes cannot be proved absolutely; but the more we assume and apply them, the more they seem to hold.

This view considers every person a human organism: an organization of Aristotle's "vegetative" functions of nutrition and reproduction; "animal" functions of sensation, movement, and, we would add, basic urges and emotions; and "rational" functions (also found somewhat in animals), with which we would rank also the higher feelings and actions. So composed, every human organism is the product of 1) what he inherited from the myriad trials and errors of organic evolution, namely, his genes; 2) his environment, which includes social influences; and 3) a special product of genes and environment, his own efforts. (The genes, the environment, and the efforts alike we assume are caused by, or follow upon, their histories, including their effects on each other. Thus one's efforts can be facilitated by memories and habits of successful efforts, and can be inhibited if one becomes *too* occupied with questions and theories of how such efforts occur.) The result is a human individual, a unique personality.

From the beginning, man's life has consisted largely in experiencing directly, enjoying, and participating in countless things from creature comforts to religion. Some of the direct experiencing, enjoying, and participating is little more than vegetative; much of it is essentially animal; and much is more or less rational. All of it, however, that is adequately humanized is integral to human life, individual and social.

Also from the beginning, according to his ability man has been eager to know, understand, and reason about not only what affects him directly but also many things which are more or less remote from his direct experience and practical concerns. This urge to know, understand, and reason is the flowering of intelligence. On the whole, it has proved good for survival and good in itself.

Together with the experiencing, enjoying, and participating, and especially with the growth of intelligence, have grown conscious use, control, and even shaping of the world and the man to the end of more satisfactory living. Such use, control, and shaping are the fruits of intelligence.

This view does not support the persistent scholasticisms that intelligence is something apart from feeling and action, and that, in human living, any of these is itself superior to the others. Feelings, in all their kinds and grades, from the most earthy to the most subtle; actions, from the simplest to the most complex; and all the functions of intelligence, from the most rudimentary knowing to the highest reasoning, are in every instance unique; yet all of them are reactions and are vital, interrelated aspects of human living.

For example: One has walked a certain forest path often enough to know the path and understand its purpose. Such knowing and understanding derive essentially from experienced feelings and actions; in this case, say, the feel of the path, its emotional flavor, and the experience of walking it. The knowing and understanding have developed as symbols, which in this case are ideas, to serve as economical substitutes for the actual feel, flavor, and walking when one is not free to traverse the real path. Moreover, the knowing and understanding always lead to really walking the path, so far as natural obstacles and competing reactions, including competing interests and ideas, are not stronger. (The stronger reaction is not necessarily the more passionate one.) When there are such obstacles or competing reactions or both—the path is not at foot, or one is weary, or one ought to be doing one's home work, or one prefers poetry—one may forget about the path, or perhaps think about it for an instant only.

Even the problem-solving level of intelligence, namely, reasoning, is essentially the interplay of feelings, or of ideas that substitute for them, as they conflict and work out the fullest expression possible for the given lot of feelings under the given circumstances. Thus, feelings toward buying an airplane may have to yield to feelings against trying to spend money that one does not have; some feelings may be inhibited by functionally stronger feelings that determine the outcome.

The best problem-solving, the most reasonable reasoning, occurs when all the relevant feelings, together with the reactions associated with all the relevant facts and their consequences, or the ideational substitutes for these feelings and further reactions, play their parts in the interplay. Only thus can the outcome be the best for the entire individual in the long run. The person who fails to think, choose, and act intelligently lacks important feelings, or facts, or symbolizing ideas, or integration, or some combination of these; hence his reasoning fails to represent and further him as a whole person.

True, intelligence is more highly evolved than the cruder of the feelings and actions. It is superior to all the feelings and actions, however, only as a parliament is superior to all the citizens that have developed it: they have developed it to work out rules and devices for the best life for all the citizens, including the members of the parliament. Progressive parliaments evolve from less to more representative, informed, and effective bodies. Progressive intelligence evolves likewise to represent and further, so far as possible, all the interests of the person.

Contemporary man seems no less vegetative and animal, and no better equipped with brains, than his later-stone-age ancestors. In so far, however, as he has advanced significantly beyond those ancestors, at least in his most enlightened representatives, modern man has become less savage and more spiritual: he has developed considerable economic security, many cultural contacts, and various instruments which enable him to use his brains far beyond any opportunities the primitive had; and he has come to live less by unexamined customs, edicts, and dogmas, and more for critically tested beauty, goodness, and truth.

Thus literature has developed from romantic stories of tradition and adventure to careful explorations and, in effect, experiments in human motivation, learning, and character. History has advanced from chanting tribal and heroic myths to tracing significant cultural trends, correlations, causes and effects. Science has grown from the limited observation, practical sense, logic, and even crude experimentation and quantification of the savage to the more systematic findings and developed methods of the modern investigator. Through that growth science has developed into particular sciences. An example is hygiene, which has progressed from superstitious charms and incantations to many workable principles and techniques.

Another field of study that has grown from ancient times is ethics. In the beginning, men's conduct was regulated only by their narrow wants and sympathies; physical facts; social taboos, approvals, and fictional goals; and precepts and punishments directed to "what is done." Many people still think of ethics as this or that sectarian code of conduct, list of virtues, and indoctrination with little real sense of what conduct and virtues are for. As the systematic science (in a broad sense of the term) of morality, however, ethics considers basically the human values, negative and positive; that is, the interests, evils and goods, dissatisfactions and satisfactions, bodily, economic, social, and spiritual; wherein the negative values may be decreased, and the positive values, increased, for all the people; and when different values conflict, as they often do, both within and between persons, by what principles the conflicts may best be resolved. Thus ethics is a critique both of individual living and of civilization, and offers enlightened perspectives for all intelligent persons.

Every field of knowledge has been produced and should be increased by and for human interests and powers; in a word, for better living. Hygiene and ethics are good examples. These fields have developed out of men's direct and indirect experiences of the worse and the better in health and happiness. Good living consists partly in enjoying any field in itself, so far as one can, through learning, advancing, and applying it.

Every field of knowledge seems to have been developed, even among the ancients, by essentially the same method: a method that is perforce truth-seeking; intuitive, imaginative, and logical; analytic and synthetic; and appreciative. Stuart P. Sherman took this method to embody the modern spirit. John

Dewey called it, especially as carried out in experimentation, the scientific method. Though much of it was practiced long ago, let us call it the modern approach.

Dewey urged that this approach be used, so far as possible, to improve our judgments about values, social, esthetic, and the rest, and to guide our actions "to make all values more secure and more widely shared." As men learn to rely less on primitive myths and tribal notions as to bad and good in every field of values; as they learn to rely more on their own powers in the modern approach, this approach "imports a new morale of confidence, control, and security." (Quoting Dewey, Quest . . . 1929 42 Minton, Living Philosophies 1931 24 Simon & Schuster).

AUTHOR INDEX

The references are to passage numbers.

The order is alphabetical by the printed letters of whole surnames or traditional sources regardless of diacritical marks; as

du Bartas	O'Neill	Süden
ibn Ezra	Ortega y Gasset	Sudermann
MacMullen	O'Shea	Vance
Mark	Simeon Ben Eleazar	Van Duzen
McMullan	St. Leger	Wisdom of Solomon

TOPIC INDEX

The references are to passage numbers. A hyphen after a number indicates one or more passages following in the text.

The order is alphabetical by whole topics; e.g.,

Humanity
Human nature